My

SPRING

Royal Times and Ordinary Lives

JEAN A. STOCKDALE

Matador
9 Priory Business Park,
Wistow Road, Kibworth Beauchamp,
Leicestershire. LE8 0RX
Tel: (+44) 116 279 2299
Fax: (+44) 116 279 2277
Email: books@troubador.co.uk
Web: www.troubador.co.uk/matador

ISBN 978 1780884 813

British Library Cataloguing in Publication Data.
A catalogue record for this book is available from the British Library.

Printed and bound in the UK by TJ International, Padstow, Cornwall
Typeset in 11pt Aldine401 BT Roman by Troubador Publishing Ltd, Leicester, UK

Matador is an imprint of Troubador Publishing Ltd

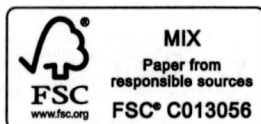

Dedicated to my loving family of the past and of the present.
Special love to Michelle, Jerry, Thomas; my brother and family;
Valerie, Terry and family.
I'm so proud of Thomas for writing the poem 'Attack' featured in the
last chapter. More from Thomas in the next book, 'My Summer',
more Royal times and ordinary lives.

About The Author

There's something great, even amazing, that happens every day of your life, but the truth is it doesn't always happen. Today, all day long, nothing really happened. Yet I want people to know that I'm here. I want to say that I'm a great person or that I'm special, but I don't think I can at all.

I'm just an ordinary girl with an ordinary life, not interesting enough for people to know about me. But I want people to know about me.

And today, even though nothing really great happened, I feel as though something great did happen.

When I started putting 'pen to paper' and writing poems and prose, my life years stretched before me in an endless line far longer than my mind could imagine. By the time I finished putting 'words to computer screen', my life years stretched behind me, unimaginable to someone still young.

I'm not a professional writer or poet and I've no university degree. But inside of me, well, there lies a story. I was born and brought up in Sheffield. As a royalist I checked memorable dates between my ordinary family and the royal extraordinary family and found that many life events of both families happened in the same year or around the same time.

And in the parallel storylines; there's fascination, there's joy, there's sorrow and guilt…and a little bit of humour!

The author writes her early poems in 'magazines' she compiled as a child. One poem is about spring and summer.

SPRING…	into…	SUMMER
light and lighter,		light blue skies,
shoots shooting,		flowers blooming,
branches branching,		'snowing summer',
fresh and fresher,		soft and softer,
shining dew,		sunny showers,
taller grass,		leafy trees,
sunny and shade,		hot sun and sand,
sheep lambing,		sheep shearing,
daffodils opening,		sunflowers growing.

(This poem is actually read across, so you might like to read it again!)

Contents

Prologue

George III, of the United Kingdom of Great Britain and Ireland, had produced nine sons, an heir and many spares, so to speak. Yet, by 1819, there were still no grandsons to take the Monarchy forward. He spoke sternly to his four eldest sons to go and find wives for the 'good of the Kingdom'. The fourth son married a widow of Saxe-Coburg-Saalfeld, who had two children already born. Together they had a daughter, a princess born fifth in line to the throne of the House of Hanover.

The princess moved closer to the line of succession after her father died and then her uncles died without heirs. George IV and William IV, two of George lll's sons, both died while on the throne leaving no legitimate heir. In 1837, a month after the princess' eighteenth birthday, the daughter of the fourth son became Queen. Albert, a young prince of Saxe-Coburg-Gotha, is brought to England with his brother to meet the young Queen. Although he had been told at an early age he would marry his English first cousin, he had no idea that by the time they met, she would be the Monarch.

Three years after their first meeting Queen Victoria marries Prince Albert. Almost to the day, nine months after the wedding, she has the first of their nine children.

Years later, the widowed Queen loses her heir presumptive grandson to pneumonia only a few short weeks away from marrying Princess Mary of Teck, the great grandaughter of George III. (She was known as 'May', her birth month).

In 1893, there were two notable marriages.

The first notable marriage, albeit arranged, was the Queen's late grandson's betrothed, Princess May, marrying his younger brother, Albert George, who had now been thrust into the limelight of the British Monarchy.

They married, having ten bridesmaids, amid much pomp and ceremony in the Chapel Royal at St James Palace. A procession of open landaus took everyone to the wedding breakfast at Buckingham Palace. After a honeymoon on the Sandringham Estate they started married life in York Cottage on that same estate in Norfolk.

The second notable marriage, a love match between first cousins, took place in the north of England. 'Notable' in terms of the author's family, that is.

They married, having no bridesmaids, in a quiet ceremony at the local church. The bride, groom and both sets of parents walked back to the bride's parents' home for tea and buns. There was no honeymoon and they started married life living with the bride's parents.

Very Early Spring

A very weary and frail old lady slept in her very grand four poster bed in a house where she and her late husband had been so happy. Her children and grandchildren heard her murmur and saw her lips twitch. They leaned forward for a sound, a movement, but it never came.

The old lady was dreaming of another century, another age, when life as an only daughter had seemed a slower and simpler way of living. How that had all changed when she was a young girl of eighteen and thrust too early into the world of adulthood and duty. An arranged 'match' had blossomed into love and she went on to share a devotion, a serene happiness, with her "beautiful" husband, bearing him nine "wonderful" children.

Then, all too quickly, her happy life was gone when he died young and suddenly, leaving her alone and empty inside. For many years, far too many, she had blamed Bertie, her son and heir, as her beloved husband had visited him to give guidance on his royal duties and to err his 'philanderings'. After that visit he had caught a chill which had led to his untimely death, causing a devastation she would never recover from.

In her dream, though, she felt very close to his beloved memory and to his warmth and to his love.

Her last conscious word had been "Bertie" as he had embraced her with much sobbing. A wholehearted reconciliation at the 'eleventh' hour. Then her distraught, favourite grandson, the Kaiser, took her in his arms as she fell asleep.

She never awoke from that last slumber and died peacefully. She left a country, a powerful and wealthy country and vast empire, to mourn her passing. She had reigned for the longest time and become known as 'grandmother' of the European Royals as she had arranged her children's marriages into almost all the major royal families across the continent.

Bertie had an overpowering, happy memory of his parents, once again together, holding and swinging their entwined hands as if they were the only two people in the world. He remembered when he had once had, though rarely, carefree and happy times with his siblings in vast gardens, but that was long, long ago and now he felt very alone and very old.

During his mother's long reign, he had become known as 'Uncle' to the nation and British Empire, but he would very soon hold the mantle of burden and responsibility he had longed for, and dreamed of, for most of his life.

But his eldest son, now heir to the throne, had not been born or groomed to become King. He had grown up in the shadow of his older brother, born to be King, and as they were close in age, they had been educated together. They had both toured the Empire as naval cadets. After that they had been separated as the younger son could continue in the navy while the heir apparent had to go to university.

At the young age of 28, the oldest brother had contracted influenza in a pandemic, turning to pneumonia; tragically dying from it only weeks before he was due to marry Princess May. It was decided that the time and effort it had taken to find such a sensible and obedient princess, from good Anglo-German stock, should not be 'wasted'. Prince George, the new heir, was 'encouraged' to marry his late brother's betrothed. Although they had dutifully wed, they grew to have a deep affection and love for each other.

George was invested as Prince of Wales at the Coronation in 1902 as his father was crowned King of the United Kingdom and Great Britain and Ireland and of the British Dominions and Emperor of India. King Edward ('Bertie'), though British, had some German blood as Monarch of the Houses of Saxe-Coburg-Gotha and Hanover. Although a first cousin, the Kaiser would listen to 'no-one' and started to build up his German Army.

'Bertie' had to prove himself as King at the age of 61 years, but times were changing…from rural to urban living, from horse power to motor cars…and the reforming of the British Home Fleet and the British Army. He would take a personal interest in the building up of the Naval Fleet, 'just in case' it was needed in the future.

Unfortunately, due to his mother's seclusion, the monarchy had not been seen and not been heard for a number of years. On a rare occasion 'out and about' the old Queen 'opened' Sheffield's new Town Hall as part of her Diamond Jubilee celebrations in 1897. How she had 'opened' it was the subject of conjecture as she never left her open horse-drawn carriage.

Did someone bring the ribbon tape to the carriage?
Did the tape wrap around the Town Hall and then the carriage so she could cut it while still seated?

Or, did she lift her arm and when she brought it down, a dignitary cut the tape?

(Answers on a postcard please.)

The Town Hall was a very fine Renaissance building with a 64 metre high clock tower surmounted by a statue of the Roman God of Fire, Vulcan. The Queen, plus an extensive entourage, travelled to Sheffield on the Royal Train, taking some five and a half hours with two short stops en route.

(Having sifted through the imaginary postcards, the most incredulous guess was that a ramp over the kerb took the open carriage to the bottom of the Town Hall steps and she cut the tape which was wrapped around the whole building.)

In fact, a gold key attached to an electric wire leading to the ornate tall gates was handed to the Queen and she touched the handle with her black gloved fingers. Amidst loud roars of applause and trumpet fanfares, the Town Hall's gilded gates flew open.

Incongruous to the ceremony were the brilliant uniforms of the men and the gay dresses of the ladies seated on platforms to the left and right of the Town Hall entrance. Due to the crowds of dignitaries, trumpeters, singing children, 'Uncle Tom Cobley and his dog', the Queen saw nothing of the ceremony and did not see the gates opening.

(Note: the inference that the Queen had used a remote control device from her carriage to open the gates is somewhat misleading, i.e. untrue. What actually happened was a man, dressed in Town Crier garb, turned the key in the lock and three concealed men opened the gates manually. As the Queen could not see them and they could not see her, there must have been a trail of hands bobbing in the air to signal the button had been pressed.

Worth a mention here, is where the Queen went after the Town

Hall. It was to watch armour plate being rolled at Cammell's Cyclops Works. Did the dignitaries lay on an elaborate mirror-to-mirror system so the Queen could view the rolling process from where she sat outside? No, it was reported that the Queen "...saw the rolling from her carriage." Did the carriage go onto an enormous fork lift truck which elevated the Queen high enough to look through a window? I think not, and she saw nothing.

Out of choice, I'm sure the Queen would have left her carriage, but she had been advised not to 'overdo it'.)

Back to the Queen's Diamond Jubilee, to mention that she was the first monarch to be able to celebrate 60 years on the throne. In London, the central fixture of the whole Jubilee was the St Paul's Thanksgiving Service. Famously, and true to form, she stayed put in her open carriage with its eight cream horses, declining to attempt the steps. *(Were the doors left open so that she could follow the service and sing with the congregation?)*

In fact, the clergy, dignitaries and troops came to her and the service was held around her carriage. It lasted only 20 minutes but the 17 strong carriage procession took in a lot of London en route back to the Palace, giving some 25,000 people who lined the route, the chance to see her.

The end of the Victorian era heralded turbulent times and changes in trends, traditions and technology. But first on the agenda was the setting of a higher public profile. The King made more and more public appearances up and down the country and in Europe. His charm had the 'midas' touch, bringing an upsurge of popularity for the Royal Family and making that vital connection between the monarchy and the British people.

In 1905, the open carriage was back outside Sheffield

Town Hall, this time with a King and Queen who left the carriage, walked up the steps and went inside.

This visit was part of a tour for the opening of the new university building and they left the carriage again for the official ceremony – no 'remote control' devices or 'trickery' needed this time.

(Sheffield, in the West Riding of Yorkshire, was founded as a tiny market settlement in the valleys of the rivers Sheaf and Don. Water wheels harnessed power from the rivers for the grinding mills which sharpened knives and made cutlery. By 1600, Sheffield was the main centre of cutlery production for England and had introduced silver plate processing by 1740.

Sheffield received its Municipal Charter in 1843 and became a city in 1893.

During the 19th Century, Sheffield gained an international reputation for steel production and developed crucible steel and stainless steel. The Industrial Revolution saw the population increase tenfold and by 1901 stood at over 451,000.)

The new Edwardian era saw the first of many improvements to people's daily lives, including improving education for children 5-13 years and the introduction of an old age pension in 1909 of five shillings a week (a quarter of a pound or 25p), to those over seventy of 'good character', subject to a form of 'means test'. However, medicine was still rare and costly and running water generally not safe to drink. Running water, at that time, was provided by over 300 private water companies!

(Just imagine if there had been regular 'cold calling' at your door by all those 'watermen'? There'd be a plethora of queues, jostling for customers at people's back doors. Paper sellers shouting, "read all about it… more policemen deployed on estate queue duty," and "…fights break out between queuing 'watermen' on Woollen Lane!")

Towns and cities had unclean air and smog due to most homes and factories burning coal. A day of fog and smog in the cities became known as a 'pea souper', i.e. thick soup.

A humble family in the north of England, Sheffield, had heard about the sad news of Queen Victoria's death from customers who came through their shop door. It was quite unbelievable news and a lot of people needed to see it in 'black and white' before accepting that the old, but much loved, Queen had actually died. Words on people's lips were 'end of an era' and 'nothing will be the same' and even 'will things change for the better'?

However, the northern family would soon have news of their own and they silently prayed that the new life would be a daughter, as their two sons played outside. It was not to be, and the next day a third son was born above the shop, an aunt in attendance. The father was helping out in the shop downstairs, with the young boys trying to help. It was a few hours before he could see the baby. After a few days, the mother was back serving again in the shop.

Another boy was all the more surprising for the parents, whose mothers were sisters, making them first cousins. As cousins, they had always had a strong bond of friendship. As they left school, they both courted their own school 'sweethearts'.

They met again at a family wedding. The cousins talked and talked and realised their strong bond had become a romantic bond. They finished courting their 'sweethearts' and started courting each other. Their two mothers were none too happy at first and asked them to wait. They waited two months, three weeks and two days before telling everyone of their intention to marry.

The boy had five sisters. His girl cousin had four sisters. With so many sisters between them, they had hoped for a son amongst daughters. A girl would mean help around the home, in producing homemade food and drink for the shop they managed, and a girl would have looked after her siblings. A girl would also have grown up to help them in their old age. Perhaps their next child, if they were so blessed, would be a daughter.

The small shop the parents managed sold everything from all sorts of homemade food and drink, to all sorts of hardware and small household goods; opening 'all hours'. That is, from early morning to late at night and when the shop appeared closed, customers went round to the back door. Sweets, cakes, bread, pies, pasties, biscuits, lemonade, ginger beer – all homemade.

Lard and butter would be delivered in large, open, metal tubs. Lard and butter would be cut by a large knife and 'paddled' into a rectangular shape by wooden spatulas, then put on thin greaseproof paper on the weight scales. Dripping was made from cooking meat and sold like lard and butter. Dripping sandwiches, for some reason, would be folded lengthways whereas for other sandwiches it was across the width.

Meat was sliced by hand and cooked straight from slaughterhouse 'off cuts'. Food and cooked meat would be wrapped between two small greaseproof sheets, then wrapped again in newspaper. Fresh meat was only sold from a butcher's shop.

The shop had shelves to the ceiling with dry goods, hand packaged in a thin brown paper. Dry goods ranged from seeds, flour and sugar to currants, herbs and tea. To reach the higher shelves there was a small, wooden stepladder.

In a gap between the shelves was a curtain leading to the back sitting room-cum-storage area. This also served as a shop when it was closed at the front, hence the label 'open all hours'.

On the counter or floor were the metal tubs of lard and butter and a large bowl of dripping. To one end of the counter was a wooden till which went 'ting' every time it opened to put money in and take change out. In front of the counter were large sacks containing potatoes and salt, as well as boxes of hardware goods such as candles. Salt was in block form and chipped off to be weighed and sold, (grated at home). It was a very 'full-looking' shop, brimming over with food and goods.

Household items ranged from homemade soap to sand for cement. Candles were big business, pre-electricity, and there were many different sizes of candles. Other popular items were scrubbing brushes, mop brushes, buckets, bowls, small steps, kneeling mats, polishing cloths – in fact anything the 'modern' housewife needed! Irons, made of heavy iron the shape of today's electric irons, were also sold.

These irons were heated on the top of a metal grid on the open fire and using a cloth, for the heat, a woman would take it off and iron her clothes. When it was too cool, it would go back on the heat. Some households had different weighted irons, depending on what was being ironed. A cotton sheet would need a heavier, larger iron.

Corner shops could be found, well, on corners. That is, nearly every corner of a cross road or at the end of a side street.

(When walking around old, terraced streets today, houses on street

9

corners can be seen bricked up on one side, or bricked up with a small window, where once had been the large window of a 'corner' shop.)

Corner shops were visited at least once a day, especially for fresh bread and food. It was pre-fridge days but a cellar head or the cellar steps at home acted as 'cold storage'. If a house had no cellar, a cold flannel would be kept on top of the milk in the larder or pantry, or it would be placed in a bucket of cold water.

However, a corner shop may not actually be 'on a corner' and could be within a row of houses, but would still be known as a 'corner' shop or 'beer off' (an off licence.)

The northern family's corner shop was in a small, back-to-back terraced community. Small pavements with whitened front steps and in between several houses were covered 'gennels' ('g' pronounced as in 'gem' and is taken from the word 'gunnel',) or passageways, leading away from the road into paved courtyards. Along the back wall of courtyards would be a row of outside toilets, one per household.

When the houses and toilets were first built, a toilet was not allocated to each house but, over time, a family would claim the one nearest their house as their own. They were known as 'closets'. When visiting, someone would say, "Jus' goin' to' closet." Or, "Jus' goin' cross yard."

If the person took a newspaper or book with them, then he or she would be going 'for a while'. If 'your' closet was occupied and it was needed urgently, then a random empty one would be chosen. Outside closets were not locked from the outside, but were kept closed by a 'sneck'. Some might have a bolt on the inside for privacy.

In winter, the closet cistern would often freeze so when

you went to the closet, you'd have to take a bucket of warm water to pour down the closet seat after usage. They could be cold and damp places – not somewhere anyone would take a book to read while 'ablutioning'.

Behind the closet door hung squares of newspaper with a piece of string through a hole in the squares. One square per visit. Some courtyards had back to back closets to match the back to back houses. The usual number was three back to back making six, but if there were seven or eight houses then at 'peak' toilet times it could be a case of 'musical closets'. If there was no bolt, the closet user had to hold the door or sing.

Some corner shops kept a ready-made stack of newspaper squares but most had gone brown, not from use (?), but with lack of use as no-one had a spare farthing (a quarter of an old penny) to buy ready torn squares.

(A farthing was a very small copper coin. Two farthings made a halfpenny and four made an old penny. It's very difficult to compare that sort of 'small change' with today's penny, but a farthing may have equated to ten decimal pence. A thre'penny piece was silver and actually had some silver content at that time.
Twelve pennies made a shilling.)

One thing not sold in corner shops was milk – remember, no fridges. A milk cart pulled by a horse would bring round large cans of milk with pint and half pint measures. Women would go out to the cart with their own jugs to be filled with one or more measures of milk (it was always women who went out for the milk.)

The milk cart would come round twice a day, more often in hot weather. The word 'hygiene' was unheard of and some milkmen would 'top up' their milk with water or local pond water. From time to time, a milkman would be caught 'topping up' his milk and be prosecuted (there were no 'milkwomen'.)

Those living on or near a farm, could enjoy warm milk straight from the cow.

Christmas decorations were sold in the shop, by way of coloured paper chains which children would stick together with a paste made from flour and water. A lot of salt was sold round the clock which was especially used to keep meat fresh in salted water. People would buy small joints of beef a week off Christmas (it was cheaper) and keep it in salted water down in the cellar.

Fresh meat was always kept on a table down in the cellar, but had to be quickly moved when the coalman came (no such word as 'coalwoman'.) The outside grate was lifted off by the coalman and he would lift a sack of coal from the lorry and throw it down over the hole, then shake the sack for all the coal to go in the hole (no apology for the rhyme!) The slang name for the coal hole was 'coil oil', pronounced like 'coil oil'.

When he'd finished, a woman would go and pay him or be given 'tick' (owing the money.) Whoever was in the house might help out with shovelling the coal into a neater mound so that the woman of the house could clean the table to put the meat back.

Large, poor families, many extended and related to each other by blood or marriage, were regular customers in the shop. Some parents would send in young children, usually girls, who were expected to remember what they were buying and have the right money though very often they were just short of the amount needed and hoped to get away with the odd farthin'. Most times, the shop owner would keep a note of what was 'on tick' and ask the mother on her next visit.

Imperial money used at that time was known as 'pounds, shillings and pence'.

(A 'copper' would be a penny (written as 1d) or 'coppers' – two pennies (2d):
12 pennies made one shilling (referred to as a 'bob' and written as 1s), and
20 shillings made a £1 (quid).
A 'tanner' was sixpence (half a shilling – 6d);
'thruppence' for 3 pence – 3d;
'tuppence' was 2 pence – 2d).

A farthing would pay for a ride on a tram.

A halfpenny would buy a postage stamp or a small loaf. A quid, at the turn of that century, would buy a week's shopping, the coal, some clothes, a trip to the cinema and still have change. One shilling (1s) was worth 5 new pence (5p).

Two sisters, born a year apart, came into the shop nearly every day, not always to buy something and, on occasions, were given a few broken biscuits or bread and dripping. The third sister, of a year and a half, was staying at a nearby aunt and uncle's public house. Their mother was due to give birth any day and the two sisters had been asked to go and buy some soap.

In the shop, the eldest girl said how much their father was hoping for a boy this time, but the next day a fourth daughter was born. She was born different from other children and had a hole at the bottom of her spine (later known as spina bifida.)

As she grew older, the third sister took on the role of helping her as she could not walk or go to school. Later she would teach her to read and write.

Very few families owned their own home. The girls' parents rented a terraced 'two up, two down' house with a shared front courtyard with the usual row of outside closets, one per family. Children would sleep in one bed and toddlers slept in a cot until they got too big. A newborn baby would be put into a drawer with knitted shawls made from left-over wool. Bath time was once a week in front of the open fire, two children to a tin tub of lukewarm, soapy water.

The tin bath 'ritual' would come round every Friday evening. The bath would be kept either at the cellar head or hung up on a wall down the cellar steps. A steady stream of boiling water from pots and pans to'ing and fro'ing from the open fire would be poured into the bath. A bar of soap thrown in to soften it. The two youngest, whether crying or not, would go in first and be washed then dried by an older sibling.

The same ritual for the next two. A couple of pots of boiling water may be used at this point to top up the bath level. After drying down the latest glum looking child, it was fresh pyjama or nightie time – after the once a week bath it was also time for the once a week clean underwear. Older children would go in after each other and if they bathed themselves, as a concession to a bit of privacy, the mother would go and put the squeaky, sparkling youngsters to bed.

Parents would bath after all the children had gone to bed or older children sent into the front room. But, if it was winter, it would be warmer to go to bed than sit in a freezing front room.

Men coming home from work each night would have a strip wash to the waist and then get changed into their old clothes, ready to eat.

Men spent long hours at work, either grinding cutlery or in small steelworks, in this largely urban end of the city. They would not take part in any work associated with the home or the bringing up of the children. Some men might play with their children but otherwise it was 'women's' work. It was women who would be seen 'out and about' with their children, shopping or visiting other family members. Washing clothes would take a whole day, Mondays, using a 'dolly posher' in a large, upright tin container or washtub.

(A 'dolly posher' was a long wooden handle with three wooden prongs on the end and used for washing clothes in a wash tub, or the tin bath. The 'posher' was manually turned inside the tub or lifted up and down to clean the clothes.)

After the washing was done, it was 'whitening of the steps' time. With a 'donkey' stone (made of pumice), women would whiten all steps up to the front or back garden and especially the house steps. There was a lot of pride in having whitened steps. If a visitor 'smudged' the white line, it would be whitened again as soon as possible.

If a 'donkey' stone was 'wearing out', women would try and listen for the shouts of a 'rag and bone' man from the street. He would call out, sometimes ringing a handbell, "any ole rags, bring out yer rags." He would keep small household items on his cart, some of which would be 'donkey' stones, and exchange an item for the rags.

Ironing the clothes would take nearly a whole day, on Tuesdays, using at least two irons. One would be on the fire heating while the other was being used. Baking bread, pies and buns was done most mornings. For tea, it might be vegetable stew, once a week including a few pieces of meat; or dumplings in the stew or corned beef hash. Hungry between meals? Then dry bread or with jam or dripping would be 'on offer'. If lucky, there may be a broken biscuit or two.

In the final days of a woman's pregnancy, female family members would come in and help with the children and chores. No-one living in this poor neighbourhood could afford a doctor or midwife.

A sister or mother would assist a local woman acting as midwife at the birth. A new mother would be back on her feet and 'carrying on' as usual, within a day or two of giving birth.

The third of the four sisters can remember going to her uncle's public house to stay and she knew when she returned home there would be a new baby. From the age of three, each time she had to stay there, she remembers thinking, "I'm going to have a brother or sister." A fifth sister was born, but she had secretly wanted a brother.

The uncle and her aunt lived in and managed the local public house and would send their two small boys into the corner shop for food and occasional treat.

One day, the eldest boy from the pub came into the shop and said their mother had fallen down the cellar steps into a crate of ginger beer bottles. They wanted to buy their mum some sweets for when she came home from the hospital. A little bag was carefully filled with sweets, in near silence. Unknown to the children, at that point, was that her neck had been broken in the fall.

Sadly, she never did come home from hospital. The little

bag of sweets was gently placed on her coffin by the two boys. The girls' father and his bereaved brother were helped out by their sister who hadn't married. She then moved into the pub to look after her brother and his boys.

Later that year, the third sister went to stay in the public house again, and thought, 'a new brother or sister'. This time she had a little brother; she felt so happy, but everyone seemed so glum. Also, she couldn't understand why her stay continued. Eventually, the aunt now living at the pub said the little baby boy was ill and that no-one had seen the baby, save mother, father and a nurse who had had to be called.

The baby died at three days old. The two oldest girls took a turn in carrying the tiny coffin to the cemetery with their father and their uncle from the public house.

The third sister's next visit to her uncle and family was a shorter stay and she came home to a little brother, Frank. He was doted on and much loved, having a cheeky face and blonde, curly hair. When he started to walk he had a little brush to follow the third sister round when she mopped and brushed the floor. By the age of two he would follow this sister around wherever she went. They were inseparable, which helped her mum as she started to be sick each morning and each evening.

Just as her mum's sickness subsided and her new 'lump' started to show, Frank caught a cold and he was laid in his cot. The third sister sat next to the cot each day. As he grew worse, a nurse had to be called who said it was now bronchitis. The nurse said he would need hospital treatment and would be taken in the following morning. They would have to find the money somehow.

(A nurse was called because the cost of a doctor was much higher.)

Sadly, he never woke up the next morning. Frank was just two and a half years old. There was a long, sad procession behind the horse and cart carrying the small, wooden coffin. The third sister was devastated and her father held her in his arms for most of the way to the cemetery and she was asleep over his shoulder on the way back.

Out of the sadness came another boy, Harry, and two years later, a second boy, Walter. Longed for brothers at last for the five girls.

The three oldest sisters' schooling was hit and miss as they fitted in their chores. The fourth sister, known as an invalid, had to be taken to the local hospital once a year for doctors to confirm that she could not attend school.

The third sister, Annie, was my grandma.

In the same year as the youngest of the two northern brothers were born, the relatively new King died from heart failure following emphysema; his lavish culinary tastes and cigar smoking finally taking their toll. But his Queen, devoted to the end, would not 'give up' his body for over a week and he became the first monarch to lie in state. Queues of people, stretching back seven miles, waited to pay their respects.

Even though he had been 'acting monarch' in his mother's long seclusion after widowhood, his reign as King had been just nine short years. His mother had been a tough act to follow but he had proved himself to be an extremely popular and forward thinking King. His son, the Prince of Wales, was now a reluctant King.

It was not for the first time, or the last, that an unwilling second son was thrust into the limelight of the British Monarchy. Still shy with a quiet demeanor, he hated going out in public and dreaded, feared, the prospect of one day becoming King. But that day of total dread had arrived!

In 1911, to celebrate the crowning of King George and Queen Mary, there were national festivities up and down the country. In London three million people descended on the capital, including governors and troops from the British Dominions 'beyond the seas' who came to honour their new King. Six thousand of those millions filed into Westminster Abbey for the actual Coronation.

(In my book, that's pretty much 'full to the rafters'.)

Needless to say, only a fraction of those in the Abbey saw the actual crowning. The Archbishop of Canterbury asked, "Sir, is your Majesty willing to take the Oath?" The King replied, "I am willing." After the solemn religious pledge the King said, "All this I promise to do." He signed the Oath at the altar and sitting on the throne he was anointed on the head, the breast and his hands. He knelt and was blessed by the Archbishop. He rose and received the ceremonial robes, the swords of the state and of justice, the orb, the ring and the sceptres.

As the King was crowned, a wave seemed to break along the ranks of the peers who donned their coronets. "God save the King."

After the Queen was crowned, a sequence dance of uplifting arms, in cascading formation, took place as the peeresses placed coronets on their own heads. "God save the King."

In this Coronation year, the King had to put duty first and make the best of things. It was to be a very busy year. Before the ceremony, there had been the unveiling of the Victoria Memorial in front of tumulturous crowds and in the presence of the Kaiser on his last visit to England. Then the King invested his own eldest son, Edward, as Prince of Wales at Caernarvon Castle amidst so much pomp and ceremony it was likened to a 'mini' coronation. (He was known as 'David', the last of his seven Christian names.)

There were state visits to Ireland and Scotland where the King's popularity had never been in any doubt. He held a huge, palace garden party; he was entertained by 100,000 schoolchildren at Crystal Palace and he reviewed his armies and 30,000 boy scouts at Windsor.

At year end, the King and Queen set sail for India. George was the first King Emperor of the British Dynasty to 'appear' to the Indian peoples. Thousands upon thousands had made long pilgrimages across the country, suffering hardships on the way, to simply catch a glimpse of him. Masses descended on where he had sat only minutes before, regarding it as sacred to touch where he had touched. Everywhere the royal couple went they were met with huge displays of imperial pomp and pageantry, as well as religious fervour.

He came back a proud man in the glorious role of King and Emperor of the World's greatest power. It was not going to last for long...

Meanwhile, it was a time to celebrate the Coronation at the girls' Sheffield school. All city schoolchildren got a medal to wear on the day and a souvenir programme was given out. The programme of festivities stated, 'The whole of the school children of the city, being assembled in their respective schools, will be presented with Coronation Medals and a Souvenir Programme on behalf of the Lord Mayor, by some important Citizen who will deliver a short address on the importance of the Coronation…' The important Citizen was the Chairman of the City's Education Committee as the Lord Mayor was at the Coronation Ceremony in London.

On the actual day, 22nd June 1911, thousands of children took part or watched as the northern city's Coronation Pageant unfolded. They walked to the city centre or rode on tramcars at no charge. Each child was presented with a chocolate bar and the 'aged poor' provided with tea and entertainment in church halls. The sick and 'infirm' were sent a parcel of groceries.

The three girls wore their Sunday best dresses (their only best dresses) to school that day, but saved their chocolate to show their parents and share with their invalid sister who had remained at home with the younger children. After the procession, salute and singing, the schoolchildren walked to the nearest park to where they lived to hear a selection of band music. The sisters' strict father said they had to be home by 7.30pm but were later allowed to the top of the hill nearby to watch the local park's spectacular fireworks against the night sky and the billow of smoke from hill top bonfires. Their aunt from the pub and the two boy cousins joined them.

Schools at the turn of the century were called 'Board Schools' and used slate and slate pencils. Girls and boys had different playgrounds and entrances and, because of that, different games. Boys played marbles and would be proud of their collection. Girls would play hopscotch or play with skipping ropes. A larger rope would be held by two girls, one shouting out a girl's name. The named girl would then run in and skip with the speed varying by the girl at either end, but if she faltered she would have to take one end of the rope.

Boys and girls were separately educated, sometimes on different floors of the school. Boys' lessons were designed to equip them for earning a living and girls' lessons were on 'home making'. At 9am, the school bell would sound and there would be a morning playtime break, some children bringing a slice of bread to eat. Lunch was 12 until 2pm to allow children to go home as there was no food or drink provided in school.

Class numbers were high with pupils sitting on benches (desks were added in later years.) Teachers sat at a high desk at the front and would have a hand bell to get attention. All women teachers were spinsters as marriage was a full-time 'job'. There would be a coal fire in each classroom during winter with the live-in caretaker being responsible for starting the fires, putting coal on and clearing the ashes.

Girls at school during the 1914-18 war had to sew sacking for sandbags on certain afternoons. Also, knitting socks and other things which would be sent to the frontline soldiers. Boys continued with their normal lessons, which now included how valiant and heroic it was to become a soldier.

Children played in the side streets as there were no cars and a horse and cart would be slow enough to move out of its way. One or two end houses might boast of a 'postage-stamp' grassed area or small garden.

About half a mile from where the family lived was the city's Botanical Gardens. It featured a dome shaped glass tropical greenhouse, fountains, flower beds, lawns, trees, paths with benches, and … a bear pit. Up to the 1870s, people could come to see the two brown bears living in this pit and they could be viewed by leaning over a short wall at the top.

The bears had been removed after a child fell into the pit and was mauled to death.

After that, wire mesh was laid across the top to stop anyone else falling in but it did not stop people from throwing things down into the empty bear pit.

Grandma always insisted that she had seen a live bear in this pit when she was a young girl. In fact, she *had* seen a bear in the pit. A drunk and disorderly man had been arrested with his dancing bear at some point between 1908 and 1910. The police had not known what to do with the bear so they had put it in the pit until its owner was released from the police cells and the bear was reclaimed. As word of mouth progressed outwards that there was a bear again in the pit, visitors streamed into the Gardens to see the bear.

(Sheffield's Botanical Gardens opened in 1836. The public could visit the Gardens four times a year on gala days, for a charge, to walk around the domed glasshouses, fountains and see the two bears in the pit. In 1844 financial problems beset the society which had built it and a second society took over the upkeep. The glass conservatories were extended and the curator's house built.

However, by the late 1890s, falling income and competition from the opening of free local parks put the Gardens in danger again. In 1898, the Sheffield Town Trust 'saved the day', doing some essential repair work and then abolishing the entrance fee.)

The Gardens' lawns were not for children and displayed 'keep off the grass' signs. But children could now play safely in free local parks, all of which had extensive grassed areas.

Girls and boys played with wooden hoops which would be pushed along by a stick. It was mainly boys who played with long wooden sticks which had a rope attached at one end. The rope would be twisted around a wooden top. The stick would then be flung towards the ground and the top would spin on release from the rope. Boys might also play cricket or kick a football about. Throw and catch was played with anything that could be, er, thrown and caught.

The father from the corner shop would only ever see his three boys at play on Sundays as he held a job, of long hours, in a grinding works during the day and sometimes, but rarely, served in the shop at night. He had a permanent cough from the grinding dust and had to walk there as the tramcar now cost a half penny a ride.

(Men dry grinding knife blades and forks could expect to live until 35 years and those wet grinding rarely lived beyond 45.)

He also smoked a large number of untipped 'Woodbines' cigarettes which would not have been associated with his cough.

Breakfast was porridge, lunch was bread, and the evening meal some form of meat stew or a plate of vegetables. A half penny would buy two small loaves, though most people made their own.

In summer, when fires would not be lit to heat an oven, uncooked bread could be taken and baked in a baker's oven. The dough would be dropped off at the bakery by children on the way to school and then collected as loaves on the way back. A half penny charge buying more than two small loaves.

The three boys from the shop had to help clean, clear and serve in it, as they had no sister. Hoping to be blessed with a girl, the mother became pregnant once again. A fourth son was born, but sadly he was to die at nearly two years old.

The middle son, at six years, could pick out candles for customers by the size on the box. This system worked well until October when people started asking for roman candles! He was not allowed to touch the gunpowder fireworks which were kept in large, tin boxes.

The introduction of one half day closure per week for shops (Thursday) just sent customers to the 'back door system' more often. Customers were very poor and for that reason prices had to be 'kept down'. Broken or older biscuits were sold in a bag at a reduced price. Biscuits, like most food items, were not packaged in any way and were home made.

It was only a 'break-even' living, topped up with the father's meagre wage from the grinding works. The boys were a great help in the shop and from the age of thirteen the eldest boy would bring in a wage from the same grinding firm as his father.

The middle son, Wilf, was my grandad.

Most children who started writing with their left hand were forced to use a slate pen with their right hand. Grandad, however, had been allowed to carry on writing with his left hand.

He had an education until he was thirteen, leaving a year early. Children who were classed as bright and intelligent were allowed to leave at thirteen instead of fourteen years. *(It became compulsory in 1918 to stay at school until fourteen.)*

He was too young to go to war in 1914. He was too young to lose his father but his cough just got worse and worse. Because of his father's poor health, he decided not to grind, and got a job at a nearby steelworks. But he was not too young to smoke! At 13, he joined his workmates and became a heavy smoker of strong, untipped 'Woodbines' cigarettes.

Ironically, he would never know or realise that avoiding

the dust of the grinding works had been 'replaced' by smoking.

Grandad could play the piano, self taught, and with or without piano music he could play anything. Popular tunes he could play without music. He also played the cornet for the local Salvation Army Band, playing at local churches and the Cathedral.

Sometimes something happens that changes a family's destiny for all time. But remember, destiny has no respect for a family's roots or background.

The aristrocratic Moncrieffe family had sixteen children, eight of whom grew into beautiful young women. Most married into prominent and wealthy families, their destiny from birth. The fourth daughter, Lady Harriet, was said to be the most beautiful. In 1869, at eighteen years, she had been wooed and then dutifully married Sir Charles Mordaunt giving him a daughter, Violet. As a couple they attended parties attended by the Prince and Princess of Wales. She soon started entertaining male visitors while her husband was away.

One visitor was the Prince of Wales, 'Bertie'. On a fishing trip to Norway in a 'not so good' year for salmon, the husband is reported to have come home early and found the philandering 'Bertie' with the wayward Lady. The Prince beat a hasty retreat while the husband is said to have taken her two white horses and shot them while she was made to watch. He started divorce proceedings and she admitted that their daughter may not have been his. *(There was more than one contender for the title of 'real father' but in the eyes of the law she was still the daughter of Sir Charles.)*

The Moncrieffes, to avoid a scandal, had her declared

insane. She spent the rest of her life, some 36 years, in a mental asylum. She never saw Violet again.

(Violet eventually married and had a son who was to develop a safari park on his family's Longleat Estate. His entry in 'Who's Who' only mentions Violet's father, Sir Charles.)

Grandad's Great Uncle Bill, from humble roots, became a prominent figure with an office in the business quarter – a square of former Georgian homes – in Sheffield city centre. He was one of several men who pioneered the city's trade union movement at the turn of the century. By paying 3d, you became a member and the movement would fight for better pay and conditions in your place of work.

Grandad was told about his uncle's prominence and that he had become a sort of 'hermit' when he retired from the movement.

Uncle Bill would always be afraid of newspaper men – reporters. He also shied away from making friends, of any kind. Unknown to Grandad and his family at the time, Uncle Bill's younger sister had been with child at only 15. Before anyone could notice her 'predicament', she had been 'whisked' away by her father. One evening she was part of the family and the next morning she was gone. Her brother missed her at first, but he did not know exactly where she was and their ordinary family life went on. In fact, neither his mother nor his older sister knew where she was.

Many years later, when he had left the trade union movement to younger men, the truth that he had surpressed for so long surfaced. She had been 'put away', locked away from society. He visited the city's mental institutions vowing to find his sister. This search was started without his ailing father's knowledge.

He did eventually find her and went visiting, but she did not know him at first. Then a glimmer of recognition was switched on in her eyes and she threw her arms around him. They embraced for the longest time. She pleaded with him to take her out of there. "Everybody's mad in here, please, please don't leave me," she sobbed. "It wasn't my fault, this man made me, he made me."

Her brother turned away and wrenched, "Oh no, oh bloody no." He pulled her to him, but bile was in his throat.

"Damn it father, did you know it was rape?" But the question was lost in time, as his father had passed on.

"Not my fault, not my fault," she kept repeating as she sat moving her upper body forwards and then backwards, in a sad pendulum motion. He asked about the baby and she shrugged. Her pendulum motion increasing in speed.

He asked the matron about the baby and she looked through a large ledger, but whatever truth was in that ledger, stayed within it. The matron shrugged and said a feeble, "Sorry." 'Sorry' the ledger gave no information? 'Sorry' the baby was given away? 'Sorry' the baby didn't live? To his sister the baby had 'died' the moment it was born. She had surpressed the trauma for so long that it would not, could not, surface.

"I'll try and get you out," he said to her, not really believing it himself, but he knew he had to try.

For now though, he just had to get out, the walls were 'caving' in on his head. He pealed her arms off him and vowed again to try and do something, but he felt a sickness build from inside his gut. The guilt spilled out and overwhelmed him.

All those lost years, a lost life; her lost baby, the terrible injustice. On the way out he saw again the inhumane conditions of the institution, the locked doors, the pall of secrecy and the hunched over, thin, staring 'inmates'.

He tried, he believed he tried very hard, but in the end he met a brick wall and did not go back. He wanted to go back, he really did, but he couldn't bring himself to go back. A terrifying guilt had gripped his stomach and made his life mean nothing to him, every time he thought of his younger sister. And this was often.

She was to spend the rest of her life 'inside'. Her one and only 'crime' was to have a child out of wedlock, though the man who had committed the real crime still walked the streets. She had been dealt a lifetime of devastation as a sane 'inmate' and the despairing sadness that she never saw her baby at all. Never again to run down a wet, grassy hillside and never again to smell fresh meadow flowers. Never to love in the way she had dreamed of as a young girl.

Even more heartbreaking, if that was possible, was her desperate need for her mother, but her mother was never told where she was and it was not 'her place' to ask. Mother and daughter were never to meet again.

For the family's sake, her mother and father had kept an outward illusion of married life, but their only conversations after he took her daughter from her were perfunctory things like "Pass the salt."

The despair and guilt of her brother, that he could have done more, that he could have bulldozed a hole through that 'brick wall' lived and festered inside him until his last breath. Although technically he lived on the 'outside', his mind was imprisoned within him and his shoulders became hunched as he shuffled round the house. He died an unhappy, broken man.

An act by an unknown, selfish man had wrecked a family's life, a family of five and an innocent baby. His father could have given support, could have shown love, but he had locked his daughter up and 'thrown away the key'. His mother was deprived of a grandchild and of her own daughter. In fact, his mother was deprived of any grandchildren as her other two children did not marry, or more likely, chose not to.

The 'something' which happened to shape Grandma's destiny was the War. Without the War, she would have lived her life in Oldham, with unthinkable and unwritten consequences.

Grandma's Aunt Polly, her father's older sister, worked in a mill in Oldham and had found Grandma a job there. Working in a mill was regarded as 'good money' and most of her earnings would be sent back for the family. She was put on a train to live with her aunt and work in the mill, but she did not want to go.

Her life settled into a routine of work, tea and then bed. Work, tea and then bed – times six. On Sunday she helped her aunt with household chores. She so looked forward to having a break and going home to visit but she daren't ask when, or even if that might happen at all.

War loomed ever closer.

In the royal household, wedding invitations from the Kaiser had been received from Berlin for the nuptials of his daughter, (and great grandaughter of Queen Victoria.) Also invited, of course, was the Tsar and his family. The King, the Kaiser and the Tsar all wore military uniforms, the King choosing his German uniform for this happy occasion. They were never to meet again.

War declared.

There was talk of the Oldham mill diversifying into making war goods.

Aunt Polly was sent a telegram from her brother in Sheffield, asking, or rather telling her: "Send – *stop* – our – *stop* – Annie – *stop* – back – *stop* – due – *stop* – to – *stop* – war – *stop*". He wanted his family to stay together and be safe. Although dreading what 'war' would mean, she was happy to be back home. She had so missed her sisters and two little brothers.

A government campaign was launched for women to take over 'men's' jobs as they went to war. This gave rise to some job name changes, albeit temporary – 'Firewomen', 'Postwomen', 'Milkwomen', 'Miss engine-cleaner', and 'Porteresses'. By 1917, around a million women were doing what had been 'men's' jobs.

A lot of women working in the munitions factories saw it as the 'second best' thing to their brothers going to war. Their own 'war effort'.

Factory shifts lasted 12 hours with breaks between 9 and 10 am and then from 1 to 2pm. The shifts were over five and a half days of the week. The weekly wage was £1 and 1d. Children swapped school classrooms for the factory floor, some as young as 9 years, to bring in a wage to help their mothers while the breadwinner fought for King and country.

Women working in traditional male roles during the war years, however, gave a new view of what women were capable of. The women's pre-war suffragette movement started to be heard. They had been campaigning for the right of women to vote in parliamentary elections and some women had chained themselves to railings and set fire to mailboxes. *(Some women got the vote after the War, the rest had to wait until 1930.)*

Having returned from Oldham, Grandma started work in a small tools firm as a 'filer' which is filing tools to the required shape.

As the fashion dictated at that time, the hem of her skirt and petticoats were worn just above her ankles, which were always hidden under lace up boots. Now that she had started work, she twisted her long brown hair into a bun at the back of her neck. The cloth used for her skirts were browns and greys, worn with a contrasting white, plain blouse. A short, top coat adorned on cold days.

She met someone at the firm and they became friends, having some 'wonderful dates' along with her best friend, Nell, and her 'beau'. On one date, walking into the countryside, both couples sat a short distance apart in a grassy meadow and a shy first kiss took place. They would not have been allowed on a date without a sister or girlfriend accompanying them.

Both of their young men then went to war, which soon became known as the 'Great War'. Grandma's soldier friend wrote often. They were long, friendly letters and postcards which soon turned into messages of love. Each letter ended with him asking her to wait for him until after the war.

In a relatively short time, there were over a hundred postcards, some in sets of 2, 3 or 4 with wartime verses and sentiments, such as 'If you were the only girl in the world', 'I wonder if you miss me sometimes' and 'when God gave you to me'.

There were also patriotic cards. One set featured soldiers and the Union Jack entitled 'I love my Motherland'. The verses mentioned sons from India, Australia, Canada, Ireland, Scotland, England and Wales keeping the 'old flag flying, it's a flag worth fighting for; in unity, for Empire, Home and King'. Other sets featured, 'It's the Navy', 'Rule Britannia' and 'America's Mighty Army'.

There were brown sepia postcards with a picture of a loving couple and ones of a young woman with real hair on the postcards. There were cards showing springtime in Paris and embroidered material in the shape of an envelope with a small card inside. All the postcards went lovingly into an album.

Several of each, sent over time, had phrases like, 'I'm thinking of you', 'forget me not', 'my dear sweetheart' and 'wait till the boys come marching home'. Three sets of postcards featured couples getting married. In these later cards and letters he vowed he would never come back to England if she did not wait for him.

But Grandma did not want to wait for him coming home. She kept replying in a friendly and 'light' manner. That is, until her father said she had to let him know there would be no courtship on his return. He was a local lad and his parents later blamed Grandma as he set up home in France after the War, never coming back to live in England again.

Some soldiers from the Great War were housed in barracks and there was a large barracks about a mile from where Grandma lived. She remembers soldiers marching on the local roads and her family's pride as they saw her cousin marching with the other soldiers before they were sent to the front. Her cousin, from the public house, was just 17 years old. Her family could not imagine that large numbers of these soldiers, proudly marching on the city's main roads, would not be returning home.

The Sheffield Barracks had been described as 'the finest and best garrison in the Kingdom' and was the largest military depot in the UK since being built in 1848. One tender for the conversion work was £46,019, broken down as:

Excavating	£6,000
Masonery and brickwork	£31,000
Carpenters/Joiners' work	£4,900
Wood fitments/general fixtures	£789
Iron Founders' work	£3,275
Ironmongery	*£55*
	£46,019

(Included in these prices was six shillings for bell hangers' work in fixing four 14oz bells.) However, the actual cost totalled £124,000 and the new barracks covered 22.5 acres.

Within the complex was a five bedroom house for the Garrison Commander's family and married quarters for fifty officers' families. There were infantry soldiers' quarters; horse stables; a gymnasium; a school for 80 children; a 58 patient, two storey hospital; a granary; four cookhouses and numerous workshops. In military terms, there were gun rooms, guard rooms, detention cells and a rifle range. There was even a chapel and a small mortuary. (A garage for 26 cars and vehicles had been added in 1903.)

Over the years, the Barracks had housed many army units, including some from the Boer Wars, and then the Great War.

(The defeat of the British Army against the Zulus in 1879, encouraged the uprising of Boer farmers in 1880 and led to the first Boer War (1880-81). The Boers (who were descendants of the Dutch Settlers in Africa) lay siege to several British Garrisons hoping to starve them into submission. Troops from Britain and the Empire's colonies were sent to Africa, some in scarlet and some in khaki uniforms. The Boers wore their civilian clothes. The garrisons were relieved and the war resolved by granting the Boers a form of self-government.

The second Boer War (1899-02) involved large numbers of British troops, plus those from the colonies, being sent back to Africa. (Troops had now adopted the khaki uniform.) The British garrisons were sieged once more, but again relieved by 'weight and numbers' of the British Army. The war ended with the Boer Republics being converted back to British Colonies, with the promise of future independence.

Apologies for the 'nutshell' of information on the two Boer Wars.)

It's interesting to note, however, that the German Empire openly supported the Boers' rebellion, which included the sending of armaments and later a congratulatory telegram to the Boer leaders on the War's outcome, ie the promise of future independence. (This took place in 1907.) In the aftermath of the War, and Germany's 'enemy' stance, Britain started to establish European allies which, in fact, stood them in 'good stead' for the Great War.

(British losses in the Boer Wars were high due to disease as well as combat. The Government of 1902 realised that the majority of the troops from Britain were weak and undernourished even before leaving English soil. This realisation led to the social reforms of the early 1900s.)

At the start of the Great War, those who owned large houses and castles had their homes commandeered for soldiers who became sick or injured on the frontline. An Earl and his family who owned Glamis Castle, Scotland, saw it turned into a 'hospital' to treat wounded soldiers.

Too young to train as a nurse, the young daughter of the family, played an amateur 'Florence Nightingale' role.

A soldier whose plane was shot down overseas became friends with the young daughter's brother in a German Prisoner of War Camp. They were imprisoned for two years. On their release, her brother invited his soldier friend to convalesce at the castle instead of going back to his native Australia. At the castle her brother introduced her to his friend and the three became inseparable.

The three of them shared 'wonderful times'. It is said that the soldier and the young girl shared a shy first kiss. At the end of the War, however, social barriers came back and the soldier found he was mixing 'above his station'. As a young child the daughter had become a Lady in a wealthy, aristocratic family. There could be no courtship.

(*Elizabeth Bowes-Lyon, ninth child of Lord and Lady Glamis, was not born a Lady. She was Hon. Elizabeth until her grandfather died in 1904 and her father became the Earl of Strathmore.*)

A year after the Great War had ended, the young northern girl, Annie, started courting John, the youngest of the three brothers from the shop. Her older sister, Emily, was courting the middle brother, Wilf. Sometime later, Annie confided in sister Minnie how much she liked Wilf. Minnie told Emily. Emily decided to end the courtship which had been 'walking out' rather than anything else.

(*'Walking out' would be today's equivalent of 'going out' with someone. Courtship was more serious, but not as serious as becoming betrothed or engaged.*)

Annie then breaks off her courtship with John. Meanwhile, Grandma's best friend, Nell, introduces her brother to Minnie and they start courting. Have you followed that?

Let's recap, Emily and Annie are single again. Wilf is not single – he's now courting a girl called Alice. Minnie is betrothed to Nell's brother. Best friends were to become sisters-in-law.

Emily, acting as matchmaker, mentions to Wilf, serving in his family's corner shop, that Annie likes him. Emily then asks Annie to buy something, knowing that Wilf is still serving in the shop that evening. Annie goes into the shop, they chat and he says he is serving the following evening.

Annie calls in the next evening. Walt ends his courtship with Alice and asks Annie to go 'walking out' with him. He feels guilty about Alice, so he tells his brother John that she likes him. John asks Alice out.

At last, Grandad is courting Grandma! John starts courting Alice. Many years later, I was to learn of an unspoken jealousy and distance between the two women.

The sisters' strict father allowed no boys to call at the house. The girls would leave the house in twos to meet boyfriends but would always stay together. Courtship at that time was walking, sometimes linking arms, or going to a dance with the girl being accompanied by a sibling or friend or be part of a foursome.

Throughout the courtship of my grandparents, one of her sisters or Nell would be with them. They could not afford to go to the pictures very often, as the cost to watch anything was a full penny each. They also walked everywhere as the tram cost half a penny.

They were very much in love, but would never be alone until their wedding night.

The northern girl was born in the year the great Queen died. The southern girl, a lady from the age of 4, had been born at the turn of the century, ninth of ten children. Her father, the Earl of Strathmore, forgets to register her birth and is fined seven shillings and sixpence. She is looked after by a nurse and is raised in the family home near London. Holidays are taken in Glamis Castle, Scotland. Ironically, she meets the man she will marry at a children's birthday party in London – he is ten, she is five and gives him the cherry off her cake.

During the war years, as a safety precaution, and whilst Glamis Castle is being used as a military 'hospital', the family live there.

A year after the War ended, the young Lady from the Scottish castle was launched as a debutante in London. There were rounds of dances and house parties, all chaperoned, and the beautiful debutante very quickly had suitors. She danced with them but no friendship kindled. A debutante friend introduced her to a gentleman who was equerry to the second son of the King. The shy Prince is reported to have said to a close friend, "I fell in love today."

(A debutante, French word meaning 'female beginner', is a young lady of aristocratic or upper class background who had reached the age of maturity. All debutantes reaching the age of 18, in white evening dress, would be presented to the reigning monarch, by way of tradition dating back to the 1700s. It marked the start of a season (the summer months) filled with glittering dance balls, weekend hunting parties, house parties and other social gatherings up and down the country. The aim of this 'coming out' was to meet and marry a rich young man.)

A house party at her parents' Scottish castle – included

on the list of invites is the King's second son, Albert George, 'Bertie'. They danced and talked together. Later that year, when the debutante's mother became very ill he proved very supportive and visited them in Scotland.

Their courtship blossomed, but due to everything that the marriage would bring for the young girl, she was afraid that she would never be able to 'think or speak or act' freely ever again. Prince Albert's marriage proposal to Lady Elizabeth, in the spring of 1921, was turned down. They continued to see each other and corresponded.

The following year, as a favour to her brother 'Bertie', Princess Mary asked Elizabeth to be her bridesmaid. She wrote to him after the wedding, they met, but a second proposal was turned down. They did not see each other and did not correspond.

By the end of 1922, all but Albert himself had given up on the idea of them being friends again, let alone marrying each other. Elizabeth had many admirers and one particular beau, James Stuart, equerry to the Prince. Fate, or call it what you will, helped out as well as Albert's family as James left for 'pastures new' in America.

'Bertie' was reported to have said, "I'll give it one last shot." In early 1923, his next proposal was neither turned down nor accepted. A turning point even so. He joined the Strathmore's for the weekend, proposing 'continually' from Friday until he was accepted on the Sunday evening. Up to that point, they had been glum indeed, but after the word 'yes' it was open happiness and radiant smiles.

Early Spring

A grand wedding was going to take place in the capital city. The bride would be wearing a wedding dress of ivory chiffon; a traditional, full length gown, with a fashionable, but unshaped lace bodice, and matching silk shoes. A long train was worn in traditional style of that day, made of Nottingham-lace. The groom's wedding suit was cut from the finest cloth, adorned with shining new shoes.

Eight bridesmaids joined a large number of guests to see the happy couple get married.

A small wedding was going to take place in a northern city in a local church. The bride would be wearing a wedding dress worn by the bride's mother, traditional for the 1880s, and was brought out of its tattered box of moth balls and torn, paper-thin tissue paper. The hem was 'tapered' up as a small gesture to 'modernise' it. New ribbons were threaded through her old, worn shoes.

The wedding suit was darker than the groom preferred but had been the only one which fitted in the pawn shop. He had splashed out on boot polish to spruce up his shoes and no rain on the day would mean dry feet.

Eight guests, no bridesmaids, saw the happy couple get married.

In the south, a golden carriage took the bride and groom

to their wedding breakfast. They then greeted their guests one by one as they arrived in their cars and horse-drawn carriages. Sparkling, vintage wine in the finest of matching, cut glasses served to toast the happy couple. A meal of several courses followed. The couple left for a two part honeymoon, the latter ten days in Scotland.

The small northern wedding party walked from the church to the groom's parents' back room. Homemade lemonade in glasses and mugs served to toast the bride and groom. Potted meat sandwiches, pork pie, iced buns and cups of tea in a 'running' buffet followed. There was no honeymoon.

In London, they started married life living with her parents as their chosen home in Richmond Park was deemed 'too far' from the city centre. Work sometimes took them up and down the country but as long as they were together they did not mind. Carefree summer holidays were taken in Glamis Castle with other members of the family.

As the King's second son, he could look forward to many more years of dutifully meeting and greeting the British people, up and down the country, alongside carefree family holidays. Effect: content.

His elder brother, the heir to the throne, had just gone on a mammoth tour of the Empire. Effect: sensational success.

At the same time, their father was embracing and forging links with 'ordinary' people, in the light of increasing unemployment and a new socialist government. Effect: becoming known as the people's King.

In the north, they had started married life at the groom's parents' shop. There were two small bedrooms on the top floor, one for them and one for his mother and a brother still at home. Effect: cramped. (Sadly, his father had not lived to see him marry.)

The groom still worked long hours in the local steelworks and the bride had to give up her filing job after marriage, though she helped out in the shop. The mother now had the 'daughter' she wasn't blessed to have. Any holidays for the newlyweds, few and far between, would be a day at the seaside.

Three years after marrying, the happy royal couple were, at long last, expecting a baby. After debilitating morning sickness and confinement problems they were blessed with a daughter, born at home with family doctors, midwives and nurses in attendance.

She was a very pretty baby with clear blue eyes and a wide, generous smile.

Three years after marrying, the excited northern couple were, at last, expecting a baby. After protracted months of morning sickness they were blessed with a daughter, born at home with only a midwife in attendance.

She was a quite pretty baby with hazel eyes and a warm smile.

Nearly a year later, however, the royal parents were parted from their little girl for several months while touring abroad as part of their royal 'work'. They missed her first steps. After returning, they moved into a home of their own at 145 Picadilly, a large Georgian town house near to Hyde Park. They were ecstatic to announce a further pregnancy, at long, long last; a second daughter who was born at Glamis Castle. The father proudly referred to his family as 'we four'.

The northern father had been out of work for some time,

but now he had an overseeing role in an engineering tools firm. He looked forward to coming home after work and then spending each Sunday together as a family. They both were delighted in their little girl's first steps. 'We two' had become 'we three'.

The life changing events of 1936 propelled the royal father into a world he had never wanted or been groomed for.

A stammer, when speaking, became worse but his wife's calmness and support helped enormously. 'We four' moved into a palace when the girls were ten and seven.

The palace, now their home, suffered bomb damage in the Second World War. In fact, a total of six bombs were to hit the palace. They set an example and cut out luxuries.

The eldest daughter would go on to become Queen.

'We three' moved into a northern terraced home with a small garden, not a courtyard, but still with an outside closet. By the start of the Second World War, they kept chickens in their back garden for fresh eggs as food was rationed. They tried to have a luxury item of food as often as possible, but most times the 'luxury' had to be a meal made with their own eggs.

The daughter in the terraced home was my mother, Annie.

Like Princess Elizabeth, mother was born in between the two world wars.

Both babies were born in the middle of a coal miners' strike and recession, the like of which the country had not seen before. By April 1926, the long and bitter dispute in the coalfields was moving rapidly towards its climax. The miners' leader had made an impassioned speech, summed up by the phrase, "Not a penny off the pay, not a minute on the day." But looming 'in the air' was the general strike which would halt industries and services for nine long days.

As if the Home Secretary of the day wasn't busy enough; he received a call in the early hours of the morning of the 21st April to attend a royal birth. He was far from feeling any kind of celebration, but it was a duty he could not shirk and went quickly to the bedside of the Duchess of York. Her parents, the Earl and Countess of Strathmore, just happened to be the most prominent coal owners in the country.

Why the Home Secretary needed to be at the birth of a minor member of the Royal Family was a mystery steeped in the tradition and custom of the British Monarchy. There was a general belief that the Home Secretary would provide a validation of the birth, that no 'switching' of the baby had taken place and no treachery was afoot. According to the newspapers the next day, he was deemed to have been "… present in the house at the time of the birth…" One thing was certain – there was no sleep for anyone in that house, that night.

It was a difficult birth, despite the very best of medical attention. The newspapers' code for a caesarean section was used, "…and a certain line of treatment was successfully adopted." The risks of such an operation at that time were immense and as a consequence would limit the number of children the Duchess could have in the future, making it very unlikely she would have a large family. The fact that this might inhibit a male being born to the Yorks was not regarded as important. The King's eldest son and heir was young and healthy, and expected to marry and have the requisite 'male heir, and spare'.

The princess was born at 10am and, although third in line to the throne's succession, she seemed as remote from becoming Queen as, say, putting a man on the moon! Before the Act of Settlement in 1701, the princess would not have taken precedence over any younger brothers of the King. It was this Act that had led to Princess Victoria, who's father was deceased, taking precedence over the younger brother of William IV.

Had the northern birth suffered the same complications, mother and/or her baby, may not have fared so well. Amongst other factors there would have been a life threatening time delay in seeking further medical help for the midwife in attendance.

Grandma had registered her expectancy at the GP's surgery so that a midwife could be appointed. There was no doctor's examination, no tests done, no interview with any doctor or midwife. In fact, she did not meet the appointed midwife until the day of delivery.

Mother's birth, after a long labour, was a natural one at home in the bedroom, the appointed midwife in attendance. Helping with the sterilisations, towel fetching and supplying of water was her eldest sister. Grandad was smoking and pacing in the living room.

Grandma stayed in bed three days (bed rest would have been at least a week, possibly two, if a hospital birth.) One of her sisters called each day to help wash the baby, do the shopping and cook Grandad's tea.

After two weeks in the afternoons the newborn was wheeled round the park and local shops in a large perambulator by Grandma's mother or a sister.

The afternoon stroll for the baby princess was with a nanny rather than her own mother. A 'nanny' in the north meant the baby's grandmother.

Both babies wore 'no frill' garments and were mainly dressed in white, sometimes with pink trimming. Cotton was the favoured material for most of their baby clothes, representing cleanliness and purity. On cool days, the northern baby wore a hand knitted, white matinee coat with matching hat and tiny bootees tied with pink ribbon.

In 1930, the Duke and Duchess of York went to spend the summer in Glamis Castle to await the birth of their second child. As the Prince of Wales was still unmarried, the Royal Family hoped for a son, 'just in case'. The Scottish birth meant the Home Secretary had the width and breadth of the country to travel to be present, or in close proximity to, the delivery room. He reached the Castle amid a thunderous thunder storm with only hours to spare.

A girl was born on 21st August, the first royal baby to be born in Scotland for over 300 years. Lady Elizabeth wanted to call her 'Ann' but her husband did not. As they dithered over the name until October, parents all over the country had registered their new daughters by surname only until the royal names were announced. The news came through, at last, that the baby would be named 'Margaret Rose' and Princess Elizabeth, or 'Lilibet' as she was affectionately known, said she would call her 'Bud'. When asked why she replied, "Well, she's too little to be a rose, she's just a bud."

The three girls were growing up in terraced property, but there the similarities ended. The Sheffield property was a 'two up, two down' house on a back to back estate. The London property at 145 Piccadilly was a town house, reportedly with 25 bedrooms, including the servants' quarters.

The royal nursery was on the top floor, consisting of a

day room, a night (bed)room and a bathroom. The mother wanted to spend as much time as possible with her little daughters, but the requirements of royalty soon produced long parental absences and the nanny's role grew.

The northern 'nursery' was a corner of the parents' bedroom. Mother and baby spent almost all of their time together. Nanny, the maternal grandma, carried out the 'walking of the pram' duties in the afternoon.

Up to the age of three, my mother's head leaned to one side as she was born with a shoulder bone joined to a neck bone. The hospital doctor said it would not get better but worse, and eventually she would not be able to hold up her head. An operation could sever the bones. My grandparents did not like to think of their daughter being operated on at such an early age but neither did they want her to grow up with a deformity.

Grandma blamed herself for little Annie's deformity in the form of a superstition she believed happened during the pregnancy. She had slipped on the bottom step of the stairs and felt pain in her neck which she had rubbed for a while. Where she had rubbed was the very spot where the baby's shoulder bone was joined to the neck. Grandma always said that if she hadn't rubbed her baby's neck would not have been deformed. It was a total belief and regret that did not diminish with the passing of time.

Grandad remembered as a child, after an accident to his foot, his mother had been asked to consent to have his foot amputated. She had refused, and had kept refusing, and his foot had eventually got better. This was remembered, but there were still many months of indecision with their daughter before consenting to the operation.

It was a resounding success! Mother was left with only a small length of criss-cross scarring, from the stitches, to the right of her neck. She would grow up to hate all photographs taken before the operation as they showed her head leaning to one side at an awkward, and unflattering, angle.

Money was in short supply in many households and in the aftermath of the general strike, grandad lost his job. He was 'laid off' with hundreds of other men from a number of the larger steelworks. There were queues at job exchanges and outside large factories and works each morning. Among the flat capped throng of men looking for a job, any job; was flat capped grandad.

(The recession had resulted from the 'fallout' of the nine day general strike in 1926 involving the coal miners who were protesting at the mine owners cutting their wages in order to 'pass on' the falling price of coal. Newspaper coverage of each 'side' was split, with one newspaper calling the strikers 'revolutionaries'. The King took exception to this suggestion and was reported as saying, "Try living on a coal miner's wage before you judge them."

The strike was due to free imports of German coal (part of the 'war deal') the loss of export markets as a result of WW1 and because of heavy domestic use of coal through the war, resulting in many coal seams becoming depleted.

In London, there was no shortage of volunteers to take the place of the strikers – volunteer railway guards, omnibus drivers and signalmen, to name a few. The volunteers were steam-lorried into the capital or they slept on the premises. A milk depot was established in Hyde Park with food and petrol convoys being given armoured vehicle escorts or soldier guards. British 'good sense' prevailed and the strike was called off.)

Some industries suffered from the strike, including the

heavy industries in Sheffield leading to a recession by the end of that decade. Many Sheffield steelworkers lost their jobs and livelihood, grandad amongst them.

After a fruitless few weeks of walking and searching and disappointment, he started to try more local, smaller, firms. This eventually proved fruitful as there were less flat capped men looking for jobs outside small engineering/small tools works.

He was given a job in the machine works of a small tools firm. Within a few years, grandad was made works manager and given a car to use as he drove around to promote their tools in large shops and warehouses. The big black car had 'Al Capone' type ledges under the front doors on either side of the car. Grandad kept it shiny clean and it was his to use on Sundays as well, which meant that he could fish at various local rivers and reservoirs. If fishing locally, he would go alone but farther afield the family would go with him.

To start with, mother and daughter would sit on the river bank with him and then go for a walk and shopping, if near a village or town centre. At lunchtime, rejoining grandad for a picnic of sandwiches, pork pie and homemade cake or apple tart. They would ask him to lift up his 'keep net' to see what fish he had caught. The net was large enough to keep the fish underwater and the rod-type handle on the riverbank would be weighed down. Around tea time and before setting off back home he would empty the fish back into the water, free again to swim away.

Tea at home might be homemade meat pasty or pie or chops of meat with potatoes, vegetables, Yorkshire pudding and gravy. Sometimes, dumplings in hash or pieces of meat in the hash. On Sunday, if going on a fishing trip, a meal would have been pre-prepared by grandma before setting off, keeping cool on the cellar steps. In the evening, grandad or mother might play the piano or they might all play a card game. Whoever played the piano, grandma would be sewing or knitting while she listened.

A night out for all three would be a visit to one of grandma's sisters for a cards night, or a rare visit to grandad's married brother's home. His older brother George now played semi-professional football for a nearby town and was soon to marry.

A night out for grandad would be to play billiards at the public house at the bottom of the hill, the 'Queen's Ground'. This was conveniently next to the Phoenix Cinema and sometimes the three of them would walk home together after mother and daughter had been to see a film.

(When grandad lived in his childhood home there was a billiards hall above a shop on the main road, next to the housing estate.)

The local pub was a drinking place for men with very few women, or wives, venturing in and certainly grandma never went inside even to watch him play competition matches. grandad won cups and medals for billiards and one of the medals being solid gold which grandma put on a chain and proudly wore. The next one he won was made into a chain for mother to wear when she was older.

At least one evening in the week would be set aside for mother and grandma to walk to her own mother's home, where her invalid sister and youngest brother were still at home. Another evening, they would visit her two sisters, and their husbands, who all lived on the same hill, very conveniently. The hill was called the 'Bank, shortened from Rivelin Bank, and they would announce, "Jus' goin' to 'Bank."

They would walk up the road, twisting and weaving up two hills, along two gennels and down 'Bank. In Yorkshire, 'the' is omitted.

Grandma and mother went to church. Most children went to Sunday School with each attendance in the morning and/or afternoon being marked by a star stamped on a card – the Star Card. At the end of the year, the stars would be counted and those with good attendances would receive a book prize. Inside the cover would be an elaborate printed inscription stuck into the book of the church's name in fancy lettering. Underneath would be printed the child's name and 'prize for good attendance in …' (the year).

The Church was the focal point for many social as well as religious activities, such as Easter and the Autumn Harvest Festival, but the largest event on any local church's calendar was Whitsuntide in May.

On Whit Sunday it was the annual Whit Walk and then the Whit Sing in Hillsborough Park with children in their new clothes. An individual procession would start from each church and make their way to the main road where they would join the main Whit Walk. At the head of the main procession was the marching band, then schoolchildren, Boys' Brigade and Girl Guides. Behind each church's banner would be their May Queen and her trainbearers and the church's congregation.

As the procession passed the local hospital, everyone would detour into its grounds and stop to sing a couple of hymns standing outside the windows of wards. The procession would then meander back to the main road. People who lined the route to watch would then join the back of the procession to the local park's Whit Sing.

Hundreds, if not a thousand or more, would be in the park singing their hearts out to the popular hymns. In between singing, a vicar would say a prayer and short service and then the band would play. It was very much a 'carnival' atmosphere.

Families would picnic in the park before making their way back home at the end of the afternoon. It was very much a case of 'don't spill ought down yer top' or frock or shirt. 'Sit prop'ly' to minimise creases and 'don't sit on 'grass' to avoid green marks on pristine new clothes. The smaller the child, the greater the chance of mishap!

Older children knew the importance of keeping their outfit clean on the Sunday.

Mother had started to take an interest in her clothes and she liked to read, along with most of the nation, about what the princesses were wearing, especially around Whitsuntide. They were always dressed the same. One year, mother's Whit outfit was a coat and hat to match with shiny new shoes and to her delight saw that the princesses were wearing almost identically designed outfits. The picture of the princesses, getting out of a car with a corgi on a lead, was in black and white, which made the colour of their coats and hats a light grey.

(As their father had grown up as a 'second' son and made to feel inferior to his older brother, as heir to the throne, he wanted his daughters to grow up 'equal' and he decreed that they should always be dressed the same. Oh, what a thought – if dressing children or people in the same outfits made them equal…)

The day after, Whit Monday, was when families would visit nearby relatives to 'show off' their children's new Whit clothes and be given a 'copper or two'. Grandma and mother would start on 'Bank where there would be a cup of tea and biscuits at one sister's home and the other sister would walk up to chat and give mother the customary tuppence or thruppence for her new clothes. A usual total of five pennies from the 'Bank.

Then grandma and her newly 'turned out' daughter would visit her grandma and invalid aunt. It would be a penny from there. As they visited often, it was a 'closet' stop as well, due to all that tea and more to come! Then onto an uncle's home, 'Oh, dun't she look luv'ly – let's put kettle on.' At another relative, 'An't she grown – kettle's jus' boiled.'

That year was a good year and another eight pennies were in Mother's small, new handbag.

At Uncle John and Aunt Alice's she would play with her cousin, Barbara, while the grown ups chatted. As they didn't live nearby (though it was in the same city) grandad took them in the car. While there, they would arrange an outing or a day trip out, much to grandma's chagrin (remember Alice and Annie only had a 'lukewarm' relationship with each other.) Mother would come away with a silver thru'pence.

An average Whit total might be as much as 1s 6d, of which she would keep back one penny and her mother would put the rest into her money box for saving. (1/6d is about six new pence.)

At last, the day after was a day to wear 'old and comfy' clothes again!

That was Whit Tuesday to watch the 'Star Walk' event. This tradition began in 1922 as a race walk of 12 miles, for men and boys, around the city streets to try and encourage walking as a sport. The event was organised by the daily 'Sheffield Star' newspaper hence it being called the 'Star

Walk'. Only walking male 'novices' living within a 20 mile radius of the newspaper's building were eligible to enter. *(It took another 50 years before women were allowed to compete!)*

Wherever anyone lived within Sheffield, the walkers would walk through on the main roads to see the event as it unfolded in their 'neck of the woods'. The serious and not-so-serious contenders would be cheered and clapped as they passed. There were no trainers yet invented so walkers had to wear hard, heavy shoes often resulting in blisters.

Serious contenders would turn up early to the start in order to flex their leg muscles. They would be race walking in the required 'heel and toe' action with swivelling hips in a smooth, fast walking movement. The main rule of the race was that one foot had to be on the ground at all times, as in 'heel and toe'.

The majority of Star walkers were the not-so-serious contenders, some of whom would be dressed in football tops and shorts and the fancy dressed tended to 'waddle' along in varying speeds of walking. For the last few miles at a snail-type pace but they would get the loudest cheers to 'egg' them on to the finishing line.

'Barnsley Hill' sorted out the men from the boys, so to speak. The serious walkers slowed down very little as their elegant muscles took the strain of the hill. The 'waddlers' would straggle and start to look pretty exhausted and that was only after catching their first glimpse of the hill looming 'like a wall' in the distance.

Mother walked to the bottom of the road to see the Star walkers. After the serious walkers had, well, walked by some straddlers would stop every so often to laugh and joke with people in the crowd, one or two asking for safety pins to keep their shorts from falling down. Outside some public houses, slow walkers might be offered a drink of beer to help them on their way.

The course had been shortened to eleven and a half miles and a hot Oxo drink and medal greeted all those who finished, however quick or slow they walked.

As a young girl watching this walking spectacle it was a most enjoyable end to a weekend of 'dressing up' in new clothes and walking from 'pillar to post'. A welcome comfy, worn dress would be adorned with a straw hat if sunny. It was a chance to be part of a cheering, laughing crowd rather than the centre of attention and trying to smile sweetly after an 'oh you're so like your mother' comment.

During ordinary weeks, grandma might visit her sisters in the day or they would visit her. Never on a Monday which was wash day.

Washing clothes took all day. Well, it started the night before by half filling the tin bath with water and bleach to soak grandad's overalls. The morning's first task was to scrub shirt collars with soap against a scrubbing board before putting into boiling water to soak – collars were then detachable from shirts.

Bed linen went into the washer first which was manually filled up with pans and a large kettle of boiling water from the open fire. Grandma poured in a few soap flakes from a packet and also rubbed more soap from a handmade bar. Then she would move the lever backwards and forwards to wash the clothes. This lever was the 'new fangled' part of the washer.

Excess water would be rung out from the sheets as they were lifted out. The water is then emptied, bit by bit, from the bottom of the washer into a bucket. Then poured away and this process repeated until empty. The sheets were rinsed in the sink from running water, then squeezed, and then rinsed for a second time. Squeezed once more and then folded through the mangle.

Bed linen on the line, the whole washing process is repeated for the overalls, socks and any trousers. Another wash for the shirts and any whites and a separate wash for towels. Grandma's tops, skirts and dresses were hand washed, as well as the woollen garments. Underwear and stockings were washed by hand. Everything would be mangled except woollens and stockings.

On Tuesday it was ironing day with the 'two irons' system. In fact, grandma had a third larger iron which was used for the bed linen. An old blanket and sheet laid across the table acted as an 'ironing board'. This took the 'best part' of half a day with a break around lunchtime to go to the corner shop for something fresh to eat. Before teatime there was another visit to the corner shop.

The 'big' shopping day was Wednesday. This meant a visit to the shops on the main road and would take hours, at least half the day. Just before tea time, grandma may also visit the corner shop for bottle items which would have been too heavy to carry with the main shopping. The corner shop visiting was once or twice a day, except Sunday. No shops opened at all on Sundays.

The average weekly time spent on shopping was ten hours!

Baking was done on Thursdays. For tea, it was homemade meat and potato pie, which also included vegetables and cut up sausages, sometimes kidney pieces.

The pastry, only on top of the pie, we called 'pie', so if grandma asked if anyone wanted more pie, it would mean the pastry. Most of the baking was for the weekend.

Fridays resembled a 'spring' cleaning day as furniture was moved for sweeping and brushing underneath. Rugs would be hung on the washing line and hit with a stick to get all the dust out. All shelves, ornaments, wall pictures and clocks, the piano and anything not in a cupboard would be dusted.

Every day was 'whitening the steps' day with the essential 'donkey' stone.

Grandma wore a full pinafore ('pinny') at all times of the day and would only take it off at teatime. Washing up after tea, or any other evening chores, and it would be slipped back on. She would keep it on for the corner shop but take it off to go to the main shops. A clean 'pinny' was always hanging behind the cellar door just in case of unexpected visitors. A knock at the door and she would rush over to the cellar head and change her 'pinny' in a superman turning-round manoeuvre.

(When saying 'pinny', it was pronounced 'pinna'.)

Grandad's mother came to live with them as the brother still at home, George, had married and moved away. A bed was made up in the front room so that she did not have to climb any stairs to and from the outside closet. Sometimes she would make the 'Himalayan' journey upstairs and sleep in mother's bed when the family had 'sing along' evenings in front of the piano.

During this period, grandma had a three 'pinna' system. A second clean one hung at the bottom of the stairs in case she had to go into the 'patient' and then she would change back into her everyday one before returning to the living room.

What a dilemma if there was a knock at the door and she was with the 'patient' wearing her second 'pinny'. Would she choose to 'superman' her everyday one at the bottom of the stairs, or risk leaving the visitor a bit longer and going for the untouched 'pinny' at the cellar head?

But, it was a very difficult few years of always having to take the old lady's ill health into consideration. They got no help from grandad's brother John who only lived at the other side of the city which added to the already considerable tension between grandma and her sister-in-law Alice. The 'patient' died of pleurisy when mother was eight.

Families looked after their elderly parents as there was nowhere else for them to live. If there had been a daughter, she would have had the duty of looking after the ailing mother.

The younger brother George now played football for Huddersfield Town. The year after they had a daughter. In fact, all three brothers had a daughter as their only child.

John and Alice had been reluctant to 'take on' his mother, now their daughter Barbara was growing up (she was younger than mother.) Of course, it was one of those 'excuses' that the family accepted, but never believed 'in a month of Sundays'.

Also, grandad had the use of a car and the family lived a 'stone's throw' away from a large shopping area. In fact, everyone lived near a shopping area, as there were corner shops, er, on every corner.

The 'stone's throw' away shopping area was a parallel of two rows of shops either side of the main road. Shops selling a wide variety of fresh food, other edible provisions and household goods and services all from individual, small shops. The only shop anywhere near to resembling a large shop was the local co-operative store selling amost everything. The size depended, very much, on how small or how large the actual shopping area was.

The two rows of shops along the main road were between the family's home and grandma's childhood home. A main road had tramlines. These particular tramlines having been laid in 1877 and electrified in 1903, a year after the horse drawn trams were withdrawn. The horse drawn tram sheds, in amongst a row of shops, were then converted into tram sheds and tramlines extended into them. The first motor bus on the route along this main road, to and from the city centre, started in 1912.

Trams were also used to collect mail from the post boxes along its route. A couple of miles journey took 'the best part' of forty five minutes due to the incessant stopping for passengers and mail collections. *(Using trams to collect the post ended in 1939.)*

Every shopping area would include a post office. If a postcard had a message of five words or under, the postage would be 1d, but if the message exceeded five words, the cost would be 2d. It was one way of 'putting up the cost' in a very subtle way as a message of ten words would not 'weigh' any more than four words. Or did longer postcard messages take longer to deliver as the postman would have more to read? (Just a thought!)

At the bottom of the street, to the right of the main road, was an old toll house, still lived in, and across a side street is the large co-operative store. A large store to reflect the large shopping area. After that, a bank and a pawn shop, then rows of houses which had their front doors straight onto the pavement.

At the next corner was a public house. There were still a lot of horse and carts, and milk carts pulled by horses on the main road. These were joined by a few cars and 'every so often' a tram and bus. At that time, you could just give a cursory glance left and right and walk across any road.

A large stone-built police station had been converted into a dentists and this marked the end of that long row of shops, houses and pubs.

Crossing the road was the start of the parallel line of shops. There were a couple of public houses, a furniture store and then a row of houses before the start of the individual shops after a side road. Shops which included several butcher's shops (not together), a haberdashery (sewing and knitting) shop, bread (homemade and unsliced) shops, a post office, fruit and veg, hardware 'anything' shops, ironmongers, cards, newsagents and spice and grocery shops.

Along this side of the main road was a large archway which used to be a terminus for the local stagecoach and horses, next to an inn.

If grandma did not want any shopping on the way there or way back to her mother's, they would cut across a long road running parallel with the main road at the top of steep side roads. Along this parallel road, side streets went downhill to the main road. The right hand, much steeper, side streets, led up to another straight road with individual shops on either side, but was not a main, tramway road.

At the end of the long, parallel road which still had corner shops of course; the road sloped downhill, leading to the back to back houses of her former estate. Her home had been the middle of three terraced houses on Woollen Lane. These three had their front doors leading into a shared, walled courtyard with steps onto the pavement. This allowed grandma's invalid sister to sit outside the front door without being on the pavement.

All the other houses on Woollen Lane had their front doors adjacent to the kerb in the usual way. No-one knew why these three particular houses had been built in a 'back to front' way.

To recap, down grandma's street was the main road, to the right of which were the shops along the main road to Woollen Lane. To the left of the main road, at the bottom, led to the larger shopping 'mecca' of Hillsborough.

The route took in the Queen's Ground and the Phoenix Cinema, a row of large houses, side roads, a Catholic Church and School, the local swimming baths and Yorkshire Penny Bank. After this bank was the bridge over the river and the four street crossroads known as Hillsboro' corner.

On the opposite side from grandma's road, almost to Hillsboro' corner, stood the former large, military barracks now converted and used by 'Burdalls', the makers of 'gravy salt'.

After this 'corner' and over the bridge, the shops started in earnest. Davy's the Grocer's, the Chemists and down a side street was the slaughterhouse. On the main road, after this side street, was Mr Parker's pawnshop; Mr Hogg who sold fish and Mr Kelsey's pork shop. (What a pity Mr Hogg sold fish and not pork!) Then, Madam Bells' shop, selling beads of every description and all kinds of ornaments – a bit of an 'Aladdin's Cave'.

Next door was a herb and sarsaparilla shop and then a chip shop up two steps into what had been a house's front room. There was Mr West's butcher's shop and Mr Abbott's seed and flower shop. At the corner of another side road was Lister's, the 'beer off'.

On the other side of the road was the largest in the area, co-operative store. Next to that another butcher's shop, 'Talbots'; a shop full of knitting wools and patterns; then a second hand clothes 'emporium', next door to a larger than usual corner shop of a side street. This was Kinema Road where the Kinema Cinema stood (rhyme intended). To go in to watch a film cost 1d. On the other side street corner was a chemist shop which was also a dentists. When the Chemist was acting as the Dentist there was entertainment in there, for free!

(There was no anaesthetic in use and a pair of pliers was sometimes used to extract teeth which would indeed have been entertaining for customers. Unless, of course, you were the person in the dentist's chair!)

Next door, the post office was in someone's front room, next to the haberdasher's shop and another butcher's, 'Funks'. There was also an ironmonger's and grocery shops. One grocery shop had an unwashed floor – more potato dirt to walk on than seen on the actual potatoes.

Spice shops (spice as in sweets). The latter had shelves of glass jars which were taken down to be weighed as a customer called out what they wanted, '2 ounce of sherbert lemons', or 'tuppence worth of dolly mixtures'.

Along that side of the road, Mrs Burton's flower shop, the pikelet shop and Mr Hallet, the Barber. Then a baby linen shop, Fletchers the Bakery and Howards 'all-sorts'.

On hot, sunny days Mr Howard had a stall outside his shop selling ice cream. Ranks were often broken on the way to the Whit Sing in Hillsboro' Park for a cornet of his homemade, 'delicious' ice cream.

Along the road leading to the right of Hillsboro' corner were more shops…

Mr Ford's, gentlemen's hatters

A fish shop – with a stall on the pavement

Mr Brown's pork shop – bacon would be sliced from the side of a pig in the shop

Misses Gregory's ladies' outfitters shop *('misses' as in two spinster sisters)*

Someone's front room selling pots and crockery

A chip shop

Miss Mortimer's wool shop – wool had to be wound into balls at home

Mr Greaves, the optician

Miss Greaves, his daughter's jewellery shop

Newsagents

Tobacconist

Greengrocers, advertising one carrot or turnip or celery stick for only 1p

…was this the start of 'two for the price of one'?

Mr Wright's coalyard, with the sign 'bring your own wheelbarrow to buy coal'

Tomlinson's, Funeral Director *(no need for gimmicks here)*

Mr Cork's, cobblers shoe repairs, and inside was the 'lovely' smell of leather

In the middle of these shops was the large, imposing tram shed. At night the trams would go through the enormous doors into the double tram shed.

On the opposite side of the road were terraced houses and then a warehouse selling wood. More houses and then 'Joseph Wing Ltd', making files and engineering tools which grandad managed for Mr Wing.

Then another small tools company, 'Burgon and Ball' (*amazingly still there!*)

A 'must mention' here building, over the river bridge, is a small mill used for grinding hull, bought by German Wilson. What an unfortunate forename! However, by 1914, his son John Wilson, with a more fortunate forename, had taken over and converted it to a cornmill. (If the building had still displayed the name 'German Wilson' at the start of the War in 1914, it might have been attacked along with other shops owned by Germans or those displaying German names. German owned shops closed for the War.)

Going back on the opposite side of the road were some smaller shops, including a chip shop, a car sales lot, a public house and a small, grassed island with men's toilets in the middle. These toilets were used by male tram and bus drivers, hence no need for female toilets! The horse trough on the island was much in demand by horses pulling heavy loads of iron and steel from firm to firm. It was also well used by horses pulling the milk floats and 'rag and bone' horses.

After this island lived Mr and Mrs Jolley who made and sold their salve, very good for boils, etc. Then there was a shop where people took their bread to be baked. There was also a small co-operative in an ordinary sized shop which professed to be the 'smallest ever' co-op.

There was also a vet, a blacksmith and a wheel shop; the latter selling, er, wheels and the repair of. A shop making and selling 'polony' (a type of meat) had shut for the duration of the War as the owner was of 'German extraction' and feared it would be wrecked (the building not the polony.)

That reminds me of a saying, not in everyday use anymore, "it's all a load o' polony," meaning whatever 'it' was, it was a "load of old rubbish."

Further along opposite the tram shed was a sign above a somewhat small arched entrance, 'Hirst and Sweeting', which offered lorries, and oyster grey and red charabancs (coaches) for hire. We pronounced charabancs as 'charabangs'. (*This sign can be seen to the left of the picture in the first section of photographs.*)

It was amazing how such large 'charabangs' could manoeuvre in and out of such a small entrance from/to a main tramway road. Each manoeuvre going in or out would stop all traffic, including the trams of course. (*The road haulage part of the business later became 'British Road Services'.*)

Back at the crossroads of Hillsboro' corner, on one side was a public house and on the other, a large card shop. In the build up to Christmas, the card shop would sell decorations and trees.

Birthday and Christmas cards were postcard style up to the 1940s. Grandma would stick each annual set in an album. An early one of my mother's, in very fancy lettering at the top, 'A Joyous Birthday' and underneath a photograph of a little girl with a dog.

Another card said 'To greet your Birthday' with a hand coloured photograph of a little girl. This was from the owner of a large family owned department store, called 'Atkinsons' in the city centre. On the reverse of the card it read 'from Uncle John' as in 'John Atkinson'.

(*At the age of 26 years in 1872, John Atkinson opened a new city centre shop selling lace, ribbons and hosiery. By offering high* quality service and value for money, the shop went from strength to strength. He expanded into adjoining shops and started selling a wide variety of goods, including clothes and furniture.

In 1901, an all-in-one store was built and by 1922 there was an impressive 46 departments. The flagship store was on different levels and had a spectacular glass roof – it was a shopping experience like no other.

Despite the depression of the 1930s, department stores were 'springing' up in most large cities, not least, in London. One new store advertising a 'jumbo' sale actually hired three young elephants to walk around the ground floor and just outside to try and attract customers through their doors. However, the best advert that a London store could have was an article in a newspaper that the two princesses had visited the store. Sales of toys, clothes, gifts, books, and more, would 'hit the roof' as a result – no elephants needed there!)

If a greeting card stated 'hand coloured' it meant that a sepia photograph had been coloured by hand to give the appearance of a photograph in colour.

A postcard of two donkeys at the seaside, one with a dog on top and the other with a child riding it, had a caption "we have plenty of room at Blackpool." This card was from relatives living in Blackpool and the penny stamp was hallmarked 1932, which was the year after 'we three' had moved into their own home from grandad's family shop.

At seasides, you were as likely to see baby to half-grown elephants as donkeys, and in the family album there is a photograph of a man with a baby elephant on the sands which would have become a future performing elephant at a circus. Other popular animals, taking a bit of exercise, would be circus horses, camels and occasionally a walking brown bear, not fully grown, with a short lead of steel chains.

Seaside holidays, driving in the car, were taken at Blackpool, staying with the relatives. Sepia photographs show grandma and mother, over the years, on the sands with the Blackpool Tower in the background, one shows them licking an ice cream cornet. The first fine weather day, grandad might have said, "Let's get down on sands fer 'oliday photo', hey, go and get some ice creams!"

The year after, "Let's do melons this year and walk on seafront," still with Blackpool Tower in the background, of course.

Another year, it was mother, aged about eight, waving on the sands holding a small handbag – with the Tower behind her.

Mother's a bit older now and she suggests taking this year's sands and Tower picture. The photo' is of them under a parasol with the Tower 'jutting' out of grandad's right shoulder. "We're not lettin' you take another picture," they said. But oh dear, the one grandad takes the next year has the Tower 'plonked' on top of mother's head!

Yet another year's photo', "Hey, we've not 'ad one on pier!" So there's the photograph of mother and daughter sat on the pier with the Tower in the distance, but between them.

The first non-postcard, opening card in the album, said "Dear Husband, to wish you Birthday Gladness and happy times," and turning over the page:

"Here's wishing you a birthday bright –
Such happy hours – a heart that's light,
With joys the passing days to fill –
The coming year much happier still."

Inside the card, grandma had written only her Christian name 'Annie' with no kisses! This was no indication of a lack of love, but 'love and kisses' were absent from most cards between the couple.

A birthday card to Annie reads, 'Best wishes for your 8ᵗʰ Birthday,' but in fancy lettering, and then in italics:

"Eight long years, just think of that,
My! you are growing old;
But that is nothing, for I hear
You are as good as gold."

The postcard had a hand coloured photograph of a small girl talking to a doll and was from 'Uncle John' Atkinson, owner of the department store; though he was a family friend rather than a related uncle.

Another postcard for mother's eighth birthday was in the shape of an '8'. In the bottom circle of the large '8' was a little girl with two puppies.

"Ninth Birthday Wishes" was written inside a large '9' on the front of the postcard and showed a girl with roses. On the other side, in pen and ink, was written, "Best wishes on your birthday, from Grandma, Aunty and Uncle." That is Aunt Harriet who couldn't walk and Uncle Walt still at home.

For her tenth birthday, a large postcard with flower borders reads "Wishing my Daughter Birthday Happiness" and, underneath, thatched cottages behind a small pond with the verse:

"To wish you many glad returns Dear Daughter – on this day, With health and happiness – to bless you on your future way'.

On the other side, in pen and ink, "From Mam and Dad xxxxxxxx". Printed in the bottom right corner: "A real photograph, hand coloured."

Mother always remembered a wireless in the living room

which was often on for music or news broadcasts. The King's Christmas message had started in 1932 and had been much welcomed by the nation and countries of the Empire. He was a popular King and as a girl she recalls news items at the cinema on where the King and Queen had been visiting that week.

The King's last Christmas speech had been given only a month before he died. Now, everyone had closed their front room curtains out of mourning and respect for the King and each day people listened to the wireless for news of when the funeral might be. Mother thought how sad as she remembered the films about the silver jubilee celebrations of 1935 which were shown at all the picture palaces (cinemas).

Around that time, my mother nearly lost her life to scarlet fever, so called because of its red rash. In such pre-antibiotic days it was very serious and children had to immediately be isolated and quarantined, usually in hospital. Grandma refused to let her go into hospital, so she was confined at home in a darkened bedroom with her parents and doctor as her only contact. When she started to recover, after several months away from school, grandma arranged for schoolwork to be sent home and collected.

During this time, mother wrote in an exercise book her favourite poems: 'To the Moon' by Shelley; 'Silver' by Walter de la Mare; 'Big Steamers' by Kipling, and a poem she could recite, word for word, was 'Abou Ben Adhem' by Hunt.

'Abou Ben Adhem, may his tribe increase
Awoke one night from a deep dream of peace
And saw within the moonlight in his room
Making it rich and like a lily in bloom

An Angel writing in a book of gold
Exceeding peace had made Ben Adam bold
And to the Presence in the room, he said
"What writest thou?"
The Vision raised it's head and with a look
Made of all sweet accord, answered
"The names of those who love the Lord."
"And is mine one?" said Abou.
"Nay not so," replied the Angel
Abou spoke more low and cheerily said,
"I pray three then put me as one who loves his fellow men,"
With that the Angel wrote and vanished.
The next night it came again with a great awakening
And showed Ben Adhem the names whom God had blessed
And lo, Ben Adhem's name led all the rest!'

Her own poem in this exercise book, reads:

'*Christmas Eve*
Up the chimney the tiny ones call,
Dear Father Christmas,
Please bring a big ball,
A trumpet and flute,
A picture book jolly,
A wee teddy bear,
And a beautiful dolly.'

Mother's 'worst' time and most 'boring' months were the ones when she was slowly recovering but had to stay in isolation. She had been one of the top in the class, but on her return she was near to the bottom. She joined an extra 'homemaking' class with the girls rather than her 'pre-illness', mixed class studying English literature.

The use of an often 'scratchy' pen nib and paper had replaced the slate and slate pencil grandma used to write on in her school days.

Unfortunately, mother went to a school where they would not let pupils write with their left hands as she had started to do. She was forced to write with her right hand, but remained left handed for everything else. In keeping with those times, her own mother endorsed the teachers making her write with her right hand.

Schools still had separate entrances and playgrounds for girls and boys, but there were some shared subjects, like English. The girls still learned how to sew, cook and general homemaking; with the boys doing science, woodwork and games.

Below is an account about school days in the 1930s adapted from a schoolgirl's memory of that era which mother said was very like her own.

There was a rocking chair where you could have a ride on your birthday. There was play in the sand-pit and coloured counters for sums. Next to the blackboards were duster-bags smelling of chalk, and dust would rise like clouds from them.

The playground's big iron gate was locked at dinner time (there were no school meals). There was a shed for wet days. Sparklers and coloured fireworks were a treat on November 5th, but in the infants only.

When you reached the Standards there were desks not tables. Two to a desk with about 30 in the room. Teachers told you to 'stand out' in the gangway for talking, or the shame and fear of standing in the corner with your hands on your head. If the headmaster walked in he would take away anyone standing up for the dire punishment of the cane.

We had to sit still with our arms folded or hands behind our backs and to not talk unless the teacher spoke to you. The teacher's most frequent sayings were: 'don't talk', 'sit up', 'sit straight', 'speak up', and 'go and stand outside'.

Big wicker work baskets contained our sewing. I made two handkerchief bags with chain stitch embroidery. Tuesday afternoons were bliss for me because I liked sewing but some girls' fingers were all thumbs and their sewing got grubby. The boys went away and did woodwork.

Learning to write with ink was torture. The pen nibs were scratchy and had to be dipped in too-full inkwells of powdery ink. I can still smell them, ugh. Filling the inkwells was a privilege as well as washing the leaves of the (yukky) yukka plant on Fridays.

Modelling with clay was dirty but fun. The deep stain of your chosen coloured clay took some getting off. Anyone could guess the colour I had used just by looking at my red hands or my green hands. And what I was making never looked right. A horse I made looked like a sea monster. Did I make a dragon next, no, it was supposed to be a dog. When you wet the clay I didn't like the squelching sound it made and when you were pasting, if you put too much on, it oozed out onto the picture.

There was endless repetition and chanting of the times tables and 'twelve inches one foot, three feet one yard' etc to learn measurements. Speaking of repetition, if you got a spelling wrong, you had to write it out 20 times. I loved learning poetry.

Scripture was every morning and you had to learn a psalm. Sometimes there was a small prize for learning quickly, like a sweet.

On the annual Empire Day, 24th May, the school sang hymns

and songs together then we had the rest of the day as a holiday so we went home again. On the 1935 Silver Jubilee Day of George V we ran races and played games on the Common.

Standard examinations had to be taken at a different school than your own. Some weeks later you were sent a card which said your position and which secondary school you were going to.

Payment to the schools went on numbers attending so teachers sometimes went round to get pupils into school. A boy of 9 came in one day who had never been to school and had no knowledge of words at all. Another day, two children were admitted, caravanners aged 5 and 7, and all they knew was the letter 'a'.

We had the use of a playing field some distance away and at school we had a wireless.

Local schools came to share each other's facilities, such as the playing fields and woodwork benches. The school mother went to, as in the above account, had access to a playing field but it was nearly a quarter of a mile away. The journey was not a flat one and involved going down a very steep hill, up another steep hill and along a twisting country lane. Boys from nearby schools would come and learn woodwork at mother's school.

Children learned to swim in the local 'slipper baths' about a quarter of a mile in the opposite direction of the playing fields with one steep incline to race down and then the same hill to steadily climb back up to school.

('Slipper' baths were so called because the freestanding 'bath tubs', higher at one side, vaguely resembled a slipper. The slipper baths, normally at the side of an indoor swimming pool, were for people without bathrooms to pay and use the washing facilities. There were separate 'slipper' baths for men and for women. Most people, however, saved money and used their own tin baths in front of an open fire.)

If naughty in class, the teacher might throw a ruler or rubber at the pupil. If children were very disobedient, for example talking in class, they would get 'three of the best' which was the cane or a slipper on their bottom. The teacher would say 'bend over' and then give the pupil three whacks. Some schools would give 'six of the best' and in years to come a cane would be used only on the palm of the hand. It was very rare that a girl would be punished in this way. Mother never became a candidate for any dire punishment.

Physical education in schools was deemed a priority and, wherever possible, schools were to have nearby access to playing fields.

What had been an earlier slogan of 'keep fit for the military' (this acknowledged that a large number of Britons had been unfit for national service at the start of the Great War) was shortened to 'keep fit'. New playing fields were made and open air lidos built.

(An open air lido was an outdoor swimming pool. At that time, men and women could not swim together and some pools even had an iron grill in the middle to make doubly sure there was no 'larking about'. You were allowed to talk through the grill though.)

The early 1930s saw a consumer boom of goods, including the motor car. More cars on the road led to new promotions and slogans such as the introduction of the kerb drill 'eyes right – eyes left – then quick march' to make crossing busier roads safer.

British Pathe News had started introducing sound to their broadcasts and showed the new kerb drill and 'keep fit' slogans on their newsreels. The kerb drill was demonstrated by a row of chorus girls looking right and left and then walking, in step, across the road. 'Keep fit' showed young people making use of new, larger playing fields and people of all ages jumping in and swimming in the lido pools.

At visits to the cinema there was always a Pathé News update of the Royal Family – Mother always looked forward to a story about what the two princesses were up to. At the age of 10 she greatly admired Princess Elizabeth, especially as they had been born in the same year.

Grandad called his daughter 'princess' which made her feel very regal and special. If there was anything in the newspaper about the two princesses, she would read it.

But 'everyone' seemed to be talking about Prince Edward, heir to the throne, going out with an American woman. Mother had thought that a Queen Consort had to be British until the word 'divorcee' confused her. Grandma explained that the Prince would have to choose between the throne, now that King George had died, or to marry a divorcee. Grandma added, "…and an American at that."

The newspaper headlines of 'Abdication' meant that the uncrowned King had not chosen the throne and the path of duty that had been bestowed on him from birth. 1936 was known as the year of the three Kings – George V, Edward and George VI.

(Only months into Edward's reign he proposed to marry American, Wallis Simpson, who was seeking a second divorce. It was argued that people would not accept a divorced woman with two living husbands and any marriage to Edward would conflict with his role as Head of the Church of England. In his famous abdication speech, he said he could not "…accept the heavy burden and responsibility… without the help and support of the woman I love." There's no doubt her unsuitability would have caused a constitutional crisis but the Duke of Windsor (his title after the abdication) in his Nazi

sympathiser role could have done far more damage than create a crisis.)

As the abdication sunk in and people accepted Albert George as King, and his young eldest daughter as heiress presumptive, there was a realisation that before any Coronation the family would be moving into Buckingham Palace. When told about the move, Princess Elizabeth had remarked, "What – you mean forever?" Princess Margaret had then asked her sister if it meant she would be Queen one day. Her sister replied, "I suppose it would."

(The princess was named 'heiress presumptive' rather than 'heiress apparent' as it was possible that her parents might have had another child and, if a boy, would have succeeded the throne.)

Their way of life had now changed forever and a permanent crowd formed outside the railings of the Palace. Only short weeks before, the princesses could walk in the nearby park and play with neighbours' children. A detective now accompanied them everywhere and when speaking of 'mummy and papa' they had to say 'the King and Queen'.

The King's speech impediment became a 'nightmare' when public speaking and he had to accept professional help. He was also helped and encouraged by his calm and serene wife.

The following year the girls rode to their father's Coronation in a glass coach and were privileged to sit with the widowed Queen Mary in the royal box. Princess Elizabeth watched intently (well for most of it) the three hour long ceremony in which her father had the utmost difficulty in repeating the words, "…all this, I promise to do." What a moving experience though, to see her own parents being crowned King and Queen and then to take part in the procession herself.

She wrote an essay on her experience:

"...when mummy was crowned and all the peeresses put on their coronets, hovering in the air and then the arms disappear as if by magic...but at the end of the service it got rather boring as it was all prayers. Granny and I were looking to see how many more pages to the end and I turned one more and it said 'Finis'. We both smiled at each other and turned back to the service... When we got back to our dressing-room we had sandwiches, stuffed rolls and orangeade and lemonade. Then we left for the long drive... " (back to the Palace) "...then we all went onto the balcony where *millions* of people were waiting below. After that we all went to be photographed in front of those awful lights."

A schoolroom was established for the girls which overlooked the lawn at the back of the Palace. Around the same time, three patrols of the Girl Guides were established at the Palace with girls from family friends and vetted acquaintances. This was to encourage 'normality' mixing with other girls and to provide some form of physical education.

As thousands upon thousands had flocked to London to see the Coronation and then watched the films at cinemas up and down the country, new films were being produced in Germany.

Political propaganda films were the new German 'weapon' of 1935 starting with the film 'Triumph of the Will', starring a small statured man with a 'chopped off' small, black moustache. (The moustache could have been brown, but the films were in black, white and shades of grey.) He was shown standing in a slow moving jeep with his right arm outstretched towards the sky but, as the film progressed, this lowered to shoulder height. Every so often he would fold his arm upwards, palm exposed, in a 'static' wave position. His salutes were cheered to, shouted to and devotedly saluted back to by a hundred thousand German arms.

This was Hitler, the ever growing popular 'film star' and political leader, signalling the resurgence of a mighty Germany. He had a new blockbuster about to be 'premiered' which intended to show and consolidate his power base. The sequel to 'Triumph of the Will' was the 'Nuremburg Rally'. The film showed the rally setting the 'gold medal' standard in propaganda 'weaponry'.

The rally cemented the German Army's strength in a mass rally of over 700,000 people. It showed a 'never before seen' throng of people who were fanatically shouting and cheering and saluting. It showed rows upon hundreds of rows of German soldiers, fastidious in their goose step and salute formation. The rally was a huge success, bringing millions of German people to the Nazi cause as it was shown over and over again in cinemas across Germany.

After the Berlin Olympic Games, held in 1936, the momentum of keeping fit increased and German newsreels now showed mass synchronised gym displays in stadia and fields. These showed large keep fit displays of German youth.

At first, British Pathe News presented a largely uncritical view of Hitler's Germany in terms of the keeping fit and the massive military displays. One newsreel reported "800,000 pairs of boots standing heel to toe waiting for the Fuhrer's speech."

Another newsreel commentated, "In Britain as well as in the hearts of the German people there's the same preference to the joys of peace than the horrors of war." Three days after that, Germany invaded Poland and Britain declared war.

Pathe quickly changed to statements like, "Everything we do is inspired in the absolute conviction that a great evil must be removed from the world," and the newsreels were used to, "Rally the nation against the common enemy." The Government wanted nothing left to chance and a Ministry of Information was introduced by the Government to impose censorship and commission propaganda.

War Times

As already mentioned, early in the lives of my grandparents, there was a war involving, very nearly, all of the world. Any war which included countries with dominions, such as the UK and its Empire, meant that they were also at war. Collectively they were known as 'Allies'.

Grandad remembered wanting to sign up in 1914 at the start of the Great War, as it became known, but he was too young at just 14.

In his short reign, King Edward ('Bertie') was proved right to be cautious of the Kaiser amassing his German army and that he could not be trusted. 'Bertie' could also be applauded for his campaigning of the British Admirals to modernise and add to our Navy fleet. He would not, of course, live to see the build up to the Great War itself.

It was only expected to be a relatively short war which had been triggered by the assassination of Archduke Ferdinand of Austria, the heir to the throne of Austrio-Hungary. However, the conflict soon spread to the rest of the world from the Empires of Germany, Austro-Hungarian, Ottoman (Eastern Europe), Russia and the British Isles. After the United States forces joined the rest of Europe and the Allies, they drove back the German armies and Germany agreed to a ceasefire on 11th November 1918. Well, that's the Great War 'in a nutshell'!

It was the first war that introduced trench warfare, fighter planes, poison gas and tanks as weapons of war.

At home, especially in London, anyone with a German name was shunned and shops owned by Germans were looted or wrecked, or both. Other protests included German pianos being thrown out of houses onto the street. Many Germans, known as foreigners or 'aliens', were locked up for their own protection and to stop them spying.

However, for the thousands who signed up in August 1914 they would not have expected to live in the sort of conditions that were endured in the trenches.

Lack of movement and 'stalemate' meant that the soldiers, having first dug the trenches, spent most of their time in them. They were cold, wet, vermin and lice infected conditions. There was constant shellfire and stray bullets causing random deaths at any time. Sleep came in 'cat nap' form because of the noise, fear and the 'need' to keep awake. Keeping awake, and alert, gave the best chance of staying alive.

Soldiers lived in terror of the whine, rising to a howl, of an approaching heavy shell and the fountain of mud and filthy smoke into which it exploded. There was then the constant smell of burning under the relentless 'weeping' of the skies.

Conditions sprung up like 'trench fever' (from lice infections) and 'trench foot' (fungal infection from the cold and wet). To keep the lice at bay, many men would shave off all their body hair. The mud and the wet made the feet swell and painful sores would develop, making walking very painful.

Overpowering smells came from the open cess pits,

rotting sandbags, from bodies in shallow graves and from bodies lying in the open of 'no man's land'.

Or 'dead man's land'.

Such unbearable smells, including stagnant mud, body odour and cooking smells, were all mixed with the whiff of chlorine, used to try and keep infections at bay. In fact, men could be physically sick from the stench, and the smells attracted rats. The rats were everywhere, sometimes getting into food stores.

One Great War soldier said, "Rats were sheer torture and lice were also close 'companions'. The lice would drive you crazy, they itched so much. One way to get rid was to burn them out with a fag end, sizzling both skin and 'it'. The wash tub gets rid of them as well, but they come back. It's a lousy war."

Soldiers were given 'bully beef' (like corned beef) from tins (rat proof) and would taste quite palatable if mixed with onions, but what would be added when onions ran out? Chopped up old and hard biscuits! Occasionally, plum and apple jam arrived in the trenches, contained in tins. Water, for drinking, had to be boiled and chlorine added to kill germs which would then make it taste like 'swimming pool' water. If water ran short then trench water had to be boiled. Diarrhoea and sickness were rife.

People at home knew what it was like to 'go without' and be hungry, but not to the point of *starving,* which soldiers were frequently faced with; due to food supplies not arriving, as many supply wagons were blown up en route. Rations that were left, or made it through, had to be further 'rationed' and there were even reports of having no alternative but to eat horse meat.

A third of all deaths resulted from the squalid trench-life conditions.

There were still many, many lives lost and soldiers wounded straight after emerging from a trench…in only the first ten yards.

How could anyone imagine being a soldier and seeing close comrades drop 'like flies in a trap'. Then, if still miraculously alive after a day's trench warfare to try and sleep through some of the night; knowing that when dawn breaks it could be their last dawn. Soldiers got the 'shakes' with fear and dread. No soldier could just walk away. There was no safe pathway out of the trenches and certainly no white flag arrangement for 'time out'.

Some soldiers were so desperate, so afraid, they would shoot themselves in the foot or leg so they could be sent back with the wounded. If a leg or foot injury was classed as a 'flesh wound' they would be sent back to the frontline after treatment, albeit limping. What good luck if you were classed as 'crippled' – you would be sent home.

The casualties suffered in this War are almost beyond comprehension – more than eight million soldiers, on all sides, the equivalent of about 5,500 every day.

There were rumours of a form of 'stage fright' where soldiers 'froze' when the order bellowed out to 'CHARGE'. There was no time to waste. They were either trampled from behind and then shot by a trench commander or just shot as they 'froze' in their terror.

No-one knew about 'shell shock' and how it might make a soldier mentally ill. In this war, it was a sign of cowardice. 'Cowards' were court marshalled and the sentence…to be shot by a rifle squad of 'your own side'.

A Great War soldier's story
(based on accounts from different soldiers)

On the inside I didn't want to sign up, but on the 'outside' I was frightened of being labelled a coward – even though I wasn't quite seventeen. I realised the time had come where I had to prove myself to myself.

I'd never been away from my mother and sisters, and never been farther than our next village. They had pleaded with me not to sign up, begged me, but my mind was made up.

They stood proud, I could see that, when I marched in line from the village, joining a long line from the previous village and marching onto the next. I revelled in the pride and the glory of it all, and singing valiant songs en route. I knew I would eventually have to get on a ship and sail for France, but I'd never even seen a ship, let alone the sea.

We all reported for training and waited in line to be given our uniform. I hadn't expected it to be 'made to measure', but my boots were far too big and my trousers too short. Other recruits had similar problems and we swapped around our gear until we were all pretty much comfortable.

I hated the training. We learned to run up hills with heavy packs. We learned to shoot straight, to clean out our rifles and make our bayonets shine. There was incessant marching, 'hourly' inspections, cleaning and more cleaning. Nothing was private anymore, you washed in rows, slept in rows, you went to the closet in rows and with no dividers.

We had to line up for everything. Even the practice trenches had to be in lines. "Deeper, DEEPER," shouted the Sergeant, "Do you want your heads blown off? This trench is all that will keep you alive, all you've got to hide in, God's good earth."

A wrong word, unguarded look or a 'bit of fluff on your collar' meant instant punishments. Like, ten times round the parade ground with your back pack on or fifty press-ups, with or without your pack, which depended on how 'angry' you had made the Sergeant.

Most of us thought the Sergeant was making things up to satisfy his desire to see the new recruits suffer. At that time, we didn't know those punishments were, in no shape or form, as harsh as the suffering we would have to endure.

In training, I had met up with two school pals from my village so it was good to have someone who knew you 'of old'. We could write home, but you couldn't put what you were doing or where you were. I kept my letters 'cheery' so as not to worry my folks.

As soon as I was on the ship bound for France, I was wishing, praying, to be back in the training camp. The heaving grey waves of the Channel meant I could hardly stand up to lean over the deck to be sick. I spewed so much, I thought my organs would come up next. I was not alone, my two pals were sick with me, along with most of the green-looking recruits.

A seaman said to us that we would fare better below deck and as I could feel no worse than I was feeling, we took his advice. There were five of us who made our way to the bowels of the ship and lay down amongst the terrified horses, at the mercy of their hooves. The roll of the ship was indeed much less and we stopped being sick, even having a 'cat nap' in the straw. At last, the engines fell silent and we made our way on deck.

Our first glimpse of a foreign land, but all around us was English. We alighted to see lines of our own side's walking wounded, bandaged and hobbling. Their haunted eyes stared at us and their silence spoke 'volumes' to us. One managed to say, "Good luck." From that moment onwards we knew some of us would be like them, or worse.

We camped in lines of tents and slept in rows. Distant guns could be heard with the drone of aircraft and the sky was lit up at night. We selfishly thanked God we were not underneath those lights of shells exploding. The Captain in charge of us had said that's Ypres, said like 'wipers'.

When we got to the trenches, we found the previous occupants had left them in a 'right mess'. Our first job was to rebuild the dilapidated trench wall and clear out the rats as best we could. The mud came up to my shin and it was cold and gooey. My feet had been wet since leaving the rest camp.

At last, the longed for march back to rest camp, but the Captain kept us busy – cleaning our kit, marching up and down, gas mask drilling and then we had to do it all again. My feet remained wet and paralysed. When we did eventually file into our tents, we had our letters to read while thawing out our feet.

One night a week we were allowed to drink in the local hostelry. What a blessing to drown our sorrows in beer, egg and chips. The next day's sore head was forgotten as we marched to the trenches once again.

That evening, we walked through 'Wipers' as the shelling had stopped and it was a shorter distance to rest camp. It was the first time I had seen the town we were fighting for. We were fighting for rubble and ruin and a deserted town, save for a few roaming cats and dogs. We saw some dead, mangled horses. My aching, wet feet were forgotten at the sight of their terrible wounds. No-one spoke and no-one smoked.

Next morning, back in the trenches, I was on sentry duty and locked in my own world inside a stifling gas mask. There was still a mist hanging over 'no man's land' which was like a blasted wasteland with unnatural humps. They were the unburied. I cried like a baby inside my mask.

When I was stood down, I rejoined my two school pals who had got the 'shakes'. We all wanted this to stop and for 'Fritz' to go away.

Our Captain thought 'Fritz' *had* gone away and we three were amongst the soldiers sent to find out. We stayed close behind the Captain, all of us in masks with our bayonets ready. Inching our way forward on the ground, getting wetter and muddier which, at the time, I was not consciously aware of.

We're crawling through the wire now and all was silent. We kept our heads down. Near their trenches, the Captain rolled over the edge and we followed. We're in the enemy's deserted trenches. It was easy…too easy!

Flares went up into the dark sky and anyone not in the trenches was illuminated.
Shells rained down and illumination turned into elimination. The earth splattered us with the impact and the Captain gave the 'pull back' order. I could hear whizzing and whining and a blast sent me sprawling. I couldn't hear a thing and I daren't move. Was I dead? I saw flashes of rifle fire but I was in a silent world.

Strong hands moved me forward and I tried to walk, but couldn't. I knew I was done for! The Captain was alongside me, shouting at me with words I couldn't hear, but he was pushing and pulling me. Then he went down on his knees and we looked at each other. I saw the light fade in his eyes. I don't know how I got back to be curled up in the dug out, having torn my mask off, but I didn't care who saw me cry.

My hearing returned though my other senses still felt numb. Rifle and gun shots rang out. Then an eerie silence as I thought my hearing had gone again. I couldn't find the strength to touch my ear.

The Captain was gone. One of my school pals had not returned. Someone said they thought he had been seen but he remained missing. Men were still stumbling about and dazed. We all lay exhausted. All in our own thoughts, our own horror.

I couldn't grieve. I just felt numb.

Hope ebbed away with each passing hour. My pal was out there in some crater. Or was he now one of the humps? By the first light of dawn, I knew he would not be coming back. My other pal next to me, just as numb as I was. Everyone looked numb, heads slumped or heads in hands. Our faces were streaky and wet from dirt and tears.

My sentry turn came as morning broke. With my gas mask and bayonet on standby, I had started to feel dreamy and my eyes had misted over. A voice inside my head said 'don't fall asleep on lookout' and I shook my head to keep awake.

I looked out and saw something moving at the wire.

A voice whispered, but it wasn't inside my head. "Don't shoot, I'm from Company B, coming in, don't shoot." I thought I must have been in a wonderful dream.

It sounded like the voice of my missing school pal and

louder the voice said, "Is everyone asleep?" It was him, it was really him and I knew I was awake.

"Give us a hand down then," he said.

I lifted up my hand and he tumbled down beside me. I hugged him, like I'd never hugged before. I tried to stifle my tears but my cheeks were wet with his tears, my tears, and we cried together. We sobbed in each other's arms for the longest time.

When he could speak he told me he had been shot in the knee and couldn't move, had passed out in fact. He had woken up and still couldn't move; so he had to lay still, dead to all around him. He had had no option but to wait for quiet and the cover of darkness. He had inched his way along and dragged his outstretched body forward. Stopping only to regain some strength, then edged slowly onwards again.

I called for help and he was stretchered off to the field hospital. Later on I went to see him, "How's your leg?" His answer was, "It's my ticket out of here" – his ticket back home. How I envied his injury.

★ ★ ★ ★ ★

As the Great War soldier had once been a new recruit, he now welcomed the regular batches of new, and raw, recruits. They included the French, who were marched towards the trenches in amongst a wagon train of trucks and horses pulling artillery guns. The recent, relentless rain storms had left dire conditions with only thin, mud spattered planks to walk on. When they had reached these fields of mud, all thoughts of their marching songs, camaraderie and bravado fell to the wind. They could not believe what lay before them.

Half 'caked' bodies, hooves sticking out of the mud, soldiers' faces half submerged – dirty and cold. Feet stuck up and hands reaching out of the mud in a forlorn gesture of hope. A filthy, booted leg here, a twisted arm there. An unseeing, muddy face with a dirty bandage across his forehead. Had he managed to lift his head, to get some air, in a vain attempt to stay alive?

A wounded soldier had clearly scraped through the quagmire, somehow, to find comfort in his dying moments, and was now lying with another fallen soldier in a macabre embrace. Only half of their bodies were visible, the rest claimed by the wet earth. Some soldiers' eyes still 'seeing'; closed on others, as if they had fallen asleep wrapped up in a thick, mud blanket.

Some were in contorted positions, half visible, some were clinging to the side of trenches, fully visible. Another soldier was lying face down in the mud at the end of a plank. As if he'd tripped and fallen flat on his face. All of them, mud splattered and 'frozen' in time.

Would the next batch of new recruits find *them* like this? It was a question which started in their stomach, not in their heads. Some bent over, heaving. Some were physically sick. Some cried. Most were just numb with shock, disbelief and fear, all mixed up in a jangle of shaking nerves. Their first job? To bury the young heroes they had never known.

Local young men in Sheffield who had answered Kitchener's call to 'do their bit' for King and country had been eager to sign up and be part of the same regiment, to stay together. A proud City Battalion. They sung their marching songs, they laughed and joked and they looked forward to reaching the front.

At the Somme 'front' in the summer of '16, a quarter of the City Battalion of young men were 'wiped out'. Nearly the same number of men were so seriously injured their war was also over. There were no numbers of those who did see their home city again, but the horror of 'going over the top into hell' never left them. They had schooled together, grown up as friends, had signed up en masse, and then died together.

After that, city or townsmen were not kept together in the same regiment.

Gas is a funny thing as it doesn't respect Battalions, or borders, or different uniforms. A bit of wind and the gas goes back to those who first launched it.

The Allies answer to the German gas attacks was to fire gas filled shells so they went 'straight there', too far away to 'blow back' anything. The gas, however, still permeates outwards from the reached target. It slowly kills horses, birds, civilians and any living thing without protection.

Local French people learned to carry gas masks around with them in defence of either sides' gas attacks. Their masks were rudimentary bandage cloths wrapped around their faces with two eye holes, but only effective for a very short time.

At best, the mustard gas caused temporary blindness, intense eye discomfort and floods of tears. If the latter, the soldier could use this as camouflage and have a 'good old cry'.

A French soldier temporarily blind and deaf, with an ear blown away, was taken to the casualty station by Leon, his closest comrade. They had been together since their call up, training days. The medics were picking out the 'self mutilated' soldiers and trying to help those with 'genuine' wounds. Soldiers needing only an hour spent on them would take priority over someone needing over three hours of attention.

This was on the basis that three soldiers could be saved in three hours as opposed to just one in the same precious time.

Temporary injuries, such as an ear being torn off, a shoulder smashed by a spade (spades were used in the trenches rather than bayonets) or a flesh wound, would soon have them back to the frontline. You needed the 'right sort of injury' not to go back – the loss of a foot or an arm!

Due to all this slaughter and mutilation, reinforcements from the Colonies of the Empire had been called up. From Afrikaans and Hindus to New Zealanders and Canadians, though most had been volunteers. In fact, in some colonies there were too many volunteers and names had to be drawn out of a hat. "And, the lucky winners are …!"

The French soldier is now back at the front, he knows he wouldn't want to carry on without Leon. He said, "I'm one of the lucky ones to have a friend to share ups and downs with when all around us is death, but what we miss more than anything is our women. A letter from my girlfriend Martha makes me feel human again."

He goes on to say, "Leon and I are separated for the first time – I feel like an orphan. He's been like a father to me, even though he's only ten years older and now he's gone to another Battalion. We write to each other for a while and he says he is fighting in the mountains with the snow and cold. I miss him terribly and look forward to his letters almost as much as the ones from Martha."

A good 'marriage' of the War was women and the munitions factories. In France, the female helmet makers put little notes in the rim of the new helmets. Things like, 'good wishes for a prompt and happy return to your family' and 'I hope this helmet brings you good luck'.

The French soldier misses a letter from Leon, then another and weeks go by without any word. Then he hears that he had visited his girlfriend and didn't report back. Leon is on file as a deserter. The French soldier vows to wait for him.

(After the War, he receives Leon's identity tag and fob watch in a cheap cardboard box. He said, "I had to carry on with my life, making Martha my wife. The nightmares of what Leon and I went through and survived, leaves me colder than any snow capped mountain. But, my darkest thoughts are how he might have died when they found him."

As a deserted soldier, Leon would have faced a short court martial hearing and found 'guilty'. Then killed by a firing squad, made up of his own country's soldiers, following orders.)

Leon was a casualty of War, someone who could not take the shelling and killing any longer. There were hundreds like him, soldiers of different nationalities, suffering from a mental illness not recognised at that time. Nevertheless, a hero. A hero alongside those who's short lives were to end at 'The Somme'.

'The Somme' was, in fact, the bloodiest battlefield of that War. This was because the frontline 'zig-zagged' from the north to the south of France with a wide, thick defence of barbed wire in 'no man's land'. To cross from the British side to the German side was an impenetrable wall of barbed wire.

A devastating bombardment of artillery rained down on the Germans, said to be over seven nights and seven days, which was supposed to disable the barbed wire to make rudimentary paths through it. The British soldiers were spread over the length of this frontline and told there would be minimal German resistance.

Mounds of empty shells built up. If all the mounds were added up it would total some two million spent shells. That's ten per enemy soldier. They were told the coast would be clear.

The 'coast' was not clear! Whoever told them that had got it wrong, so very wrong. It was no chess game or 'test your skill' competition. "Oh got it wrong, let's start again." Getting it wrong meant a senseless suffering and toll of innocent lives.

When the British troops went over the top of their trenches they were horrified at what they found. The massive and sustained gun and bomb attacks had failed as the enemy troops started firing from their undamaged artillery guns. The 'ten yards rule' had been blown to hell. Our troops now had to try and struggle through the barbed wire but were 'picked off' by bullets as their clothes snared. They were 'sitting ducks' – uniform and flesh torn on the wire, unable to squat down and with nowhere to hide.

Who had got it wrong? The young privates were working class lads commanded by upper class officers. Officers who were determined to win a British victory 'at any cost'. They knew the Germans were well defended, including the barbed wire 'shield', but what they hadn't accounted for was the failure of the bombardment.

Notwithstanding that, the privates were ordered to walk and to keep in their formation lines. The Germans couldn't believe their luck – 'sitting ducks' lined up row after row. It was a massacre.

Also, because the frontline was so extensive, the soldiers were spread too thinly along it, therefore, the few that made it through the wire could make little impact.

(But why did all that artillery have no, or little, effect? The sad answer was due to the War being thought of as a 'short war', so the relatively small stock piles of ammunition soon ran out. New stock had to be hurriedly made, the quality suffered, with the result that the shells did not explode on impact.

Piles and piles of unexploded bombs, along with the mounds and mounds of spent shells, were found stretching along this frontline after the War.)

It had been expected that 'The Somme' would make some soldiers heroes. It made thousands but they were left behind in a foreign field.

British Pathe showed a film taken on the first day of 'The Somme' battle. It actually showed a rehearsal of the first hour, depicting smoking soldiers smiling happily, walking up the short ladders out of the trenches and looking back at the camera. They were then shown walking through 'set up' gaps in the barbed wire. The film also showed the Allies' great artillery strength.

What it didn't show was the men getting snared in the wire trying to find imaginary gaps, and then their bodies slumping. What it didn't show was the 10,000 soldiers who fell in the first hour of the real battle. At the end of that first day, the casualities had doubled to 20,000.

Back at home, Lady Elizabeth nursed a heavy heart. A beloved brother had been killed and one was still missing.

Grandma's marching cousin, one of the boys from the public house, was killed 'coming out of the trenches at Passchendaele in 1917' (so the telegram quoted.)

The War was no longer a glorious adventure for young men. What memories of them marching in their new scarlet uniforms singing 'God save the King' to the music of the brass band and being showered with flowers. Memories now lost in time and grief.

The fighting at Passchendaele started in July with several 'stalemates' along the way. One was due to the heaviest rainfall for 30 years falling in a few days. This brought mud of quagmire proportions, so thick it clogged up rifles and even tanks. It was so thick, men and horses drowned in it. If a man disappeared in the mud, he had to be left, so as not to jeopardise others who might have attempted a rescue. Holes made from shells and filled with mud were now graves for many a poor soldier. If a horse could not get out of the mud, it would have to be shot.

Horses were as essential to the Great War as a bayonet was to the rifle. At the start of the War, there were not enough horses in Britain, some 100,000 were needed. Vets and army officers were dispatched to farms and villages all over the country to buy horses under a requisitioning order. Farms were left with only one horse as the rest were commandeered, i.e. sold, to the Army.

If a farm had four shire horses they would 'lose' three. Yet to the farmer's children they were more than plough 'pullers', they had names, they were loved. The whole family were heartbroken that they would never see their beautiful shire horses again.

Some men had volunteered with their own horses and were readily accepted, of course. They had paraded proudly together through the streets of Britain, singing 'it's a long, long way to Tipperary, it's a long way to go' alongside the marching soldiers and the band. Thrown flowers caught in the horse's mane and saddle. But no man, or beast, could imagine the horrors which lay ahead.

Getting frightened horses onto ships was a testing task for the crew, but get them on the ships they had to do. Horses were pushed and pulled up the wonky, wooden ramps, some were harnessed on board; all neighing loudly, bearing their teeth in terror. There was no time for soothing words or gently cajoling the horses, most of which had never seen the sea, let alone a ship.

Horses are known to be sensitive to their surroundings, but nothing could prepare them for the sea journey or what lay ahead. There was no time to train the horses not to react to loud gunfire. No time to teach them to standstill when a bouquet of shells rained down.

One of the few cavalry charges, at the start of the War, showed the futility of horse and man against machine guns. No man and no horse could get within 600 yards of the German's fire power. After the heartbreaking slaughter of those charges it was time to rethink, and quickly!

A horse's role became a vital one in pulling the wagons to bring goods and supplies to the frontline. Shire horses fared the best when pulling up to two ton loads for hours at a time, and on routes fraught with danger. It was like 'running the gauntlet' along country paths and lanes for hour after hour. When the wagon train risked stopping for a rest or water, they risked becoming 'sitting ducks'.

At the end of one wagon train, the horses had had enough and would not budge for the soldier driver, for neither 'love nor carrot'. What saved man and horses was actually the gunfire. It startled the horses into galloping forward and the soldier grabbed at the reins for dear life. He was bashed against the horse's legs, he swallowed mud, he was gashed, but he was alive!

Vets were much in demand for horses' hospitals which had sprung up in attempts to 'bandage' up the wounded for them to 'fight' another day. Sadly, no bandage or vet could save any horse once caught in the quagmire.

The close 'best friend' bond between horse and soldier driver would be sorely tested if a horse strayed from the wooden slats across the mud fields. One leg misjudged the pathway and caused the horse to lose its balance. As its legs sank ever deeper, the ties to the wagon had to be severed quickly.

The horse would neigh and bear its teeth, then neigh gently as 'his' master reached out to stroke its head and try to whisper in its ears. Then he would move back and turn away. Another soldier would lift the horse's front forelock of hair, if that was possible, and pull the trigger. As the horse fell sideways or its head slumped into the mud, its master's shoulders would jump at the bang and then slump in unison with his 'best friend'. But no time to grieve…the wagon train rolled on.

By November 1917, the village of Passchendaele was captured by the British and Canadian forces. The hundred days of fighting left nearly half a million Allied casualties and over a quarter of a million German deaths. *(The scale of such deaths were not publicly known in Britain until after the War.)*

(Note: there were no records of horse casualties but none, it is believed, were brought back to England. The surviving horses were sold or given away.)

Soldiers were living from day to day, never knowing when they saw the sun rise if they would see it set.

A surviving soldier said, "I wasn't shooting a man, I was shooting an object and it was that object or me. I chose me."

He also said, "If someone said he wasn't scared in the trenches and in the frontline, he was a damn liar. I was scared, shaking with fear."

A soldier in the trenches was part of a team, four or five becoming best friends; living with each other night and day, sharing everything together. One soldier said, "It was more of a love than a comradeship in a way." His team had been through so much but they never talked of 'after the war', they were too frightened, surviving the here and now.

Out of their trench, the team inched forward, rifle and bayonet ready. A shell flashed and one of the team was down; blood around his leg, but he felt no pain just numbness. He looked back, he saw one of his best friends lying behind him, wounded. He could not see the other three just beyond him, but there was a lot of smoke. The smoke slowly cleared but he could not see anything of his three best friends. The pain he felt inside was growing as intense as the pain he now felt in his leg.

A search was made for the three other members of the team. He shouted to the searchers, leg pain forgotten, "Go back, look again," and they looked again. He screamed, "KEEP LOOKING," but by then he knew it was a hopeless search. Nothing was ever found of his three best friends.

They were three of the 40,000, and more, of the Allied soldiers who were never, ever found. The two wounded comrades were sent back to England to recover, but they never recovered from the pain they felt inside, or from the guilt of having survived when their friends had not.

Was the sacrifice of all those young lives justified? What is certain is that the Germans launched a spring offensive on Passchendaele and all the ground captured by the Allies was lost.

Even so, it heralded the final period of the Great War. The Allies launched a series of offensives, or battles, along Europe's western front. One of these battles was the recapturing of the Somme. The last soldier to be killed, a Canadian, was at 10.58am on 11th November 1918.

By this time, the German armies had retreated. An armistice, or agreement, was called to cease fire. The actual signing of the armistice was at 5am in a railway carriage, and was effective from the eleventh hour of the eleventh day of the eleventh month.

However, it wasn't quite time to celebrate as the War had made the German family links with the British Monarchy a great embarrassment and, in fact, a liability. The King might have had German blood and spoken the language, but he felt 100% British. At the beginning of the War, he had remained 'quiet' and dutiful, amidst anti-German feelings turning into riots against German owned shops and goods. The name 'Saxe-Coburg-Gotha' had to go.

All German titles were dropped and a very British sounding House of Windsor was created. At the same time, 'enemy' princes with British titles were deprived of them. Other Royals followed suit, including the Battenbergs becoming the Mountbattens.

Of course the British Royal family, namely Queen Victoria's children and her children's children, had wed into Europe's royal families, some of whom were already related.

The late Queen's grandaughter, Alix, married into the Russian Royal Family taking the name of Alexandra. Her husband, Tsar Nicholas II, was a first cousin of King George. The German Kaiser was another of their first cousins.

The Great War and its aftermath had torn apart many of

the royal families around Europe, seeing 27 royal houses either deposed or abdicated, including both the Kaiser and the Tsar. The outlook for the British Monarchy looked 'bleak'.

(Of all his cousins King George had been closest to the Tsar, the resemblance to each other 'quite remarkable'. In April 1917 Nicholas turned to George for help. After an emergency meeting at Buckingham Palace, George offered asylum to the Tsar's family and a few loyal servants. Days later, on advice from the King's private secretary, he told Parliament he'd changed his mind – he said the monarchy was his first priority and he would save the House of Windsor, at all costs. He had also said if that meant sacrificing the House of Romanov and the Tsar, rumoured to be a tyrant, then so beit.

At first, Parliament said it was 'too late' to take back the offer, but the King insisted and the offer of asylum was withdrawn. It did mean the end of the Romanovs. Three months later, the Bolsheviks slaughtered the Tsar, his wife, four daughters and son, and the servants.)

The King could not, and did not, show any outward signs of grief (or guilt) that he had turned away a close family member. Instead, he 'knuckled down' to raise the profile and standing of the new House of Windsor. He and the Queen did much meeting and greeting up and down the country. Going to events, races and football matches. The King had presented a cup to the winning football team in front of 73,000 spectators, all 'belting out' the National Anthem, fervently cheering and lifting up their hats. He then created the Order of the British Empire medal, awarded on merit to non-military people.

The House of Windsor was 'back from the brink' and as popular as ever.

While the nation was still celebrating the end of the War, the King and Queen, were stricken with the loss of their youngest son, aged only 13. John had always been a delicate child of general poor health. It was said that, "…in the end he died peacefully and, while sleeping, his little heart had stopped."

Meanwhile, it was a difficult transition period for a lot of soldiers home from the War and for their families. A lot of women had carried out head of household duties and traditional male jobs. Women had succeeded in a number of jobs formerly thought to be beyond their capabilities.

The stark reality of war, and its aftermath, had touched most families, whether royal, noble or poor. Some families found it very difficult to adapt and move on. Some would never get over not knowing exactly how their brother, son, father or cousin lost their young lives, where they were buried, or even if they had been buried.

Grandma's sister, Lily, had married just before her new husband, Fred, had joined the Yorkshire Light Infantry. This unit spent time in the nearby Sheffield Barracks and would march along the main road from there into the city centre, and back, or to the train station if they were going to the frontline. They would be waved off by family and friends, not knowing who would see whom again.

Fred was one of those who did come back from the frontline. He was awarded a medal of honour for distinctive service, and although very proud of his achievement, never regarded himself as a hero.

(Heroes were the ones who did not come back. A Great War soldier said, "Too many died – war isn't worth one life.")

Light infantry soldiers are trained to fight on foot, to

engage the enemy in face to face combat, the backbone of an army. In this war, soldiers were most successfully deployed to manoeuvre in and around the constricted spaces of the trenches and evade detection. Light infantry were less heavily armed and the most common mission would be to patrol, as opposed to bombardment or ambush. They used lighter weapons such as rifles and grenades.

An infantryman would be expected to put aside his personal fear, despair, fatigue and injury. All would carry photos of their loved ones next to their ID and, in between missions, would take great comfort and renew their resolve from gazing at these photos. Fred's photo of Lily was worn and tatty by the time he came back. He had gone to war a carefree, newly married young man and he came back with a solemn, nervous disposition.

Like so many returning soldiers Fred relived his experiences in dreams, nightmares even, as a fallen comrade's face is lit up again and again by candle light at the end of a trench. Disjointed memories depict the endless chatter of machine guns which hammer out their devilish tune inside the soldier's head. Memories became overshadowed by grief and guilt, a guilt which would never leave him, even with voices of reason within his head, putting up a good argument.

The guilt that Fred had come back and his comrades had not, overwhelmed and consumed him. The man that Lily had married did not return from the War.

Even though Fred survived and he did not suffer injuries or loss of limb; he was still a casualty of war.

(There was to be no 'war baby' which might have brought some joy to the young couple's life. Year after year went by childless.)

Sheffield, Fred's home city, had suffered its first attack

from a German Zeppelin in the middle of the Great War. *(A Zeppelin is a large, rigid airship, cylinder shaped, filled with hydrogen cells.)*

Twenty four years later, the city would suffer further attacks, this time at the hands of German planes.

The Great War started to be known as the First World War (WW1) as the next global conflict loomed.

WW2 lasted from 1939 to 1945 and involved most of the world's nations. Their leaders putting all of their entire economic, industrial and scientific capabilities at the disposal of the 'war effort', including Great Britain and its Dominions from beyond the seas.

However, this war would result in the mass deaths of civilians (known as the Holocaust) and the only use of nuclear weapons in warfare.

Between 50 million and 70 million soldiers and civilians would be dead by the end of this World War. To comprehend this number of people is hard to imagine, but the whole population of the UK stands between those two numbers!

The Second World War effectively started on 1st September 1939 with the invasion of Poland by Germany. Britain's declaration of war was followed by the countries in the British Empire and most of Europe, again known as the Allies.

By May 1940, countries in Europe were 'toppling like dominoes', whether or not they had made their declaration of war.

A propaganda film showed Hitler inspecting his most coverted 'prize' – Paris from below the Eiffel Tower. Would his next film show him looking up at Big Ben?

A British invasion was a very real threat by 1940 and the

heavy bombing of our aircraft, army sites and cities from September of that year was expected to be the prelude to the landing of a German force.

War Diary and Memories

At the start of the Second World War, mother began to write in a diary. It was a surplus, complementary diary from a Sheffield wooden box manufacturer which her father had given her. The one year diary actually spanned three years of entries from 1939 to 1941.

Also included, amongst the diary entries, are mother's memories of what was happening around her from cinema and wireless broadcasts and what she read in newspapers. Mother said she wrote her war diary in her bedroom at night to try and stop her thinking too much about what might happen tomorrow.

Several advertisements in the diary, give an insight into what was being used at that time.

'Knowles Firebricks – these mechanically strong and tough firebricks stand up to high temperatures and severe conditions splendidly. May we send you full particulars and free samples?' *(These would be used as the base for an open fire.)*

'Vitrifine Stoneware Pipes and Connections – by carefully selecting and blending these Clays we are able to produce PURE STONEWARE eminently suitable for Sewerage work…'

'Knowles Fireclay Grate Backs – scientifically designed and manufactured to reflect heat in the most effective manner, these Gate Backs combine a pleasing appearance with a high standard of efficiency. We shall be pleased to quote you for Fireclay Backs…' (*As the name implies it would form the back of an open fire.*)

'Knowles improved ANTI-VAP street gully – it is the gully that provides all the approved features of modern sanitary science with simplicity of design'.

A bookmark was in the diary which read, 'Have you joined the H.B.C. (Hits Back Club)?' (then underneath) 'Membership… open to 480,000 men, women and children of the city. Object… *to hit back* by lending £4,000,000 in National Savings to provide *100 four-engined Lancaster Bombers* during WINGS FOR VICTORY Week – May 29th to June 5th.'

(The Hits Back Club was a national fund raising scheme to encourage civilians to put funds into national accounts in order to pay for bomber aircraft. £4,000,000 was the national target and towns and cities achieving their individual targets were awarded plaques. The national slogan was 'Carry the war to your enemies'.)

Other local fund raising schemes was the Red Cross 1d a week collection and volunteers would go from house to house collecting 1d (an old penny).

After the local advertisements were pages of weights and measures, metric to imperial and vice versa imperial to metric.

For example, 'one millimetre (mm.) … … … = 0.03937 inch'.

Likewise, 'one dekametre (10m.) … … … = 10.936 Yards'.

And imperial to metric: 'one mile (8 Furlongs) … … … = 1.6093 kilometres'.

Then information on 'weight of earth' and 'weight of

timber' which would have been extremely useful information (?) as the diary was with the compliments of 'John Knowles & Co. (Wooden Box) Ltd'.

Then a page on 'Stamps, Taxes and Excise Duties' and facing that 'Postal Information, &c.' First entry was stamps, not exceeding 2 oz, 1 and a half d. Postage for over 2 oz was another half penny. Postcards were 1d and postcard replies were 2d. Bills paid in the post or to give anyone money, was via a postal order which were in denominations of 6d up to 2s 6d then 1s ('s' stands for shilling) after that. Postal and money orders (used for larger amounts of money up to a maximum of £40) would be the equivalent of a future cheque.

The 1939 diary also listed postal information. It cost one and a half pence to send a letter and one penny for a postcard. It's interesting to note here that the postage rate had only increased to 1d from a halfpenny at the turn of the century.

Parcel post was six pence and an express parcel service was six pence per mile up to a certain weight and then 1d per lb (pound in weight) up to a maximum of 15lbs. A telegram sent in the day was six pence and sent at night it was a whole shilling (twelve shillings to the old pound). Motor car road tax was four pounds up to six horsepower and, thereafter, fifteen shillings for each extra horsepower. A car's engine capacity used to be referred to as 'horsepower'.

Some diary entries for 1939 had been erased and written over. On 20th June, it was recorded that, 'To-day we bought our bird and he was 6 wks old.' Rubbed out underneath was 'he cost 2d' (two old pennies). The bird was a blue chested budgie, Mother called 'Peter'.

On the same 'memoranda' page was written, 'War started September 3rd 1939.'

Like the announcement of the death of King George V in 1936, all wireless programmes were interrupted with, "This is London…"

On that day, the wireless announcement brought a sense of numbness and fear – and then frantic planning to dig big holes in gardens. Previously delivered sheets of corrugated iron, 'just in case needed', were now hastily erected in these holes, stabilised by soil or sandbags. People without gardens were issued with box-like metal shelters to use indoors or to fasten to outside walls.

Already issued gas masks were tried on again and straps adjusted. They had to be carried and kept nearby at all times. When you went to work, to the shops, to school – the gas mask went too. In some outside closets one of the family's gas masks would be hanging up behind the door. It would hang above the torn newspaper squares. *(I was always amused by the thought of yesterday's news headlines imprinted on your bottom!)*

One of the first diary entries in 1939 was of mother being a bridesmaid to Uncle Walt, the last of grandma's siblings to marry. Aunt Cath's twin sister was bridesmaid with mother. A checklist to take to the wedding would have included a handkerchief, card, present, confetti and … your gas mask. Fortunately, there was no gas mask test or alarm for the happy couple to marry looking like two alien beings in their best clothes.

(The happy couple had actually met via a blind date. Aunt Cath and her sister used to help serve in the family's chip shop and one day a friend arranged for the two young women to go on a blind date with two young men. They were to wait on the opposite street corner to the chip shop and wait for their beaus. Uncle Walt turned up and he

thought he was seeing double! Aunt Cath claimed his arm as they went walking – and that was that!)

Gas detectors were placed in some streets which were supposed to light up if gas was in the air. In fact, they were never needed as there were no gas attacks on Britain, but everyone had to be prepared. At the time this was a very real danger.

Gas-proof prams emerged which looked like coffins with an air filter on wheels.

Masks for babies outside of prams made them look like an alien from Mars. Babies had to have an anti gas attack suit which was as difficult to get the baby into as a little boy into a tin bath of soapy water. There was an air pump at the side to enable anxious parents to pump more air into this tiny 'astronaut' looking 'space' suit.

Ladies' handbags were sold with a compartment for the gas mask.

Some children used their mask to carry sweets about, which proved convenient until a gas mask drill took place and the child forgot. Result: a sherbet lemon 'sticky' hair do! Children could also use the masks as bats, as goalposts and swing them as a weapon.

Dogs were not left out and gas-proof kennels were made for canine pets. They could also be used for cats. Were there any gas-proof horse boxes? I think not unless you, the reader, can tell a different story?

Houses with a shared courtyard and no garden could not erect corrugated shelters as they needed to be dug into the earth. Families from these houses had to use the nearest public shelter, an indoor metal shelter or build and fasten a shelter to a courtyard or garden wall.

Shops selling material or curtains did a 'roaring' trade to black out any light from windows and doors, including fan lights (small windows above doors). Street lamps were shaded or put out. Trams and buses could be heard in the street at night, but eerily not seen, save for a very faint light at the front and back.

People with cars painted white stripes on the wings in an attempt to be seen while driving with no lights on.

Everyone had to have an ID card. Women would take the family's birth certificates to the local church hall and then, about a week later, would go and collect their ration books. The Royal Family also used ration books.

With the books, the woman of the family, would go and register at the local shops. (It didn't have to be a woman, but as it was a 'household chore' linked to shopping, then it was left to the wife or mother.) In the case of the Royal Family, it would have been a (female) staff member of their household.

The shopper had to exchange food coupons for whatever the shop could get; so one week you might have to buy wheat flakes and the next, loose porridge. The shopkeeper would send off the ration coupons and he would be sent the equivalent in food/goods the following week.

(Shopping was still women's work, hence referring only to women, and shopkeepers were (mainly) males though their wife or daughter might help him in the shop.)

Food wasn't the only thing rationed. Coupons were needed to buy textiles and wooden furniture using a 'points' system. 24 clothing points had to last six months and if a shop dress was bought, this used about half of those points. Hence, the 'make do and mend' slogan.

Working class women had always been resourceful in

using up scraps of material or wool. They now resented the Pathe News films about 'make do and mend' as they had always done that. The films, though, gave some good examples of how to use items from your 'rag box'. Like, 'How to patch elbows, by Mrs Sew-and-Sew'. Or sewing together four tea towels and making a dress or sewing together several pieces of 'leftover' material and making a top or skirt.

An example of sewing seven facecloths together to make a swimming costume was of little use, however, to working class women. It became somewhat 'fun' for middle or upper class women to 'outdo' each other with their, or their maid's handiwork. One news film showed a department store holding a 'fashion show' of 'made up' clothes. You can guess what class of women were shown in the audience! A clue is needed? The women wore hats rather than headscarves.

The government issued advice on what to grow, what to eat, what to mend (e.g. how to join a make do and mend group), how often to do gas mask drills and what to keep in your pocket, e.g. ID card, whistle, torch, ration books. In fact, there was a 'propaganda' slogan and advice for every aspect of people's lives, the majority of which were aimed at 'the man on the street'. Children's outgrown clothes would be passed through the family or to neighbours' younger children, which is exactly what a lot of families had to do anyway.

People would call into shops before they officially closed in case there were any 1d or 2d bargains. A few butcher's shops would sell mutton lamb bones for 2d which still had bits of meat on and could be used in a stew.

Word 'got around' that a spice shop had a delivery of

Lion's ice lollies on a Sunday evening and a queue would form round the back of the shop to buy one for 2d. There would be great excitement at the arrival of the lorry, but there were times when the lorry didn't turn up and a lot of children had to walk home with a heavy heart and dry mouth.

Pathe News broadcasting became invaluable for giving help and advice to the British people during the War. Slogans such as 'if you save gas and electricity, you save coal' and 'for more eggs save kitchen scraps' (to feed your chickens) and, of course, 'make do and mend'. Each slogan showed an ordinary family acting out a relevant scene at home.

Advice included 'what to do in an air raid'. For example, 'If you're in the open with no cover, lie down, preferably in a ditch.' The newsreel would show a man lying down in a ditch.

Another example, 'If you're within five minutes of your home, go home, but keep away from the windows,' showed two schoolboys walking briskly through their garden gate.

And another newsreel example showed a group of people with their heads raised upwards, staring at the sky, with the words 'never stare at the sky.' (Then why show a crowd staring at the sky?)

These broadcasts, alongside newspaper articles and leaflets, were successfully used to promote the evacuation of children from cities and towns and portrayed this as 'going on holiday'. The newsreel actually started with the slogan 'off on holiday' and showed children boarding trains and a nurse coming round with cups of tea. And later, the film included children alighting from trains and being greeted by new guardians. Some films showed children enjoying farm and country home life.

By the end of 1939, nearly 1.5 million civilians, mainly

children, had been evacuated from cities to the countryside. Some children were as young as seven and would definitely have thought they were going on holiday, returning home in a few days time. Of course, evacuating anyone was entirely voluntary. That is, voluntary for the adults making the decision, but not for the poor children.

Some siblings weren't kept together and two young sisters found themselves in a manor house, separated from their brother. They had to work every day polishing silver and were treated worse than servants, as they were unpaid and had no choice. Their polishing started before they went to school and this made them late for school nearly every day. Children late were given three whacks of the cane on each hand. As the girls were late most mornings, the whacks would add to their already hurting and reddened hands. After school, they returned to the manor house and more polishing, broken only by a meagre tea and, at last, bedtime.

A lot of children, though, had a great time on farms and homes where they were treated like 'one of the family'.

(After the War, some evacuees were never claimed by their parents and were adopted by their new family. They were happy to be adopted as most of the abandoned children had never heard from their parents for up to six years. Some parents had written to the evacuees' guardians asking them to take the child and they would sign any necessary papers. And some guardians kept it a secret that they had heard from their parents.

In later life, a few of the adopted evacuees would try to trace their birth parents and siblings, with varying success.)

From Sheffield, there was poor 'take up' of sending children to the countryside. To encourage 'take up', school classes could go as a group to villages near each other but only a few schools took part. Trains leaving Sheffield to evacuate children were never full. My grandparents said they knew of no-one in the family, on their street, or any friends who had sent any of their children away.

There were some children who tried to walk and hitchhike back to their homes. Two children, seven and nine years old, set off walking from Leicester and then hitch hiked – arriving back at their home in Sheffield on the same day! They weren't sent back.

By May 1940, because no bombs had dropped and no invasion had happened (known as the 'phoney' war) hundreds of children had been collected or sent for and returned home. Children returning home did not make the cinema newsreels.

Of course, it was known as the 'phoney' war only afterwards as preparations, during this time, were made to thwart the impending invasion. Street signs were removed or turned the wrong way and anti tank ditches appeared across the southern countryside. Barbed wire and mines appeared on beaches. There were roadblocks and spot checks of people's ID by the local defence volunteers (soon to be known as Home Guard.)

Newsreels at the pictures showed the swastika flag being hoisted in Dunkirk harbour and marching German soldiers through the Arc de Triumphe in Paris. Some cinema goers said how 'evil and wicked' the soldiers looked.

By June, the impending invasion seemed 'almost imminent'. The ringing of church bells was banned as this was the signal of invasion, which could be via parachutes, by sea or by air. Leaflets were distributed, 'if the invader comes' and it listed what to do and how to do it. They stated, '…on hearing the church bells, wherever you are and whatever you are doing, make your way home quickly. Stay put and stay calm'.

People had no option but to do as they were told. Those living near to the sea, attached sidecars to bicycles for the family to flee inland if necessary or to stay put and don't open the door to anyone.

Some youths, not old enough to sign up, joined the local brigade or cadet force as they could take their rifle home. A lot joined just to have a weapon to use. Others made sure their fire pokers were handy.

By September, the British were asked to be vigilant and look out for suspicious people who could be acting as spies. The slogan 'careless talk costs lives' was publicised amid a list of who and what to look out for:

- someone with a beard *(ordinary citizens get shaving!)*
- washing put out on the line in the wrong order *(was there a correct order?)*
- leaving the plug hole in after a wash *(pub landlords check the lavatories)*
- men in nun's clothes *(except fancy dress parties?)*
- masculine looking nuns with visible tattoos *(wear gloves)*
- any stranger in your street or hamlet *(or stick your ID card to your forehead)*
- those carrying box shaped equipment
- vegetarians *('everyone' ate meat and fish)*
- anyone hiding in bushes *(now is the time to buy a big dog)*
- a man asking for strange drinks, e.g. champagne cider
(note, asking for a pint of German beer would have been too obvious!)

- anyone walking about at night or with a map or without local knowledge

The wave after wave of German bombers at the start of the blitz was thought to be the prelude to the invasion. It was not thought to be 'if' the invasion happened but 'when'.

The two princesses had been secretly 'packed' off to Birkhall (Balmoral Estate, Scotland) and could only look forward to a nightly telephone conversation with their parents. Like other evacuated children the two royal evacuees desperately missed their family and, as hundreds of other children returned home, they were allowed to live much nearer to home at Windsor Castle. However, their whereabouts were kept out of the cinema newsreels.

While some newsreels at the pictures showed the German advance in Europe, there was an hour long broadcast every evening at 6pm, called 'Salute the Soldier, a cavalcade of the British Army'. People could go in and watch this broadcast and/or stay for the film. This meant people would be watching the same newsreels before and in between the films. As most people visited a 'picture palace' at least once a week, the propaganda messages on 'our island fortress' and the 'top tips' for everyday living would get across and be remembered.

The cinema newsreels regularly showed the King, sometimes with the Queen, visiting bombed cities and towns with the commentator saying, "Here is the King, an inspiration to the stricken inhabitants of this bombed city."

In fact, the King had wanted to go and fight but had been persuaded that he would be doing the 'best job' by boosting morale in the meeting and greeting of the British people, up and down the country. The role of the Monarchy in the War can't be understated as their high profile visiting bombed out towns and cities depicted, 'we're all in this together' and that 'we were fighting for King and country'.

People from all walks of life, wherever they were, would gather round the radio to hear the King's Christmas speech. They all hoped that the King's bad stammer would not prevent him from finishing what he had to say. Also, the King and Queen had decided to stay in London with the British people. However, the only person 'thankful to be bombed' was the Queen who gave the statement, "Now I can look the people of the East End in the eye."

The most damage was in the Palace's quadrangle and if more windows had been closed, there may have been injuries from shattering glass. In the area, one policeman said to the Queen, after bowing his head, "A magnificent piece of bombing if I may say so ma'am." She smiled back.

Buckingham Palace's Royal Chapel also took one of the bombs which went through the roof, wrecked the altar and sent twenty tons of debris through to the basement.

The Royal Family was extremely popular through the War and the damage done by the abdication was repaired.

The King and Queen went to stay with their daughters at the weekend, whenever possible. The most popular of the closely guarded locations was Windsor Castle as it was nearest to home. Another 'secret' location was Sandringham, or the time the princesses were there was secret.

There were still photographs of the family together or of the princesses playing in a park. Even though staged, it showed that 'family life goes on'. There were newsreels at the cinemas on the Royal Family at work and at home.

There had been quite a number of requests for Princess Elizabeth to speak or make a wireless announcement which would be aimed at the children of Britain.

After several rehearsals to master her breathing and phrasing, on 13 October 1940, she broadcast: "Thousands of you in this country have had to leave your homes and be separated from your father and mother. My sister Margaret Rose and I feel so much for you, as we know from experience what it means to be away from those we love most of all. We know, every one of us, that in the end all will be well." Finally, in the carefully worded script, there was an exchange between the sisters, "My sister is by my side and we are both going to say good night to you. Come on Margaret, good night," and a smaller voice then said, "Good night."

Mother listened with her parents and she felt that the message had been meant 'for her'. It gave mother, and her mother, a sense of 'we're all in this together'. The somewhat 'sloppy' broadcast had been a huge success and endeared young and old to the princesses and the Royal Family.

Wartime also brought new sounds, including high pitched 'up and down' notes from sirens fixed to certain buildings. Hearing that siren would signal the start of an air raid and people would rush into their air raid shelter or the nearest public one if not at home. (Or, if nowhere near home, they could always lay down in a ditch.)

At the end of the air raid, an even noted siren would sound. People would wait an extra few minutes in silence before making their way out, fearing what they might see outside – was their home still standing? Many, many hours were spent in air raid shelters.

Large buildings such as factories or Bassetts, Sheffield's

large sweet manufacturer (during the war, a munitions factory) would have one of the air raid sirens attached to the building. If anyone was near one of these sirens it was ear-piercingly loud, which made everyone rush into the shelters so the noise would be deadened as quickly as possible. People at the bottom end of the local park would run across the road and use the factory's large air raid shelter, covering their ears to the high pitched sound as they ran. Mothers with children having to forego that luxury as their hands had to usher or carry the little ones.

As sweet factories turned to manufacturing arms, sweets were rationed 'for the duration' to 4 ounces per week, whatever size family you had. There were 'D' coupons for 2 ounces of spice and 'E' coupons for 4 ounces. So if 4oz of spice was wanted but only 'D' coupons were left, the shopkeeper tore out two 'D' coupons.

The first commodity to be restricted in 1941 was petrol and from the year after, there was no civilian petrol. Tinned meat was also restricted and tax duty increased on everything from tobacco to sugar. Basic food rationing started with bacon, butter and sugar, followed by meat, tea, jam, breakfast cereals, cheese, eggs, lard, milk and canned fruit as well as fresh fruit. If apples were available, the shop usually restricted these to one apple per family. Newsprint was restricted. All soap was rationed (good news for little boys.)

A typical weekly ration was 2 ounces of bacon; one egg; 2 ounces of margarine (hard cooking variety) and 2 ounces of loose tea *(tea bags not 'invented'.)* Butter was only for children under five and pregnant/nursing mothers (2 ounces was just less than a quarter of 500 grams.) All foods were the same price anywhere as set by the Ministry of Food.

Families with gardens took to keeping chickens to provide eggs, due to the rationing of only one fresh egg per week! An egg isn't an item which could be halved to have later, is it? Most people had to resort to using dried egg powder.

People started to keep a Christmas box which filled through the year with 'bits and bobs' such as lace, ribbon, paper, string 'ends', buttons and a spice or two.

Newspaper made crackers (without the bang) were tied with string or ribbon and a nice spice 'surprise' prize inside. Strips of paper to make chains across the room. Folded up paper made into patterns and painted on sprigs of holly.

(New tongue twister: nice spice surprise prize inside; nice spice surprise prize inside; nice sprice supersize pies inside... Do try this at home!)

When it came to Christmas food, there was advice to keep a storage jar which was slowly filled with dried fruit, sugar and anything which could be saved to make the Christmas pudding or stuffing.

(War time recipe for Christmas pudding: grated carrot, suet, flour, sugar, grated potato, breadcrumbs (from a stale loaf), currants and dried mixed peel. All mixed with a solution of water and dried eggs.)

Note: Christmas puddings sent over to our soldiers contained real ingredients and real eggs...and well deserved!

(Typical recipe for stuffing: grated carrot, powdered egg, suet, breadcrumbs (again from a stale loaf), grated nutmeg and a few sultanas. This concoction was mixed together and then stuffed into the Christmas chicken.)

Note: Turkeys were in short supply, except on farms or if a turkey could be obtained on the 'black market'.

People made use of every available channel to buy goods

for Christmas. Honest British people turned into 'racketeers' in the build up to Christmas; for example, a miner exchanging his ration of free coal for a turkey or chicken. Some people, of previous good standing, would even resort to stealing when an opportunity arose. Those working on a farm or in a grocery shop might make use of such an opportunity.

The government authorised extra rations before Christmas, advertised as 'Food Flashes'. "Roll up, roll up, get your extra rations here…take home one and a half pounds of sugar and eight pence worth of meat, four pence fresh and four pence corned beef…" Still on production of ration coupons, of course.

"Roll up, roll up – for a child or pensioner, get your extra half pound of spice."

(Pensioner meaning anyone 70 years or over.)

Although potatoes, vegetables and bread were not rationed 'for the duration', they were difficult to buy and the bread was very poor quality. Registered vegetarians got extra cheese so those who particularly liked cheese would register as a vegetarian.

('For the duration' was a phrase which sprung into use meaning 'during the war' and using the phrase meant you didn't have to use the word 'war'.)

As already mentioned, clothes and furniture were also rationed. The government issued 'rules' for making clothes, such as jackets had to be single breasted with minimal buttons and pockets. No turn ups on trousers. No unnecessary frills or trimmings, though the padded shoulders stayed put. The range of 'utility clothes' were endorsed with the hallmark 'CC41'. Utility furniture also had this hallmark.

People entitled to buy utility furniture, via the points system, were newlyweds, those setting up their first home and victims of bombed houses. There were 22 pieces of utility, wooden furniture including, a dining table and chairs, easychair, kitchen cupboard, bed, cot, wardrobe and dresser – all in oak or mahogany. Carpets were hard to get, but if you were lucky, the furniture seller may let you choose a coveted carpet 'from the back'.

When visiting newly furnished homes, there was no need for polite phrases of 'oh, I do like your furniture' or 'that dining suite goes so well with that cupboard' – as all utility furniture looked the same!

For the duration, goods such as cameras, alarm clocks, china and lawn mowers could not be bought from anywhere. There was no restriction on alcohol, but public houses would regularly run out of beer.

Rattles would be sounded for gas attacks. There were no church or school bells as they were to be used as a warning of invasion. Many street and road direction signs were removed or turned round to point in the wrong direction so the enemy would get lost in any invasion!

The very real threat of invasion in the early years of the War had lead to the forming of the 'Home Guard' – this consisted of older men or men exempt from call up due to illness. They kept alert and patrolled their local area for anything suspicious in a similar way to the much later neighbourhood watch schemes.

A lot of schools had to close as all the male teachers went off to war – even though it was an exempt occupation. So did they prefer to fight than to tackle 2C on a Friday afternoon? Many pupils 'escaped' school during the War, and the fact that only two out of three children had a school to go to! Quite a number of closed schools were used as 'Home Guard' bases or air raid warden posts.

Stories of schools being bombed were few and far between, fortunately. One school was hit by a land mine in the evening, but luckily, it was empty at that time…or was it? Who should be rescued from the rubble? The headmaster and a female teacher – were they marking exercise books? Were they planning tomorrow's school lessons? The answer? They said they were 'fire watching'! A likely story…

Now try the following true or false stories:

1. Munitions factories were disguised as duck ponds to fool enemy planes?
2. The Government urged people to save their milk bottle tops to be turned into Lancaster bombers?
3. Rationing finished when the War ended?
4. Small heaps of manure were left around schools in case of fire?

(Answers at the end of this section)

Let's look at some of the government's 'daft' rules of the time:
- men's suits could only have three buttons;
- women's heels could be no more than 2 inches;
- fancy belts and elastic waistbands were banned;
- use less elastic for women's knickers which was fine for slimmer women but not for those with a fuller figure – did plumper women have to wear 'baggy' knickers?

(No they didn't, but it meant 'bigger' knickers cost three coupons and not two)

- car sharers got extra petrol – all a person needed to do was place a sign in the car window, 'I give people lifts'! Hey presto, more petrol.
- coal was rationed but not gas ovens. People would sit around a lit gas oven for warmth when they ran out of coal.
- bath water had to measure no more than 5 inches – did an inspector come round to houses with a ruler, "I'm just here to measure your bath water?" (I think not!)

In Germany, however, rationing or 'daft' rules were brought in before the War. One rule was to only have a bath on a Saturday or Sunday – who would be policing that rule, we wonder? German people could only buy certain items from distribution centres, e.g. toilet paper, in efforts to avoid theft.

Everyone had to do the 'Hitler salute' unless you had no arms at all. One child with a broken arm was told by a teacher that he need not do the salute. When he was asked why he didn't salute, he said his teacher had told him he didn't have to – the teacher was arrested and taken away. *(After the War, it was learned that the teacher was shot.)*

German wireless stations would broadcast propaganda in English, meant to reduce morale, but it made British people more determined to do everything they could 'for the duration'.

On British wireless stations, weather forecasts were stopped as it could give the enemy vital clues of when to fly or not to fly. Why didn't the broadcasters give weather forecasts the opposite of the actual weather? The forecast could have been given as 'a lovely sunny, clear blue sky, good flying conditions', when it would really be foggy, raining and windy. This decoy weather could have led to enemy planes in a lot of trouble...?

Some radio stations, such as Radio Luxembourg, had to stop broadcasting.

The Home Guard would help out anywhere and be invaluable when their towns or cities were bombed. Everyone pulled together, known as 'blitz spirit', as the bombing became a 'way of air raid life'. People would use understairs' cupboards, cellars, under large kitchen tables, in outhouses (sheds), and local caves. In London, hundreds of people would 'bed down' on the tube's underground stations. Although the latter was not allowed, the authorities would bow to people pressure and keep up morale by turning a 'blind eye'.

One cinema newsreel showed the blitz spirit where everyone helped survivors safely get out of bombed buildings. It did not show any horrors of war or badly injured people. It also filmed placards 'open for business' in front of shops where the glass window had gone or owners would be seen selling from the pavements in front of their bombed shop. A newsreel even showed a woman typing from a chair on the pavement as a man wearing a suit and bowler hat said to her, via the commentator, "...and my new address is..."

'Spirit of the people' broadcasts interviewed those who showed bravery when their homes were bombed or showed steadfastness in the aftermath. Local at home heroes were 'born'.

Like in the Great War, advertisements used posters and newspapers to encourage young men to sign up and older men to join the Home Guard. Everyone was expected to be patriotic and positive, doing all they could. One slogan was 'whether you are in uniform or in working clothes you are crusaders of the home front'. Those in the army, navy and air force were 'fighting in the battle for civilisation'.

Women aged between 17 and a half and 45 years were encouraged to join the WRNS (Women's Royal Navy Service, known as the Wrens) or the ATS (Auxiliary Territorial Service) with the slogan 'show some pluck and sign up'. It was publicised that Princess Elizabeth had signed up for the ATS.

As in WW1, women were once again called upon to undertake a wide variety of jobs. Single women between the ages of 17 and 24 were 'called up' and given the choice of joining women's services, civil defence or a civilian job deemed essential to the war effort. They stepped into thousands of roles as men were sent to fight overseas. Women had vital jobs in munitions factories and in the Sheffield steelworks making parts for guns, tanks, ships and planes.

There were also advertisements for housewives and mothers to take on spare time jobs in the evenings and at weekends, whenever they could arrange childminding. A journalist in one newspaper went to interview a wife and mother whose story was meant to encourage other women to 'sign up' for war work. The article, now rather threadbare, was saved by my mother who had actually saved it for the sewing pattern on the reverse!

Spare-Time War Work
Do your bit, even if you can only give a few hours each week…

"When you've a six-year-old in the house you don't need an alarm clock, so I'm not afraid of over-sleeping and being late for my work on Sunday mornings. Sunday is the only day I have free for a war job, because on that day my sister comes in to look after the children.

We have an early breakfast and by 7.30 I am away, for unless I clock in by 8 I shall be reprimanded and forfeit a quarter of an hour's pay.

I heard of this spare-time factory work through a friend who works in a bank. She put me in touch with the Bank Officers' Guild, who found me the job. I dreaded it at first as I had never done factory work, and at first I found working a foot press boring. In time, however, I began to understand more about the work, it became surprisingly interesting and, like most mechanical work, it has a rhythmic quality which is soothing and pleasant. And it's fun to find yourself getting quicker and quicker – especially when you look at your clock card and you see that a bonus has been added to your day's pay.

I was a bit scared of the hundred or so faces I saw in the press shop on my first day. But I soon made friends, first with the workers on either side of me, and later with others I met in the cloakroom and in the canteen. And what a jolly crowd they are! There are all sorts of people in my factory – a charming woman of sixty-odd whose paintings have hung in the Royal Academy; a toy maker whose business failed because of the War; girls who have been factory hands since they were fourteen; typists, shop assistants, domestic workers and housewives like myself from every walk of life. I love the feeling of real 'equality'."

(Sadly, that last phrase was short lived! After the War, when men

returned, they claimed 'their' jobs back and any housewives still spare-time working were sent 'back to the kitchen'. Society was a long, long way from equality as it was still a 'man's' world when it came to work and a woman's 'place' was deemed to be in the home! It took until my mother's generation to allow working after marriage but it was another generation on top of that before women returned to work after children. Even then, it was not uncommon to wait until your youngest child was seven before getting a 'little' part time job.)

The article continues…

"There's not much time for talking – even if we could hear above the humming and banging of machinery – but over our dinner in the canteen we exchange news and views. I find this dinner time gossip stimulating.

On Sundays we knock off at four, which means I am home in time for an early tea with my family. At first I found the work very tiring, but now I've become accustomed it, I am only comfortably tired. Yes, I can honestly say I enjoy my war job. I enjoy the comradely atmosphere, I enjoy the satisfaction of doing a strange job well and I enjoy the mid morning cup of tea more than any cup of tea in the week. I enjoy the walk in the neighbouring gardens with one or more of my friends, and most of all I enjoy the feeling that every pressure of my foot on the press brings victory a fraction of a second nearer!"

(There was then a paragraph on how to apply for 'Spare-time War Work' and be sure to 'enclose a stamped addressed envelope for the reply'. There was also a paragraph on 'out-work' if a mother had no-one to look after the children and it encouraged you to let the children 'help the production drive' at home.)

The article ended with this paragraph…

"So women and children of all ages could 'do their bit'

for the war effort! And remember, you get the satisfaction of bringing victory a fraction of a second nearer!"

(What an article – it gave mothers of small children a way to help with the war effort, it gave them a feeling of 'equality' and…it brought victory that bit closer. Quite a statement!)

What the story omits was how dirty and dangerous working in munitions factories really was. The explosive chemicals would turn women's skin and eyes yellow and their hair orange. Even worse, if that was possible, the potent raw bomb materials, including sulphur, could cause lasting yellowing of the skin and hair. Many workers were nicknamed 'canaries'.

The smell as women walked through the factory gates made some heave, even turn back. Explosions were common and machinery dangerous.

Yet the selfless working of women and men in such hazardous and life threatening conditions to provide armaments and bombs for our army was just as invaluable as using the end products on the frontline. Women all over the country were 'doing their bit'.

Aunt Cath became supervisor to a female 'army' of street lamp lighters as the men signed up or were conscripted into the Allied Army. Uncle Walt carried on as best he could as a wholesale distributor of fruit and vegetables – despite some weeks not having very much to distribute.

Back to mother's wartime diary, and an entry for December 1939 showed that mother had seen the film, 'The Four Feathers' at the Empire (*Theatre*) and 'Ali-Baba and the 40 Thieves'.

('The Four Feathers' film is about an officer who shows cowardice and is given a feather each from fellow officers. He is then given the

fourth feather from his girlfriend which is the 'last straw'. Off he goes to war in a foreign land to prove himself so he can give the feathers back having shown bravery and courage.)

On 1st January 1940, my mother recorded the weather as, "frosty", then on the 3rd, "cold and frosty." On the 5th, Mother went to Aunt Lily's for tea and wrote, "then I went to a whist drive." On the 6th, "I went into town to-day."

On the 13th it was "an icy day" and "I went to the Kinema'to see Lupina Lane in Lambeth Walk."

('Lambeth Walk' is a musical comedy, starring Lupina Lane, based on an adaption of 'Me and My Girl'. The story is about a 'chancer' from Lambeth Walk, London, who is found to be the long lost heir to a title and castle providing he can prove he has enough 'aristocratic bearing'. Things are going well until his girlfriend, from Lambeth, turns up who is somewhat 'overbearing' in cockney.)

On the 15th she wrote, "To-day the Barrage Balloon went up for the first time" which was about half a mile from home.

(A barrage balloon was a large, hydrogen filled balloon launched from a lorry. 293 were strategically placed around Sheffield to protect against enemy bombs. Aeroplanes would have to fly higher, which reduced the accuracy of the bombs being dropped.)

Twenty seven anti-aircraft guns had been put in place around Sheffield to force the German planes to fly higher. These guns acted in the same way as the barrage balloons, in and around the city. Similar to the arrangements made in the city for WW1.

Sheffield steel factories were set to work manufacturing weapons and ammunition for the war effort and turned out the raw materials and munitions that kept much of the country's armed forces fighting. As a result, the city became a target for German bombing raids.

To cope with moving all the increased amounts of large equipment, an elephant was brought in to pull the carts which carried the heaviest of the steel and other material.

To 'man' the factories while the men were fighting, women were brought in. They rolled the steel, they operated machinery and, in fact, worked on anything and everything. For their war efforts, the women were paid £5.8s3d per week. *(What they didn't realise until after the War, was the men had been paid a much higher wage…for the same work.)*

One of the large steelworks was home to the only hammer in the land capable of turning out crankshafts for the Rolls Royce engines fitted to our fighter planes. Our planes with these engines were the ones which won the Battle of Britain. Had the German planes bombed this steelworks it would have done irreparable damage to the country's war effort.

On 16th January 1940, mother wrote, "It was very cold and frosty." "Snow" was written in every day's entry from the 17th January right through to the 6th February. In fact, mother recorded the snow as, "9 and a quarter inches thick." That seemed extremely accurate – maybe she used a ruler in the snow?

On 25th April mother wrote, "Grandad died," (her mother's father and the great grandad I would never meet.)

It was custom for a coffin to be placed in the front room until the funeral. Mother's grandad was no exception and he was brought back in an open coffin to stay in her grandma's front room. Cards with black borders were sent out informing relatives that he had died and giving the funeral arrangements. As everyone lived nearby, the cards were hand delivered.

All adults wore black, with the widow and close female relatives wearing a black veil over a hat or their head. Mother's grandma and her grandad's sister wore the black veils. Due to the cost of the black veils, his daughters did not wear them. Children were not expected to wear black.

There was a service in the church and then a service at the graveside during which all men had to take their hats off, whatever the weather. Everyone's front room curtains were drawn from the time they knew of his death until after the funeral.

Often, when there is a death in the family, there is a birth. Aunt Cath and Uncle Walt had a little girl and the diary records, "Valerie born on the 15th of October" which was just over a year after mother had been their bridesmaid. In her diary, she had written a poem about being a bridesmaid:

'A memorable day
Remember that memorable day,
As a bridesmaid there I stood,
As the car drove down the street
To the church up the yonder road.'

Towards the end of 1940, mother wrote, "Uncle Walt was called up in the Air Force and was to be stationed in Swindon."

From another diary entry, the couple and their small baby had travelled to his base after he had been home for a few days leave. He had started training as a rear gunner, but thanks to his wife's stance of proclaiming, "Oh no, you're not going to be a rear gunner," Walt had gone and pleaded with his commander that this had been vetoed by his wife who was on site to see him if necessary. The commander accepted the request – better than to suffer the wrath of a wife and new mother!

Walt was then stationed at air bases in North Africa. Of course, like all soldiers corresponding with home, they were not allowed to give their exact location or what they had been doing or what they were about to do. This was in case any post fell 'into the wrong hands'.

Grandma received regular postcards from her brother during the War. These included black silhouette pictures of soldiers with a message on the parchment-type postcard. The pictured soldiers were usually stood about smiling, talking, having a cup of tea and smoking – they were never 'in a tank' or 'in battle'. He would sign himself as 'Uncle Wally', as 'Wally' became his wartime nickname.

Sheffield suffered its heaviest bombings on 12th and 15th December 1940.

On that first night in Sheffield city centre, it seemed like any other night when the air raid siren had sounded. People in theatres and cinemas continued to watch the show or film. People in public houses continued to drink, play cards or throw darts.

People at home would still go into their air raid shelters but if the raid continued towards midnight, a lot of families, grandma's included, would come out of the shelter, put their night attire on and then go to sleep in their own beds.

Mother wrote on the 12th, "heavy raid on the city, Kinema bombed, Hawksworth Avenue bombed, parachute on wires near Gilpin St. Land mine. Blanchards bombed." Blanchards was a large furniture shop on the main road, not so far away from home.

The Kinema Cinema was in amongst the nearby local shops and streets. A land mine had exploded causing extensive damage to half of the cinema and in that half, the roof had collapsed on those who were seated and still watching the film.

(Unknown to mother at the time, it was also near to father's home and in this cinema, on this night, his 15 year old sister Jessie had been watching a film with her girlfriends. The air raid siren went and people looked around as one or two stood up to go. The cinema announced that they would continue with the film but anyone was welcome to leave and go home or to a nearby shelter.

Jessie's friends decided to stay but she thought, "I'd better go home so my parents aren't worried" and she left to walk the short journey back. The next day she learned that the cinema had been hit by a bomb and parts of the roof had collapsed. Her friends were amongst the dead. Her decision to leave had saved her life. A close call.

Jessie would later go back to the rebuilt Kinema Cinema (rhyme intended) with a girlfriend from work, and meet her future husband who was the film projectionist. She was immediately charmed by his charm, quick wit and good looks. He promised her a job and she became an usherette there, selling ice cream.

Another close call happened in father's family's shared, flagged courtyard. Their air raid shelter was shared with neighbours and fixed to the side of the house and along the side wall of the yard. (Their home was on the same estate where my maternal grandparents had grown up, but at the opposite side.)

While in the air raid shelter a bomb dropped nearby in the blitz, bringing down their chimney pot, down the chimney breast and through the bedroom fireplace. It brought bricks, dust and soot billowing into the room. The same mess billowed out through the room downstairs. A lot of clearing up, but they still had their house and their lives.

Father's younger brother Fred, aged eight at the time, was in the same air raid shelter with the family and said he needed the closet. He would not use the bucket. He was bored, everything was quiet outside, and he intended to bounce his ball in the yard. Having only gone a few steps from the shelter, a line of tracer bullets ricocheted along the back wall and outside closets. Boredom over, and needing a change of underpants, he rushed back into the shelter.

The all clear went at 4.10am the next morning. Families in the courtyard emerged from their individual corrugated shelters to inspect the bullet holes along the back wall and there was another line of bullets above the passageway.)

Recorded in mother's diary on the 13th December was, "Aunt Lily and Aunt Minnie evacuated. Aunt Minnie at our house. Blanchards still burning." (Aunt Lily had walked on to her mother and her sister's home to check they were alright and then stayed there.)

On the 14th December, "Dad was evacuated from work – everybody goes from Holme Lane. A man disconnected land mine 7 secs before it should have exploded."

(Now, that *was* a close call.)

Holme Lane was the long, main road cutting through Hillsborough Corner, consisting of works, garages, shops, the tram sheds and people's homes. The 'close call' land mine would have destroyed the whole of that area, including grandad's work at Mr Wing's and 'Burgon and Ball' next door. Also, the homes of the two aunts and their families on Rivelin Bank (known as the 'Bank), located behind the Burgon works.

The 15th December diary entry read, "Second heavy raid on the city, big fire at works, nearly all the men coming home. For the first time since the war has been on we had the alert in the day from 1-15." The day after, "Aeroplanes keep coming over we keep hearing bangs don't know whether they are delayed action bombs. Frightening. Today the cars on Holme Lane have started running."

(Note the word 'frightening' in amongst the factual account of the bombing. It wasn't referring to a scary film, it wasn't referring to someone making you jump, it was a reference to not knowing if the next bomb would land on your family home and if those in the home would survive. Frightening indeed.)

It's certainly difficult for anyone too young to have lived through this time to imagine how terrifying and life changing this period of the War was. For each drone of an aeroplane heard, bang or no bang, mother said they held their breath in the ensuing silence as it could have been one of the delayed action bombs and blow them up. Mother said that they would be sat in the air raid shelter, trying to sew or read, with aeroplanes flying overhead and then after hearing a bang, they would hold their breath and look up at the ceiling, willing it to stay put.

Any shaking or an underground thud and they would hold their breath again in case it resulted in the collapse of a chimney pot, or worse.

(An aunt of mine (father's future sister-in-law) who was five at the time had chickenpox and, therefore, was not allowed in any air raid shelter. Her mother and two sisters all stayed behind in the house, sheltering on a mattress at the cellar head. On their heads, they donned upturned saucepans for extra protection should this be needed. Their mother had made the three girls 'siren suits', all in one trousers/top and hood, which were slipped on over pyjamas or clothes in the event of an air raid.

Nine months after their father returned from the frontline, a fourth sister was born.

The aunt's mother was one of thirteen children with an interesting pattern of births – three girls and then a boy, three girls and then a boy, three girls and then a boy. Was the last sibling a girl or a boy? True to the pattern, it was a girl.)

On one of the Blitz nights, the aunt's home area was bombed as the local shops and homes followed the line of the city's river. It was thought that enemy planes targeted rivers and large roads in the belief that factories or works were situated on either side. They had been mistaken along that stretch of the river. A nearby row of houses was hit and the area's electricity and water went off for several days.

Only one home in the area had a supply of fresh water, which came from a tap in the cellar. Anyone who needed water had to queue on the cellar steps and through the family's sitting room to fill pans and jugs. No tin bath in front of the fire for that family! Just think, the family is having their tea and the queue comes out of the cellar head, snakes round their table and out of the back door.

The next day, while her mother collected water, the aunt and a sister walked over to the bombed houses and she remembers seeing bodies and limbs in the rubble. They ran quickly back indoors as they should not have ventured outside so neither could mention what they had seen. The War had become very, very real for a small five year old girl and that memory would never, ever leave her.

In fact, there were countless deaths of people who went onto bombed sites, either to try and collect any belongings they could find or they were 'looters'.

These deaths were classed as 'unnecessary', especially as some were children playing and then falling down holes and getting buried.

The aunt remembers walking to school with her sisters and seeing a mass of rubble where a church had been and the house of her school friend had been 'flattened'. When she got to school she learned that her school friend and all her family had been killed in the house.

Another school friend had a lucky escape. The school girl's grandma, mother, her sister and two brothers were sheltering in the cellar of their home. Without hearing anything and without warning, the ceiling came down and trapped the girl's shoulder, arm and chest. Her little brother was underneath her and seemingly unhurt, but the cellar was filling up with water from a burst main. She was unable to move and unable to save her brother as he gurgled in the water and then drowned. She kept shouting and the rubble was eventually cleared and she was treated for a broken pelvis, broken arms and a crushed chest. Only her older brother and she had survived.

After that, the sisters used to walk home from school, very slowly, in case they found their home a pile of rubble. When they rounded the last corner and saw their house still standing they would run, hard and fast, to get home.

Small children who should be happy and carefree had to set off in a morning not knowing if they would come home to rubble, or worse. My aunt said that her focus had been on seeing the home still standing and hadn't thought beyond that.

My aunt said, "It was very frightening especially when you started to hear bangs and from an upstairs window to look out and see white lights in the sky and more bangs. I didn't feel it was really happening, it was so unreal. Some homes had their fronts blown off, exposing furniture and pictures still hanging up. You felt like a child who'd opened the front of a doll's house. One house still had a picture above it's fireplace with the words 'Home Sweet Home' in different embroidered colours. Pitiful looking children walked slowly alongside young and old women pushing prams piled up with clothes and pans. My mother said they were the homeless who had tried to salvage belongings from their bombed homes."

A bombed Marks and Spencers store had defiantly opened up in the Locarno Dance Hall and a nearby grammar school had been turned into a shelter for the homeless. People brought old prams, clothes and food to the shelter. Large or extended families were allocated a school classroom, but otherwise families had to share. A local doctor volunteered his services to treat the wounded.

Some people turned up at the shelter with nothing but the clothes on their backs. Those bereaved would turn up dazed, not knowing what to do and not wanting to eat. Others would walk about in the daytime and then return to their makeshift home in the evening.

A fireman's family sat at home, day and night, waiting for him to come home. On the third day another fireman offered to go round the hospitals. When that proved fruitless he started to search the mortuarties. In a makeshift mortuary he recognised his fellow fireman's belt on a body.

Bombs respected no-one and there were reports of machine gun fire and people being shot as they tried to escape from falling buildings. The gun fire came from the air. Those who had escaped a bomb's destruction, which included children, were then shot down in the street like animals.

Feelings ran high in shops as customers and members of the Home Guard started saying 'now let's give it back' meaning why don't we (our country) bomb Berlin. Although expressing sorrow for the civilians who would be caught up in the bombing it now seemed enough was enough. By this stage of the War, there never seemed to be any doubt in people's minds that Britain would win.

A slogan appeared in Sheffield's local newspaper, 'keep calm and carry on'. In fact, it became a national slogan.

Some people were even trying to 'keep calm and carry on' each night of the Blitz. The audience evacuated from a city centre cinema was advised to go into Marples Hotel as there was a network of cellars there, though not an official shelter. Some people sheltered in the doorways of C&A Modes and when that took a direct hit, they just crawled out from the rubble, brushed themselves down and 'carried on'.

There weren't just buildings and rubble around, but shop contents, debris, rubbish, parts of trees, overturned cars and trams on fire. One tram from the High Street had just been swept away like a toy train and ended up on its side further down the road. Another tram nearby had caught fire from a burning department store.

A policeman and a volunteer kept guard outside a store's window display, minus its window, as the broken mannequins still wore their expensive fur coats.

On 17th December, my mother's diary entry was, "3rd spy executed. Sirens went at 2 o'clock in the afternoon. I was at Aunt Minnie's. Dad came to see if I was alright, all-clear went at 4 o'clock."

Her dad had walked about a mile home, in the middle of the air raid, to find that his daughter was at her aunt's, behind where he worked. He walked back to 'Bank and then they walked home together.

The Spy Story

Two spies were executed on 10th December and the 3rd spy on 17th December 1940. The reason for the delay was that the third spy had appealed. Although he withdrew the appeal, it had 'bought' him a further week of life. All three were hanged at Pentonville Prison.

Spy no 1, Jose Waldberg, aged 22 years, was born a German. Spy no 2, Karl Meir, aged 24, was a Dutch National of German extraction. They had landed on the south coast in a fishing boat which had been pulled by a German minesweeper. They sailed to within a short distance of the coast and launched a dinghy. Each spy had a wireless transmitter (but not a receiver), a revolver, material for secret writing, local maps and £60 in £5 notes.

Meanwhile spy no 3, Charles A Van Den Kieboom, aged 26 and a Dutch National born in Japan, had come ashore with the same equipment and money. It is believed that he was accompanied, but no trace of him or them were ever found.

All three spies' cover story was that they were refugees. Their 'story' was when the invasion happened they would go with the civilian population and still send back information. They were given a password to use when contacting the invading forces. Their mission was to report troop dispositions and armaments, aerodrome activities and anti-aircraft defences.

However, all three were captured within hours of landing.

Meir fell into conversation with an air raid warden and, when asked for his ID, told him the story about being a refugee, saying, "We landed here last night." As he had said "we", the warden became suspicious and Meir was arrested. Under interrogation he told police about the other two. Waldberg was then arrested.

Meanwhile, Kieboom had been challenged by two police officers as he was carrying 'suspicious looking' equipment across the road. Kieboom was arrested.

Between them coming ashore on 3rd September 1940 it had taken just over three months for their arrest, interrogation, the trial, conviction under the Treachery Act 1940 and then their execution.

(There were other spies executed through 1941. The planned invasion thwarted at every turn!)

In mother's diary "Nothing to report" was written on the 18th December and the day after the entry was "We put Christmas tree up at night." A clear indication that 'normal living' took place in between raids and other events. For example, written on the 20th, "To-day I had some bootees" *(these were ankle, zip up, dark brown suede boots),* "sirens went at 6.40pm stopped in shelter until 11.40pm. All clear 12.40pm."

By leaving the shelter at 11.40 to go to bed, before the all clear had sounded, they had risked their lives. Yet it had only been two days since one of the major blitz nights had occurred in the city, losing many lives and destroying much property. It seemed to mother, a strange decision by grandma to put sleep before safety.

In the next diary entry for the 22nd, mother reported, "Sirens went at 6.35pm. We were at Aunty Lily's and uncle told us we had won a prize in a raffle, all-clear went at 10.30. Sirens went again at 1 o'clock. All-clear went at 6-30pm."

On the 23rd, "Sirens went at 7.15pm. All-clear sounded at 1.30am. We never heard all-clear." They were asleep, of course, but safe.

Let's recap:
Sirens went – get into air raid shelter.

Win a raffle prize. All clear and leave the shelter.

Sirens went again – get into air raid shelter. All clear – troop out of shelter.

Make a cup of tea.

Sirens went and slosh, slosh – take tea into shelter. Yawn, yawn.

Zzzzzzzzzzzzzz

Or a simpler recap: in, out; win prize; in, out; in, out; make tea; in, out; zzzzzzzz.

Such times of going in and out, in and out, of the air raid shelter were so mentally and physically exhausting that the all clear sometimes went unheard as everyone had fallen asleep. Or, people were so exhausted they left the shelter for their beds, regardless of the risk. Then in the midst of this long day and night, the surprise prize in the raffle was a very welcome bar of chocolate!

Newspapers reported, "Christmas 1940 – the worst is over!" That was not to be, as London was severely hit on 29th December.

On Christmas Eve, the diary read, "Dad's going on nights." Mother and daughter went to sleep at Aunt Minnie's. From that day and over Christmas, Mother wrote, "No sirens." On the 27th, "We went in town and saw all the ruins – there had been 55 aeroplanes in 15 minutes going on one of the blitz nights."

Mother said that she had never seen such devastation and it was unbelievable that one bomb could destroy so large a part of the city centre. She said it was like looking through grey coloured glasses, everything was coated with dirt and ash. So much rubble, overturned buses and trams, and the debris made it look like a cyclone had whisked everything up and then strewn it all about.

It is believed that the actual mission of the planes was to destroy factories along the river but the stretch of river hit was residential at either side. Near to that was the long road going through the city centre which was thought to have been mistaken for the long road going through the industrial part of the city. The later planes carrying the higher explosives saw the fires and dropped more bombs. A 500kg bomb completely destroyed the large department store, C&A Modes.

Across the road from the C&A store, Marples Hotel had some of its upper windows shattered. This seven storey hotel was a popular, busy drinking place and as usual, on the unsuspecting blitz night, it was full of people. As the siren had rang out at 7 o'clock, a lot of people had carried on drinking and being merry, but injuries from flying glass had now made people alert and wary of their safety. The injured were treated in the network of cellars running under the hotel.

More and more people made their way into the hotel's large cellar. People felt safe in this underground network of cellar chambers especially as they could carry on drinking and playing cards. And, the building's structure was untouched after the devastation so close by. Also, a lot of people thought that the chances were slim of another bomb in almost the same place as the flattened department store.

A neighbour of one of grandma's sisters was walking through the city centre on her way home as the siren had started. She turned towards the hotel, but then thought 'I'd better go home as my mum is on her own' and she turned away and walked home. That concern for her mum would save her life.

There was drinking and singing in the hotel. Most had no choice but to stay anyway as another department store next to the earlier bombed one took a direct hit. That bomb took out the ground floor windows of the hotel injuring many people inside. This sent more people down into the cellar network for cover and to have their wounds dressed.

Still a lot of people thought 'no chance another bomb round 'ere, we're safe inuff'.

An hour later, that same evening, the hotel suffered a direct hit. The seven storeys collapsed like a pack of cards, leaving utter devastation and carnage.

People first on the scene in the morning could not take in what had happened or knew how best to start looking for the many people trapped underneath. Where the bombed hotel had stood was now a 15 ft high mound of rubble and debris. The road between the hotel and stores had been obliterated. In fact, it was several hours into the morning light before the authorities and volunteers started looking for survivors.

Rescuers were also dazed onlookers, saying "Where do we start?"

And start they did, with shovels and bare hands. From the rubble, some were stretchered out. Some could only be put into black bags.

By the afternoon, it was discovered that a single chamber's roof had withstood the bomb and seven men were miraculously brought out injured, but alive. Two of them actually walked away, not leaving their names, and were never traced.

The exact number of people who perished still remains unknown – 64 bodies were eventually recovered, along with body parts from others, and the official death toll was put at 70 people. There were reports of children in the cellar, but the youngest victim found was a 22 year old woman.

At the beginning of that fateful year, for the safety of everyone, the gathering of a lot of people in one place had been banned. So cinemas, public houses and other entertainment centres had been ordered to close. That lasted all of two weeks and they were re-opened.

Up to December's blitz nights people had become so blasé about hearing the sirens and it being a false alarm that most would continue to drink and chat in the city centre pubs. On the first night of the blitz people were talking about Christmas rather than the War and even when the siren sounded at 7pm, people carried on talking and walking or whatever they were doing.

In cinemas, people would stay and continue to watch the film after the warning siren had sounded with only one or two leaving.

People in a near full, 400 seated cinema were steadfastly viewing the film when the roof caught fire. Everyone decided that they didn't really care how the film ended and they all stood up to go. However, there was no panic as they all left in an orderly fashion and made their way to nearby shelters. Unfortunately, some of the film goers had made their way to the Marples Hotel. (After the blitz nights, all cinemas and theatres were emptied by the police once the siren sounded.)

At the other end of Sheffield city centre two large, flagship department stores were razed to the ground in the 'blink of an eye' in the blitz.

Next to these flattened stores, there was also a direct hit on the longest standing family department store, Atkinsons. Here, the bomb had left only two pinnacles standing amongst smouldering rubble and twisted metal.

By the time of the War, 'Uncle John's' two sons had taken over the running of the store and in preparation they had built a bomb-proof, thick metal vault in the bowels of the store. Each night the irreplaceable customer ledger books, invoices, till receipts and other paper work were locked safely in this vault.

Although the store was reduced to a mass of rubble, all the vital paper work detailing the customers who had bought goods 'on tick' would be locked securely away. Atkinsons was owed thousands of pounds in credit. The store could now ill afford to lose that amount of owed money.

But wait, all that had to be done was to clear away the rubble and find the impenetrable, underground vault. A few days later and the debris was cleared around where the vault had been built. The vault door was exposed.

The family and some of the staff stared at the door of the vault, but they weren't staring at a closed, secure door. They were shocked to see that the door was ajar. Realisation of what that meant was slow to dawn on the small gathering. It was clear that on that fateful night the responsible but hapless, member of staff had been, er hapless, and forgotten to shut the door.

The entire contents had been lost and destroyed by the ensuing fire and smoke. The family didn't have a clue who owed them the thousands of pounds they would need to start again. Was a Nazi bomb about to bankrupt 'everyone's' favourite store? Amazingly in the days that followed, people queued to pay back the money they knew they owed and 80% of what was owed was paid back, voluntarily.

The Atkinson family defiantly set up a portacabin, across the road from the store's shell and displayed a notice of 'shop open as usual'.

Various store departments had started to open all over the city – in a church, in a cinema, a school room and even in a kiosk outside the railway station. The store and staff (I'm sure it would have included a now forgiven 'Mr Hapless') showed tremendous resilience at these 'outposts'. The Star newspaper's editor made space for the Atkinson family to use a floor of their premises as their office. Later on, a former shop and restaurant was bought by the family and it really was 'business as usual'.

At the front of the actual site they erected boards the full width of the flattened store and then installed glass and behind the glass they displayed their wares and bargains and advertised where to go for the other store departments.

(Atkinsons was re-built, where it fell, and is still there today as the last of the family run department stores.)

Fires in the city centre, on both blitz nights, were out of control down the two main roads – every building had either been bombed or was on fire. The heat in one department store was so intense that the wall buckled. Another department store, Walshes, caught fire after the air raid was over from surrounding buildings. Just on this street alone there was a mound of twisted and mangled steel structures, hanging or falling, amongst tons of rubble, including shop contents, burning cars and trams.

Sheffield had endured nine and a quarter hours of bombing on the first blitz night and a further three hours on the second night. Despite anti-aircraft gunners on the ground no German plane was shot down.

A total of 660 lives were lost and the greatest single loss of life was in the hotel. Some 1,500 people were injured. Over 40,000 were made homeless and 3,000 buildings had to be demolished with another 3,000 badly damaged.

For those still with a home, over 300,000 people were left without water. 50 electricity sub stations were out of action and thousands of telephone lines were damaged. Boys and young men were asked to volunteer as messengers to keep communication channels open around the city centre.

An air raid on one of the following nights included the industrial parts of the city but the damage was not serious enough to affect production of its wartime armaments.

It left Sheffielders even more determined to put everything they had behind the war effort. There were stories of bravery and close calls, but many said that they had 'held their breath' numerous times and some had 'been too afraid to be afraid'.

As a result of bombings up and down the country, a German invasion was still a real threat. Wartime censorship on the total numbers killed or injured added to speculation that a lot more people had been affected by the blitz nights.

Grandma and her daughter hated grandad going on nights as they were so terrified of being alone through the night for fear of air raids or an even worse threat from an invading force. No-one felt safe at night in bed and my mother said she was sometimes too afraid to fall asleep.

New Year's Day 1941, mother recorded, "We went to Aunt Lily's for the night and before my dad went on nights we heard the police whistles. Later we heard all-clear. Sirens again at 10 o'clock all-clear 2.30." As Aunt Lily lived round the corner to where grandad worked, grandma decided they would stay overnight, rather than be on their own at home. Mother also wrote, "Uncle Fred poorly, doctor came."

Walt was home on leave and on the 3rd he "came to our house and sirens went at 7.10 all-clear 7.40." More time in the air raid shelter over the next two days but "no sirens" recorded on the 6th January. Mother also wrote that the "King and Queen visited the city."

On the day of the Royal visit, the Lord Mayor with the King and Queen walked amongst a large Sheffield crowd, talking to numerous people who had come out to greet them.

The former Lady Elizabeth never forgot her much earlier grief of losing her brother in the First World War and now, as Queen, she was able to identify with other families who had lost loved ones, especially those who had lost a soldier son, father or husband.

Normally, on Royal visits, a route would be made with barriers or ropes and people would line the route. On this visit, there were no ropes, no police cordon and no path cleared through the throng. A few police officers walked behind them but did not try and move anyone to let them through.

The King and Queen continued to talk freely to people they came across. They walked towards a black car in the distance, but it took quite some time for them to actually reach it. As they edged nearer to the open car door they were still stopping to talk to different people. Some people became emotional and the Queen would take their hand briefly. After they got in, a path for the car opened up. There was a lot of 'hanky' waving and cheering as they inched away.

On another occasion, Winston Churchill visited the city and spoke from the Town Hall's balcony to a 20,000 strong crowd below. He gave his legendary 'V' for victory sign. The roar of the crowd was as deafening as it was defiant.

The new year brought a new phrase, 'grim optimism', as the blitz spirit was sorely tested up and down the country. There were stories of heroism and of grief. One family torn apart by the first of two blitz nights in another northern city, told how a mum and her three girls were squashed in the understairs cupboard for over 5 hours. Mum went to get everyone a drink from the kitchen. The garden and kitchen suffered a direct hit. The young girls had lost their mum.

Another family of a mum, dad, four girls and three boys were sheltering in the communal area of their tenement building with many other families. At the end of the blitz nights, there was only mum, one girl and two boys left. The mum's one year old baby died in her arms but the one growing inside her, miraculously survived. The two nights of bombings were Saturday and Sunday and on the Monday, the resilient adults returned to their wartime jobs!

In my mother's diary, she reported that during January and February of the new year, the sirens would sound 'nearly every day'. On 12th February, there was a gas attack alert and mother spent the afternoon in the shelter at school wearing her gas mask. She carried her mask in a box with a shoulder strap making it easier to carry the bulky object. The benefits of the many air raid and gas mask drills at school were now being realised, though it had been an alert and not the 'real thing'.

The local barrage balloon caught fire on the 23rd February and the diary reads, "Engines rushed from all-over to put it out."

Sirens sounded at least twice a week through the year. After some air raids mother would record, "Guns firing, think bombs have been dropped." One day in April, the school sirens went at lunchtime so they had to leave their food and go into the playground shelter. "We stayed in until tea time" and by the time they had got their things together, "Parents were waiting at the school gate, as if by magic." Her mother was one of the waiting parents.

"At home, we had a card from Uncle Walt." On the front of this one was a large sailing ship with 'Greetings' at the top and at the side:

"**R**oll

 On

 Boat" to the side of the ship, spelling 'ROB'.

Underneath was the message, "Good Luck, Ann, from Uncle Wally xxxxx."

Walt was involved with both battles at El Alamein in North Africa as part of the RAF ground to air missile team. The second battle from 23rd October to 11th November 1942 was an extremely vital one for the Allies in keeping the Suez Canal open and in safe hands. The Suez Canal was controlled by the British Empire and, at all costs, this had to be protected, mainly because of its access to the Middle East oil fields.

(The Suez Canal is an artificial sea level waterway in Egypt connecting the Mediterranean Sea with the Red Sea. Before it was opened in 1869, ships had to go all the way round Africa.)

The Axis forces in North Africa consisted of German and Italian troops, but they were now overstretched and exhausted as well as being seriously depleted in numbers. No reinforcements could be expected any time soon due to protracted battles elsewhere. On the other hand, the British Allies, joined by the Americans, were resupplied with men and materials from the UK, India, Australia and New Zealand.

As usual, in any build up to an offensive there are decoys and deceptions. In the build up to this second battle there were a number of deceptions designed to confuse the enemy Axis Command. One was the dumping of waste materials (packing cases, crates, etc.) under camouflage nets to make them look like ammunition dumps. They were spotted and watched by the enemy, but as they didn't subsequently move or change in appearance, they were ignored.

Another deception involved building a pipeline further south than the attack was going to be. Axis Command estimated the finish of this pipeline would be the start of the attack. Of course, it was a dummy pipeline not meant to continue being 'built' after the real attack date.

A 'coup de grace' reverse deception was started. This consisted of dummy tanks made from plywood which marched along over jeeps. In another area, away from the planned offensive, the reverse of this was taking place with the real tanks made to look like dummy tanks of plywood.

Due to this ingenious reverse deception of the Allied forces, the enemy Axis Command split their 'seriously depleted' soldiers into north and south teams. They also had very limited food supplies and, with hardly any fuel, both enemy teams were, in effect, 'grounded' in their split positions.

After a 20 day battle of ground and air superiority, the Allied victory was all but total. The victory still came at a 'price', claiming 13,500 British, Commonwealth and American lives.

On the ground, each day's battle would be a battle in itself for the rank and file of soldiers. Even if there was no great physical effort of running over ground or marching with firearms, as was the case for Uncle Walt's team, the mental and emotional stress was felt in abundance. A new day's sunrise and heat brought new challenges and fears; with thoughts of 'will I see the sunset again' and 'when I fall asleep would I wake up'.

Uncle 'Wally' had a best friend, Jack, who he had been with from the start of his service. They had even gone home on leave at the same time, playing cards en route. Jack had a baby boy only two months older than Walt's baby daughter. Jack was from further north, near Newcastle, and at first his accent had been difficult to understand. However, he had said the same about Walt's Yorkshire accent.

They had laughed about what 'sithi 'ere' had meant in Yorkshire slang, which was listen here or come here. With Jack it was just a question of talking a bit s l o w e r.

When sleep wouldn't come at night, even though exhausted, they would talk about their earlier lives. Jack's job had been in a brewery on the factory floor and after the War they had agreed to have a pint of 'his' brew. Walt had told him about his job in the market trade of fruit and vegetables and that he was known as 'the banana man' as he sold more bananas than any other fruit. (He wouldn't have sold any in the War if he'd been at home as there were none to sell.) They agreed to meet up in 'civvy street' and have a pint and a banana together.

There was no vestige of privacy left between them as they had been sick together, they had laughed together, they had helped each other in dire conditions, including ablution needs. They had shared food, drink, cigarettes, clothes and deep grief as comrades fell. They had cried, sobbed and they had hugged. Shared love and shared comfort.

On this morning, Jack had relieved himself and joined Walt for breakfast. Jack was a bit down and Walt saying, "Full English is off the menu today" did not cheer him up. Walt relieved himself and they both had a cup of tea together. As milk was powdered, they had both acquired the taste for black tea. On this morning, Jack burned his tongue on the hot liquid.

They could hear the sergeant shouting instructions and what the order of the day was. Today, the two best friends, with their team, were to help those who were defusing mines by moving equipment and earth for them. Ah well, something different today. But, today was different. Today had no tonight for one of the friends.

The two pals worked together into the afternoon and it was hot, sweaty and thirsty work. Then without warning a blast threw one of them backwards. He was on his back and opened his eyes but they were unseeing – blind from the flash of a mine. He moved his arms outwards to try and feel the ground with his hands. The gravel felt loose but he couldn't see it. He screamed from deep within himself, his mouth opened, but no sound came out.

Someone helped him up. A team mate asked, "Can you stand?" He stood but his legs concertina'd downwards. He is carried. "We're in the tent," a voice said. The voice's hands bandaged his eyes. "Jack," he asked. "No, I'm the doctor."

Wally's thoughts whirred inside his mind.

I could hear shuffles and shouts and the doctor by my side disappeared. I touched my bandage and then stretched out my arms. I felt a straight material at both sides – I was laid on a trolley of some kind. I moved my hands down my body and the tops of my legs hurt so badly. My hands felt skin where my trousers had been, but I didn't remember losing my clothes. I had my pants on but they were wet and sticky to the touch. I didn't care.

A female voice asked me if I could sit up, and I did, sort of. She moved my legs sideways and over the trolley bed. I shuffled my bottom forward, she helped move my legs over the trolley side and my feet touched the ground. So far so good. I stood as she held my arms. She asked, "Can you walk?" I moved my right foot forward and then my left. "Good, I'm taking you to sit on a chair through here." Her hands were gently resting on my right arm and her gentleness seemed to give me the strength to move forward.

Wally said, "Jack?" There was no answer as he went back into his own world. *Time seemed to stop as I sat there, slumped. I waited and waited and I think I nodded off. A background of muffled voices startled me and I became aware of people coming and going in front of me.*

Time had no meaning.

"How are yer mate?" Wally recognised the voice as a member of his team.

"Where's Jack?" he asked.

"He's in the tent…but…" and the team member's voice tapered away.

"I'm taking off these damn bandages." Said Wally as his hands went to his head.

A firm "No" came back from the gentle nurse.

He stopped in his tracks.

"Please wait," she says softly, and he waited.

The nurse then said, "You have to keep them on overnight."

Wally dropped his head. All fight had gone. He later

slumped off the chair and onto the floor. His mind was blank but sleep did not happen as all he wanted was to hear Jack's voice again.

Wally did eventually fall asleep and a blanket had been placed over him. Early the next morning as he began to wake up…

Tender hands moved me sideways and started to unravel my eye bandages. There was a blinding light as I slit open my eyes. I shut them again. My eyes were now tiny slits and I could see shapes walking about. To my side was a man on his side facing away from me, nearly all covered by a blanket. I reached out, "Jack?" Quieter, I said again, "Jack?"

The man, whose hair had resembled Jack's, turned onto his back and tilted his face towards me. He had a bandage over his head and one eye. His one good, uncovered eye looked at me blankly and his mouth opened but nothing came out. My heart sank – it wasn't Jack. The rest of the man's face was red and blistered. I looked at my hands and they were red. I felt my face and I knew that it was also red and blistered.

The nurse came along the line of men on mattresses as she sat someone up and gave another soldier a drink. She sat the next man up. Wally slowly tried to sit up for when it was his turn. "Come on Walt have a drink," said the gentle nurse.

"Where's Jack, do you know?"

"I'm sorry," she replied.

"Take me to him please."

"Drink this" and he took a sip of water. His mouth was dry but the water dribbled down his chin. The nurse carried on down the line of injured soldiers.

Time seemed to stop again.

I slithered down the mattress. I thought time had really stopped. I started crying from somewhere deep within my chest and then tiny wet tears welled up in my aching eyes and dripped down my cheeks.

Later, but I wasn't sure how later, two team mates came and squatted in front of my mattress. I could see they looked glum. One held his head in his hands as he made silent movements backwards and forwards. The other said… "We've lost Jack." I stared back in silence for the longest time.

Wally broke the silence with, "He's lost in battle?" Both men shook their heads, looking down.

A realisation was sinking in and I slowly lifted the blanket over my head and I wanted to cry but I just felt numb. I felt sick, so sick. My legs ached but they felt like jelly at the same time. All I could picture was a baby boy who would never see his dad.

★ ★ ★ ★ ★

(In later life, if Walt allowed his memory to go back, he would become quite emotional and his whole body seemed to drop and become smaller. His eyes would glaze over, his head dropping down and he would lose his voice. A solitary remembrance that no-one else could share. He saw his best friend as the war hero. Not men like himself or his brother-in-law who had returned.

He would say very little about his hero friend. What he did say, was that part of him had died with Jack in Africa.)

In early 1943, grandma received a parchment postcard depicting a laughing picture of three soldiers drinking from mugs and smoking. Underneath the picture it read, "Christmas Greetings from the Mediterranean, from Uncle Walt xxxxx." He was out of Africa.

In mother's diary there were quite a few entries saying,

"No sirens today." The city's sirens were to sound, genuine or false, between 18th August 1940 until 28th July 1942. That's nearly two years of, at best, uncertainty and anguish. At worse, two years of intermittent fear and feeling sick from nerves and dread. All the anxiety and stress of getting into an air raid shelter, wherever you were. They were also times of listening and of hoping, and times of togetherness.

The diary had recorded on 2nd August 1942, "Uncle Fred in hospital."

Next to the last entry in the diary was the sad news, "Uncle Fred passed away." He had been a distinguished and honoured soldier in the First World War but did not make it through the next. He had started with bronchitis, turning into a chest infection and then pneumonia, dying at only 47.

Friends and family who had known Fred before WW1 said that only "half the man" came back from the War. Aunt Lily had said, "the man I married did not return from the War." They had a loving marriage but it was not blessed with the children they had hoped for.

The last entry in the diary was the following poem:

Our Christmas Present
On Christmas Eve if Jerry comes
We'll make him pay for what he's done,
We'll go and chase him on the run,
And tell Father Christmas to give him no fun.
To Hitler I would like to send a letter,
But I don't think it would make it much better,
What notice would old Adolf take,
He'd only throw it down the cellar grate.

Mother had already left school by 1942 but due to the War she had not been working. Grandma did not want her to start work. Mother was determined it was time to work. Grandad asked her to come and work at his firm in the office. Mother wanted to be independent and make new friends. Grandma said, "I want you safe, please don't work."

The subject seemed to be dropped, so grandma thought. Until mother announced, "I'm going to work at Wigfalls, you know how near it is to home," but her mother retorted back, "not near enough." Mother was determined to start work. Grandad said 'his bit', but to no avail.

Grandma insisted her daughter walk back home as soon as a siren sounded and, to please her, she said she would. Although in easy walking distance she had no intention of running back home when the sirens went. Wigfalls' air raid shelter was attached to the courtyard wall behind the store. That's where she intended to go in an air raid.

Not so long after starting work, the siren sounded and the staff and one customer went into the shelter. As soon as the all clear sounded the staff went back to work. It was strange how the same customer would appear in the store within ten minutes of any all clear sounding. The staff downstairs got used to sending the customer upstairs to the office. Yes, it was grandma checking all was well.

Wigfalls, an electrical retail store, was at the start of the local shopping 'mecca'. It was the flagship store of a chain of three shops around the city. Above the store was the office. Mother's job was to work out the wages, collect the money from the nearby bank and then 'divvy' the cash into packets. Once a week, a worker from the other two shops would collect the wage packets to take back for their shop's assistants.

Mother liked working there and received 15 shillings a week, *(that is, 75p)*. She gave all of it to her mother who would give her 5 shillings back.

The job was good experience but after several months mother started looking in the jobs section of the local newspaper, unbeknown to her mother. A junior wages clerk at a large, local steelworks was being advertised as 'good money', that is over a £1 per week.

A headed letter kept as neat and clean as if it had been typed yesterday, stated:

Dear Madam,

Referring to your application for situation as Junior Clerk in answer to our advertisement in the Sheffield Telegraph 'Y21'.

Kindly call for an interview as early as possible, and oblige.

Yours faithfully,

Director, George Clark.

Mother 'obliged' and was offered the job. She was delighted. Grandma was not delighted as it was farther away from home by about half a mile and then down a side street from the main road. However, the steelworks was very near to grandma's childhood estate and where her mother and handicapped sister still lived. Mother reminded her of that, which seemed to placate her.

A headed letter arrived for mother which was handwritten this time:

Dear Miss …,

Referring to your recent application for situation as Junior Clerk and subsequent interview.

We confirm your appointment herewith at a commencing salary of 25/– per week and that you commence your duties with us on Monday August 30th *at 9.30 A.M.*

After Monday your hours will be 9 A.M. to 5 pm with 1 hour for lunch.

Yours faithfully,

Director, George Clark.

The salary, 25 shillings or £1.5s.0d *(that is £1.25p)*, was an increase of ten shillings per week, *(remember, 20 shillings to a pound)*. Ten shillings could still buy a week's food shopping. Or a new skirt. Mother could also afford to go to work on the bus, though it was only four stops away. She planned to walk it in good weather.

For the first week, mother actually allowed half an hour for the journey but after that she could leave the house as late as 8.40am and still walk there for 9am.

The three settled into a new routine at home. Mother left for work at 8.40am, Monday to Saturday. Grandad set off in his car for work at 9.00am on the same days. He nearly always returned home for lunch.

Except on a Saturday, mother arrived back at 5.20pm unless she had called in on her grandma and aunt on the way home. Grandad was home by six. Grandma laid the tea on the table at 6.15pm, sharp.

On Saturday, mother finished at 12 noon and usually met her mother to go shopping. Grandad finished some time between 12 and 1. He was used to getting his own lunch on Saturdays. That is, calling at the chippy before he drove home.

At work, mother could even forget that there was a 'war on'.

(Answers to the true and false quiz:

1. *true – munitions factories were disguised as duck ponds so that enemy bombers couldn't pick them out;*
2. *true – used milk bottle tops were recycled and made into Lancaster bombers;*
3. *false – many things stayed rationed until 1954;*
4. *true – manure was used to throw on burning schools or other buildings.)*

War Stories

So many stories have been told about WW2, including some as part of mother's war diary and memories. The following account is from the Dunkirk evacuation.

Most adults have heard of the Dunkirk heroes, but there were many 'forgotten', fallen heroes left behind in Japan, Asia and Africa, to name only three.

Many battles in and around Dunkirk took place as the German advance marched and fought their way to the town. There were thousands upon thousands of retreating Allied soldiers who were in danger of being trapped on the coastline. A massive evacuation programme was launched and decoy battles planned.

The German advance had to be held off as long as possible to allow over 800 vessels, some in flotillas of navy and private ships, coming and going again and again over the channel, in the shadow of darkness. The private ships included, merchant boats, fishing boats, pleasure craft and lifeboats.

A quarter of a million troops, made up of British, French, Polish, Belgium and some Dutch, crowded into a beach head 25 miles wide and 6 miles deep. Only 5,000 troops, mainly French, were in the rearguard, stretched across that frontline width.

The French Admiral, in a bunker near Dunkirk beach,

wanted to hold onto Dunkirk, but the British Major General had his orders to evacuate everyone except those holding the rearguard and the decoy points.

On 31st May 1940, the British public heard from the BBC the first details of the story unfolding, "all day and all night members of the undefeated British expeditionary forces have come home and are coming home. Allied forces are still holding a rearguard line on the coast…"

Also listening to this was the Cold Stream Guards Platoon Sergeant at a decoy point, one of many, on either side of canals further along the coast. He was in charge of a platoon at only 25 years old, largely due to being able to speak German. He thought the Allies were beaten as the 'waiting' game continued and he assumed the Germans were resting before their assault.

The wounded are taken to the last casualty clearing station still operating, near the coast between the decoy canals and the Dunkirk beaches. In the front of the station, the British bury their recent dead.

Meanwhile, the Platoon Sergeant in the 'waiting' game, reflected…

'Boredom is endless,
Boredom takes energy,
it takes time.
Boredom takes courage,
but he had no courage when he was bored. He lights another cigarette'.

The platoon had set up guns on roofs of deserted houses and were watching and waiting and smoking. They had been told to last out as long as possible.

They had some trucks, hidden around the back of the houses, but knew that it would be touch and go whether they would make it back to the beach in time to get on 'the last ship' home.

Dawn on the 1st June 1940, some 40,000 Germans draw ever nearer to the 5,000 Allied rearguard troops.

The last casualty clearing station runs out of anaesthetic. The 'red cross' trucks reload wounded soldiers at the station and drive to the beach head. On arrival, the truck driver sees that the wounded he brought hours earlier are still lying where he placed them. When the truck driver enquires about the plight of the wounded he is told they weren't a priority as they "take up more room on the ships." He could understand that, giving priority to able bodied men, but yesterday the wounded had been able bodied men themselves!

German planes were bombing the ships in the channel and out of 41 destroyers, only 9 remained in use. Thousands died at sea.

Of the thousands who did make it back to English soil, a small number stayed at the port scanning faces for their brother, their father or father-in-law. One was searching for his twin brother. The 'waiting' game at home.

And the 'waiting' game continues at the decoy canal positions. The platoon is running out of cigarettes.

Some Germans are spotted in a field some distance away and guns shoot out from the house tops. The Germans then advance but hidden behind a line of civilians. "Hold your fire," the sergeant shouts. As they get nearer the Germans shoot some of the civilians and the platoon opens fire again. The Germans pull back and hide. More waiting. Artillery guns are set up in the distant fields. Spasmodic firing hour after hour. The 'waiting' game is over.

An impossible situation. Still the British order is to stay and hold, not to evacuate in their trucks. One British soldier decides to run for it. A rifle shot rings out and he falls. He is shot down by his own side! A shameful act of war is sometimes hard to talk about or write down. A poor, young soldier, so scared, so 'out of his mind' that he had felt there was no other option than to run away.

Those who ran were treated as deserters. They were shot rather than helped or shown compassion.

At the casualty station, over 200 wounded still remain but they needed three officers to stay behind with them. There were no volunteers and names were drawn out of a hat. The three unlucky 'winners' shake hands and hug the leaving soldiers.

At the decoy point, after thirteen hours of steady shooting, the Germans push forward their firing line. The Platoon Sergeant is badly wounded and the man next to him lies dying. When darkness falls, the sergeant is stretchered out into a 'red cross' truck and left at the now quiet and subdued casualty station. He hadn't been taken to the beach head as only the walking wounded and those who could sit up are given places on the fleeing ships.

Dawn on the last day and the last ship had left for Dover. Those left behind would have to wait for nightfall to see if any ships returned. Numbers left? Perhaps a few stragglers? Over 8,000, mainly British and French troops, were still fighting at the decoy canals or in the rearguard.

At Dover, the order went out to send all available ships back across the channel. A clearing up operation was started on the ships by mopping the decks of blood and water.

At Dunkirk, the order came through at last: "British expeditionary forces evacuate." Forces at the decoy canals made their way to the beaches. Some of the forces from the rearguard pulled back onto the beach. The very last, packed ships sail for Dover.

Dawn breaks, the Germans capture the rest of the rearguard soldiers and the wounded at the casualty station. The Platoon Sergeant has been propped up against a wall outside. On the way in, a German gives him some water and a half smoked cigarette which he had asked for in German.

He escaped capture, forgotten about as he sat there. But his recovery, thanks to French sympathisers, was a slow process as an arm and a leg below the knee had to be amputated. He went on to help organise escape lines across Europe and then he returned to France with Allied troops in 1944. He was awarded the Distinguished Service Order for Valour at Dunkirk.

Taken from one of Churchill's speeches after Dunkirk, "...a war is not won by evacuation," but it had saved over 300,000 lives! It was just unfortunate that a few had had to be left behind for the safety of the fleeing thousands.

More than a quarter of the escaped, expeditionary forces would go on to make up the core of the Allied Army through the War.

★ ★ ★ ★ ★

The next story, so to speak, is in February 1943, when it was the turn of the Germans to need some form of 'escape' or evacuation as the Russians advanced towards Stalingrad. The German soldiers had retreated and retreated back to

Stalingrad, many of whom had been crushed under the Russian tanks as they hid in trenches or tried to run.

The Germans were up against the freezing temperatures of a Russian winter and their supply lines were cut off, leaving them without food. They had to eat what few horses had survived so far and melt snow to drink.

A plane took off with a German Officer on board, bound for Berlin, to plead that Hitler give the order to surrender, but Hitler would give no such order. He sacrificed his men, rather than 'sacrifice' Stalingrad and he ordered them to fight until the end. His soldiers feared they would be shot by the Russians. They weren't. In fact, 91,000 German soldiers disobeyed orders and surrendered.

Over 80,000 of that number would be killed in the dying embers of the fighting, or by starvation or the freezing conditions.

The Russians' food rations per soldier were halved so there was more food for the new captives, but the intense cold and near starvation would result in more deaths than by any fighting around Stalingrad. Those who survived such grave conditions were sent to concentration camps in Russia. They were not released until 1955 and even then only a few thousand made it back to their German homeland.

One German widow said after the War, "I died too at Stalingrad but I had to live for the sake of our daughter." Another widow said, "I could not bury him and I could not stand by his grave and I still can't live with that and still wonder if he is alive or dead."

★ ★ ★ ★ ★

The D-Day landings in Normany started a year later in June 1944. The landings were in two phases. Firstly, an airborne assault landing which included British, Canadian, American and Free French troops. And secondly, an amphibious landing of Allied infantry and armoured divisions onto the coast of France.

Those evacuated from Dunkirk, and more, now formed part of the invasion force to reclaim land and people.

It was the 'turn' of the German Army to be spread 'too thin' in divisions all over Europe, including 157 in Russia alone. A significant number of the divisions were depleted in numbers due to intensity of fighting, some by up to 50%, according to German records. German soldiers were ordered to the fortifications along the French coastline of the English Channel, about 30 to each, called 'nests'.

Posted at Nest Number 62, *(code named Omaha Beach)*, were 31 Germans and a Lieutenant. Nest Commanders lived in an occupied French house and the Lieutenant at No 62 took one of his soldiers as a valet to live in the house's attic and be at 'his beck and call'.

The German soldier's story

At aged 19, I'd studied at agricultural school in 1942 and then drafted into the German Army. I didn't want to become a soldier but I knew I had to make the best of it. All I wanted to do was work my father's farm for when it would be mine.

It was hopeless to think that you would survive your tour of duty. I, and those with me on the basic training, saw no hope of survival.

In August of that year, I was sent to be a dispatch rider in the infantry division. As a farmer's son, I had trouble getting used to life in the barracks. If you said anything, it was 'shut up when you talk to me'. If your sentence started 'I think...' they would say 'leave your thinking to the horses, they've got bigger heads'. It was 100% blind obedience. A stray word or gesture and you were punished immediately.

New orders came through and we travelled by train to the French coastline and were assigned to different fortifications along the beaches. My fortification or nest number was 62 with thirty other men and a Lieutenant, who told me I was going to be his valet. I went to live in the house with the other nest commanders. I had my own room in the attic and I loved my time living there. I became really good friends with the Lieutenant. He was more than a friend, more like a father to me, even though he was only eleven years older than me.

Sometimes he would take me with him into town and when we passed a village, we stopped and would be given locally picked grapes and drinks. Most times we never made it into town, as the villagers plied us with delicious picnic food and local wine. In town, the commanders would visit cabaret shows and pick up women – they were the times when the Lieutenant had to leave me in the house, but he said being in the town was like 'paradise'. We knew it was a temporary 'paradise', but we hoped the British and Americans would land somewhere else, not where we were.

Each morning the Lieutenant and I went to inspect 'our' nest and I checked my position which was a machine gun to the right of the nest, underneath a camouflage net. We then stood on the embankment looking over the sea. The rest of the soldiers lived in the nest.

One day in early June '44, we were put on red alert and all of us had to stay in the nest. A few days later, there was a bombardment from big ships out at sea but the bombs all went behind us. We never felt in any danger but we had some debris falling on us, that's all. The bombardment from the planes seemed to be aimed at the beach itself, but again no bombs fell near us.

The American soldier's story

All we knew was there was a war going on 'over there' and that Hitler was taking over many countries, including Russia. 'Pearl Harbour' brought us into the war. I got my papers in 1942 and after some basic training found myself boarding the Queen Elizabeth in New York, bound for England. It was the first time I had been away from home in all of my 20 years, except for about 50 miles away visiting relatives.

It was like being on a floating hotel with 15,000 men. We had to make our own entertainment like boxing rounds, playing cards, kicking a ball about and smoking and talking in our smaller groups.

I didn't want to go to war, but there was no other option. After landing, we had practice runs over assault courses in the south of England, including walking through swamp water. I was drafted to a machine gun platoon and had to carry two heavy machine guns, one in either arm and attached to my belt to take some of the strain. No-one knew anything about an invasion or said when it might be.

We were told two days before, on 4th June, that we were moving out and travelled to the coastline in our platoons. There were small prayer services along the harbour. 155,000 of us 'stood' ready on the English beaches for the dawn of D-Day and the Allied invasion.

(The Queen Elizabeth had been launched in 1939 as a cruise

ship, named after the King's consort, Queen Elizabeth. With the onset of WW2, the conversion from ocean liner to troop ship took place in Singapore and Sydney, replacing sun beds and chairs with strengthened decks which allowed for all those marching, heavy boots. High class crockery and silverware tissue-papered away. All removable décor was…removed! Superstructure 'bits' were 'sliced' off.

Her sister ship, Queen Mary, had a similar conversion and both were repainted in 'war' colours, i.e. grey.

There were anti-aircraft guns on the upper decks, the stern had anti-submarine protection and around the ship several guns with high and low angled mounts. Two of the latter were placed 'in front of the bridge' (I assume here that 'in front' means 'on top' unless those on the bridge had to duck and weave their heads in order to see where they were going!)

Hitler tried to destroy both ships, in vain of course, by offering the Iron Cross and 250,000 US dollars to any U-Boat Captain who could sink one of the Queens.

As a troop carrier, the Queen Elizabeth carried more than 750,000 troops and sailed some 500,000 miles. Soldiers had to sleep in shifts as there weren't enough bunks for everyone to go to bed at the same time.)

The German soldier's story

My orders were to keep firing until I had nothing left to fire with. I was told when the water was up to their knees start firing and don't stop.

I could see that a big ship had stopped some way out and soldiers were coming down a ladder on either side, two at a time. They moved forward in a dark anonymous, slow moving mass. Then I could make out bobbing heads and shoulders as they came towards us.

I know they had parents and I was sorry for them, but I wanted, above all else, to see my own parents again.

I started firing from my unobstructed view and my clear line of firing.

The American soldier's story

There was no greater sound than the silence of our landing craft. We sat, just smoking or not. We were part of this war now and I couldn't turn back.

We had been led to believe that the bombardment had taken out the German positions and we would have little resistance. My orders were to get to the shoreline as quickly as possible.

My neck, back and armpits were wet with sweat before I even entered the water. When the ramp came down we were neck deep and had to hold smaller men up over the waterline. I emptied bladder and bowels in the water, certain I was facing death and I would never see my parents' loving faces again.

Those who reached the sand, were hit and fell. Those still in the water were hit and drowned. My best mate fell and I felt an impulse to help him, even turned my body towards him, but what could I do – drag him and risk us both being killed anyway? I moved on.

I reached the wet sand and I fell as bullets hit me, looking up from the sand and I swear that I saw a helmet of a lone gunman who was mowing us down like 'ninepins'.

He was showing no mercy and his firing was relentless. Bodies were heaping up at the shoreline where I was. I dragged myself to an embankment where a few survivors crouched down.

I looked back, still with the side of my head on the sand, and there were bodies laying in the sand almost as far as you could see. Many more bodies were revealed when the tide went out. I felt sick in a way I'd never felt sick before.

(The American soldier was taken to a field hospital and survived three bullets. He got to see his parents again.)

The German soldier's story

All I could think of was my orders to "hold your positions 'til the last round of bullets." Every man who left each ship was in our line of fire. Those wounded but still in the water, drowned. I could see the blood flowing in the water. Bodies piled up, two metres high. I had no choice but to keep firing, there was no way to avoid it. My mouth was dry, my groin wet with sweat and stale urine.

Out of every fifty shots, only five or so would miss. It was 3 o'clock and I was now using a rifle. I saw that a helmet was in view over the embankment and I shot at his helmet which bowled over down into the sand and he fell forward. (Since then, whenever I shut my eyes he falls over again and again.)

At 3.30, the order came to pull back and with those left at nest 62 we ran back. We waited for the Lieutenant but he never came. We ran back to the house.

There was no pride in what we did and I've had a lifetime of guilt and self loathing. Just thinking back, I feel sick to my stomach.

(The German soldier survived and saw his parents again.)

★ ★ ★ ★ ★

By August 1944, Allied troops reached Paris and in September, American soldiers entered Germany. The Americans, and Russians, had to take Berlin 'street by street' in long, drawn out gun battles around bombed buildings, rubble and debris.

Meanwhile, the largest ever civilian revolt in history had been taking place by the Polish population against the Nazis. In January 1945, Warsaw was liberated by the Russians.

Concentration camps were liberated. But thousands were so emaciated, so weak, they would not survive the liberation, welcome though it was. At Dachau, like others, the Germans had rounded up the 'inmates' who could walk, gave them a piece of bread and shouted, "March!" After more than two hours continuous walking they were allowed a few minutes rest. Those who could not get up again were shot.

One survivor from Dachau said that he would lie next to a dead man, sometimes for a few days, in order to eat his ration of food with his own.

Colditz Castle was liberated. Among the liberated Allied officers at the Castle was the nephew of King George VI and first cousin to Princess Elizabeth. *(At the time of the Viscount's birth, he was sixth in line to the throne.)*

Victory was 'round the corner'! A welcome peace made possible by fallen heroes. Heroes who would not be forgotten by their loved ones and the heroes who returned.

One Canadian soldier spoke with humility after the War, "Heroes are the guys who didn't make it and heroes are the guys who're wounded. Not me. I'm no hero. I made it." Another said, "I tried to do two things – stay alive and do my job. I'm not a hero but I served with heroes."

WW2 ended when Allied troops captured Berlin and the

Germans unconditionally surrendered on 8th May 1945. Japan's unconditional surrender followed the nuclear bombing of Nagasaki and Hiroshima. A tragic end to so much tragedy and loss of life. But the truth is, from tragedy, future lives and a democratic way of living were saved.

VE Day in Europe is remembered on 8th May each year. Victory in Japan (VJ) Day is celebrated on 15th August.

Remembrance Day is marked by the ending of WW1 in the 11th hour, of the 11th day, of the 11th month and two minutes of silence is observed at 11am throughout the UK, most of Europe and the Commonwealth. After 1945, it also marked WW2, becoming known as 'Poppy Day'.

For that two minutes silence, everyone and everything would stop: factory production, cars and buses in the street, trains would halt, people stood with their shopping, and wireless programmes interrupted – everyone would stop what they were doing and bow their heads, in remembrance.

"Too many died – war isn't worth one life"… said one Great War soldier who survived that war.

Trams at Hillsboro' Corner

Maternal great-
grandparents

Maternal grandma

Grandma's 'invalid' sister and
brother Walt

Aunt Lily's husband. Fred.
Honoured for distinguished
service in WW1

WW1 postcards sent to grandma from 'her' soldier

The soldier's WW1 postcards turned into marriage proposals

Brothers John and Wilf (grandad on right)

Grandad in his Salvation Army band uniform

Wedding of grandparents, 1923.
l to r: A. Lily, U. Harry, grandad, U. George, grandma, U. Johm
and A. Minnie

Grandad ready for work

Grandma ready for
housework in her 'pinny'

Mother just before her neck
operation

Mother and 'baby' in the
garden at home

Mother and daughter pose
outside her school

A heavy smoker of Woodbines
untipped cigarettes

Two of mother's birthday cards

Mother's Whitsuntide outfit

1939, bridesmaid to U. Walt

Grandma's brother Walt and his
best mate, Jack, from WW2

Winner of the best dressed paddler
contest, U. Walt and daughter Valerie

THE GIRLS RECKON THEY CAN DO ANYTHING
WITHOUT US MEN
NOW-A-DAYS

BUT CAN
THEY?

A cheeky war postcard

Mellow, reviving, smooth and full-bodied — a stout of supremely fine quality

Return your bottles — please!

MACKESON'S STOUT

sets you up wonderfully

STRANGE BEAUTY TEST

AMAZES 10,000 WOMEN!

POSITIVE PROOF that you can look more beautiful in 30 seconds

A SENSATIONAL OFFER!

Before the 'invention' of the Trades Description Act

HOW LONG IS A CUP OF TEA ?

ABOUT TWO MINUTES if you have a NEW WORLD No. 1430 Gas Cooker with its high-speed boiling burners. Lovely to look at and easy to clean, this newest model raises the famous NEW WORLD cooking standards to even higher levels. Soon available at your Gas Showrooms.

PRODUCT OF Radiation Ltd

NEW WORLD *Cookers have the PIGGLY, as fitted ONLY to RADIATION appliances.*

NEW WORLD No. 1430 **GAS COOKER**

A cup of tea only takes two minutes with a New World Gas Cooker

Mars ARE MARVELLOUS

THERE'S A MEAL IN A Mars

Marvellous that anything so nice can be so full of real goodness too. But, as you see, Mars bars are packed with all those good things that nourish, energise and sustain you.

Note: MARS is a marvellous meal

SILVER SHRED is here again! This delicious Jelly Marmalade made from ripe juicy lemons is now in stock at all good grocers.

ROBERTSON'S

Silver Shred

Lemon Jelly Marmalade

James Robertson & Sons (P.M.) Ltd. Makers of 'Golden Shred' PAISLEY · MANCHESTER BRISTOL · LONDON

EXTRA PRESERVE RATION May 23rd–June 19th Try SILVER SHRED for a refreshing change

Offer of extra rations from Silver Shred – early concept of 2 for the price of 1?

A man gets real pleasure from PLAYER'S

No caption needed!

How to get rid of that sore throat – have a cigarette!

Lips that stay put, even after smoking!

'In-Between' Diary

The next significant diary of my mother's was post war by a couple of years and heralded the start of her 'going out'. The phrase used in the Debutante world was, of course, 'coming out' but it also meant an 'in-between' time. This 'in-between' time would be the start of going out with friends while still going out with your parents to the shops, on holiday, walking and seeing a film. This phrase gave way to the 'teenage years' used by the next generation and after.

Interestingly, the first few pages of this 'in-between' diary as the earlier 'wartime' diary, featured information on weights, measures and postal rates. Letter stamps were now two and a half old pence, postcards 2d and reply postcards 4d. Letters to 'Navy, Army and Air Force Abroad' was only one and a half old pence.

There were now telegraph money orders for sending money to countries of the Empire ('except Newfoundland' which cost less money to send). Sending money to 'Foreign' countries would also cost less, 'except Cuba' which cost more money to send.

Before getting to the diary dates, there was a page on:
– first aid information (example: breathing difficulties – 'douch chest with cold water'); *(er, would the cold water not send someone into shock?)*

- meteorological notes (fall in barometer: 'cold increasing, in winter, snow');
- GMT and time zones (same time as Great Britain: Eire, France, Belgium, Portugal, Spain, Gibralter, Morocco, Gold Coast);
- useful constants and numbers (length of the seconds hand Pendulum, Greenwich is 39.139 in.);
- sunrise, sunset and full moon times; *(werewolves take note!)*
- important dates in history which started with the first Pharaoh in 5000BC and ended with VJ day on 15 August 1945.

The actual diary entries are written in fountain pen and still in the diary is a small 'diary blotter' from 'Ford's Blotting Paper'. Underneath that was written: 'obtainable in 23 colours from all Stationers' – the one in the diary is a pale green colour, with dried ink blotches.

The diary date is in bold and then any explanations are in italics.

Sat 1 Jan – Went to Dan's house to tea. We had a drink in Crookes with Alice and Louis *(friends)*, then Dan and I came back to our house.

(Dan was the son of family friends. Alice and Louis lived about half a mile walk from 'our house'.)

Sun 2 Jan – Dan came to our house, we all went to Cath's house to tea.

(Cath is Aunty Cath, married to Uncle Walt, but in conversation Mother would refer to her as 'Aunty'. At either side of their house on 'Bank was Aunt Lily and Uncle Fred, and at the other side lived

Aunt Minnie with husband Frank and son Frank. So when Aunt M. is visited, it would mean the others were as well, written as "etc" in later entries.)

Dan and I went to their house for a bit and then back to Cath's.

Mon 3 Jan – went to work. Dan and I went with mother and father to track club.

(This was club night at the local greyhound track.)

Tue 4 Jan – went to work. Dan came to meet me at the office and we went to the Regal to see 'Oliver Twist'. After we went to Dan's house, met Ken's wife.

(The 'Regal' was a cinema in Sheffield city centre. Ken was Dan's older brother who had married the year before.

Films were advertised as 'continuous performances' so if the start of a film was missed, you could stay until the whole film had been seen. In fact, you could watch the same film over and over and stay in until it closed. It was 4d for a child (that is less than 2p) and if the film was classified as an 'A', then children had to be accompanied by an adult. Children used to 'hang around' the front of cinemas asking adults to take them in, which a lot did, as long as the child had enough money.

The cost for adults was 6d in the front few rows and 10p at the back and in the balcony.)

Wed 5 Jan – Went to work. Dan came down for me and we stayed in.

(That would be Dan waiting for her outside the works' office, then walking to 'our house' and staying in. The front room was used on those 'staying in' occasions and they would have talked, read, listened to the wireless or my mother would have played the piano.)

Thu 6 Jan – Went to work. Went to the station to see Dan off. Stayed in at night and wrote to Dan.

(Dan had been called up into National Service for 18 months.)

(I will miss out diary dates which read 'went to work. Stayed in all night' and 'went to work'. Also, entries like 'went to Aunt L. and Aunt M.' or to her 'Grandma's', the latter of which would include invalid Aunt H.)

Mon 10 Jan – Went to work. Went to Eversley House dance, not very nice, came home about ten thirty.

(Eversley House was a large, old house (now Grade II Listed) used for dancing. It was within the shopping area of Crookes. Each district had its own small shopping area, the larger ones having cinemas and public houses.)

Wed 12 Jan – Went to work. Went to the Palace *(Theatre)* with Mother and Dad to see the pantomime, 'Cinderella'.

(Palace Theatre, audience capacity 1600, was opened in 1898 and reopened in 1913 as a cinema as well as a theatre.)

Thu 13 Jan – Went to work. Went to the Phoenix *(Cinema)* with Mother to see 'I Love Trouble'.

(The title suggests it might have been a comedy but it wasn't. A wealthy man hires a detective to investigate his wife's past. The detective discovers his wife was a dancer and left her home town with an actor. She had then stolen £40,000 from the club where she worked. The husband found out about this and to avoid a scandal killed his wife. He was using the detective to try and find someone from the wife's past to frame for the murder.)

Sat 15 Jan – Went to work. Went shopping in town *(city centre)* with Mother. Went to Eversley House dance.

Wed 19 Jan – Went to work. Went to Mr Ryan's funeral during the morning. Went to the Regal with Mother to see 'The Huggetts Family'. ('Here comes the Huggetts'.)

(The first of the Huggetts Trilogy, a British film, about a working class English family. Jack Warner starred as head of the family and his three daughters used their own first names in the film – Petula Clark was Pet Huggett. A 'flightly' cousin was Diana (Dors). Such light comedies were very popular with British audiences still feeling the impact of World War II.)

Sat 22 Jan – Went to work. Went to the local shops and then to Grandma's with mother. Went to Eversley House dance.

Sun 23 Jan – Went a run in car with Mother and Dad. We went to Aunt M. etc. in the evening.

Mon 24 Jan – Went to work. Went up to Dan's house.

Sat 29 Jan – Went to work. Went in town shopping with mother. Went to Eversley House dance. Gilbert there.

(Gilbert had been someone with whom she had 'walked out' with a few times in the year before.)

Sun 30 Jan – Went to Dan's house to tea. Ken and Joan there.

Mon 31 Jan – Went to work. Went to the Scala with Gilbert to see 'Daughter of Darkness'.

(Scala Cinema's audience capacity was 1,020 but within a few

short years it was demolished to make way for a city centre road improvement scheme. The film is about a honeymooning couple who arrive at a European Hotel. The middle aged Concierge is sure he saw the woman when he was a little boy but as she looks no older, assumes he is mistaken. A Countess arrives and becomes obsessed with the newlyweds. However, three deaths later – the groom, the Countess and her companion – the bride is left free to stalk new victims! Hardly a light comedy…)

Sat 5 Feb – Went to work. Went to town straight from the office with mother. Went to Eversley House dance, not very nice, came home at 10.20pm.

Sun 6 Feb – Stayed in all day. Wrote to Dan in the evening.

Thu 10 Feb – Went to work. Went to the Palace Theatre with Mother and Father to see 'Snow White and the Seven Dwarfs'.

Sat 11 Feb – Went to work. Went to town shopping with mother. Stayed in at night.

Tue 15 Feb – Went to work in the morning, wasn't very well so I had the afternoon off. Stayed in all night.

Wed 16 Feb – Went to work. Went with Mother to greyhound stadium. Fallen out with Dan.

(Nearly two years of National Service, though there were visits home, seemed a long time for a young woman to wait and who still wanted go out. Dan had not been happy that she went out dancing while he was away.)

Thu 17 Feb – Went to work. Went with mother and dad to the Palace to see 'Hello from S.E.A.C.'

(This stands for South East Asia Command and was a film about that Asian Command unit in WW2.)

Sat 19 Feb – Went to work. Went shopping down Brightside *(popular shopping area with a large department and clothes stores.)* Went to Eversley House dance.

Wed 23 Feb – Went to work. Sent Dan the ring back. Went with mother to the Phoenix to see 'To the Ends of the Earth'.

(This was an American film which starts with a Government Agent on a coast guard boat off California chasing a ship, but the captain panics and sends 100 Chinese slaves on board to a watery grave. The agent goes to Shanghai to try and track down the ruthless captain and discovers a huge drug smuggling operation. He believes the drug ringleader to be a woman and follows her to 'the ends of the earth' to Cairo, Beirut and Havana, in order to stop the drug smuggling.)

Sun 27 Feb – Went with mother and dad to Aunt L. to tea. After, went to grandma's *(by car.)*

Tue 1 Mar – Went to work. Went to the Regal with mother to see Margaret Lockwood in 'Look Before you Love'.

(This film, starring the English actress (1916-1990), was a romantic girl meets boy story set in a hotel in Rio.)

Sat 5 Mar – Went to work. Went in town *(shopping)* with mother. Went to Eversley House dance – Ralph was there.

(Mother courted Ralph just after the War. He was five years older,

had been an Allied soldier and always wore his uniform on 'dates'. After 'falling out' with Ralph, mother had kept a 'soft spot' for Ralph by keeping his photo and small mementoes. On the reverse of the photos, the writing of Ralph's name had been rubbed away with a rubber, leaving a small mess of pulp. The photos, on thick card, were unaffected.)

Sun 6 Mar – Went with mother and dad to Aunt M. etc. in the evening.

Mon 7 Mar – Went to work. Went to Greystones *(Church)* dance with Ralph (Walt's firm's dance.)

Thu 10 Mar – Went to work. Went with mother to grandma's.

Sat 12 Mar – Went to work. Went in town shopping. Went to Eversley House dance – Gilbert there.
   (I can't keep up – dancing with Ralph, Walt and then Gilbert…)

Sun 13 Mar – Stayed in during the day. Went a walk with Gilbert in the evening.

Sun 15 Mar – Went to work. Stayed in at night. (Clothes came off coupons.)
   (As previously mentioned, rationing started in 1940, initially caused by German submarines sinking ships bringing supplies to Britain, causing severe shortages. Food was rationed until 4 July 1954.)

Sat 19 Mar – Went to work. Went to town with mother,

bought a bedroom suite. Went to Eversley House dance –
Walt was there.

Sun 20 Mar – Went to Bridge Street with Walt to see a Polish
film. Went with Walt to the Hipperdrome to see 'Boomerang'.

*(The Hippodrome was opened in 1907 and was another theatre
that later reopened as a cinema.)*

*(The film 'Boomerang' was based on a true story. A priest is shot
in the street and an ambulance takes ten minutes to reach the badly
wounded priest who later dies in hospital. A vagrant, and discharged
soldier, is found near the scene with a gun. He's arrested and then he
confesses to the crime. The prosecutor, on investigating, finds the
vagrant's gun could not have shot the priest, despite his 'confession'.
The vagrant is proved innocent and is released.)*

*Note: have you noticed that whoever mother 'bumps' into at a dance,
the next day or week she goes to the cinema, another dance or for a
walk with them? For example:*

*   ***-29 Jan,** Gilbert at the same dance…two nights later, went to the
Scala with Gilbert;*

*   ***-5 Mar,** Ralph at the same dance…two nights later, went dancing
with Ralph;*

*   ***-12 Mar,** 'bumped' into Gilbert again…next night, went
walking with Gilbert;*

*   ***-19 Mar,** Walt at the same dance…next night, at the pictures
with Walt.*

★ ★ ★ ★ ★

Tue 22 Mar – Went to work. Went to the Phoenix with
mother to see 'Life with Father'.

(However, father would have been next door in the local public house playing billiards.)

Wed 23 Mar – Went to work. Went to the Regal with Walt to see 'Mother wore tights'. *(Surely that would have been a film to see with mother?)*

(The film was a vaudeville variety show of comedy and singing sketches).

Sat 26 Mar – Went to work. Stayed in during the afternoon. Went to a dance with Walt at night.

Sun 27 Mar – Went in car with mother and dad to Matlock *(Derbyshire.)* Stayed in at night.

Tue 29 Mar – Dan's birthday. Went to work. Stayed in at night. Received a letter from Dan's mother, answered it in the evening.

(That was a letter to say that they, his parents, were sad that they had broken their 'engagement' and to keep in touch. Mother's reply thanked them and wished them well. 'Engagement' is in quotes as Dan had given her a ring but had not discussed with her parents so it would not be classed as a binding engagement.)

Wed 30 Mar – Went to work. Went with Walt to the Hippodrome to see 'No room at the Inn'. *(A theatre play.)*

Sat 2 Apr – Went to work. Went to town with mother. Went to a dance with Walt.

Sun 3 Apr – Went in car with mother and dad to Buxton.

Went to the Regal with Walt to see 'Well I never'.

Wed 6 Apr – Went to work. Went to the Empire with mother and dad to see 'Would you believe it'.

(This film was a black and white 'slapstick' comedy, like Keystone Cops or Laurel and Hardy.)

Thu 7 Apr – Went to the Speedway with Walt. *(Speedway was motorbike racing at the greyhound stadium.)*

Sat 9 Apr – Went to work. Went with Walt to a dance.

Sun 10 Apr – Went in car with mother and dad to Castleton and Hathersage. *(Villages in the Derbyshire Peak District).*

Mon 11 Apr – Went to work. Went to Aunt M's then went with mother and dad to the track club.

Thu 14 Apr – Went to work. Went to the Speedway with mother.

(Things seemed to be settling into some kind of 'walking out' cum 'courtship' with Walt. But hold on, just back from National Service was a very shy young man called Joseph who returned to work in the steelworks side of the firm where mother worked in the wages office.)

Good Friday 15 APR – Went to work, finished at lunchtime. Went to Aunt L. then went to grandma's. Went with Joseph to the Regal to see 'Luck of the Irish'.

('Luck of the Irish' is an ironic phrase as the Irish are known to be unlucky but its origins are actually based on luck. The phrase dates back to when a high number of Irish migrants struck gold in the

American West when prospecting for gold.

So the storyline of the first film on the first date of my mother and father was a romantic comedy of a young American man who meets a beautiful young woman and her leprechaun friend on a trip to Ireland. Oh dear, he has a wealthy fiancée back in New York! He returns home only to bump into the beautiful woman and the leprechaun. He's torn between his Irish roots and the beautiful woman or the wealth he can enjoy in New York. I wonder which he chooses, bearing in mind leprechaun's are lucky!)

Meanwhile, Anne was in a real life drama of Walt vs Joseph. Let's see who won through in the end…

Sat 16 Apr – Went in town with mother, had dinner in town *(Atkinsons.)* Went to the Palace with Walt to see 'Walls of Jericho'. *(Ah! Walt's still 'in the picture'.)*

(This film is a girl meets married boy 'soap opera' set within the walls of a university in a place called Jericho, Kansas.)

Sun 17 Apr – Went in car with mother and dad to Ollerton *(Clumber Park in Sherwood Forest.)* Met Walt and went through Endcliffe Park and Whiteley Woods.
…what about Joseph?

Easter Monday 18 Apr – Stayed in during the day. Went with Walt dancing.

Tue 19 Apr – Went with mother and dad to Henley Lake Amusement Park, near Huddersfield, in the car. Went with Joseph to the Regal to see 'Euraka Stockade'. *At last, it's Joseph's 'turn'.*

(A British film about an 1854 rebellion by Australian gold

miners which was crushed by the authorities. It took its name from the Euraka Hotel, which was burned down as part of the film.)

Wed 20 Apr – Went to work. Went to the Palace Theatre with mother and dad *(to see…?)*

Thu 21 Apr – Went to work. Went to the Speedway with Joseph.

Sat 23 Apr – Went to work, stayed in during the afternoon. Went with Walt in the evening to the Hippodrome to see 'Somewhere in Politics'.
…is it time to tell Walt something?

(This film is an unabashed 'knockabout' British comedy involving a house being double let to two tenants, one a married couple and the other a sister and two brothers. They try and share the house and make 'the best of things' amid lots of domestic slapstick. The two lots of tenants are rival supporters of the two local election candidates, hence the title.)

Sun 24 Apr – Went a run in car with mother and father to Ladybower. Went for a walk with Joseph through the local park.

(Ladybower is a reservoir which took two years to fill with water and was the largest in Britain at the time of completion in 1945. The King and Queen attended the opening ceremony in September of that year and performed the 'cutting ribbon' ceremony.

Two Derbyshire villages had to be 'drowned' to make way for this reservoir – Ashopton and Derwent. The latter village's church steeple was left in tact as a memorial to the two villages, but was blown up in 1947 amid safety concerns.

In times of drought, the low water level reveals Derwent's packhorse bridge, some cottages and the remains of the church and steeple.)

Mon 25 Apr – Went to work. Went to the Kinema with Joseph to see 'A Foreign Affair'. *A good sign, walking with Joseph yesterday and then today…*

(This film is set in occupied Berlin, where an army captain is torn between an ex-Nazi café singer (Marlene Dietrich) and the US Congresswoman (Jean Arthur) who came to Berlin to investigate GI morals but did not know of their 'foreign affair'. One gaffe is that Jean, unmarried in the film, wore her wedding ring almost throughout the picture, even in close ups!)

Tue 26 Apr – Went to work. Went to Cath's and Aunt L.

Wed 27 Apr – Went to work. Went to the Regal with Walt to see 'Paradine Case'.
…it's now time to let Walt down gently.

(The film is an American courtroom drama set in England, directed by Alfred Hitchcock. An English Barrister (Gregory Peck) falls in love with a woman who is accused of murder. The plot unfolds of how this affects the Barrister's relationship with his wife.)

Thu 28 Apr – Went to work. Went to the Speedway with Joseph and we took Valerie with us. *(Reminder: Valerie is her young cousin, daughter of Uncle Walt and Cath.)*
At last, Joseph is meeting a family member. Bye bye Walt!

Sat 30 Apr – Went to work. Went to the Hippodrome with Joseph to see 'The Guinea Pig'.
(A 24 year old Richard Attenborough played a 14 year old boy

in this British film! The working class boy won a scholarship to a public school and he meets snobbery and punishments as he strives for acceptance. Note: Attenborough must have looked exceptionally young at 24 to play a boy of 14!)

Sun 1 May – Went in the car to Workshop and Retford. Went walking with Joseph.

Mon 2 May – Went to work. Went with Walt to Cutlers Hall dance.
…did you let Walt down gently this evening, or even not so gently?

Tue 3 May – Went to work. Went with Joseph to the Regal to see 'So this is London'.
(A 1939 British comedy about an American who clashes with an Englishman over the merits of their respective countries, only to find their children have fallen in love with each other.)

Wed 4 May – Went to work. Went to the Palace with mother and dad.

Thu 5 May – Went to work. Went to the Speedway with Joseph.

Sat 7 May – Went to work. Stayed in during the afternoon, went to Aunt L. to tea. Went with Joseph to the Kinema to see, 'The Pirate'.
(An American musical. Manuela, played by Judy Garland, is destined to marry Don Pedro, a man she doesn't love, while she dreams of being swept away by an infamous Pirate, Mack 'the black' Macoco. A handsome pirate, played by Gene Kelly, comes to town as

part of a travelling circus. Manuela visits the circus and she falls for the pirate. Don Pedro convinces the authorities that the pirate is Macoco ,who is wanted for stolen treasure, and he is arrested. To cut the swashbuckling story short, evidence comes to light that Don Pedro is the real Macoco and he is arrested, leaving Manuela to marry her circus pirate.)

Sun 8 May – Went with mother, dad and uncle Walt in the car to Bakewell *(Derbyshire)*. After, went with Joseph for a walk up Stannington and little Matlock.

Mon 9 May – Went to work. Went with Walt to a dance at the City Hall.
…so Monday is 'Walt's night'!

Tue 10 May – Went to work. Went with Joseph to the Palace, Union St, to see, 'Johnny Belinda'.
(An American film based on a true story and was the first time rape had featured in a storyline. A young Jane Wyman starred, who was 'deaf and mute', faced the consequences of lies and rumours after being raped. Agnes Moorhead co-starred as her aunt. Jane received an Oscar for her performance.

My aunt – the five year old from the War – was also watching this film with a girlfriend. As the rape scene unfolded, a neighbour in the audience, jumped up and shouted, "You dirty dog." Both girls were very embarrassed at the outburst and, after the film, quickly made their way out so the neighbour didn't see them.)

Thu 12 May – Went to work. Went with Joseph to the Speedway.

Sat 14 May – Went to work. Went to the shops with mother. Went to the Regal with Joseph.

Sun 15 May – Went in car with mother and father to Ollerton. Went with Joseph to the Hippodrome to see 'The Two Sisters from Boston'.

(An American musical comedy about two sisters with Broadway aspirations who first find work in the same 'downtown' saloon.)

Mon 16 May – Went to work. Went to the City Hall dance with Walt.

…it's Monday, and it's 'Walt's night'!

Tue 17 May – Went to work. Went to the Phoenix with Joseph to see 'My Wild Irish Rose'.

(This film was in glorious Technicolour and was nominated for an Academy Award. The film traces the rise of an American tenor to stardom at the end of the 19th Century/beginning of the next.)

Thu 19 May – Went to work. Went to the Speedway with Joseph.

Pattern emerging here: Monday is 'Walt's night'; Tuesday is 'cinema night' with Joseph and Thursday is 'Speedway night' with Joseph.

Sat 21 May – Went to work. Went in town shopping with mother. Went to the Regal with Joseph to see 'Whispering Smith'.

(Alan Ladd stars in this American western as an iron-willed railroad detective. He goes after a train robber but develops an interest in the train robber's wife!)

Sun 22 May – Went with mother and dad in the car to Ladybower. Went with Joseph to the Star Cinema *(near the city centre)* to see, 'Bond St'.

(British drama about a bride's dress, veil, pearls and flowers bought in London's Bond Street and tells the secret story behind each item.)

Note: the weekend belonged to Joseph!

Mon 23 May – Went to work. Went with Walt to the City Hall dance.

…but Monday belonged to Walt, again.

Tue 24 May – Went to work. Went in the park with Joseph and then to the Kinema to see, 'Summer Holiday'.

(An American musical starring Mickey Rooney. This film was nothing to do with a group of young people having a holiday on a red London bus, i.e. the 1963 British film with Cliff Richard.)

Thu 26 May – Went to work. Went to the Speedway with Joseph.

…and Thursday is speedway night with Joseph.

Sat 28 May – Went to work. Went in town and down Attercliffe shopping with mother and dad. Went with Joseph to the Hippodrome to see 'Bonnie Prince Charlie'.

(A British historical drama with David Niven as the Prince, about the 1745 Jacobite Rebellion and his part in it.)

Sun 29 May – Went with mother and dad to Southport in the car.

Mon 30 May – Went to work. Went with Joseph to a dance at Eversley House.

This Monday: Joseph – 1; Walt – 0.

Tue 31 May – Didn't go to work, had a sore throat and cough so went to Doctors.

Went with Joseph to the Phoenix to see 'Mr Perrin and the Traill'. *(Can't have been that poorly then?)*

(A British film drama – an elderly schoolmaster is upset when a new young teacher (John Mills) arrives and proves popular with pupils but the rivalry leads to a tragic conclusion.)

Sat 4 Jun – Went in town with mother in the morning, had lunch in town. Went with Joseph to the Empire *(Theatre)* to see Allan Jones, then went to the News Theatre *(city centre cinema)* with Alice and Louis.

(This was the start of the weekend Bank Holiday for Whitsuntide – Sat to Tue.)

Sun 5 Jun – Went with dad to Aunt M. etc. in the morning. Went to Joseph's to tea, after tea Joseph and I went to Endcliffe Park and Forge Dam.

(Uncle Walt and family had now moved to the 'Bank' next door to Aunt Minnie and Aunt Lily – visiting made easy!)

Note the serious courtship event: "went to Joseph's for tea."

Mon 6 Jun – Joseph and I went to Belle Vue for the day on the train. Went to Belle Vue Speedway in the afternoon.

Note: Mondays – game, set and match to Joseph. Er, Walt who?

Tue 7 Jun – Watched the 'Star Walk' in the morning. Joseph and I went round on the Circular Bus. We went to the Regal to see 'The History of Mr Polly'.

(This film starred John Mills and was based on an HG Wells book – the first to be adapted after his death in 1946.)

Thu 9 Jun – Went to work. Went to the Speedway with Joseph and his father. Mother came later. Joseph and I went for a walk in the park.

(Family members join the 'courting' couple, then the family are abandoned for a 'walk in the park'!)

Sat 11 Jun – Went to work. Went with mother to Aunt E. *(Grandma's sister Emily.)* Went with Joseph to the Kinema to see 'If I had my way'.

(An American musical starring Bing Crosby who takes charge of the daughter of a fellow construction worker killed in an accident. He takes her to New York to find her uncle but he has a rundown restaurant and no money. He tries to help the girl and her uncle by making the restaurant a success,)

Sun 12 Jun – Went with Joseph in Graves Park in the afternoon. In the evening we went in Millhouses Park and then Hillsboro' Park.

Things to do when courting – visit three parks in one day. Let's hope they wore sturdy court shoes for all this walking. Pun intended with the court shoes.

Sat 18 Jun – Went to work. Went to grandma's with mother. Went with Joseph to the Regal to see 'A Yankee in King Arthur's court'.)

(An American has a blow on the head and wakes up to find he

has gone back to the time of the legendary King Arthur – based on a book by Mark Twain.)

Sun 19 Jun – Went to Aunt L. to dinner. Went up Bradfield with Joseph. In the evening we went up Rivelin.

Note: things to gain from courting – fitness through lots of walking.

(Bradfield is a small Derbyshire village with a cricket green, park, river paddling and picnic area, a village shop/tea rooms and post office. Following the river round would lead to Rivelin. Known locally as 'up Rivelin'.)

Mon 20 Jun – Went to work. Went with Joseph to the Regal to see 'The Blue Lagoon'. *(Two children are shipwrecked on a desert island and fall in love while growing up.)*
…Mondays are now, well and truly, 'Joseph's night'.

Sat 25 Jun – Went to work. Joseph came to our house for tea. After tea we went to the Hippodrome to see 'Man Proof'. *(A 1938 romantic comedy.)*

Small note: our diary 'heroine' and Joseph have now had tea with both sets of parents.

Sun 26 Jun – Joseph and I went with mother and father in car to Saxilby. Joseph and I went to Lincoln.

Large note: Joseph invited on the Sunday run out and fishing trip in the car. The courting couple were dropped off at Lincoln and then collected on the way back.

Mon 27 Jun – Went to work. Went a walk with Joseph 'up Rivelin', we also called at Aunt L. and Aunt Cath's, etc.

Courtship note: now Joseph has met all of the 'etc' family on 'Bank.

Wed 28 Jun – Went to work. Went with mother to the Ideal Homes Exhibition in town.

(The Ideal Homes Exhibition of 1947 was the first to be held after the War (it had been suspended from 1940 to 1946) and there were smaller exhibitions in other cities. Unfortunately, most of the furniture on display was still not available to buy and to do so involved adding your name to a long waiting list. There were displays of prefabricated housing which was 'put across' as the quickest way to rebuild houses after the War.

Visiting the London Exhibition that year was Princess Elizabeth and Prince Philip, giving it their 'seal of approval'. They saw the launch of the microwave and a lifesized replica of Eros, which was still absent from Piccadilly Circus.

1947 was also known for its winter of extreme weather, with snowdrifts of 14 foot in Norfolk. Snowdrifts were so deep that soldiers had to use flamethrowers in attempts to clear the snow. There were even icebergs off Great Yarmouth.)

Sat 2 Jul – Went to work. Went in town with mother. Went with Joseph to the Hippodrome to see, 'Forbidden'.

(A thriller set in Blackpool about a man in a loveless marriage who peddles lotions and potions. He falls for the candy floss seller and they start an affair. Wife finds out and confronts her, who confronts him. He leaves some lethal tablets for his wife to take but changes his mind and heads back home. Too late, she's already dead, but unknown to him, it's through natural causes. He panics, disposes of the body, then flees to the Blackpool Tower. In hot pursuit is the police and all the action at the end of the film is at the top of the Tower.)

Sun 3 Jul – Went with mother, dad and Joseph to Trent Lock in the car. *(Trent Lock is by the Notts canal.)*

Sat 9 Jul – Went to work. Went with Mother to Grandma's. Went with Joseph to the Regal, to see 'The Lost Moment'.
(An American film starring Agnes Moorhead as a 105 year old recluse who was the young lover of a famous poet who wrote her many love letters. Her lodger is an undercover publisher trying to get hold of the love letters and in the process, falls for her niece.)

Sun 10 Jul – Went with mother, father and Joseph in car to Cleethorpes.

Tue 12 Jul – Went to work. Dan rang me up at the office. Went with Joseph to the Empire *(Theatre)* to see 'The Five Smith Brothers'.
(The previous year, the five brothers had done a summer season at Blackpool. They served in WW2, but shortly after returning, one brother was killed in a road accident. His replacement took the dead brother's name on stage. Three had been professional footballers and now, as five brothers, they did a singing and variety act.
It was somewhat ironic that all five brothers had served in, and survived, WW2 to return home, start entertaining together and then have one brother killed in a road accident.)
Dan ringing up – was it a 'how are you' call or 'are you free to go out' type of call? Either way, it was still Joseph's night.

Sat 16 Jul – Went on firm's trip to Blackpool for the day on the train. Mother, Joseph and Joseph's mother went.
Note: it was a 'bit of a Blackpool week' – seeing the Blackpool brothers and then the firm's trip.

Family note: both mothers on the 'getting to know you' trip. Although both women grew up on the same estate and were part of large families, Grandma now had the 'upper hand' in terms of better lifestyle, e.g. living in a house with a garden and a car.

Sun 17 Jul – Went with mother to Cath's and Aunt M. etc. Went with Joseph to the Hippodrome to see 'The Light that Failed'.

(A 1939 British film about a London artist who is losing his sight and he struggles to complete his masterpiece of a cockney girl, story based on a Rudyard Kipling novel.)

Tue 19 Jul – Went to work. Went with Joseph to their house and then we went for a walk.

Thu 21 Jul – Went to work. Went with Joseph to the Speedway.

Sat 23 Jul – Went to work. Went in town with mother. Went to the Regal with Joseph to see 'The Perfect Woman'.

(A British comedy – a scientist creates a 'perfect woman' and his niece pretends to be this artificial woman when taken out by a male escort.)

Sun 24 Jul – went with mother and dad and Joseph on a trip to New Brighton and Mersey Tunnel.

Mon 25 Jul – Went to work. Went with Joseph to the Empire to see a French Show, very good. *(Oooh, la la!)*

Tue 26 Jul – Went to work. Went with Joseph to the Regal to see 'Enchantment'.

(British drama starring David Niven who retires to the house he was brought up in and looks back on his life and lost love.)

Wed 27 Jul – Went to work. Went down to Joseph's house, then we went for a walk to the park and Botanical Gardens. *(Taking in the bear pit, minus the bear.)*

Thu – Speedway night, took Valerie.

(Valerie, can remember going to Thursday's Speedway night on quite a number of occasions with Anne and her boyfriend, Joseph. She said there was something about the roar of the motorbikes and the smell of the dust and fuel which made an exciting night out.)

Sat 30 Jul – My Birthday. Went with mother shopping in town, had lunch in town. Joseph came to tea and Cath, Uncle Walt and Valerie.

Sun 31 Jul – Went a walk with Joseph in the afternoon up Middlewood and to Claywheels Lane. We went to the Hippodrome in the evening to see 'Jungle Princess'.

(A 1936 American film about a hunter in Malaya who is attacked by a tiger and his guides run off leaving him for dead. He's saved by a beautiful young woman who has grown up in the jungle and they fall in love. NB: was she a 'female Tarzan' character?)

Mon 1 Aug – Went with Joseph in the afternoon to the fair in the farm grounds of Granville. We went to the Phoenix in the evening to see Stewart Granger in 'Woman Hater'.

(This weekend was the Summer Bank Holiday, Saturday to Tuesday.)

Tue 2 Aug – Went with Joseph to the Regal to see 'Dear Octopus' and 'Marry me'. Came to our house to tea, then we went to the stadium to see a horse show, speedway and fireworks.

('Dear Octopus' is a 1943 British comedy starring Margaret Lockwood, a member of a 'well to do' family reunited for a golden wedding party.

'Marry me' is a British comedy film about a journalist who goes undercover to matchmake couples.) Note: both films about marriage!

Wed, Thu, Fri – Went to work.

Sat 6 Aug – Went to work. Stayed in during the afternoon. Went with Joseph to Union St Picture Palace *(a cinema)* to see, 'Emperor Waltz'.

(A musical starring Bing Crosby. A travelling salesman meets an Emperor's daughter in Vienna, they fall in love, and they try to overcome social differences.)

Sun 7 Aug – Joseph came to our house in the afternoon. After tea, I went down to Joseph's house, we played cards.

Mon 8 Aug – Went to work. Went with Joseph to the Regal to see, 'A Boy, A Girl and a Byke'.

(Romantic comedy about 'boy meets girl at a bicycle club' – bit of a clue in the title, of course!)

Tue 9 Aug – Went to work. Went to the Kinema with Joseph to see 'Intrigue'.

(American drama – death and intrigue in Singapore. Review quote 'forgettable'!)

Sat 13 Aug – Went to work. Went to town with mother. Went with Joseph to the Kinema to see 'The Street with No Name'.

(American crime drama about a deadly crime gang and an FBI Agent. This film sounds 'forgettable'!)

Sun 15 Aug – Went for a walk in the afternoon with Joseph then went to Joseph's for tea.

(Going to Joseph's for tea was very different to 'tea at home', mainly due to his siblings, two sisters and three brothers 'coming and going' which made it a busy tea time. The older brother with learning and social difficulties would disappear upstairs when any visitor arrived.)

Mon to Fri – Went to work and in the evenings, long walks or staying in and on Friday evening, visited Aunt M's, etc.

Sat 20 Aug – Went to work. Went to town with mother. Went a walk with Joseph to the park.

Sun 21 Aug – Went with Joseph to the park in the afternoon and in the evening another park.

(All this to'ing and fro'ing around the local parks – saving up for anything?)

Mon 22 Aug – Went to work. Went to Union St Picture Palace with Joseph to see 'Disaster'.

(An American film about a rescue from a high rise building hit by a plane, based on the real life Empire State Building being hit by a plane at the end of the WW2.)

(The real life account – one foggy morning, a B-25 bomber was

being flown over New York on the way to Newark Airport. The pilot asked for a weather report and was told, "I can't see the top of the Empire State Building." He continued flying but dropped altitude to regain visibility, but in doing so he had to avoid several skyscrapers. Oh dear, he was unable to miss the Empire State Building, tallest in the world at that time.

The 10-ton bomber smashed into the 79th floor creating a huge hole. Then the plane's fuel exploded and hurtled flames inside and outside the building. A survivor said she was on the edge of the fireball and shouted to a co-worker engulfed in flames, "Come on Joe, come on" and he walked out of it.

The crash caused a lift to plummet to the bottom, but miraculously the two women inside were alive. Not so lucky were 11 office workers and the 3 crewmen who were killed. 26 others were injured.)

Sat 27 Aug – We went to Blackpool for our holidays. Mother, father and Joseph. Joseph and I went in the Pleasure Beach in the evening.

(Ah, saving up for the holiday…of course.)

Sun 28 Aug – Went into Stanley Park. Went to Fleetwood.

Mon 29 Aug – Went to *(Lytham)* St Annes. Went on the Promenade. Went in the tower. *(Note: capital letter for 'Promenade' and then small letter for 'tower'.)*

Tue 30 Aug – Went on the Promenade. Went to the Tower Circus.

(Blackpool Tower Circus was a spectacular show, featuring slapstick clowns, performing wild animals, bareback horse riding, high wire walking and acrobatic acts. The finale was the floor being lowered

and water then filling the round stage and a spectacular water show took place, including performing seals.

The animals were kept in cages at the top of the Tower, much too small cages, I might add. There is still the Tower Circus and water show, but minus the wild animals and the cages are long gone.)

Wed 31 Aug – Joseph and I went to the speedway at Fleetwood.

Thu 1 Sep – Joseph and I went in the sea. In the evening, we all went to the Ice Drome. *(That was to watch a show and nothing to do with any personal ice skating.)*

Fri 2 Sep – Went to Fleetwood Market, and to Knott End *(to reach the latter was via a ferry across the estuary.)* In the evening we went to the new Opera House to see Charlie Chester *(a comedian)* in 'Midsummer Night Madness'.

Sat 3 Sep – Went shopping in Blackpool. Then we came home. Stopped at Hyde on way. Dad won an electric clock *(at a prize bingo)*. Joseph and I went to their house. *(No sleepovers in those days, Joseph either walked her back home or her father collected her in the car.)*

Sun 4 Sep – Joseph and I went a walk up Denbank in the afternoon. Went for a walk in the park in the evening.

Mon 5 Sep – Went to work. Went with Joseph to the Regal to see 'A Letter to Three Wives' with Kirk Douglas.

(The female narrator of the film writes to three wives saying that she has left with the husband of one of them. They have flashbacks

which intimate why each wife might be the one deserted. Based on a book called 'A Letter to 5 Wives', but the film 'lost' two of them!)

Fri 9 Sep – Went to work. Went with Joseph to the Kinema to see 'Polly Fulton'.

(Wealthy Polly, played by Barbara Stanwyck, is engaged to a dependable lawyer everyone likes. Then Polly meets a brash young man who dislikes Polly due to her wealth. BUT, they soon fall in love and marry. He goes to war and is rumoured to be having an affair. Meanwhile her ex-fiancé, who has married her best friend, is killed in the war and she gives comfort to her friend. Brash husband returns and they confront each other.)

Sat 10 Sep – Went to work. Stayed in during the afternoon. Went with Joseph to Bertram Mills Circus.

(One of the best, if not the best, travelling circus. It had over eight performing elephants, begging, turning round, playing dead, walking with forelegs on each other and 'handstands' using their trunk to balance. Performing lions and tigers (not together) with the lion tamer putting his head in the lion's mouth! As many as twenty horses in the ring, trotting round in two opposing circles; formation dancing in twos, bareback riding on one or two horses and walking on their two back legs. This was as well as the usual high wire acts, acrobatics, jugglers, clowns, a woman snake charmer, sword throwing, etc.)

Sun 11 Sep – Went with mother, dad and Joseph in the car to Saxilby. Then went with Joseph to their house.

Wed 14 Sep – Went to work. Went with mother and dad in car to Ladybower *(the reservoir – see 24 Apr.)*

Sat 17 Sep – Went to work. Went shopping with mother. Went with mother, dad and Joseph to the Palace Theatre.

Sun 18 Sep – Went for a walk with Joseph. Went for a walk to the park in the evening with Joseph and then we went to our house.

Mon 19 Sep – Went to work. Went with Joseph to the Regal to see 'Golden Eye'.

(American comedy crime mystery – a gold mine is losing money but suddenly starts to make money. Charlie Chan, with his 'gang', pose as tourists and find that all is not well. The mine is a 'front' for criminal activities. This is a Charlie Chan detective movie and does not, in any way, resemble a James Bond film!)

Wed 21 and Fri 23 Sep – Went to work. Stayed in at night and did some knitting.

Weekend – Lots and lots of walking...lots and lots of talking...an occasional 'peck' and holding of hands.

Mon 26 Sep – Went to work. Went with Joseph to the Hippodrome to see 'The Case of Charles Peace'.

(British crime film about Charles Peace, a notorious Sheffield burglar and murderer. He was eventually hanged in 1879, aged 47 years.)

Wed 28 and Fri 30 Sep – Went to work. Stayed in at night. *(Saving up for the week's holiday?)*

Sat 1 Oct – Started my holiday. Went with Joseph to Blackpool on the train to see the illuminations.

Sun 2 Oct – Stayed in all day. Joseph came up in the evening. *(Walking and pecking activities, around the parks, curtailed due to the early, dark evenings.)*

Mon 3 Oct – Went with mother shopping. I went a run on my cycle. Went with Joseph to the Empire in the evening.

Tue 4 Oct – Went with mother in town shopping. Went with Joseph to see 'Good Morning Boys'.
    (British 'slapstick' comedy about a roguish head teacher who bets on horses with his pupils and teaches them nothing. They visit Paris where they outwit a gang of crooks trying to steal the Mona Lisa.)

Wed 5 Oct – Went with mother to Worksop for the day. Went with mother to Uncle Walt's in the evening.

Thu 6 Oct – Went with mother to Chesterfield for the day, shopping. Went with Joseph for a walk in the park.

Fri 7 Oct – Went with mother to grandma's in the afternoon, then I went to meet Joseph. Stayed in at night.

Sat 8 Oct – Went shopping and then to Aunt M. etc. Went with mother in the afternoon shopping *(shopping again?)* Went with Joseph to Eversley House dance. Bill, Alice, Louis, Gilbert and Walt there.
(Who wasn't there would have been a shorter list, er, just Ralph and Dan weren't there!)

Sun 9 Oct – Stayed in all day. Joseph came up in the afternoon and stayed for tea.

Mon 10 Oct – Dad's birthday. Went to work. Went with Joseph to the Regal to see 'That Lady in Ermine'.)

(American musical, in colour, set in 1861. A ruling Countess' country is invaded by a Hungarian Army. Her lookalike ancestor comes alive from a portrait and 'saves the day'.)

Tue 11 Oct – Went to work. Went with Joseph's mother and father to see 'Jungle Fantasy'. *The party included Joseph.*

(A musical about a tribe of females in the jungle led by a fearless Queen.)

Sat 15 Oct – Valerie's Birthday (now aged 7 years). Went to work. Went with mother and father to the Cemetery, then to Valerie's for tea. Went with mother, father and Joseph to the Palace Theatre.

(Have you noticed that 'Mother' was always 'mother', but 'father' would sometimes be 'dad')

Sun 16 Oct – Went with Joseph to their house. We went for a walk at night in the park. *(It was early evening before it went dark as most local parks were locked after dusk.)*

Mon 17 Oct – Went to work. Went to the Regal with Joseph to see 'Don't Ever Leave Me'.

(Petula Clark starred in this black and while film. She is kidnapped by an elderly crook who tries to prove he isn't 'past it' in terms of committing crime. She is a bored young woman and when the crook loses his nerve with the kidnapping, she gives him the confidence to go through with it.)

Wed 19 Oct – Mother's Birthday. Went to work. Stayed in

at night. *(They had a birthday party tea for the three of them.)*

Sat 22 Oct – Went to work. Went to the cemetery with mother and dad. Then to grandma's. Went with Joseph to the Empire to see 'The Delta Rhythm Boys'.

Sun 23 Oct – Stayed in all day. Joseph came up in the afternoon and in the evening. *(Joseph had called in the afternoon, not been invited for tea so he went home and then came back in the evening.)*

Weekdays – The usual entries of 'going to work' but then the more unusual entries of 'staying in'.
...saving up for anything? Holidays all gone so what could it be?

Sat 29 Oct – Went to work. Stayed in all afternoon. Went with Joseph in the evening to town, then we came to our house and stayed in.

Sun 30 Oct – Went for a walk with Joseph in the park and the woods. Went with Joseph for a walk, then we went to their house.

(It was generally known that courting couples used the shade of a tree to do a little pecking. They sometimes held hands and sat on a park bench, but there was nothing beyond a 'pecking embrace'. However, the strict chaperoning of her mother's generation had now gone.)

Thu 3 Nov – Went to work. Went with Joseph to the Palace Theatre to see, 'The Nude Look'. Father & Mother also went.

(This was a theatre production which did not have any nudity in it whatsoever, hence the title, 'Nude Look'.)

Sat 5 Nov – Went to work. Went in town to dinner with mother *(lunch)*. Went with Joseph to their house, mother and dad came down later. Went with Joseph, Fred and Bert to see a bonfire. *(Two of his brothers)*.

Serious note: both sets of parents in the same house and at Joseph's home!

Sun 6 Nov – Went a walk with Joseph in the afternoon. Then went to Joseph's for tea.

Mon 7 Nov – Went to work. Went with Joseph to the Regal to see Shirley Temple in 'Mr Belvedere goes to College'.

(A black and white American comedy starring a 20 year old Shirley Temple. She plays a university journalism student trying to get a story from a genius student attempting to get a four year degree in one year for a friend. If the story is leaked before he gets the degree he will be expelled so an unlikely friendship is formed until his degree and she can print her story. Note: the storyline doesn't sound very funny!)

Fri 11 Nov – Went to work. Mother went to have some teeth out. Stayed in at night.

Weekend – Walking (and talking) with Joseph.

Mon 14 Nov – Went to work. Went with Joseph to the Regal to see 'Escape to Happiness'.

(Ingrid Bergman plays a young woman waiting for a music

scholarship in Paris. Leslie Howard plays a married man who meets her at a concert in his home town of Stockholm and they start an affair. To cut a 77 mins film short, she wins the scholarship and as he drives to Paris to be with her, there is a terrible car accident which changes their destiny…)

Wed 16 Nov – Went to work in the morning, came home poorly, went to Doctor's, got Influenza. Went to bed. Joseph came to see me.

Thu 17 Nov – Stayed in bed all day. Joseph came to see me in the evening.

Fri 18 Nov – Stayed in bed all day. Joseph came to see me.

Sat 19 Nov – Got up at dinner-time *(lunchtime)*. Stayed in. Joseph came up in the evening.

Sun 20 Nov – Stayed in the house all day. Joseph came up in the afternoon and stayed to tea.

Mon 21 Nov – Stayed in bed. Doctor came, got Intercostal Neurology. Joseph came to see me in the evening.
    (Intercostal neuralgia is caused by nerves/trauma or can be from an infection with symptoms including pain around the rib cage and difficulty in breathing. Her cold/influenza could have brought on the symptoms of this condition. Equally, it could have been brought on by her increasing nerves from the anticipated impact that the growing seriousness of the courtship would have on her parents, especially her mother.)

Tue 22 Nov – Stayed in bed. Joseph came to see me.

Wed 23 Nov – Stayed in bed, got up a bit at night. Joseph came to see me.

Thu 24 Nov – Stayed in bed during the morning, got up in the afternoon.
Note: Joseph had a night off from visiting.

Fri 25 Nov – Got up, but stayed in house. Mother went to have the rest of her teeth out.
(Before free and the advancement of dentistry treatment, people had all their teeth taken out and false teeth fitted after the gums had 'settled down' over a period of about three months.)

Sat 26 Nov – Went to Doctor's *(at the bottom of the road)*. Stayed in rest of day. Joseph came up in the evening.

Sun 27 Nov – Joseph came up in the afternoon and in the evening we went for a walk, then went to their house.

Mon 28 Nov – Went to work. Stayed in at night.

Rest of the week pattern – Went to work. Stayed in at night. Joseph came round in the evening, except Friday.
Note: very serious savings going on with all the 'staying in' diary entires.

Sat 3 Dec – Went to work. Went with mother in town shopping. Went with Joseph to the Phoenix to see 'Vote for Huggett'. *(One of the 'Huggett' films.)*

Sun 4 Dec – Stayed in all day. Joseph came up in the afternoon and stayed to tea.

Weekdays – Went to work. Stayed in at night or Joseph came up.

Sat 10 Dec – Went to work. Went in town with mother. Went with Joseph to the Palace Theatre. *(To see…? Must have been forgettable.)*

Sun 11 Dec – Went with Joseph a walk in the park, then went to their house for tea.

(Mother liked the 'hustle and bustle' of Joseph's house which made her own Sunday teatime at home seem 'too polite', e.g. as if the Vicar had called.)

Tue 13 Dec – Went to work. Went to the Phoenix with Joseph to see 'Whispering City'.

(A reporter hears that a famous actress is dying in hospital after being run over and she tells the reporter that her husband was not killed in an accident but was murdered. The reporter finds herself in web of intrigue and corruption. She befriends a lawyer but is he really the murderer? As she gets closer to the truth, the lawyer hires someone to kill her, but the hired man finds he can't kill her. Instead they fall in love.)

Sat 17 Dec – Went to work. Stayed in during the afternoon. Went walking with Joseph in the evening.

Sun 18 Dec – Stayed in all day. Joseph came up for tea. *(Still saving up for something – is it for Christmas?)*

Tue 19 Dec – Went to work. Went with Joseph to the Palace.

Sat 24 Dec – Went with Joseph in town during the morning. Went with mother shopping , then to grandma's. Went with Joseph in the fair, then to their house, then to Aunt M. etc.

(Wow, packed a lot into Christmas Eve – ah, saved up for Christmas of course!)

Sun 25 Dec – went to Aunt M. to dinner. *That's Christmas dinner which included the etc families on 'Bank.)* Joseph came for me and we went to their house for tea, later back to Aunt M.

(So the courting couple walked to his house, about a mile from Aunt M.'s. They had tea at Joseph's, then walked it back – both times passing near to 'her own home'. At the end of the night, Grandad drove them back, dropping Joseph off at his house – no sleepovers, remember.)

Mon 26 Dec – Went with mother to grandma's. Met Joseph and we all went to Cath's to a party. *(Joseph had walked from his house to her Grandma's home and then the three of them walked to the 'Bank.)*

(The party was at Aunt Cath's, Uncle Walt's and Valerie's home with Aunt M and family, and Aunt L there too. Aunt E living a half mile the other way joined them with her family of two boys. After the party, grandad gave people lifts home.) Note: no restrictions on drinking alcohol and driving in those days!

Tue 27 Dec – went to town with Joseph, came back and had tea at our house, then we went to the Phoenix to see 'Gallant Blade'.

(An American 'cinecolor' film set in 1648 at the end of the thirty

years war in France. The war's hero and his loyal lieutenant are delighted but the Marshall of France plans to plunder Spain. The 'gallant blade' is presented to the lieutenant to use against the Marshall as they both march towards Spain. En route the lieutenant rescues a 'damsel in distress' and wins her heart, only to realise that she is betrothed to the Marshall. Cue the swordfight!)

Note: there was not the usual concentration in the film by our hero and heroine as they knew what was going to happen after the film…

In the diary, between brackets, was written, 'we told Mother and Father we were going to get married'.

What a shock announcement as 'Mother and Father' thought it was going to be 'we're going to get engaged'. Remarks like, 'congratulations' and 'good news' were a little reticent to emerge, to say the least.

(After Joseph left, her mother asked her to wait until her false teeth were ready.)

Note: all her teeth had now been taken out, but the gums still had to settle before false teeth could be fitted.

The couple had even set the wedding date, subject to booking the church, for Saturday 30th March the following year and my mother would not hear of putting this date back or of even asking Joseph if he minded a delay.

(One reason for the date not going beyond that financial year was 'down to money'. If a couple got married before the end of March, they received the married couple's tax allowance for the whole of that year, i.e. from April the previous year right up to the date of the wedding. Getting married on 30th March gave them maximum tax rebate.)

An argument ensued between mother and daughter and previous 'words' and disappointments voiced about 'Joseph not being good enough' surfaced once again.

There's no doubt that Joseph and his family were very poor, having six children in a small, back to back house with a shared courtyard. The four boys sleeping 'top to toe' in one bed in the back bedroom, including the eldest 'handicapped' boy. In the front room the two girls slept together.

My grandma would remain angry and bitter that on the wedding photographs she had no teeth. However, unless you knew she had no teeth in, it was undetectable in the photographs though she could not afford to smile. Of course it wasn't just the photographs, the 'no teeth' embarrassment was every time she forgot and then smiled. Also, every time she spoke she thought her mouth 'caved in' slightly at both sides.

She did not, therefore, look forward to being 'mother of the bride'. Nor did she enjoy the day when it came. And because she did not enjoy the day, when it came, then 'father of the bride' did not enjoy it either. He 'put on a brave face' and smoked heavier than he normally did.

My mother was set on the date, unfortunately. Even her own father saying 'his bit' did nothing to put the date back. The year's tax rebate overrode every argument for the couple, but grandad offered to 'help them out'. But, like all young couples, they wanted to start the marriage with a 'bit of money' behind them rather than be 'helped out' from day one.

Thu 29 Dec – Went to work. Went with mother, father and Joseph to the Palace to see 'Babes in the Wood'.

(This was the seasonal pantomime with pre-booked tickets as, out of choice, the four would have become two. It was a strained evening all round.)

Sat 31 Dec – Went to work. Went with Joseph in town. Came back to our house and we had a party. Joseph's mother and father came. Aunty L. Aunty M. Uncle F, little Frank. Cath, Uncle Walt and Valerie. Valerie stayed the night.

Happy New Year…

Note: in the previous year to the diary, mother had courted Ralph, five years her senior, who had been 'called up' for active service in the War. He had been the 'perfect' gentleman and someone with whom her parents had hoped she would settle down with. But, he was not 'the one'. Mother had also 'walked out' with Gilbert.

At the beginning of the diary year, mother was engaged to Dan. They fell out and mother returns the ring.

After that, there's lots of dancing, cinema going and walking out (and about) with different male friends which had included Gilbert and Ralph.

Then, in the middle of the year she meets 'the one' and becomes engaged again by the end of the year.

In fact, Anne and Joseph had what can only be described as a 'whirlwind romance' – meeting, walking out, courting, becoming engaged and getting married in less than a year!

★ ★ ★ ★ ★

During the year of this 'in-between' diary there was a three part serialisation by a daily newspaper of 'Falling in Love, 'The First Kiss' and 'The Problems of Courtship'. This 'new and instructive' series for the fathers and mothers of tomorrow' is summarised here and gives an insight into post-war courtship – its joys and its problems.

The first arcticle on 'Falling in Love' starts with:

'Because your father and mother loved each other, you were born. They met each other when they were young and the liking which they had for each other gradually grew into a deep and lasting emotion. We call that emotion 'love'. It's quite different from that you feel for your mother and father or brother and sister. One day you too will meet somebody whom you will want to share your life with and with whom you will want children.'

It calls the time between meeting and marrying, the 'testing time of courtship.

'Falling in Love' goes through the changes that happen in boys and girls as they reach manhood and womanhood. It explains that an egg forms inside a woman but because she is 'too young' it quickly dies and passes out of her body. The egg being 'removed' takes about four or five days and happens once a month. *(There's no explanation of what this egg looks like and one might actually think it's in the shape of a chicken's egg.)*

Meanwhile, the glands of boys are developing, making them 'high spirited' and deeper voiced with 'downy' hair starting to grow on their cheeks. The article states, 'Within his body, too, changes take place: and the seed, which could help change the egg of a girl into a baby starts to be manufactured.'

Mother read this article to get an idea of the physical side of a relationship and how a baby is formed. This is because anything to do with the 'birds and the bees' and horror of horrors, sex, was a completely 'taboo' subject between herself and her mother. What did mother learn, or not learn, from the article?

Well, she would have learned that there's an egg which leaves her body every month while men form some sort of 'seed', but what happens to their 'seed' is not part of the article. Does a boy's 'seed' leave his body each month? Mother was more confused after reading this first article than before!

The second of the series, 'The First Kiss' starts by distinguishing between a kiss or peck on the cheeks and the first kiss of lips upon lips, seemingly to last 'for a timeless minute.'

It gives a statement that '…nobody can love more than one person at one time.'

Really? And what's that to do with a 'first kiss'?

The article then asks the question, 'How will you know it is indeed love'? The answers given are:
– you will want to make each other happy;
– no sacrifice you could make would be too great;
– you will feel contented and restful when together;
– you will be miserable and restless when apart.

'The First Kiss' makes the point that not so long ago it was difficult for a girl to be with a young man on her own. That was certainly true during grandma's courting years when she had to be chaperoned. It also states that a kiss before being engaged used to be thought of as 'improper', and goes on to say, '…things are very different now – kissing is almost a convention. An embrace under a tree is so commonplace that nobody takes any notice.' (*So that's why my parents did all their courting in local parks – to embrace under trees!*)

This second article also mentions the practical side of a relationship – ah, it's the bit 'we've all been waiting for'. But it's about cooking, cleaning, earning a living, providing a home and bringing up children. *(So the physical side of a relationship is the cooking, cleaning, homemaking and bringing up children – am I missing something here? All must be revealed in the third and last of the series…I can't wait!)*

This last article on 'The Problems of Courtship' begins with: 'When you are in your early teens certain changes occur in your body which make it possible for you to fall in love and have children.' *(So far so good.)*

It goes on to say that the 'Joining together of a man and woman is called 'sexual intercourse' but it's prime purpose is for the making of children.'

The article emphases that civilised people have long considered it wrong to have intercourse before marriage. Two explanations are given:
– a girl will lose the respect of men and the chance of finding love and marriage;
(nothing about what 'men' might lose if the reverse happens.)
– the possibility that a child is conceived without being married. It clarifies that the baby has to be put into a special home which looks after him and brings him up.

(Tragically, some unmarried mothers had to live their lives locked away, without their baby, and eventually had to be classed as 'institutionised'. As was the case of the sister of grandad's Uncle Bill who never even saw her baby before him or her was taken away.)

The explanation of sexual intercourse? Well, it's caressing sensitive parts of the body, including lips, breasts and thighs. *(And…)* It all becomes clear in the very next paragraph.

'Physical contact with these parts, in the form of kisses and caresses, stimulates us into love-making.' Then the article concentrates on the dangers of kissing if the kissing becomes too passionate, as in, '… boys will want to carry the love-making further.' (*Further? Further than love-making? Have I missed something here?*)

Meanwhile, mother wishes she had never started reading the articles, but wait… She thinks, 'if I keep them, I'm sure everything will become clear later on, like if my husband-to-be gets passionate under a tree. I can then stop him and when I get home, re-read the articles.'

Further along the same page, 'Courtship is the springtime of life. The period between engagement and the wedding day is a time when lovers assess their responsibilities and plan their home together.' The term 'lovers' did not mean that they had done more than kissing under the tree – remember it's before the wedding day.

(*All that 'park walking' my parents did and sometimes three parks in one day! It was all done to talk about and plan their home together…plus a bit of tree 'pecking'!*)

The third article concludes with, 'If you are still not sure about the physical side of courtship then you should visit one of the marriage guidance councils or read some of the excellent books that have been published so that you're not shocked and distressed on your honeymoon.'

How could any young person need further advice after reading these three informative articles on 'Falling in Love', 'The First Kiss' and 'The Problems of Courtship'?

A shorter summing up of all three articles can simply be written as the 'boy meets girl' story, they fall in love, they court each other, get engaged and share their first kiss under a tree. Then the couple get married and can finally share a practical and physical relationship, like cooking, cleaning and caressing, oh, and along comes a baby.

The articles also give an insight into the kind of newspaper advertisements of that post war era, bearing in mind there were still short supplies of many everyday things as war rationing continued.

One advertisement stated that 'Mars are marvellous – there's a meal in a Mars.'
And that a Mars bar is 'packed with all good things to nourish and sustain you.'
The advert also gives a description of all the 'good things' in the bar, like 'sugar, malted glucose, milk chocolate and a caramel layer of sugar.'

A 'Silver Shred' advert, depicting their famous golliwog, offers an 'extra preserve ration' during May and June. Is this offer of two jars of 'Silver Shred' marmalade for one ration coupon, the earliest concept of two for the price of one?

There are a couple of cigarette advertisements. One features 'safer smoking' with a tip stating that their brand is made specially to prevent sore throats!

A lipstick advertisement says that this particular brand will make your lips stay 'adorably lovely' even after kissing or smoking. And that the lipstick won't leave a 'painted' layer but a 'thrilling film of exciting colour.'

The enjoyment of living was, at last, starting to creep back into everyday things.

Just Before Spring

The northern girl had continued her education through the War, which was conducted in either the school or teachers' homes, sometimes helping her mother, sometimes comforting each other in times of great stress during the War. However, they regarded themselves as very lucky when compared to others nearby who had lost their homes or loved ones or both.

By the end of the War, the northern girl had become a young 'in-between' woman as her diary has shown.

The southern girl had continued her education with her sister, during the War, in the relative safety of Windsor Castle. They were a comfort to each other as their parents were away during the day.

By the end of the War, the eldest of the two sisters had become a young woman.

On VE Day, the northern young woman had walked into the city centre with a group of girlfriends but had told her parents they would be at the local cinema watching Pathe News broadcasts of the last days of the War and the start of all the celebrations. It was the first time she had wanted to sneak out like that.

It was the first time she had seen so many people. Everyone danced and shouted and linked arms in long lines around the streets. No cars or trams, just joyous, happy people, jumping and yelling for joy. There were men in uniform amongst the throng and one had given her a first, very brief, kiss on the lips. She had never felt so elated and carefree. That feeling would stay with her for a long, long time.

VE Day in the capital city and thousands upon thousands of people thronged outside the Palace and right up the Mall. The King and Queen, with the princesses, had made more than one appearance on the balcony. Then an appearance with the Prime Minister and a roar so deafening from the crowd you might hear it in space when he did his legendary 'V' for victory sign.

The Royal young woman, in her ATS uniform (Auxiliary Territorial Service), had thought her sister's suggestion to go out into the crowd a great idea. On any other day it would have been unthinkable, untenable, impossible. With a group of ATS uniformed friends and a plain clothed police sergeant, the princess sisters made their way down to the street and were quickly absorbed by the crowd. It was the first, and last time, the older sister would ever be able to sneak out like that and not be recognised.

It was the first time she had been amongst so many people, young and not so young, uniformed and in civvies, all jumping, shouting, yelling, singing. Oh, the freedom to be invisible in a crowd. No cars or buses anywhere, just a huge throng of people, just everywhere. To be an ordinary girl in a uniform just for this one time. She linked arms with strangers, jumping with them, singing with them, doing the Lambeth Walk and then the hokey-cokey with different groups of people.

To be on a palace balcony with your sovereign parents and sister, waving to thousands upon thousands who are endlessly chanting 'for he's a jolly good fellow'; then an hour later to be 'ordinary', to be swallowed up in the throng, to be invisible. She had never felt so elated, so alive, so free, than at that moment of her life. That feeling would have to last her forever.

They made their way back to the palace railings and started a chant of 'We want the King' knowing that they could supply the King. One of the party was sent inside and within minutes, the King and Queen were on the balcony, cheering and waving back at them as part of the crowd at the railings, but still 'invisible'!

The young northern woman had started her first job as a wages clerk in Wigfalls electrical shop selling, well, electrical goods, including wireless sets. She started going to dances with another office clerk. They met two young men in uniform and began 'double dating'. Soon, both women were courting their 'demobbed' soldiers and sometimes they would go out separately, for a walk or to a picture palace.

The woman's mother and father were now delighted with this 'nice young man', Ralph. He was so good mannered and he had fought in the War. But, he was not to be 'the one'.

The young northern woman had applied for, and was successful, in getting a wages clerk's job in a small, local steelworks for more money.

In her new job, one of the tasks each week was to count out the workers' wages and put the money into little brown envelopes called 'packets'. She wrote the amount and the worker's name on the outside of the packet. One by one at the end of pay day the workers would come through into the office to collect them.

One young worker collecting his pay, not old enough to have been a soldier in the War, had just returned from his National Service. He would blush, stutter a thank you for his pay packet and make a quick exit. Sometimes, just before the blush, she would see a very faint smile forming on his lips but he would look quickly down. Her stomach was churning and churning and her chest felt tight.

(The young, northern man had received his call up papers in 1946 to serve at least a year. Once issued with a uniform, new recruits had to bundle up their civilian clothes and send them back home. Part of the training was to fold sheets and make up beds in a specific 'regimented' way and each morning your bed and uniform were inspected. Bed and kit had to be 'just so' with buttons and boots shining like mirrors.

After breakfast, it was drilling and marching time. Incessant marching up and down and learning how to salute – the arm being raised the longest way up and then the shortest way down. Very disciplined, morning, noon and night.

Walking along one evening back to his billet, he hears a voice booming out, "Are you cold?" "No, sir," he replied while saluting. "Then don't walk with hands in your pocket – five times round the parade ground, NOW." "Yes sir," he says as he sprints away to start the laps of punishment.

He trained to be a medic and was posted to Italy, travelling by train. He thoroughly enjoyed the time he spent abroad, his only time abroad. Loving the camaraderie, making new friends, the work, and the 'sightseeing', but all too soon it was time to re-enter 'civvy street' having done an 18 months 'stint'.)

After the War's celebrations, the Royal woman worked

as a junior member of the ATS. She took a course in vehicle mechanics and learned to drive.

She also had to accompany her parents, visiting places, meeting people. At a wedding, she met again a young man who had an endearing smile and charming eyes. They talked about his different naval postings during the War and how he had been in the Far East as the Japanese Fleet had surrendered. He was very handsome, very dashing and very 'worldly' in a quiet, unassuming way. Her stomach had a fluttering butterfly inside and her chest kept feeling tight.

One day, the young man asked if he could walk with her in the nearby park and the young woman agreed. He was delighted and she felt very happy. (The plain clothed police officer remained a discreet distance behind them.)

Meanwhile, in the northern firm's office one day, the young man asked the young woman to explain a query he had about his pay. She was delighted to be talking to him at last, even though it was about work, and they smiled shyly at each other as the queue of workers formed behind him. He left very red faced and she felt very happy.

One evening, as the young woman was leaving the office she noticed that the young man who blushed was waiting at her bus stop. His face went very red as he asked her if he could take her to the pictures (he had been saving up to take her out.) She said yes and they walked to the picture palace. She knew she had fallen in love.

She introduced him to her parents who were polite and genial. When she was alone with her parents, they said how disappointed they were. They had a car now and she could afford to go to work on a bus. He came from a large, very poor family and he had to walk everywhere. She reminded them of their past, their struggles, their near poverty.

One evening, the Royal woman met again the young man at a dance, though pre-arranged, and because of royal protocol were both accompanied by friends. They danced and danced and they talked and talked. She was falling deeper in love, if that was possible.

The Royal woman formally introduced him to her parents who were polite but distant. Of course, her Royal parents had informally known him since he was a small boy, one of the few youngsters who had been invited to her birthday parties as she grew up, and vice versa. As a boy he had lived at Brook House, Park Lane with his Uncle, Lord Mountbatten. As a girl, most of her early parties had been held at home – 146 Piccadilly.

When she was alone with her parents they said his background was not suitable and that he was 'foreign'. She reminded them that he had spent most of his life in this country including his school years; had served in the British Royal Navy and that they shared the same great, great, grandmother.

Was it during this evening that the Royal young woman 'confessed' to her parents that they had corresponded throughout the War and that the young man had visited her at Windsor Castle in periods of his navy leave during the War. (If her parents had known, the general public had certainly not known.)

In fact, at only 21 years, he had been the youngest First Lieutenant in the Royal Navy serving in the Mediterranian and Pacific Fleets. He was mentioned in despatches for his service during the Battle of Cape Matapan (in occupied Greece) where he controlled the searchlights.

(In March 1941, British and Australian Royal Navy ships intercepted and sank or severly damaged Italian war ships off the Greek coast. Deception played a key role in the success of the Battle. The anchored flagship had advertised an evening party (which was never meant to take place.) That afternoon, the Admiral had arrived with an overnight suitcase and checked in at a nearby golf club seemingly to stay overnight. Instead, he surrepticiously left the club for the ship.

Luck also played a part for the Allies as the Italians had failed to spot, by plane reconnaissance, that there was more than one ship in the area, and they thought that ship was busy 'partying'. The Italian ships had no radar so they had to rely on 'sight' which was nil in the dark, of course. That night, the Allied Royal Navy ships were able to close in without detection and their searchlights illuminated their enemy for them to be fired on with accuracy. The searchlight aboard the Valiant was operated by a young prince. Note: survivors from the Italian ships were picked up by the Allies as they left the area.)

The princess was taken on a long, extended family-cum-Royal Family tour of Africa in order that she may make the 'right decision' when she came back. From her own point of view there was only one 'right' decision but she had agreed to wait until her 21st birthday.

The 'long, extended family holiday' was the second, if not the first time, the princess had set foot outside the UK. In the 1930s, she was considered too young to accompany her parents on foreign tours and then it was too dangerous to travel abroad during the War. Visiting Africa with its diverse terrain, cultures and race, gave the heiress presumptive an insight into her future Commonwealth duties. The two sisters remarked, "What opulence and what a great variety of delicacies to eat." The change from a country still restricted by food rationing to an endless delight of different foods, meals, Dutch pastries and fruit, was 'incredulous'.

They stayed in a special 'white train' which travelled around the different locations. Although South African society was rigidly divided on racial grounds, this did not stop the Royal Family meeting and mixing with people of all races, even attending a 'coloured ball' in their honour.

On their return from abroad, much debate and difficulties were expressed with regard to the prince's 'foreign' nationality. There were other 'problems' such as his standing within the Greek Royal Family, now reinstated in Greece, and not least his name from the House of Schleswig-Holstein-Sonderburg-Glucksburg. Informally, he had been using his uncle's surname, Mountbatten.

His British nationality was 'rushed' through, surname formally changed to Mountbatten and there was a timely publicity announcement that he had only lived in Greece for several months of his life and could not even speak the language.

(Ironically, due to an Act passed in 1705, all descendants of the Electress Sophie of Hanover were British subjects, but this was not researched or known at the time of the 'rushing through'. You could not, of course, nationalise someone who was already a British citizen! The prince was a descendant of the electress through Queen Victoria, who was the couple's shared great, great, grandmother, making them third cousins.

Philip's mother, Princess Alice, was born at Windsor Castle in 1885 and her great grandmother was Queen Victoria. From birth she was profoundly deaf, but due to the efforts of her own mother she spoke clearly by the age of 18 and could lip read in three languages.

At King Edward VII's Coronation, she met and fell in love with Prince Andrew, the youngest son of the King of Greece. They married in 1903 and settled into the Royal Palace in Athens. Ten years and four daughters later, the princess had proven to be very popular with an increasingly anti-monarchy Greek public.

During the First World War, she left her family for the frontline to help organise battlefield hospitals and nurse wounded soldiers.

In 1917 the Greek Royal Family were exiled, returning in 1920. Alice gave birth to a son in 1921 on the kitchen table of their country home in Corfu. He was sixth in line to the Greek throne. The year after, the King fled the country but Prince Andrew was arrested, tried and convicted by revolutionaries and faced the death sentence. A last minute reprieve allowed the family to flee onto a British Warship (which had come to their rescue) – with their baby son in an orange box acting as a cot. They had lost their fortune and purpose.

For the next few years the family lived in Paris supported by rich relatives. In 1928, aged 43, Alice converted to the Greek Orthodox Church and became obsessively religious and spiritual. A little eight year old boy was taken on a picnic by his maternal grandma and when he came home, his mother was gone.

Unknown to Philip she had been admitted to a mental asylum where she would stay for several years, having been diagnosed with schizophrenia. From 1930, Alice and Andrew were estranged but remained married.

Philip was sent to boarding school in Britain with school holidays being spent with his uncle, Lord Louis Mountbatten. It took the tragedy of a plane crash in 1937, killing one of his sisters and family, to bring Philip and his mother together again. The funeral took place in Nazi Germany. At the head of the cortege was Philip's three sisters' husbands dressed in Nazi military uniform.

As the Greek Royal Family were now reinstated, Alice wanted

Philip to join her in Athens. It was a difficult choice for such a young man to make as he had dreams of serving with the British Royal Navy. He fulfilled his wish and Alice had to be content with helping the poor and homeless of Athens. During the War, Alice was in the difficult position of having three son-in-laws fighting for Germany and a son in the British Navy.)

The now untitled naval officer was stationed in Greenwich. At public functions, Philip and the princess had to dance separately and arrive/depart separately. At home, the Royal woman played 'over and over' the hit record 'People will say we're in love' from the musical 'Oklahoma'.

As Prince Philip, he had proposed to Princess Elizabeth in 1946 at Balmoral, but because of all the 'problems', the King could not give his consent until April 1947 when he announced the couple's engagement. In a 'Wedding Preview' special edition of the 'Picture Post' (price 4d) he was referred to only as Philip.

In 1949, the northern woman was told to have a long courtship so that she might have opportunities to meet someone else and 'forget' about him. At home, on the new gramophone (like a large sideboard with a record player and wireless inside) there was 'non-stop' playing of the hit record 'People will say we're in love' from the musical 'Oklahoma'.

As the 'in-between' diary entries show, after a very short courtship, mother had announced to her parents that they were engaged. They were married the following spring at the start of the new decade, living nearby but not part of the same estate as their respective parents and grandparents had lived in.

(As mentioned, father's grandparents, first cousins, had grown up on the same estate as both my maternal and paternal grandparents.

Father was one of six children. It was customary to name the eldest girl after her mother, in this case Jessica, and the eldest boy after the father which was Joseph. Father's older sister took her mother's name but the next child, a boy, was given a different name, Colin. He was not expected to live but did. It was father, the next son to be born who took the name of his father. A girl next, and then two more boys.

The eldest son had learning difficulties and from age seven his mother would walk him to the local special school, some distance away, and then walk back home. In the afternoon she would repeat the journey to collect him. She could not afford to pay for the tram journey.

A revelation which emerged years later was the fact that my paternal grandparents were not married at the time of their first child, Jessie.

Both parents had attended Jessie's birth registration as the father's details were on her birth certificate. But on this certificate, the mother's surname was different to the father's surname and there were different columns for the signatures of both parents, if unmarried. So on Jessie's birth certificate were two different surnames and the signatures were in the 'unmarried at birth' column. As both parents' details were on the certificate the child could take the father's surname which she did. They married between that birth and the birth of Colin.)

Life after the War was still austere and hard, whether you lived in the north or the south, whether working class or Royal.

There was still food rationing, such as 3 pounds of potatoes per person per week. Food rations, per week, included: 7 ounces butter/margarine, 1 egg, a half pound of sugar, 2d worth of tinned meat, 2 rashers of bacon and 2 ounces of tea. An average family of four would normally have used these quantities per day, not per week.

(Remember, '10d' old money of meat would buy a lot more than today's 10 pence new money!)

Some tinned food would be priced in points as well as money (note: most rationed food used a coupon system.) Potatoes were rationed after the War to 3lbs per person per week.

Bread was also rationed after the War, not during the War, between 1946/48. This was because the bread had been of very poor quality and it was hoped that rationing would improve the bread. Sausages were still rare and contained a high content of (poor quality) bread.

Many people living through this period said that the food rationing was more stringent than in the War as bread and potatoes were not rationed until after.

Many gardens were now vegetable patches but still on the menu would have been nettle soup and salad with dandelion leaves. Those with longer gardens would have continued rearing hens for a weekly supply of fresh eggs. Some fruit was still in scarce supply and a lot of children had never seen a lemon or banana.

Amongst newspaper advertisements around that time were 'Hints for mothers on planning children's meals.' One advert was about using children's points – 'Don't forget youngsters with the blue ration books still get priority for milk. Use the blue ration book points for canned fish or meat, dried milk and eggs, tinned beans or peas. Also potatoes, as a wholesome food, can be used to fill up the corners with lightly cooked greens.'

Another advertisement was aimed at 'young workers' and read, 'While children at school get their school milk, youngsters out at work need their National Milk Cocoa every day! Remember, this nourishing drink is available to all young people up to twenty-one at their place of employment or Youth Clubs.'

(Such advertisements were issued by the Ministry of Food.)

Whalemeat, and snoek fish from South Africa, was not rationed but it did not 'catch on' (pun intended) as very, very few people could stand the intense and peculiar 'fishy' smell. People would 'do without' rather than eat it. They said whalemeat was a 'worrying' grey colour and tasted 'ghastly'. It was repeatedly said that 'it tasted worse than it looked!'

Many advertisements promoted remedies for indigestion and constipation, due to some of the food combinations of that time, such as 'Radiant health and vitality, the 'bile beans' way. Free yourself from constipation, biliousness, and similar ills with Nature's Gentle Aid, Bile Beans.' And, 'For comfort after eating, chew a couple of 'Milk of Magnesia' tablets and they are handy to carry in handbags or pocket.'

One advert aimed at women stated, 'If you want to get that pre-war feeling, you could drink Wincarnis, the wine that does you good.' Or you could 'make mine Myers, the rum that's matured and bottled in Jamaica, and for a 'beautiful morning' have a toast to the beautiful song Oklahoma.' This latter advert was specifically aimed at men and appears to encourage a morning drink of rum!

In every newspaper there was also the customary tobacco and cigarette advertisements. 'Choose your favourite from the six Four Square tobaccos – each a balanced blend of vintage leaf.' And, 'Go on, have a Capstan' which shows a hand offering an open packet of cigarettes. Also, 'A man gets real pleasure from Players!'

Back to food, those who could not keep hens for fresh

eggs had to buy dried eggs made into scrambled eggs which a lot of people had to acquire the taste of or 'do without.' Hence, the popularity of chickens 'home grown' in gardens for fresh eggs every day.

Electricity in homes was intermittent with some towns and cities 'switching off' electricity for a day per week. Candles were used. Buckingham Palace, as part of that household's conservation efforts, had only a limited supply of electricity. Candles galore were used.

The British Empire, in the glory days of Queen Victoria, covered a quarter of the earth's surface. The post war vulnerability period, saw the protracted dismantling of the Empire. Independence was granted to India and Pakistan, amongst others.

(India had been the 'jewel in the crown' of the British Empire. In 1931, Gandhi led the fight against the British to pave the way to independence. He even travelled to England to 'champion' India's cause, but independence was never on the home agenda. Then WW2 and the Indian people fought side by side for the Allies, but they were fighting to keep Britain and Europe democracic, which they were denied in their own country. In 1947, Lord, or Earl, Mountbatten became the last Viceroy of India. Independence led to much bloodshed between Hindus and Muslims, and the assassination of Gandhi in January 1948.)

As the lights of our country went on once more, one struggle ended and another began. The struggle to rebuild the cities and towns destroyed and to rebuild people's lives shattered by lack of food and money, and the loss of loved ones.

Clothes, new or second hand, were still in drab and grey colours as clothes rationing continued by way of a points system. Towards the end of the war and just after, points increased on clothes to such an extent that it took a whole year's points to buy a coat.

Bombsites had grass and flowers growing over them. The great freeze of 1947 saw snow come down which didn't go away. Everyone's priority was to keep warm, but there were still endless queues for food and commodities. Even so, money still went a long way and a fiver would get you a holiday at the seaside. Income tax was running at 10%.

There was change of all kinds, including a Special Roads Act which granted roads for motorised traffic only and would not be a public right of way. This was to be the start of motorway construction to the exclusion of bicycles and horses.

The National Health Service, from 1948, offered medical and hospital services provided free at the point of use and financed from central taxation – 'security from cradle to grave'. Eligibility for care included temporary residents and visitors to the country. Family allowances were also introduced for second and subsequent children of 5 shillings a week (equivalent to 25p in today's money but not in value.)

There was still virtually no crime – 'mugging' was not even a word! No-one locked their back doors, except at night and to go on holiday. No-one would dream of locking their car doors, even at night. It was a safe world in post war Britain.

Soldiers had been promised their jobs back so a publicity and propaganda campaign was started, aimed at women leaving their war work. This was in direct contrast with the campaigns before the war aimed at women taking on such work. Women were now being encouraged to 'step away' and

ATS girls were sent on a 10 day course on how to cook, sew and look after their home and husband. Pathe News showed women taking part in the course and then waiting at the train station for their men to return home. Propaganda fell just short of saying a woman's place was in the home.

During the War, a quarter of all homes had been damaged or destroyed. A massive house building programme to reconstruct and replenish lost housing got underway. As with any building projects, it was slow and the homes were needed straight away. Families took over army huts and some squatted in empty flats. Up and down the country, prefabs, quick to put together and on one level, were hastily built and were called 'homes while you wait'. They were like small, detached bungalows with their own gardens. Prefab estates soon took shape.

The need for housing became even more acute with the post war baby boom!

As post war celebrations had made way for the long, hard road back to prosperity, there was a glimmer of brightness, of cheer – Princess Elizabeth's wedding to Philip (still plain 'Philip'.) There was a rising tide of sentiment towards the young couple and the sense of a storybook romance.

Ration coupons were still needed for her dress material with the Government giving all brides 200 extra coupons. The dress was of pure silk and designed by Norman Hartnell. It was publicised that the material and accessories, such as the pearl embroidery, were all 'home grown'. In fact, the dress was made of Chinese silk, but as it was from Hartnell's own stock, it was deemed (dubiously) 'home grown'. There were eight bridesmaids and two page boys.

The princess started her wedding day much as she had

done ten years before for her father's coronation, looking out of Buckingham Palace in her dressing gown. Despite the cold November morning she would have seen crowds of people down the Mall already gathered and waiting for a glimpse of her in the glass coach.

Philip, having renounced his Greek and Dutch royal titles and accession to the Greek throne, could only have his mother and uncle, Lord Mountbatten, at his own wedding. His three surviving sisters, married to German princes who had fought for Germany, would not be amongst the guests for fear of inciting any 'anti German' feelings which might mar the day. His father had died of heart failure in 1944 while staying at the Metropole Hotel in Monaco.

The Abbey congregation was two thousand strong and made up of premiers and presidents, members of parliament, Commonwealth dignitaries and Governor-General. Also, foreign royalty, crowned heads, 'exiled' heads – in fact, a who's who of royalty from around the world.

After the signing of the register, the new HRH Duke of Edinburgh bowed to the King and Queen, the princess dropping a low curtsey with her train billowing out behind her.

The happy couple settled into their horse drawn glass coach like Cinderella and Prince Charming; making their fairytale way back along the Mall to the 'golden castle' amid trumpets trumpeting and flags flying. Thousands lined the route, cheering and chanting, loving their part in this fairytale pageant.

The 'fairytale' bubble seemed to burst at the Palace with an 'austere' wedding breakfast for 150 guests. At the end of it, the King made no speech just raised his glass and said, "The bride."

(The 'austerity' of the reception food had received much publicity in Pathe News broadcasts at the cinema and in newspaper articles. This was amid fears that the public, still struggling with food rationing, might think badly of any luxuries. In truth, it was an excuse for the 'rank and file' of the British people to be happy again and to feel proud of our Royal Family.)

A TV camera placed over the Palace forecourt had captured the departure of the carriages and their return and another camera over the Abbey was for the shots into and out of the Abbey. The television apparatus had been described by the press as 'television's magic crystal'. The wedding was broadcast the same evening while the film and broadcasting materials were flown around the world.

It was even shown in a surviving, 4000 seated cinema in Allied occupied Berlin and was fully booked, seven days a week.

Almost the entire British population had to settle for listening to the BBC radio live commentary of the wedding as there was only a handful of 'magic crystal' sets. Indeed, most of that population would not have heard of a cinema screen being made small enough for living room viewing.

(An event which had full BBC live coverage was the London Olympics. This had been postponed in 1944 and then went ahead four years later without Germany and Japan (they were not invited to compete – I wonder why?) They were nicknamed the 'Austerity Games' as no new venues were built and existing accommodation used rather than an Olympic Village. However, the Games and its star, Fanny Blankers-Koen a Dutch housewife and mother who won four gold medals, were seen by few on the few television sets.)

On the day of the wedding some television highlights made their way onto 'small' screens, but the 'rank and file' had to watch it over the coming weeks on Pathe newsreel films at the cinema.

Schools up and down the country celebrated the Royal Wedding with feasts of cakes and buns even though head teachers had been urged to be as 'modest' in their spending as possible. However, there was community singing, dancing and fireworks which made up for any 'modest' school festivities. It was a chance for everyone to escape austerity and take delight in a sort of 'family feeling'.

The happy couple enjoyed a honeymoon, first of all in 'Uncle Dickie's' house at Broadlands, in the New Forest. Then they made their way, by train, up to Birkhall (Balmoral Estate, Scotland.)

Their first choice of a country home at Sunninghill Park, Ascot, was gone after being gutted by fire some months before they married. They leased a furnished home in Windlesham Moor, near Windsor Castle, (previously sold for £40,000 in 1942), but was not immediately ready to use. Set in 58 acres of land, it had a reception hall, dining room, a 50 ft drawing room, a Chinese room, five main bedrooms and a nursery with two adjoining guestrooms.

Their London residence was Clarence House, but having been severely bomb damaged in the War it needed major renovations which would take nearly two years. So they returned to live with the bride's parents at Buckingham Palace.

There were thousands of weddings, small and large, some still austere and some more lavish, which took place up to and beyond the start of the new decade. At the start of this new decade was the year my parents married.

At the time, couples had to marry in their local parish

church, that being St John the Baptist. The church dates back to 1872 and was built at a cost of £3,600, having a seating capacity of 600. After the church was consecrated in 1874, the vicar became chaplain to the soldiers in the military barracks. Each Sunday, troops would march to St John's for the service and then march back. This continued until the barracks closed.

A public house had been built next door to the church, then terraced houses alongside that. At the other side of the church – Owlerton Greyhound and Speedway Track (locally known as 'the dog track'.)

People arrived at the church by walking, bus or tram. Dad, the best man and the rest of his family had 'splashed out' and come by tram as the church was on the main (formerly marching) road.

Grandad's black car made three trips with his brother driving. The first trip brought the driver's wife and the youngest brother and his wife. The second trip had brought the bridesmaids and mother of the bride. The final journey brought grandad and the bride.

Mother wore a new, long white dress and veil, thanks to the 200 extra clothing coupons for brides. Unintentionally, but traditionally, arriving at the church a little late (due to the car's three trips taking longer than planned.) Her veil billowed in the wind and grandad was in his best, and only, suit. A photograph showed them running up to the church. They stopped at the door to straighten the veil. There were two grown up bridesmaids, a cousin from the bride's side of the family and the groom's younger sister.

Father wore a new suit, but one he would wear to weddings and funerals for many years to come. His younger brother was best man and wore, for the first time, a suit and tie.

A family member with a camera took some 'impromptu' pictures outside the church. The formal photographs were taken in front of the long curtains in the front room of my grandparents' home, just before the wedding tea. There were no large group shots of all the guests, as there was no space for large group shots. One photograph shows the happy couple. Then the couple with the bridesmaids and best man.

Other pictures were taken in a photographic studio and showed the happy couple with their parents, bridesmaids and best man. Also, a picture of the newly weds. Grandma would have liked a photograph of the bride and herself but due to her 'mouth predicament' it was just the bride on her own.

Due to her predicament, grandma did not smile on any of the photographs as she still awaited her false teeth. Both cheeks were very slightly 'caved in', almost undetectable. To grandma, though, they were 'ravines'.

Tea and buns were 'laid on' for the wedding guests. Not everyone had come back which was just as well as there was still very little 'arm' room to eat or drink anything.

Grandma wore a new dress with her best coat over it. She didn't take off her coat as though it was a symbol of 'extra cover' for her mouth. Sadly, her new dress was kept hidden from 'guest viewing' and guaranteed admiration. It was a brown and white top with a fringe of material (peplam style) over the joined skirt, to give the effect of a suit. The neckline was v-shaped with her gold cross and chain adorning her neck.

She talked in a muffled tone, like she was practising to be a ventriloquist. "Bun anyone?" she said through lips hardly moving or opening. Nothing crossed her lips until all the guests had gone as that meant opening her mouth. That is, opening to put something in, followed by ungainly 'pressing down' gum movements to get the food ready for swallowing.

As guests left, the new 'ventriloquist' would quietly say, "Thank you for coming," and, as her arm was behind grandad and he said the same thing only louder, it looked like he was acting as her 'dummy' in a variety stage show.

The happy couple enjoyed a short honeymoon in Blackpool, (short, as in the following day and night, coming back the day after.) They returned to live with the bride's parents. This was in a terraced house, set in a small back garden with a shed and outside toilet. Inside the house, there was a kitchen/living room with doors leading to a cellar and a front room. Upstairs were two double bedrooms with stairs up to an attic.

Whether a person is born in a northern city, into an ordinary family, or into the Royal Family, a newly married couple is happy, most anywhere.

The northern newlyweds, both brought up in small, terraced homes, thought nothing of living with the bride's parents as was tradition, in those days, while saving for a home of their own. They looked forward to happy, future times together when they could buy or rent their own home and, if blessed, to have children.

The Princess had grown up in a similar, close family group, and also started married life living with her parents.

The Royal bride looked forward to many happy, carefree years of marriage and, if blessed, to have children. In fact, the happy couple were blessed with a boy a year later and two years after that a girl. A month before the first child was born, the King issued 'letters patent' declaring that any of their children could use the style and title of Prince or Princess. This would have been inherent if Philip had still been officially a Prince.

Prince Philip, his former title unofficially being used again, continued with his naval career in Malta and the Princess joined him, living in married quarters there. Apart from having to leave the children in Britain, they enjoyed a near 'normal', carefree married life while stationed in Malta.

Sadly, it could never be 'normal' with their young children hundreds of miles away, but at that time it was thought that babies were not strong enough to withstand the rigours of air travel and changes of climate.

The year after the northern wedding was the year of the Festival of Britain, a welcome relief from the devastation and hardships of the war years, and the struggles through bleak, post war years. It was originally to commemorate the Great Exhibition of 1851, but as no-one knew what could be afforded or what a new exhibition should contain, a committee was formed.

This committee included relatively young men and one woman rather than the usual older, male ministers or officials. But where in London could it be held? "Hey, let's choose one of the many bombed-out sites!" The south bank of the Thames, now an extensive wasteland, was chosen.

The extraordinary festival took shape and was advertised as 'the future'. It certainly captured the imagination of the country. Walking round the innovative designs and features, people spoke excitedly that this was like 'the future'. It was a celebration designed to show how a country battered by war and death could carve out a new future through science and innovation...while still having fun!

There was an elongated canoe shaped 'skylon' which became a lasting symbol of the festival.

There was all the fun of a funfair; circus sideshows; elaborate water fountains; giant displays of art; marching bands; parades; entertainers and clowns; gymnast displays; singing and dancing and an evening of ballroom dancing. Inside a large dome were visions of what Britain could look like in the future. A new beginning. Some said it was a brave new world. It was certainly a tonic for the nation.

The committee, and helpers, were still finishing the festival through the night of the last night before it opened. That winter had been one of the wettest on record and everywhere was still sodden. In fact, rain greeted the dawn on the 3rd May 1951. As no-one had thought to invite the committee to the opening ceremony, they had to watch from behind a hedge.

Through this hedge, the soaked committee members saw the King and Queen arrive in a state coach pulled by magnificent horses. Behind them was a procession bringing other members of the Royal Family.

Meanwhile, stuck in the lift, were some dignitaries, including the Lord Mayor of London. He announced arrogantly, "It won't start without me." Then the national anthem started up and it did start without him! They were rescued in time to hear the end of the King's speech, "...and I now declare the festival open."

(Hopefully, the Lord Mayor wasn't asked any questions about the King's speech. He may have had to make a general comment such as 'interesting speech' or 'good choice of words'. Or did he just play

safe and say, "Thank you for opening the festival!")

The King and Queen, Princess Elizabeth, Prince Philip and other senior Royals walked around, with the Lord Mayor, and met the people there on that first day. They were the first of many, many thousands who marvelled at what the dome contained – sections on discovery, science, exploration and outer space.

(That description sounds very similar to the different themes in Walt Disney's Disneyland which opened in Los Angeles in 1955!)

At the end of the festival there were fireworks and patriotic songs such as:

'And did those feet in ancient times, walk upon England's mountains green…'

with a very proud last verse being sung to 'raise the roof', '…I will not cease from mental fight, nor shall my sword sleep in my hand, 'til we have built Jerusalem in England's green and pleasant land'.

At the very close came an even louder rendition of the National Anthem.

The funfair and sideshows remained open, for a small charge per person, to allay the costs of the festival. There were also, 'mini' festivals up and down the country so that thousands outside London could be 'part of' the festival celebrations.

That same year, it was also my parents' first wedding anniversary and mother wrote a poem to celebrate it:

The Magic of Love on your First Anniversary
There's a wonderful gift that can give you a lift
It's a blessing from heaven above!
It can comfort and bless – it can bring happiness

It's the wonderful magic of love.
Like a star in the night, it can keep your faith bright
Like the sun, it can warm your hearts too
It's a gift you can give, every day that you live
And when given it comes back to you!
When love lights the way, there is joy in the day
And all troubles, are lighter to bear
Love is gentle and kind, and through love you will find
There's an answer to your every prayer.
May it never depart from our two loving hearts
May we treasure this gift from above –
You will find if you do,
All your dreams will come true
In the wonderful magic of love.

The greeting card Mother sent had a picture of flowers on the front cover with a card popping up from an envelope saying 'Our WEDDING Anniversary', ('wedding' was in capitals.) Inside the front cover were two bells with an entwinement of blue ribbons and red flowers. At the top of the main page in pale blue glitter – a 'cinderella' shoe with the heel in a horseshoe and an entwinement of white ribbons. *(A horseshoe depicts good luck and one is usually presented to a bride on the day of the wedding.)* The verse underneath read:

Our Anniversary
All that made our WEDDING DAY so happy
All that drew our hears beneath LOVE's spell
Wake anew this morning as it blossoms,
May the years their happy records tell
And God grant the love we bear each other

Grows yet stronger as we onward tread,
May our dreams come true in LOVE'S own Kingdom,
Bright as those we wove when we were wed!

Underneath was a sprig of mistletoe, then mother wrote in her distinctive, neat handwriting, *"To my dear Husband Joseph on our 1st Wedding Anniversary.*
With All my darling Love. From Ann xxxxxxxxxxxxx" (ending with a dozen kisses.)

His card back to 'Ann' can't have been memorable or worth keeping. (I'm sure he would have sent one!)

Since starting work, Annie had become Ann. She later added an 'e' changing it to Anne. Father was known by everyone as 'Joe' and it was 'Big Joe' at work, due to his 6' 2" height, but mother always called him Joseph.

Mother also saved a booklet on 'The Good Wives' Guide' of the 1950s. The following illustrates how wives were expected to be at home and to be prepared for the homecoming of their husbands from work.

"Have dinner ready. Plan ahead, even the night before, to have a delicious meal ready, on time for his return. This is a way of letting him know that you have been thinking about him and concerned about his needs. Most men are hungry when they come home and the prospect of a good meal (especially his favourite dish) is part of the warm welcome needed.

Prepare yourself. Take 15 minutes to rest so you'll be refreshed when he arrives. Touch up your make-up, put a ribbon in your hair and be fresh looking. He has just been with a lot of work-weary people. Be a little gay and a little more interesting for him. His boring day may need a lift and one of your duties is to provide it.

Prepare the children. Take a few minutes to wash the children's hands and faces (if they are small), comb the hair, and if necessary change their clothes. They are little treasures and he would like to see them playing the part. But, try and encourage them to be quiet.

Make the evening his. Never complain if he comes home late or goes out to dinner, or other places of entertainment, without you. Instead try to understand his world of strain and pressure, and his very real need to be at home and relax.

Your goal. Try to make sure your home is a place of peace, order and tranquility where your husband can renew himself in body and spirit. Make him comfortable. Have him lean back in a comfortable chair or have him lie down in the bedroom. Have a cool or warm drink ready for him. Arrange his pillow and offer to take off his shoes. Speak in a low soothing and pleasant voice.

Remember he is the master of the house and as such will always exercise his will with fairness and truthfulness. You have no right to question him!"

Obviously, mother wanted to be a 'good wife', to learn how to 'be prepared' and to be a 'little gay' when her husband came home after a 'work-weary' day.

What better sequel to the earlier articles on 'falling in love' than to read and save, 'from an egg to a baby', printed for parents to be 'explained to children'. There were also three articles on 'how a baby is born'. Although these were advertised as pages 'for children young and old', it was the first time mother had read details about the start of a new life, how that develops inside a woman and then how the baby is born.

Although mother and daughter had a close relationship, grandma never talked about the 'facts of life' with her, even before her wedding day. Mother had asked her questions about her own birth and been told 'you were a big baby' and 'I had a lot of morning sickness but never needed a doctor' and 'you were born at home with a midwife there'.

The 'how a baby grows' articles also fell short of actually saying how an 'egg' gets into 'mummy's tummy' or how the baby leaves the mother.

The articles discuss animal mating. They explain why some birds sing beautifully and why some have beautiful, coloured feathers. For example,

"It is when the peacock is seeking a mate that he opens his wonderful feathers, blue and green and shining purple as if to show his beauty to the female. It is when the turkey gobbler wants the turkey hen to mate with him that he raises his tail feathers like a fan and gives a gobble call while his wing feathers spread out until they scrape the ground."

How could this be related back to a man? Maybe something like: he struts his legs and sticks out his chest, pounding it with his fists in 'tarzan' formation.

Or: the man raises his arms in a male pirouette movement and yodels in his best soprano voice. (I could see a female 'taking flight' if a man started yodelling at a dance!)

Then the final article brings these animal mating techniques back to humans,

> "…many of the brave deeds that men and women have done they have done for love of each other, and much of all that is beautiful in life is beautiful because of love."

The article briefly mentions that the male usually tries to place the sperm in the body of the female, but there is no detail on how that occurs or even a hint of any preceding act of intercourse.

A child or adult could still be left wondering if a baby came out of a woman's naval or 'bottom', mmmm. Or how does the man try to *"…place the sperm in the body of the female"* – could it be via the (overrated) naval or even rubbed onto her stomach like a 'cream'?!

The final paragraph reads,

> "You come into the world because your mother and father loved each other so much that they started you growing as a baby."

So that's how… er, did I miss something?

Underneath the heading 'How a baby is born', is a picture of a baby being carried by a stork with a boxed paragraph:

> "Goodbye, Mr. Stork! Now we all know that the silly stories about the stork, the gooseberry bush and the

doctor's little black bag aren't true. The real and true story of where we come from and how we were made is much more beautiful – and much easier to understand. Don't you agree?"

Oh, I agree it's perfectly clear (?) I think not!

I'm sure more people would have understood how a baby is born if there had been a bit more detail about how and what starts a human baby growing in mummy's 'tummy', as opposed to a mating story about peacocks and turkeys. Luckily, the question 'don't you agree' was left unanswered as many readers, I'm sure, would have commented 'no, I don't agree'!

(I've never heard of the 'doctor's little black bag' myth! Presumably, it goes something like, 'the doctor turns up and brings out a baby from his little black bag'!)

But, the message which comes across loud and clear from the articles is that animals mate and a human mummy and daddy love each other and then an egg grows inside, and then a baby is born. Now what's hard to understand about that?

MY SPRING

A weary and frail and very ill gentleman slumbered in his great bed. He gave a murmur and then a faint smile passed his lips. His wife leaned forward to catch his awakening, but it never came.

He was dreaming of how happy she had made him though they had gone through a very bad time. He had been let down by his older brother. He had then been thrust into a world he had not been groomed for or expected to enter. His thoughts came forward to wish that his eldest daughter was here now but the memory of her was a peaceful one, feeling at this moment very close to her.

He never awoke from his slumber. Many, many people would mourn his passing. Not least his eldest daughter far away in a foreign land to be told the devastating news by her husband. She remembered when her father had waved her off at the airport, looking very tired but with no hint that she would never see him alive again. She wished she had been told before her trip just how gravely ill he was, though no-one had suspected that he would pass away so soon and so suddenly.

There were words she would have liked to have said again; words of love, comfort and hope. She wished with all her heart that she had been at his bedside.

The Princess, now Queen, thought she would have many more years of 'carefree', married family life, especially as her father was only in his mid-fifties. That was not to be as she was thrust into the limelight of the Monarchy while still grieving the sudden loss of her father.

Her aeroplane back from Kenya was delayed by some 24 hours due to thunderstorms. She was seen to be pale and tearful from the plane window, but when the time came to alight at the end of the journey, she was calm and poised.

Solemn bells pealed in churches. It was in a small district of a large northern city where a humble family household could hear the bells from their local church.

The daughter and son-in-law in the northern household had been hoping to start a family. They were still living with the daughter's parents saving every penny for their first home together which was not uncommon in those days.

On that cold winter's morning, the daughter was thinking how sad it was that the great King had died so early in his life. She had an inkling, though, that a new life had started inside her.

She had noticed small changes in her body – her breasts were tender and seemed a little swollen and for the last few mornings she had felt a little nauseous. She knew from her own mother that during her pregnancy she had been sick in the mornings.

A visit to the surgery would have to be made. There were no appointments, you turned up during opening hours – morning, afternoon and evening – and waited to be seen. Or not seen, as a thick fog of cigarette smoke greeted visitors to the waiting room.

(The advantage of the NHS was now evident by way of GP's

surgery queues which were never seen before 1948. No-one need worry again about calling out the doctor or going into hospital. Although it is somewhat taken for granted today it was a revolutionary change at the time, especially as the service was not means tested.)

In the local surgery, at the bottom of the street, there were three general practitioners (male) and a nurse (female). On arrival, you reported to the receptionist which doctor you wanted to see, or if you wanted to see the nurse. Then you took a seat at the end of the queuing system. There were several rows of chairs, filled with people and children. Some coughing, spluttering, blowing noses or in bandages or visibly in pain. If you didn't go in with a cold, you might come back out with one! In fact, everyone coughed from the dense smoke swirling about, except the smokers it seemed!

When the receptionist shouted the doctor's name, the next person in the queue for that GP would get up, knock at his door and go in. Then the next person would move up a chair and the next one would take that chair and everyone would get up and move to the next chair. It was a sort of Mexican wave of bobbing people still in a half sitting position, sliding sideways. The scraping of chairs could be heard while all this took place.

What always sprung to mind was one of her dad's favourite songs of the time, 'Bobbing up and down like this; oh it can't be wrong when it feels so right – bobbing up and down like this'. If the song was sung at a concert, the whole audience would 'bob up and down' to the chorus. If her dad was playing it on the piano, he would bob up and down from the piano stool.

(The song is from the sea shanty 'Sons of the Sea', made popular by Peter Dawson, an Australian who became a concert singer in

Britain. When he sang it at a theatre, he would shout out comments to the audience, such as, "Hey, you're a couple of bobs behind.")

Another doctor's name was called and the person next in line would go towards his door. The very second the person's bottom left that chair, the whole surgery 'Mexican waved' their half erect figures sideways and sat down again. Scrape, scrape, scrape went the chairs.

Do try this at home. It's an extremely comical process.

While waiting and 'half moving' along, there were no magazines to read, no music playing – everyone just sat there with their own thoughts or smoking or talked briefly about the weather with the person on the next chair. Occasionally, a man may be reading his newspaper. *(No-one fell asleep as you had to stay alert for the 'Mexican wave' procedure!)*

Sometimes, the moving chairs waiting system would break down if, say, a row of people didn't move or there were only a couple of rows of people and they stayed where they were. "Dr Daniels." Several voices would talk at once.

"Are you next or is it me?"

"Aren't you next?"

"No, I came in after Mrs So-and-so, she's next."

"I came in before that, I think it's Mr Hue-and-cry."

The receptionist would repeat "Dr Daniels" and a person would inch towards his door as if expecting to be challenged. Sometimes they were challenged and angry words would be exchanged which brought the doctor out to see what was happening. He would then choose the nearest person to the door and the atmosphere in the surgery was palpable in its temporary silence, save for a cough or a splutter.

If there were no vacant chairs, people would stand and queue. On a busy day, the queue would go out of the front door, down the steps and onto the pavement. In anticipation of queuing out in the street, I suppose you had to be ready with a big hat or scarf or wear a big, grey coat with the collar turned up, if you didn't want to be recognised.

(The doctors' surgery was eventually converted back to a house. Years later, I asked what happened to Dr Daniels when the surgery shut. I was told, long before the surgery closed, that he took his own life by putting an electrical appliance into his bath water. He was found dead in the bath, above the surgery where he lived. I was also told there was a lot of gossip. The nearest the gossip got to acknowledging the reason why he took his own life was the phrase, 'that's why he never married'. Any sexuality different from a man/ woman relationship was complete 'taboo' to talk about or be open about, in those days.)

Everything was still black and white, very post war. Some food was still rationed or difficult to buy. The excitement and joy of the Royal Wedding, and then the Festival of Britain, had disappeared in time.

As the King's health had deteriorated, Princess Elizabeth had taken on more and more of his official duties but there was no hint that he was so near the end of his life. The Princess and Prince Philip had embarked on an extensive Commonwealth visit to Australia and New Zealand, first stopping off at Kenya, the first leg of the tour.

In 1837, Princess Victoria had been in her nightgown when told she was Queen. In 1952, Princess Elizabeth had become Queen while in a tree house at Treetops in Kenya. In the morning, the Prince was told first and, according to an aide, it looked like 'the whole world had dropped on his shoulders'. Then he quietly broke the news to the new Queen.

On that same day, back in Britain, the picture broadcast on the television at the start of the grave announcement was of a murky, foggy and grey London over the Thames. The Houses of Parliament flag was at half mast. The speaker said, in solemn tones, "It is with the greatest sorrow that we make the following announcement. From Sandringham at 10.45am today, the King, who had retired to rest last night in his usual health, passed peacefully away in his sleep."

The previous week he had taken his family to Drury Lane to see South Pacific where nearly 3,000 people had stood and cheered as he entered the Royal Box.

The previous day, the King had been shooting rabbits, one of his favourite occupations. He went to bed with his usual cup of cocoa. He wasn't a well man but he had survived a serious operation to remove a lung at 56 years of age. Only the Queen had known he had lung cancer, but even so, death had come as a terrible shock.

An emergency Cabinet meeting had been called for 11am on the day he died where it was decided to hold the Accession Council that afternoon. This Council agreed the wording of the Proclamation of the new Monarch, the first in the absence of the Monarch since George 1 in 1714 (who, incidentally, was the first King of the House of Hanover.) Proclamations echoed round the world and were read out in parliaments and state capitals and within the Commonwealth by Governor-Generals or other officials.

The Queen was officially asked that morning, while still in the Kenyan Lodge, what she would like to be called. She replied, "Elizabeth of course." When getting ready to leave, she said to her Lady in Waiting, "I've ruined everyone's trip." Her feelings of duty were still deep inside, despite her heavy grief.

The press had been asked not to take any photographs as the motor car procession left the Lodge. They lined the route, some with stepladders, some with stools to stand on. Not a single camera was used.

On the plane journey home she asked an official, "What will happen when we get home?" No-one had realised that the new Queen would not know. In fact, a subdued greeting took place on the home tarmac from a row of prominent political figures. The Queen and her Consort went to Clarence House and were met by Queen Mary, who curtseyed and kissed her grandaughter's hand (to her great embarrassment.)

Her first public appearance was for a meeting of the full Accession Council. At this gathering the Queen said in her speech that she will take up her task, "…which has come to me so early in my life." She spoke with a clear and firm, but charming voice. It is ironic that so soon into a monarch's grief and loss, people had to welcome and celebrate the new 'arrival'. Here was a young and beautiful new Queen ceremoniously at the head of a plethora of old and even older gentlemen of the Council.

It was deemed at this Council that the Queen should be known as the 'Head of the Commonwealth'. The phrases 'Imperial Crown' and 'Queen of the British Dominions beyond the Seas' were dropped. Her new title, as well as Head of the Commonwealth, would be 'Queen of the United Kingdom of Great Britain and Northern Ireland and of her other Realms and Territories'.

For months after, there was a black cloud of grief for the King with no-one being more devastated than his widow and former Queen, Queen Mary, the new Queen and Princess

Margaret. All four wore heavy, black veils over their hats for the funeral. Queen Mary, in full length Tudor mourning dress, looked like a figure from another century, while the slim, young Queen was on the brink of a new Elizabethan age.

By the end of the year, however, there was a slow, building excitement towards the Coronation. That year had heralded the dawn of a new Elizabethan era. The new optimism in the War's aftermath had taken on a 'new pace' after the Festival of Britain. It had duly dipped during the months of mourning but was now growing again, faster than ever.

Such was public support for the young Queen that she insisted the route from Buckingham Palace to the Abbey be extended to allow more people and children to see them on Coronation Day.

It was reported that the Royal Wedding had been a 'rehearsal' for the Coronation, even that the Coronation was a sequel to the Festival of Britain. And the Coronation of such a young Queen was heralding a new future for the nation as she had so many adult years ahead of her.

One of Prince Charles' first memories was of his mother practising in the Palace ballroom using sheets pinned together as her 21 foot train. Balanced on her head, to get used to its heaviness, was the crown. Any other small child might have thought their mum was playing 'dress up' or 'I want to be Queen for the day'.

His mum would be Queen for her "…whole life, beit short or long…"

There was a rolling programme in the build up to Coronation Day of shops, homes and buildings being decked out with the colours of the Union Jack. Town Councils organised street parties and events. School children were 'in a frenzy' of painting and modelling – all getting ready for a 'mid-summer' Christmas.

A shabby, postwar capital, now decorated, uplifted everyone. A craze for periscopes, designed to help small people see over taller ones, spread quickly in London.

The 'invasion' of the capital began a week before the day. Traffic got so congested that the police stopped all non-essential traffic within two miles of Westminster. In the last few days, nothing was reported in the press or on Pathe News, but Royal related features and information. One news heading, 'All of this and Everest too' was a reference that Mount Everest had been conquered, but the reverence it should have been afforded was 'glaciered' over! *(...snow on top of a mountain, 'glaciered'? Never mind.)*

A huge garden party was held with such an array of people it was likened to an Hollywood epic. There were sultans, sheikhs, bishops, generals, African tribesmen, lords and ladies, to name a few. Hospitality for the Commonwealth leaders reached a climax the day before *the* day.

By this time, there were half a million people sitting or 'bedded' down by the side of the streets between the Palace and the Abbey.

As the gold state, horse drawn coach set off, two little figures could be seen waving from a Palace window. Prince Charles would be the first British child ever to see his mother being crowned Monarch. The little Princess, deemed too young to attend, would be staying behind.

The religious and spiritual part of the ceremony made way for the crowning. The crown hovered above the

Queen's head and then was thrust onto it. This triggered the self crowning of the peeresses, which had so impressed Princess Elizabeth in 1937. This was followed by 'God Save Queen Elizabeth, Long Live Queen Elizabeth, May the Queen Live for Ever'.

Unlike a Queen Consort, the husband of a reigning Queen is not crowned, but the Queen wanted Prince Philip to be involved in the Coronation. They knelt side by side for the blessing and took holy communion together.

(When the Prince had officially renounced his title at the time of their wedding, one of the other renouncements was his Greek Orthodoxy for Anglicanism, in preparation for when the Queen would inherit her title of Head of the Anglican Church. No-one imagined that prudent move would be realised within five short years.)

A young Prince Charles arrived for part of the Ceremony and the Queen Mother had some difficulty in restraining him. One minute he was over excited and animated and the next he was so bored his head sunk into his hands. Apart from these two extremes he understood that he must not speak loud, sing, laugh, move too much or throw his arms about.

Back at the Palace, two small children joined their parents on the balcony and waved to thousands upon thousands in the crowds, stretching all the way down and beyond the Mall. Little Princess Anne stood on a small stool to see over the parapet.

Meanwhile, up and down the country, street party fever was at its highest pitch. The 'keep calm and carry on' slogan back in the winds of time as neighbours now came together around trestle tables decked with party food and union jacks. Red, white and blue bunting hung across streets, bridges, shops, houses and gardens and anywhere bunting could be draped across. There was much singing and dancing and merriment.

A 'must' for every street party was 'Coronation Chicken' which had been specially introduced for the Coronation. It consisted of pieces of chicken in a mayonnaise sauce.

Housewives from two ends of a road setting out their separate parties, looked across to see if 'their end' was the best decked out, had the best food and who was the loudest in its celebrations. All in good fun and good humour!

Those who could 'tune in' to the BBC for the ceremony did not need periscopes.

Grandad was one of the thousands who bought a television set for the ceremony. They had a houseful of family and neighbours for the broadcast. Each family had brought something to eat and grandad supplied the drinks. A happy, celebration party was enjoyed by all.

Even though a lot of people had invested in a television, there were still only two thirds of homes with a set. Yet 20 million people had actually watched the ceremony – in their own homes, other peoples' homes or at the cinema.

All television programmes were in black and white and the early sets were 'disguised' as furniture. The set grandad bought stood on legs and had two concertina-type doors which opened like a curtain when it was going to be switched on. Knobs were used to switch on the one and only channel. (It wasn't until 1955 that commercialised TV gave everyone a second channel.)

Food and clothes rationing had ended the year before, in 1954, and a few more people were investing in a refrigerator and a 'new fangled' electric washing machine, which included an electric ringer to squeeze water out of the clothes.

Only 10% of households had a telephone. Someone might be able to afford a telephone, but if family and friends still had no 'phone, who would you call? *(No joke about 'Ghostbusters' here, as the film hadn't even been thought of!)*

Leisure time at home was reading, playing games, piano singalongs, listening to the radio or watching television. Hobbies included knitting, needlework and gardening for women and playing billiards/snooker or darts, smoking and drinking for men. In grandad's case it was playing billiards, the cornet and piano; and his love of 'gadgets'.

Gadgets such as the reel to reel tape recorder and a gramophone turntable for his growing collection of gramophone records. (1952 saw the first top 20 record chart in the New Musical Express.) Grandad had made sure that the television had a built in radio so that the wireless was 'demoted' to the front room – was he one of the first people in Britain to have an electric radio?

(Gramophone records, made of vinyl, were 12 inches and played at 78 rpm. A much earlier machine played records at 78 rpm and for some reason continued with that number of revs per minute rather than a more rounded number, eg 70 or 80. By the mid 50s, record players had three speeds of 78 rpm, 45 rpm and 33.3 rpm. The latter was the new LP speed and 45 rpm became the speed for 7 inch single records and for EPs, which were extended versions of singles.)

There were still 'singalong' nights with grandad playing the piano. Valerie can remember visiting with her mum and dad and enjoying these nights round the piano. If it was a Friday or Saturday night, Valerie would stay the night.

'Singalong' songs included, 'It's a long, long way to Tipperary' and 'Knees up Mother Brown', and, 'What shall we do with a drunken sailor'. Also, 'She'll be coming round the corner when she comes, when she comes, singing aye aye yippee, aye aye yippee, singing aye aye yippee when she comes!' They always added an extra 'yippee aye' at the end.

Grandad loved George Formby and used to sing one of his songs in George's distinctive voice. 'I'm leaning on the lamp post at the corner of the street in case a certain little lady comes by, oh me, oh my, in case a certain little lady comes by'. Grandad's collection of records grew, and included songs by George Formby, Gracie Fields, Vera Lynne, Bing Crosby and music from Glenn Miller. After hearing tunes a few times, grandad could play them on the piano.

In the shops, sales of gramophone records increased along with gramophone machines which were not 'plugged' in at that time, i.e. they were not electric. Early gramophones had a lever at the side which had to be wound up in order for the record to play. When it needed winding up again, the singing would go all slow and distorted. This was one of grandad's earliest gadgets and the top was held up while a record played. Next to the turntable were wooden compartments to hold records.

A combination set of record player and radio was known as a radiogram with cupboards underneath to store the records. These were only a little smaller than a sideboard but made from the same oak or mahogany wood. Radiograms used electricity so they needed to be located near a socket. Each room only had single sockets, two if lucky, but usually only one. The radiogram and the television were plugged into a double plug in the room's single socket.

Most homes now had a vacuum cleaner, that is, a push along, non-electric cleaner, known as a 'Ewbank' (the maker's name.) Electric vacuum cleaners were around, but they were very expensive.

New household goods were being introduced, such as electric fires and toilet paper (goodbye to the news imprinted on your bottom.)

New household goods and 'gadgets' were promoted at the annual Ideal Homes Exhibition in London and reported in newspapers around the country. A cocktail cabinet with the door folding over to create a bar counter seemed to be a cross between useful and a 'fad'.

When a top lid was lifted from another cocktail cabinet, the inside 'trolley' shape was lifted up to reveal drinks, glasses and shakers. Two tier trolleys on wheels became popular to put food on and then move into position for serving while watching television. Great, but costly, ideas.

Dining tables which could move up and down by adjusting a lever, turned into a coffee table. Chairs that stacked were introduced, made with ply laminated wood as that material could produce a curved chair back or curved arms.

Housewives were 'not forgotten' with the introduction of food mixers, one of which was the Kenwood 'chef' food mixer (though very expensive at first). Also, on show at the exhibition were ironing boards and standalone plug-in heated radiators. The phrase 'you've never had it so good' springs to mind of this 'boomtime' post war era.

Austerity was giving way to prosperity, at last.

The new Elizabethan era had arrived and heralded a more modern Britain.

Out with the old:
– Wireless

- Boiling water on the open fire
- Manual wash tubs
- Gramophones.

In with the new:
- Television
- Radiograms
- Electric kettles
- Twin tubs.

So what could we see in the kitchen on 1 January 1950?
A freestanding sink with a cold tap, small hot water boiler above the sink, fresh food larder-cum-cupboard or door/curtain leading to cellar, washtub/dolly posher and mangle, oven next to open fire, scrubbing brush, carpet sweeper (Ewbank).

And what had replaced these by 31 December 1959?
A fitted sink with hot and cold water taps, fitted cupboards covered with formica, automatic kettle and toaster, twin tub, standalone cooker, a 'Hoover', and in some homes, a fridge and a Kenwood 'chef'.

At the start of the decade, money was still tight and a housewife was spending many hours in the kitchen. She was 'more than ready' for a labour saving revolution.

By the mid-50s, washable formica surfaces and a fitted kitchen had saved a bit of the housewife's time and introduced some colour. A twin tub washing machine was a very expensive £95, the equivalent of a small car. To buy a fridge was the equivalent of £1200 today, so it was not surpising that only one in ten households were able to afford one.

But wait, wages were going up and taxes coming down! By 1955, wages had doubled to an average of nearly £12 per week with income tax dropping from 9 shillings in the pound to 7 shillings. In the government's budget of April 1958, purchase tax was halved. Manufacturers of twin tubs and fridges were happy people. Between April and December 1958, 400,000 fridges 'ran' out of shops and into kitchens.

With a twin tub, a housewife could walk away from and even leave the kitchen to do something else. Unfortunately, the machine had to be moved into position near the sink each time of use and a rubber pipe attached to the hot tap. Another rubber pipe went into the sink for surplice water to drain away when spin drying the clothes, hence calling it a twin tub.

An advantage of all this homemaking, cleaning and shopping was making it easier for a housewife to keep slim. There was also the walking involved with shopping and walking the children to school and back. On average, housewives were still involved in their domesticated lifestyle through the whole day. The only relaxation she might possibly be able to fit in, was listening to Housewives' Choice on the radio or Mrs Dale's Diary, alongside having a cup of tea or a quick lunch.

The phrase 'a woman's work is never done' remained very true, even with the new labour saving devices and the 'invention' of the weekend. A woman continued to wash, keep house, make meals and look after children, every day of the week. As always, it was a 'man's world' of Saturday sport – fishing, rugby, football and racing pigeons, cars, horses, dogs and bicycles. Some sports spilled over into Sunday like fishing and pigeon racing. Three quarters of the adult (mostly male) population had a regular 'flutter', mainly on the 'gee-gees'.

Vast numbers of working class men were either going to football matches or pigeon racing. On the way to Hillsborough football stadium, a long stretch of the main road was flanked by a steep hill with shanty-type dwellings. (As a child I thought they were the homes of the very poor.) These elaborate sheds were homes of pigeon fanciers. Each week, they would box up some of their pigeons and put them on trains for the guards to release them at their destination. Then this steep hillside would be packed with men and boys looking up to the skies for the return of their prized racing pigeons.

Further down the road, thousands of men and boys (very few girls/women) would be packed into the football stadium, all looking up and down and from side to side, as the football is kicked and headed about. My dad and grandad were two of the spectators.

Although not ideal to start married life, living with one set of parents, grandma was there each day to help and support mother, while the men went to work and on Saturday they went to the football match. Grandma was likened to say, 'if it's good enough for the Queen to have lived with her parents when she first married then it's good enough for you'. Mother would smile at the comparison.

Meanwhile, mother was now feeling sick every morning and too tired to do anything in the evening. Grandma cooked the tea and made sure that mother was eating 'plenty' – "You're eating for two now", she said. Drinking stout (alcoholic), as well as milk, was recommended for expectant mums. Mother didn't like stout but drank some regularly anyway. She continued to have small glasses of sherry to 'keep her mother company'.

There were no 'health warnings' for an expectant or breastfeeding mother to stop or cut back on alcohol, in fact, drinking stout and Guinness was actively encouraged while pregnant. Again, no 'health warnings' about smoking for anyone, anywhere.

Dr Daniels at the surgery confirmed her pregnancy was going well and explained what would happen next. *(GPs only had funding for two examinations per pregnancy.)*

This was a visit to the Clinic in town to register a hospital birth and decide which hospital. Mother and daughter went for the one farthest away from home because Nether Edge Hospital had just opened a new maternity wing.

(A Victorian hospital was built in 1841 and later, on the same site, an old hall was converted into a workhouse. After workhouses were abolished in 1929, the local council turned the two largest ones into 'flagship' hospitals – Nether Edge and the City General. In 1934, Nether Edge Hospital opened an additional 32 bed maternity block. The maternity accommodation was much improved in 1950 by the building of a new maternity wing. However, there was still the 7 or 8 days of bed-rest for the new mothers and their babies were breastfed every four hours, all at the same time. The only noise that could be heard was the sound of sucking and guzzling.

There were only two antenatal clinics for the whole city so expectant mothers, a lot with small children 'in tow', had to travel across town. At best, this sometimes involved a two bus journey. Or worse, mothers with large prams had to walk and push them considerable distances to get to the clinic as perambulators did not fit on buses or trams. Also, whether a baby or child was asleep or not, prams and pushchairs had to be parked outside the clinic.)

Antenatal 'appointments' were also at the city centre clinic. It was down a small, cobbled street off a main road with the

Clinic at the bottom of a 'deadend' cobbled lane. Mother and daughter visited together and although only one bus journey was needed, the clinic was quite a walk from the nearest stop.

Use of the word 'appointments' here is somewhat misleading, as there were no pre-booked appointments for antenatal care. Expectant mothers had to turn up, join a long queue and wait and wait. The wait was sometimes as much as six hours! The rows of seating were in cramped and uncomfortable conditions. Just the sort of thing to avoid if heavily pregnant, but the experience was repeated at most clinics up and down the country.

The antenatal care involved being interviewed and a chart drawn, by hand, to show the necessary tests and when they should be taking place. The tests were done by nurses and examinations by doctors. A sample of urine was tested, there and then, over a bunsen burner – the resultant smell was terrible and very unpleasant for women who were often feeling queasy from the long 'stuffy' wait.

You can just imagine what the queasy feeling, 'bloated' woman's blood pressure test result would be? Yes, blood pressure running high!

Privacy in cubicles was negligible with a flimsy curtain at one side of the examining couch and a flimsy curtain at the other side, which faced the seated queue of mothers, their mothers, babies and children.

Nearer to the time of the birth, antenatal 'appointments' were at the hospital. By the time of these appointments mother had finished work, leaving at the end of her seventh month.

(It was the 'norm' to leave by the sixth and seventh month of pregnancy, dependent on the woman's job. It had been the 'law', up to WW2, forcing women to leave work on marriage.)

Three months before mother's confinement a letter arrived from the Midwifery Superintendent, Maternity Department, Nether Edge Hospital.

'Dear Mrs. Stockdale,

As you are due shortly to enter Nether Edge Hospital for your confinement we think you might like to meet the staff beforehand, so that when you come to us in labour you will already know us.

Many mothers have their first baby without fully appreciating this wonderful experience, and so we should like to have a short talk to answer just the things you want to know about having Baby. If you understand what we shall do to help you and what we shall expect of you, then you will look forward to Baby's birth with confidence.

We hope you are interested and will be able to come to see us on Tuesday week, at 2.45 p.m. The porter on duty at the Lodge will direct you to Milner Ward.

Looking forward to seeing you.

Yours sincerely'

Mother was in her last few weeks at work, but she left at lunchtime to catch the bus to the hospital. She visited alone to be able to ask the sort of questions she wished, without the embarrassment of having her own mother sat next to her. Mother and daughter had never, ever, discussed anything intimate about sex or having a baby.

Mother's replacement at work was called Brenda who had, ironically, been working with an aunt, on father's side. Brenda had left her 'old' work to start a new 'career' as a wages clerk, but vowed to keep in touch with the aunt. As mum finished her job to have me, Brenda's new 'career' was just getting started.

(That is, until Brenda married, then her 'career' would be renamed a 'job'.)

Brenda was now the one to give out the firm's wage packets to the workers, including my father.

Fathers did not attend any antenatal 'appointments', and there was no such thing as 'paternity leave'. They were still excluded from any involvement. It was still unthinkable that the father should be at the birth of his own child. They were left to pace and smoke in a hospital waiting room.

There was no such thing as 'maternity leave'. When a woman had a baby she had to return to work full time or not at all. There was a 'stigma' that married women who returned to work after having a baby, for whatever reason, was taking a job 'away from a man' and would only be working for 'pin' money.

In the new wing at the hospital nurses wore cotton gloves as well as gowns and masks when changing babies as well as at births. The gloves were changed for each mother and baby, resulting in piles of white gloves waiting to be boiled and laundered. Nurses had their own sterilising kit, including towels and instruments, which they made ready in a tin to take into any delivery.

Cots were made of strong, thick canvas which could be taken off the metal base for laundering after each baby.

There was no 'special care' for premature babies, save a heated cot and oxygen if needed. What they did have was tender loving care, for example, having their skins rubbed with oils.

Mother's contraction pains started and it was 'red alert' time. Grandad rushed out to start the car while grandma rushed upstairs to get the already packed bag. Father had already gone to work.

At the hospital, grandad stayed put in the car – it was no

place for a man! Grandma walked with her daughter to the maternity ward's booking desk. They had to say 'goodbye' there and then so that the pre-birth procedures could take place.

Grandma went out to the car and they decided she should wait at the hospital while grandad went to father's place of work. Grandad then waited in the car until father was allowed to leave and he was duly dropped off at the hospital and grandparents drove back home. Grandma said it was 'the longest few hours of her life just waiting at home'. Remember, no telephone at home.

The pre-birth procedures included shaving the 'bikini' area, having a bath and then the enema in the bottom area. Next stop, the toilet.

Once mother gained control of her bowels she was shown to a bed near the delivery room. She lay on her side but was turned on her back during each painful contraction. The bed had two high, metal stirrups at the bottom – ready and waiting for her legs to be 'strung up' for the birth. The midwife gave encouraging instructions, like 'push hard', 'rest rest', 'breathe and push', 'push hard again', 'again'. Gas and air ready, but it was not used very much as it slowed down the 'pushing'.

I burst into life at 7.35pm, weighing a sturdy 7lb 10oz. The nurse softly punches her stomach a few times and the red, gory placenta plops out.

I was washed and clothed before being held in front of my mother for her to see me for the first time. I was then placed in the cot of thick canvas.

It was only when mother was out of the delivery room and wheeled into a recovery room that father was summoned from the smoky waiting room and he first saw me as a babe in a swaddling, but tight, hospital shawl. He did not feel able to pick me up, though he said he had wanted to.

Still at home and deciding, 'we can't wait another minute', grandad was despatched to the nearest public telephone box to ring the hospital. After what seemed another long wait, grandad burst through the back door like a superhero. He said, through his panting breath, "It's a girl." Back they 'flew' to the hospital.

Mother and baby stayed there almost two weeks which was the normal length of 'internment' (I mean confinement.) The first seven days was 'bed rest', necessitating the use of bed pans. The cot was wheeled in for each baby's breastfeeding and cuddling and then wheeled out to sleep in rows of cots. Two nurses would sit at a table, reading, playing dominoes or cards to pass the time. Smoking was still allowed at nursing stations.

If a newborn woke up in the night the nurse would wheel the cot back to the mother and wake her up to breastfeed the baby.

There were strict, limited visiting times and only two visitors at the bedside at any one time. The two visitors were usually the new mother's mother and the new father. Grandad was the 'odd one out' who stayed outside the ward, but as he was the car driver he was essential to the visit. Near the end of visiting time, he was allowed to walk in and say 'hello'. Then a handbell rang out. And it became 'hello… goodbye'. Grandma and grandad walked out to leave the new father to give the new mother a private kiss.

After twelve days grandad came to collect mother and baby in his car. He was lucky enough to have the autonomy in his job to be able to make personal journeys during the day. Grandma sat in the back and mother sat in front with her new baby cradled on her knee. I was wrapped in a home knitted shawl. Father saw me at home after he arrived in from work.

After tea, grandma and grandad went into the front room for the evening to give the new family some privacy. Even with the fire in the front room, the living room would have been warmer. Bedrooms were cold as the fires were left unlit. For my benefit, a two bar electric fire was bought for the bedroom to be plugged in an hour before being laid in the wooden cot.

Mother had said that it was instant and complete love when she saw me for the first time, washed and tightly wrapped up in the hospital shawl. She had touched her lips to my face, my head and wispy hair and my tiny fingers. She had delighted in the sensation of my tiny lips on her swollen nipples and how such a miracle had felt so natural.

Mother would breastfeed me in bed or in the downstairs room not being used. While that took place, only father would be expected to go into the room and only to see if mother needed anything. There was no breastfeeding outside the home, save one or two rare occasions on a Sunday 'day out'.

On such a rare day out, grandad had to choose carefully where to park in order to give mother as much privacy as possible when she breastfed in the car. She had to manoeuvre 'the act' under a shawl with a rug wedged through the window as an extra shield.

Sundays normally consisted of mother and father pushing me in the pram through the roads and round the parks. That is, after the Sunday roast dinner served at lunchtime and cooked by grandma. The new parents had to be back home for my feeding time.

Mother helped out with the weekly wash day and ironing. Every day was nappy washing day. Dirty nappies went into a tin bucket of bleach and then rinsed through, by hand, before being put into the non-electric washing machine. They were mangled through, hung out to dry and ironed the same day. Nappies were large, terry towelling squares held in place by safety pins.

Traditionally, men did not change any nappies, but father occasionally did. Grandad, from the generation before, traditionally did nothing in the home, but I'm sure if he had been asked, he would have helped out in the home.

Very, very occasionally he set the tea table. He never washed pots or did any gardening. If asked, he went to fetch food items from the cellar like meat, milk or butter.

Grandad's only 'duty' in the house was clearing the ashes, lighting and keeping the open fire going. He used to put a large newspaper sheet in front of, and completely covering, the fire, which he said acted as a vacuum to get the fire going. This paper would get sucked in before going brown and then alight.

There were times when this caught fire too soon and he had to poker it into the fire quickly.

If someone threw anything into the fire by mistake, he would put his hand in to get it, frightening me, but his hand was always unscathed. When I got a bit older, he would say, "Don't you do that." To me, he seemed to have fireproof hands.

At the end of a year of breastfeeding, grandma swathed mother in tight bandages around her chest, saying, "So that the milk dries up quicker." When the bandages remained dry all day, that was the time they weren't needed any more. Mother said when her milk had finished, the breasts went hard and painful for a week or so before softening but they remained a little 'saggy', she said.

In household terms, there was still the great divide between men and women. The greatest difference was that the man would go to work and married mothers would be all things in the home. For a man to carry an umbrella or to ask for a glass of wine was to put his virility *in* question. Beards were *out* of the question.

In the home, women still spent the equivalent of a man's working week on housework, even with the introduction of some labour saving devices! Housewives and mothers still had no time to spare on 'leisure'.

A man's leisure time seemed to be any time outside work! One pastime was to go for a drink in the local. Father would now sometimes accompany Grandad to the Queen's Ground local pub, especially if he was in a billiards tournament which would be used as an 'excuse' to go.

Men wore overalls in steelworks, engineering works or on the factory floor. Father wore overalls which would be taken off at the end of the day. Grandad sometimes wore an overall over his suit trousers and shirt. Father's job was the 'dirtiest' and he would wash his face before going home. At the end of the week (after the Saturday morning's shift) he would take his overall home to be washed. Grandad did not have to work Saturday mornings, but usually 'called in'.

Male dress code in an office job included wearing a white shirt with detachable stiff collar and cufflinked cuffs. Wearing a soft collar and the man would be labelled 'disrespectful' and 'lacking in ambition'. Particularly in London, if a man had worn a striped shirt, he would have been asked why he was still in his pyjama top. In the north, a man in a striped shirt would have been told to go to a mental asylum which would not have been said in a polite way.

Being 'gay' was still about laughing and having fun! Remember, Mother had to be a 'little gay' when father came home from work.

Newspaper opinion polls were becoming popular. Each week a newspaper would pose a question to its readers and they had to write in with their opinion.
(Or ring to in if they happened to own a telephone.)

A Sunday newspaper ran an opinion poll on 'what school do you think Prince Charles should go to'. The answers ranged from 'it's none of our business' to 'we trust the Queen and Prince Philip'. There were no printed opinions about schools. The Royal Family was loved and cherished almost everywhere in this country, but people seemed introvert within their own family lives.

Just imagine a country where doors are left unlocked; bicycles are propped up anywhere; there are no locks on motorcycles and cars are left unlocked; children play in the streets, they climb trees and get into skirmishes.

Where is this country, you ask? It's Britain in the fifties! Although there was a general 'stiff upper lip', north or south of the border, it was a safe place to live.

The new tradition of going on holiday for the weekend or for the week was being firmly established, but if making the journey by car there were queues through most towns. Although motorway building had started, there were still no ring roads around towns or cities.

There was also a revolution about to happen…Britain was under attack, not from an enemy force, but by an American rock and roll invasion. Rock and roll changed Britain's youth forever. The teenager was 'born'.

The first teenagers were 'Teddy boys', smoking and swaggering in their brightly coloured jackets and blue suede shoes. Women wore full skirts, flat shoes and ankle socks. It was, however, seen as 'common' to go out with a 'Teddy boy' because of their reputation for causing trouble. 'Nice' girls wore knitted twin sets.

Most teenagers seemed to be electrified by Bill Haley's 'one, two, three, four o'clock rock around the clock' song. The American imported rock and roll and jiving the night away was here to stay. Britain's Marty Wilde sang 'why must I be a teenager in love'. With more and more people buying a television set, 'pop' stars were becoming household names.

Of course, I was still too young to know anything about rock and roll, Bill Haley or jiving teenagers.

Spring Memories

Although not a memory, as I was only three weeks old, I was christened at Sheffield City Cathedral. It was not the local church, but as Grandad played the cornet in the Salvation Army Band once a month at the Cathedral, he asked if his first grandchild could be baptised there. The Reverend agreed and I got a very grand start in life!

My godparents were Aunt Minnie, her son Frank, and dad's younger sister who had been bridesmaid at their wedding. It was tradition to have three godparents with at least one from either side of the family. For a boy, he would have one female godparent and two men. A girl would have two female godparents and one male godparent, as I had.

My mother wanted me to be called 'Carol Anne' but as it was nowhere near Christmas, grandma thought it was an inappropriate name. My grandma would have preferred me to be called 'Annie' but as a compromise I was christened 'Jean Anne'.

Photographs were taken outside the Cathedral on a fine and warm day though family members were formally dressed in best coats. It was tradition for babies to be christened in their grandmother's and mother's christening gowns. Mine was a full length gown of silk with a patterned netting over it. Aunt Lily had crocheted a christening shawl and I wore little knitted booties.

If I had been born a boy, I would have worn the same gown and booties. In fact, a generation ago, boys were dressed as girls up to about three years old. This was particularly noticeable in Royal Family portraits showing small children, and if there was no explanation of who they were, the toddlers all looked like girls.

Mother told me I had seen the Queen when she visited Sheffield, as part of her tour of Yorkshire, in the early fifties. I thought I had a memory of mum and I running down the street to wave to the Queen. On the main road travelling at a snail's pace was a cavalcade *(I like that word)* of big black cars, and from one the Queen and Prince Philip waving to crowds lining the route.

Sadly, it was one of those memories that was not an actual memory. I very much wanted it to be a 'real one', but I know that I would have been too young. The memory of mum and I 'flying through the air' down the street with her shouting 'we'll miss her, we'll miss her' is one which became a 'real' memory over time. I seemed to remember the Queen waving as I was held up in my mum's arms.

That day in Sheffield took the Queen and the Prince to the Town Hall and, as part of the visit, they stepped out onto the balcony to wave to the throng of people below. That old, Victorian custom of looking round the Town Hall without leaving the carriage was thankfully left in yesteryear.

Their procession of cars then went to the River Don Steelworks (later known as 'British Steel') and from a glass 'office' that had been built for the occasion, they looked at the rolling steel being cast.

Then the cavalcade made its way from the steelworks to the Hillsborough Football Ground, home of Sheffield Wednesday FC, via the main tramway road where mum and I had stood waving.

(In 1898, the lease on the football club's former ground had expired and Wednesday, established in 1867, was looking for a new home. To the rescue came the owner of Hillsborough Hall who made the club a proposition of ten acres of land at Owlerton. The Owls had a new ground…and a new nickname from 'Owl'-erton, pronounced locally as 'olerton'.

The first football match was in 1899 opened by the Lord Mayor who was billed to 'kick off' the match at 3 o'clock. The announcement advertising the match, included: 'Admission 6d, boys 3d'. 'The Stand (to sit) 6d extra'. Wednesday beat Chesterfield 5-1 as was only 'right and proper' as it was 'our' day.)

In the football ground for the Queen's visit was an eager sea of 43,000 schoolgirls and boys, some sat in the stand and some stood up on the kop. (I understand children from the grammar schools were the ones seated.)

Some three thousand children marched and counter marched across the pitch, a display which they had been practising for weeks. Then the children formed a giant Union Jack with the appropriately coloured cards over their heads. Then with the same cards, but reversed, made the words 'Welcome to Sheffield'.

The Queen then toured round the pitch in an open Land Rover which had a platform for them both to stand and wave to the schoolchildren.

There are one or two other stories which could serve as an early memory of mine – playing outside on the postage stamp lawn at home and pushing a doll's pram along the tiny paths from the house through the narrow network of paths in the flower garden. The garden was fenced with a gate which was held with a tiny 'sneck'. Another memory is of me pushing a horse on wheels around the paths. The horse could also be sat on and it had a fluffy white mane of hair.

There were now five of us living in my grandparents' terraced home, the end one of three. It was on a street which started as a gentle slope from the main tramway road, growing in steepness and becoming a '1 in 10' hill at the top. It was definitely a 'pull' up to the top. However, there were cobbled short cuts, 'gennels', twisting and turning between the steep roads. In fact, most side roads were cobbled.

Across from the front of the house was a straight road which twisted away downhill in the distance. There were two corner shops called 'beer off's' which were also known as 'off licence' shops. They were on the same road but a short distance apart. 'Beer off's' had a large grate in front of the shop. This could then be lifted so that beer kegs could be rolled down into the cellar as early 'beer off's' sold beer in containers that customers were encourgaged to bring back and use again.

Cutting across the end of the downhill road was the main road with the trams and buses running alongside an ever growing number of cars. That was the main road the Queen's cavalcade had travelled on.

Shopping, still very much regarded as 'women's work', was a lengthy business as there were numerous shops to go in, to 'chit-chat' and gossip in each one. Grandma would talk to anyone, even people she didn't know – in the street or on the bus. I would ask, "Who was she?" and her reply was, "I don't know."

A typical shop queue conversation went something like:

"Eyup, a bit cooler today than yesta'day," *('eyup' is a form of greeting)*

" 'ope it dun't rain, I've left weshin' awt,"

"Ah think sun'll come awt in a bit,"

"Queue's goin' slow in'it?"

"Jus' left Funk's an' queue to' door," *(Funk's the butchers)*

"Mrs Dodd spent one an' a penny on meat, all bits an' bobs," *(that is 1s.1d)*

"Oh, she goes on an' on," *(talking)*

"Las' week I went to Funk's an' she wer' up front,

"Did yer knaw she's 'avin' another?"

"nooo…"

" 'eard 'er sister tellin' Mrs Pike," *(as an aside and in a whisper)*

"That'll mek' four little 'uns," *and amid some 'tut tutting' the front of the queue was reached at last.*

Most shop goods still had to be weighed out so even at the front of the queue there was always an opportunity to 'chit-chat' with the shopkeeper. Wicker work baskets got quite heavy and I would always end up carrying something or other, which I didn't mind.

The first big shop on this main road, to the right of our street, was the co-operative store. High, dark counters stood around each of the three sides from the entrance, assistants behind each one. Counters were on three sides with tinned and packet goods on shelves going up to the ceiling behind one counter.

The facing counter had all the fresh foods, including butter and lard in big wooden or metal tubs for the assistant to take a 'blob' out and weigh onto greaseproof paper. Then they would be 'paddled' into shape, taking further time. No-one minded queuing for what was a lengthy process per customer as everyone talked to everyone in the queue. It was a way of life.

('Self-service'? What on earth was that?)

On the right was the bakery counter with all sorts of bread, rolls, pies, pastries and pasties, buns, cakes and everything homemade from a lemon tart to large custard pies.

I was pre-occupied, as I was fascinated by the overhead payment system and would normally stand in the middle of the store looking up. Money would be put into a tin container (it had a tiny glass 'window') and 'fired' upward on a wire, which would take the money container along the overhead wires. They criss-crossed to a ceiling-high, glass box where an assistant would take out the money and a piece of paper. He (this was always a man) stamped 'paid' on the paper, counted out the change, put it in the canister and sent it whizzing back along the overhead wires. It would whoosh along the wiring and down a chute to the appropriate counter for her (this was always a woman) to take out the change and give to the customer.

I loved that shop and never wanted to go. I used to stand with my head upwards watching the containers whizzing and whooshing backwards and forwards overhead while my mother or grandma did their shopping. I remember saying nearly every time, "Call back fer me I wanna stay 'ere," but they would not leave me behind.

Shopping for food and groceries, and for anything else, was still carried out in different shops, even though most main roads with shops had a large co-operative store. There was a shop for hardware, ironmongers, a shop for laces and shoes, shops for clothes, cards, newsagents, paper, carpets, a shop for drinks and 'nik-naks', a shop for knitting and sewing wools.

Shops selling second hand goods and clothes, pawn shops, pet shops, fruit and veg shops, cobblers, knife sharpening and key cutting shops. Home made bread and cake shops and of course a post office and chip shops (as in 'fish and chips' but we would just call them 'chip shops'.) There were public houses dotted along the main road in between the shops.

As previously mentioned, at the side of one large public house which had been an inn, there was a high archway leading to a large courtyard. This had been a terminus for horse drawn stagecoaches.

Back on my street, I can vaguely remember on some days, a man's loud voice shouting, "Any old pots and pans," sometimes ringing a hand bell. I can remember running out when hearing the bell and seeing people taking out their unwanted 'nik-naks' and clothes to him in exchange for a copper or two or a 'donkey' stone.

Looking back now, it feels like I was a child glancing through a window almost closed on a bygone age where 'rag and bone' men with their horse and carts rattled along the cobbled streets. Small boys were running around freely in the road. Backdoors were still unlocked in the day. You could hop on and off a bus or tram at the back, even when it was moving. Prams with babies in could be left outside shops. Cars could park almost anywhere (not on tram lines obviously.)

Washing clothes would take the whole of Monday and ironing the day after still used irons heated from an open fire.

In other words, wash day without a washing machine and ironing day without an electric iron.

I was unaware that my grandparents would have been considered 'posh' to own a car, television and gramophone. The car was actually 'owned' by grandad's work, but the neighbours did not know that.

To the left of 'my street', led to a larger shopping area, still with all the smaller shops, but this area included picture palaces (cinemas), a large Woolworths store (purpose built after being a bomb 'crater' for several years), a ladies' underwear shop, a ladies' fashion shop, a café, a large purpose built post office, newsagents, spice shops, two banks, a Chinese restaurant above a shop, chip shops, pubs and a large co-operative store (this one having 'normal' cash tills).

(The only shops left today from my early childhood are the two family butchers (Funk's and Talbot's), the flower shop, a fish and chip shop with its original name, the large co-operative store which now includes the post office, and one of the two banks.)

On the way to this larger shopping area was the public house where my grandad played billiards and snooker, drank beer and smoked his untipped Woodbines' cigarettes. He won trophies and medals playing billiards.

(Anyone could smoke anywhere, including hospital wards, school staff rooms, cinemas, shops, on buses, trains and aeroplanes, at petrol stations and of course in all workplaces.)

Next to grandad's 'local' there was a cinema. There were three cinemas in the area and the one next to the 'local' had been named after the owners, two brothers called 'Phoenix'. One of the brothers had died from the 'flu pandemic in 1918 and the other brother had run it until 1956.

(The Phoenix was run briefly by another cinema owner and then

closed in 1960 and like a lot of cinemas and other old buildings, was demolished and the site reopened as a petrol station.

The 'flu pandemic of 1918 to 1920 is believed to have started in the disease ridden trench and other atrocious conditions of WW1 and because it was deemed 'war related' several countries imposed a media blackout, including Britain. This blackout was partly to keep morale high, but partly to keep life as 'normal' as possible in the War's aftermath. Soldiers returning home to their various countries, it was thought, may have helped spread it around the globe. There were even cases reported in the Antarctic. Between 10 to 20% of people who caught this strain of 'flu, died from it. In Britain, schools were closed with hospitals and undertakers alike unable to cope. At its peak in Sheffield, over 100 sufferers per week were dying from it.)

In one story from the 1950s, a 15 year old boy who had been allowed into the Phoenix to watch an 'X' rated film (for over 18s) and a local sergeant and policeman had checked for underage cinema goers. They found the underage boy and duly interviewed the owner and the cashier. It was the cashier, not the owner, who was fined 7/6d *(7s 6d which is less than 50p)* and given a warning.

One of the other three cinemas, the Kinema, had been bombed in the War and then rebuilt. I remember going to watch Pollyanna there as a small child, which was the first film I can remember watching at a cinema.

(Hayley Mills played Pollyanna, an orphan girl, who came to live with her rich Aunt. Pollyanna makes lots of friends, young and old, but her Aunt forbids her from attending local fundraising events which she does not agree with. She defies her Aunt and, on returning, climbs up a tree to get into her bedroom window, but she falls and loses the use of her legs. Lots of townsfolk come and visit Pollyanna and her Aunt sees how popular she is. Her Aunt's 'lost' sweetheart

arranges for Pollyanna to go away and have an operation which will repair her injury. She returns months later and can walk, much to the delight of all the townsfolk, and her Aunt finally 'gets together' with her 'lost' sweetheart.)

At the side of the Kinema, was the large Woolworths store. Next to that, was a small, cobbled lane leading to a public house with its front opening onto the road round the corner.

(Sadly, this cobbled lane is long gone, making way for a covered shopping mall.)

When walking to this shopping area, our turning point to return on the other side of the road would be the Woolworths store. On leaving that store, we crossed over the road to come back on the other side, always calling into the post office. Back at Hillsborough we would cross that and go over the river bridge. Then passed the Midland Bank *(HSBC)* and Hillsborough Swimming Baths where I would learn to swim from school.

(The swimming baths is now a public house. The pool is covered over (it was cheaper than filling it in) and the slipper baths are now alcoves with tables/chairs with the overhead balcony retained.)

On the way back home, the route took us alongside the barracks, *(now a gravy salt factory.)*

(The outer walls of the Sheffield Barracks still bears the water marks from the Great Flood of 1864 which devasted that area of the city. The dam wall of one of the nearby reservoirs collapsed, sending gallons of water rushing through the farms and streets, destroying almost everything in its path, and killing 270 people in its wake.)

Half the iron railings had been sawn off during WW2 as raw material to use in the munitions factories. Did 'they' have enough iron and left the other half of the railings? Or did 'they' think that the barracks might have to be brought back into 'war service', hence being needed as a defence barrier? Whatever the reason, the wall with no railings was walked on by children, myself included.

My grandparents' house, where I lived for the first three years of my life, was typical of that time. The front door step, whitened with the essential 'donkey' stone, led to a small paved area and a small wall with the spiky 'chopped off' railings. The privet hedge was kept trim and at adult waist height. To go around the back was via a car-less driveway as this belonged to the Jones' end house.

Grandad's black car was parked in the street and was never locked, day or night.

Car runs included days at the seaside or inland towns for fishing, usually on a Sunday. Anyone could travel how they wished and there was no limit on the number of people in the car; though six was a comfortable 'maximum' number, three in the front and three in the back. Small children could even sit on the driver's lap. Babies were held in someone's arms or laid in a carry-cot.

Grandad's car was cherished and lovingly washed each weekend. A photograph showed grandad washing his black car with a sponge and my pushchair positioned in the middle of the road for me to watch him. There was no through traffic and he was the only car owner on the street, and in the area. Within a few short years, a pram and a baby parked in the road would be unthinkable.

I have no memory at the seaside of my fingers being trapped in the pushchair on a seaside pier, but my parents delighted in reliving the story. The arm of the pushchair folded down for storage and I had been put in the pram ahead of the arm being properly secured. It was half secured with four tiny fingers trapped inside. While I cried and cried, in much pain, my father had said, "Wait, I want to take a picture" which he did and in so doing lengthened my distress. That story was told every time the photograph was shown around.

Back to the row of houses – all three had back doors leading onto a path with their garden opposite, all with a tiny wall and a 'snecked' gate. Between the house and the path leading to 'our back door' was a shed, set against a high wall with a small 'postage stamp' lawn in front. The shed walls were made of brick and the roof of corrugated iron which had been the family's air raid shelter.

The path around the shed and lawn, led to the outside toilet (called a closet) with whitened steps, of course. The next door neighbour's closet was farther away and joined our's by the back wall so their closet door was facing away from the path and garden.

I remember thinking, when a little older, how whitening steps seemed a complete waste of time. People, including children, were expected to step over the whitened part of the step to keep it white. I vowed I would not be whitening any steps when I grew up but in reality it was one of the customs which would be long gone. In fact, the 'donkey' or pumice stone used to whiten steps weren't as readily available once the 'rag and bone' men disappeared.

A second shed was at the bottom of the garden which was called an 'outhouse'. This was where the chickens had lived up to the end of the Second World War, plus a few more years; now unused and run down. I only remember remnants of feathers inside (where I wasn't allowed to go but did) and lots and lots of white bird droppings. I also remember the unpleasant, sort of sweet smell, which made my nose itch.

It wasn't a garden to play ball in but you could wander through the tiny paths in between the flower beds and imagine you were someone else, going somewhere. The paths in between the beds weren't wide enough for my doll's pram but the paths around the garden were.

The back door, with whitened step, was not locked during the day and would only be locked before going to bed (it was also the 'norm' not to lock back doors even when 'popping out' to the corner shop.) Another custom long gone!

In next door's garden there was still their corrugated air raid shelter between the end wall and the greenhouse. Living there was a couple, older than my grandparents, who had a grown up son still at home.

In the end house was the Jones' couple, younger than my grandparents. They built a carport but didn't buy a car. They had an inside toilet put in, but Mr Jones still had to use the outside closet. They were the only people on the street to have a telephone. Mrs Jones always had rouge cheeks and wore red lipstick. She didn't go to work, which was unusual for a woman who didn't have children to look after.

I overheard mum and grandma once saying, that Mrs Jones was 'talked about' as she 'entertained' male visitors in the house during the day. I remember thinking why would she be talked about for having visitors?

On Mondays the washing lines, garden after garden, were full of wet, clean clothes blowing in the wind. Except Mrs Jones, who didn't have a washing line.

All northern housewives and mothers wore a full pinafore over whatever they were wearing, at all times of the day. This would stay on for the corner shop but would 'come off' in the evening when all household chores had, at last, been completed. Except for Mrs Jones who had never been seen in a 'pinny' (pronounced 'pinna'.)

On Fridays, it was beans on toast at tea time as most of Thursdays baking was 'for the weekend'. We would have fish and chips for Saturday dinner (lunch) so that my dad and grandad had 'a good meal' before going to watch our football team. If we lost, then dad would not want any tea. Nothing stopped grandad from eating his tea.

In the north, lunch is called 'dinner time'. Around five o'clock is tea time.

Breakfast is still at breakfast time, cereal or toast, with a 'fry-up' on Sunday mornings. Supper is still at supper time, usually hot milk or 'Ovaltine' and a biscuit. If you went to bed at 8 o'clock then supper time would be just before that. If you went to bed at 10 o'clock, supper time would be just before ten and so on.

The oven was next to the open fire in the living room. To the right of this was the sink with just a cold tap. It was a stand alone sink, with curtained shelves underneath. Attached to the left of the sink was a draining board above a cupboard that grandad had put together, made of wood. Above the sink was a small hot water boiler with a separate tap. There was just enough room to get to the sink, at the side of the 'new fangled' washing machine, which had a lever inside that was pushed from side to side to wash the clothes. Attached to it was a hand operated mangle (ringer) for squeezing water out of the clothes.

A large table was centre stage in the living room with the sideboard and the television against the other two walls. A door led to the cold, 'dank' cellar (the steps were the household's 'refrigerator') and another door led to the front room and stairs.

There were two double bedrooms on the next floor and then a creaky, twisting staircase to the attic. Oh, how I loved that attic. So many interesting bygones of photos, old clothes and heirlooms. I wasn't ever allowed in for very long before I heard my nannan, as I called her, shouting up the stairs, "Come down you'll get dirty," or "Come down here where I can see you." Sometimes, after a fair bit of nagging, we would go up there together and the story behind a dress or the rickety bamboo cupboard would be told. One of the dresses was grandma's wedding dress which looked thin and delicate, but still very beautiful.

The story of the rickety bamboo cupboard was that grandma's mother had found it in a second hand shop as the owner said it was from Africa. She bought it and Walt, still at home, had been sent to the shop to carry it home. He knew the owner had given his mother 'a yarn' but he dutifully took it home and let her think it was from Africa. Ironically, it was where he would serve in WW2 which made the cupboard doubly sentimental to his mother, my great grandma.

When grandma was looking to furnish their new home, years before, her mother had insisted she take the cupboard for one of the bedrooms. It was now used as storage in the attic. When Walt was furnishing his own home, he had not taken up grandma's offer of handing 'back' the 'African' bamboo cupboard.

There was a porcelain topped cupboard which grandma

said had originally been in their bedroom to hold the wash basin and jug. When water spilled on the cupboard top it was easily wiped, rather than spoil a polished surface. They had eventually been able to afford a matching bed, wardrobe and dressing table. It was then demoted to the attic and used as storage.

There were two cardboard boxes of 'stuff' which had been brought from grandad's parents' home at the time his mother went to live there. Grandma didn't like me looking in them so I had to rummage rather than look properly, just in case she was making her way up to the attic. There was no 'sneaking' into the attic as the stairs were bare and made creaking noises. A bit older, and I would wait for grandma to hang out the washing or go to the closet, then I would rush up and get a 'head start' in the attic. Until the call, "I know you're up there so come down 'ere."

The front room of the house was only used for visitors from outside of the family or if grandad or mother played the piano. The fireplace, once open, now had a three-bar gas fire in it. There was a settee with an arm which could be released to drop down for lying on. The armchairs were chairs with arms as opposed to comfy easy chairs, but they matched the settee. The front door was only opened if anyone was rushing out to the 'jingling' ice cream van or grandad was using it to carry out buckets of water out to wash the car.

When grandad was poorly he slept in the front room. Grandma was never poorly and had never been to a doctor for herself.

I regret that I was still too young, some years later, to save anything from the attic when the house had to be emptied.

(A compulsory purchase order had been issued for the three terraced houses.) Despite pleading with my mum I wasn't allowed to keep anything back from the house clearance people.

At the time, I particularly wanted to wrap up and store under my bed some framed pictures from the front room of reindeers and stags in the wood – the sun would shine through the bay window onto these majestic creatures.

Some more years later, they regretted 'letting them go'. Grandma or mother would often say, "We let too many things go fer next to nowt," and I would reply, "I wished you'd let me keep the pictures." They'd both slowly nod their heads wistfully and our minds would take us down 'memory lane'. If grandma mentioned the 'piano' it would sometimes lead to 'words' (as in the expression 'they had words' which did not quite qualify as an argument.) Grandma could not accept that there was 'no room' in our house for the piano.

(I know that mother tried to retrieve the pictures from the shop on the main road which had carried out the house clearance but the owner, a man called Irvin, said they weren't for resale and that they were adorning his hallway. Those mourned pictures had to remain 'down memory lane'. Likewise, the piano, as that had already been sold, "Going to a good home," said Irvin to mother.)

One early memory while living with my grandparents was of grandad washing his new cream Hillman Minx, registration number RVO 502. I can't remember the big, black saloon car he had before that and now he had the first non-black car in the area. It was still the only car on the street.

I also remember having an imaginary friend called 'Minnie Mun' and running from the front room to the back door with her in hot pursuit. Mum said I 'ran before I walked' and that I was 'into everything'. One of her favourite nicknames for me was 'giddy kipper'!

I can recall events, but not how we got there or how we got back. In the summer, I remember playing with my cousins in the local park. My father's eldest sister had a boy and two girls at that time. We would run about and kick a ball, then have a picnic. My dad would push we three girls one after the other on the swings.

Dad's younger brother, Bert, still lived at home with the eldest 'handicapped' son (the term used then). He remembers their annual holiday when the four of them would go on a three stage bus journey from Sheffield to the other side of Worksop to visit family. The second bus was from there to Lincoln, then a bus to Skegness. They would stay two or three days in a 'B & B' (bed and breakfast) and then come back, using the same '3-bus' system.

Bert would visit dad at his in-laws' home, then dad would return the visit back to his childhood home at least once a week, especially as it was so near to where he worked. I can't remember his mum and dad ever visiting, it was always dad on his own going there or we would visit them as a family of three.

I've no memory of moving with my parents to a home of our own and I probably just stayed with grandma while it happened. The new home was about half a mile from my grandparents' home and I can't remember ever going between the two homes by bus. We walked there and back or we were brought back in grandad's car.

The new house, classed as semi-detached, had a front, lawned garden and a shared path through a passageway. As the passageway roof was the only thing joined to the next house, it made it a semi rather than detached. The house at the other side was joined at the sides, making it, by appearance, a terraced row of houses.

The 'front' door was actually at the side of the house in the middle of the passageway. The new front room and the front (side) door were again, rarely used. In the front room was an old settee and two, unmatching, armchairs which used to be in my grandparents' front room.

Along the wall opposite the front room's fireplace, was home to my toys. This included the wooden horse on wheels which grandad had made – it's mane was still white but not so fluffy now but I loved that horse. My other toys included two pot dolls, formerly my mum's, a pram and blankets, and a growling teddy bear. Mum knitted some tiny clothes for the bear and for the dolls.

In that same room, was a big bay window with no view, save looking at a small front lawn with a border of rose trees and a high privet hedge. In the gap at the end of the passageway, there was a narrow view of the road and the houses across. They had no front garden, only a small paved area between a short wall and their front door. All the garden walls had spiky stubs where the iron railings had once been.

To the left and opposite our row of houses was a 'short cut' road towards another estate and countryside beyond, which included the local cemetery. To the right of our row was a cobbled cul-de-sac. Almost opposite the cul-de-sac was a winding road downwards towards the local infant and junior schools.

The new home's stairs were quite steep, but not as steep as my grandparents' stairs. There was a bedroom either side and a bathroom, with a toilet, down a long corridor. Up some twisting stairs was an attic. The attic was used as storage and for the TV aerial, not as interesting as my grandparents' attic.

The sitting room had a cupboard going under the stairs which acted as the pantry, next to that was the table and chairs against the side wall and at the front was an open 'Baxi' fire. Along the back wall was a sideboard. No settee, as that was in the front room, rarely used. At the other side of the fireplace and 'katy-cornered' was the new radiogram with the TV on top.

(*Despite mum and dad advocating pay in full 'at all times' for anything – except buying a house – the new radiogram was bought on credit. The credit agreement showed they paid £20 deposit with the balance payable over 29 weeks at £2 per week and one week at 10/6d. Total cost, including credit charge of £7/2/6d, was £78/10/6d. Note: average weekly wage was £15.*)

There was a 'big' chair for watching children's hour on TV. There was a different 'Watch with Mother' children's programme each afternoon. Monday was 'Picture Book', where a lady with a soothing voice said, "Are you sitting comfortably boys and girls, then I will begin…" and a story or activity unfolded. One activity was to show a tray of things and then it would be covered with a cloth. After uncovering the tray, children had to guess what item had been taken away.

On the other days of the week there were different puppet shows.

On Tuesday, the only one using glove puppets, 'Rag, Tag and Bobtail'.

Rag, was a hedgehog; Tag, a mouse and Bobtail, a rabbit. Occasionally, five cute, little baby bunnies would make an appearance and in one storyline, after playing with mud-pies, Bobtail could not get the bunnies clean again. In the end, though, the mud was washed off!

Wednesdays: 'Bill and Ben'.

Two 'flowerpot men' with face, arms and legs, one was Bill and one was Ben who lived at the bottom of a big garden. They had a sunflower (or was it a dandelion?) friend called 'Little Weed' and a tortoise called 'Slowcoach'. They used some 'made-up' words, like 'Flobbadob' (flowerpot) and 'babab lickle Weeeed' (elongating the 'ee') meaning 'bye bye little Weed' at the end of each show.

Thursdays: 'Andy Pandy'.

Andy, a marionette, appeared with his friend 'Teddy', a teddy, and 'Looby Loo', a rag doll. Andy and Teddy lived in a picnic basket. At the end of the show, a woman would say, "It's time to go home, come on Andy say bye bye" and he would wave while the woman sang "Andy is waving bye bye, bye bye." Then, "Come on Teddy say bye bye" and he would wave as she sang, "Teddy is waving bye bye, bye bye."

My favourite, though, was 'The Woodentops' on a Friday.

The 'Woodentops' were a wooden farming family with boy and girl twins, a baby, and 'the very biggest spotty dog you ever did see' called…wait for it… 'Spotty Dog'. They had a different 'farmyard' adventure each week. Such as the sheep have escaped and Spotty Dog 'saved the day' and rounded them all up.)

Back to the sitting room, next to the radiogram and TV was a small window overlooking the porch. Then a sliding door, between the sitting room and the kitchen, which lent itself to swinging back and forth on the door handles with your legs lifted. Crockery was kept in a standalone 'kitchen unit', very stylish and modern at that time. There was a small table and one chair, oven/hob, sink with cold tap and draining board. Under the sink was the usual curtained shelves. Above the sink was a small boiler for the hot water.

(Central heating, what's that?)

Washing clothes would be done in the sink and bed sheets

done in the bath. Water was squeezed out through a stand alone ringer operated by turning the handle and pulling the clothes through. The suction pads underneath the ringer were pressed onto the draining board and the water from the clothes flowed into the sink. Mother's first electric washer (top loader) had a ringer attached which folded into the machine when not in use. The ringer was still operated by hand.

It was a small washer necessitating several different washes, rinsing each wash twice, squeezing and mangling, then hanging up on the line outside. There was also the time it took to checking if dry, the bringing in and folding, and then hanging more washing out. Not forgetting the hand washing of woollens and delicates.

The back door went into a wooden and glass, enclosed 'porch'. Outside was a paved area and two doors to the left. One was the outide toilet, and the other was for coal, as there was no cellar. After the paved area was an above average long garden.

One day at the new house, my mum asked me if I would like a little brother or sister. At first I said a sister but I remember standing in front of the fireplace, changing my mind and saying, "No, I want a brother."

When I was older, mum told me that she had some morning sickness with me, but with this second pregnancy, it was morning and early evening.

The City's Public Health Department issued a list of essentials to be collected together for a home confinement (birth). Mother had saved this list which read:

2 towels and face flannel	1 large jug, 1 small jug
tape or sanitary belt	bowl, and bath for baby
clean old linen	pail

clean newspaper and brown paper	chamber
soap for mother and baby	2 medium sized pudding basins
vaseline	2 jam jars
safety pins	tin for baking dressings
needle and cotton	pan with lid
nail brush	bed and linen for mother and baby

I don't know to this day what use the jam jars would have been put to, but there was a pencil tick alongside all the items except the jam jars and vaseline. A statement was written at the bottom of the list that 'baby is NOT allowed to sleep with mother…' and a warning that if no cot or pram could be afforded, a box or drawer could be used for the newborn.

Mother also saved a booklet issued by the City's Health Department from my own birth on 'Feeding and Rearing Babies'. It seems strange to have used the word 'reared' as it conjures up thoughts of animal rearing.

On the first page, there's dietary advice for the expectant mother. "Her diet should be light and nourishing. Oatmeal porridge, pea soup, lentil soup, wholemeal bread, cocoa and plenty of milk are excellent things for her to take. She should not take unsuitable food such as pastry, new bread, pickles, pork or anything which she knows does not agree with her. She should take her meals at the usual times and not have 'snacks' in between."

The booklet gives advice on what to wear. "Warm loose clothes should be worn during pregnancy. Stays (meaning corsets) should not be worn during the later months, unless loose, or specially made, but a broad belt of flannel attached by suspenders to the stockings should be used as a support to the abdomen. In pregnancy there is a tendency for the veins of the leg to become swollen, and suspenders should be used instead of garters, because garters increase the swelling of the veins."

It was all advice not needed today apart from the wearing of warm, loose clothing.

At the section on preparing the breasts for 'suckling', it advises using a bowl/pudding basin and vaseline if the nipples are depressed. Vaseline had not been ticked on the above list because mum had already breast fed.

The booklet's next section is on 'Feeding' and states in bold 'the only safe food for every child until it is about nine months old is its mother's milk'. Underneath, 'For the first day or two the baby requires no milk, nor other food of any kind. It should be put to the breast occasionally during the first two days of no more than two minutes at a time for fear of the nipple being made sore.'

Nowadays, babies are not referred to as 'it' and the advice that a baby was not fed at all for the first two days seems really strange! This section also states, "…the giving up of breast feeding and the commencement of artificial feeding is such an important step that it should NEVER BE TAKEN EXCEPT UPON THE ADVICE OF A DOCTOR." Can you imagine going and queuing to see the GP in order to say, "can I please wean my baby?"

To completely frighten women from bottle feeding, the booklet states, "Bottle feeding at the best is a very poor substitute for breast feeding. The risks run by the bottle-fed baby may be summarised as follows:

- a liability to all kinds of digestive disturbances, which may result in impaired digestion for life;
- a liability to rickets, with deformities lasting for life;
- an increased liability to adenoids;
- a greatly increased liability to death during the first year of life from diarrhoea;
- a lack of vital resistance, causing it to succumb more easily to the various diseases which it may contract;
- interference with the proper development of both the temporary and permanent teeth, with effects lasting for life;
- liability to scurvy;
- liability to contract tuberculosis by being fed on the milk of a tuberculosis cow.

No wonder very few women bottle fed their babies, the consequences would seem very frightening, quite a few lasting for life! Even death by 'diarrhoea'!

More than likely, new mothers would breast feed for around a year in order to go straight onto bread and butter so avoiding the dreaded bottle feeding of cow's milk! Needless to say, my brother and I were breast fed for nearly a year.

What advice was there around for my grandma who breastfed my mother for two years? Her own mother, who produced milk for several years at a time, was breastfed with her nearest siblings for nearly four years which was the 'norm' for large families at that time.

The booklet continues, "Weaning. The child should be weaned about the ninth month; but it is better to avoid weaning between the middle of July and the middle of

September so the baby may escape the danger of diarrhoea."
(Presumably because of the hot (?) summer months!) The
substituted food, after weaning, is given as "… bread and
milk, or milk pudding or bread and butter."

However, at the back of the booklet, it does relent and
there's a section on bottle feeding, but only on the advice of
the doctor. It stresses that there is no advantage in 'using milk
from one cow' but it is recommended you use a 'reliable,
local dairy farm'. "A teaspoon of fruit juice is recommended
daily and a good substitute is scraped, raw swede turnip."

But, (and it's a big BUT), don't give the baby a "raw
potato, turnip or unripe fruit to suck". As if any mum would
give a baby a nice raw potato or unripe plum to suck?
Remember though, that a mum can give a baby a raw *scraped*
swede turnip as it's a good substitute for fruit juice!

Disadvantage: any teeth coming through might be
pushed back in by chomping on a raw *but scraped* turnip.
Advantage: if money's tight then mums could use the *scraped*
raw turnip over and over again, but not *unscraped* potatoes or
turnips.

However, as the baby gets older (9 to 18 months),
mothers can start introducing "mutton broth, bread and
dripping or bread fried in bacon fat" (the latter two seem
quite bizarre and totally unhealthy by today's thinking.)

On the back page is a drawing of a cot substitute, which
is a three-sided wooden box nailed to the parents' bed – at
the mother's side, of course.

I've no memory of my mother's larger stomach but one
day I went to stay with my grandparents for a few days and
when I came back, I had a little baby brother. He was 8lb 1oz
and born jaundiced so the midwife had to call a doctor.

The reason he was born 'yellow' (as in 'born jaundiced') was because mother was blood group rhesus negative and father was rhesus positive so the two incompatible blood groups 'fought' against each other in their new baby. This only affects second and subsequent children, rarely the first born. Some babies need blood transfusions but , fortunately, our new baby did not and his pallid colour disappeared.

I called my grandma, 'nannan'.

On returning home, nannan and I stood at the entrance to the living room. I held tightly onto her hand at first as I remember feeling 'funny' then mum put out her arms and I ran into them. The 'funny' feeling I later interpreted as being 'left out'. I never saw my friend 'Minnie Mun' after that.

Waiting for me in my little wooden chair (which had been my mum's little wooden chair) was a large doll with long blonde, plaited hair. She had a beautiful face, walked and talked, saying "Mama." Mum said it had been her doll and was now mine. I was excited at choosing a name for her, but mum said her name was 'Elizabeth' and 'that was that'.

I went over to the pram and introduced baby Philip to Elizabeth but he was too interested in falling asleep.

Grandad taught me to sing all the nursery rhymes before my mother taught me to read. He would record my singing on his latest 'reel to reel' tape recorder.

After about three nursery rhymes, my voice became 'chanty' and I said 'again' in an elongated tone. Grandad's voice can be heard saying, "Don't get silly." My 'normal' voice returned as I continued with 'Mary had a little lamb'. Sadly, there are no recordings of my brother singing nursery rhymes.

My mum taught me to read before I went to school and

at five I already had a long list of reading books with pencil ticks alongside. These included the 'Janet and John' books. Sadly, she had no spare time, and perhaps no patience, to do the same for my brother.

The 'Janet and John' books were about a brother and sister. On each page was a picture of a boy and a girl doing different activities, such as 'Janet and John go to the fair', 'Janet and John go on holiday', 'Janet and John visit the shops'. Words to the pictures kept being repeated; for example, 'Janet saw a puppy', 'John saw a puppy', 'Janet picked up the puppy', 'John picked up the puppy' and so on.

My first book was 'Spot and Spam', a Tom Thumb book, with a picture of a cute puppy and kitten on the hard, front cover. The front was red and the back was blue. (*I'm not sure why I'm using the past tense as I still have the book.*) The top left of the cardboard cover is chewed away, thanks to my baby brother who thought books, or anything, were 'nice and tasty'.

Spot is a male puppy and Spam is a female kitten. The first chapter 'Spot goes to Work', starts with Spam saying he is a lazy puppy and Spot accuses her of 'not doing anything' either. (*NB: when older, they could have had 'kippies' or 'puptens'!*)

In answer to Spot's accusation, Spam says she sings by the open fire to cheer people up and then chases her tail to make them laugh – that's her 'job' and she asks Spot, "What do you do?" Spot consults Peter Spaniel who says that he is not going to work, "I'm going to sail my boat."

Spot spots 'strong dog wanted' in a shop window (so he can read then!) At the address, Mr Frog (must be a grown up hence the 'Mr') says, "You're not big enough." Spot then spots Mrs Duck with a full basket of shopping. "I'll carry that for you," he says. At her home he also helps her put the things away and Mrs Duck gives him tea and iced buns. (Whoever heard of giving puppies, dog biscuits?)

Then he took Mrs Duck and her ducklings swimming. (So Mrs Duck has ducklings – were they home alone while she shopped?) Call the Duck Police.

In the duck pond, Spot looks so cute trying to swim with the little ducklings.

The next chapter is 'Spot flies a Kite', but to cut a short story shorter, Mrs Moo Cow watches Spot trying to fly a kite which sticks in a tree. Spot cries and then Spam turns up and saves the day by going up the tree for the kite. Happy Spot and happy Spam. Mrs Moo Cow gives them tea and cake.

Inside the knarled front cover, in blue shaky ink, is written, "To Jean Anne on her third Birthday with love from Mrs Dean."

Mr and Mrs Dean lived in the middle of the three terraced houses with my grandparents' house on the left and the Jones' on the right. Had the Deans grown to look like each other, over the years, or were they related? They were both the same height, same slim build and with wiry, short grey hair. Though Mrs Dean's hair was slightly longer, still wiry, but giving the appearance of being 'unkempt'. She always wore a full 'pinna' which she still wore to the corner shop.

The Dean's grown up son lived at home and never spoke or smiled. I was told, 'he didn't hear or speak and never went to school'. He now never left the house except to sit on a chair outside the back door on warm, not hot, days.

Mr Dean, senior, never left the house except to tend the garden's vegetable patch in and around the greenhouse. Hindering his plantation was the redundant Anderson air raid shelter behind his tomato glass house as it was referred to.

Mrs Dean never left the house except to go to the corner shop and to tend the garden's small flower bed just inside the garden fence. I suspected she would have still visited the shops on the main road, if only to buy clothes and the book 'Spot and Spam'.

All three families used their salutations with each other, 'mornin Mrs Dean'. The son was never called a name, so no-one knew it, but when talking about him he was referred to as 'Mrs Dean's son'. Despite the Deans and my grandparents knowing each other for some thirty years they never got onto first name terms.

The Jones were a couple not to be blessed with children and had moved in 'only recently' – if ten years can be regarded as 'recently'.

Mrs Jones was a buxom woman with big hips and a small waist. She wore pencil skirts above the knee and 'flouncy' blouses. One or two of the blouses pulled open at the bustline. Even when going into the garden or going out to the mobile grocery van, she had her customary red lipstick on and 'tottered' on her high heels. Mrs Jones did not wear a full or any sort of 'pinna'.

In the daytime, different cars could be seen parked outside their house. I was told, 'she must have a lot of brothers', which I believed at the time as both grandparents had brothers and dad had several brothers.

While shopping with Nannan, names used in conversation with other women, to describe Mrs Jones, were 'flighty piece', 'playing fast and loose' and 'shameful'. Phrases about her included, 'skirt up to her bottom' and how she 'let's the street down'. Comments were always followed by face-pulling and ' tut-tuts'. It seemed, to me, that no-one liked Mrs Jones.

Nannan and Mrs Dean would only 'pass the time of day' with her and nothing more.

My brother could not later recall either the Deans or the Jones. He has a 'faint' memory of Mrs Dean walking across the front yard and down the path to their closet.

I loved my baby brother and would stand on tip toe to see him in the large pram.

He sucked his thumb and held a little piece of cloth to go to sleep. The 'cloth' had been a little first born cotton hat. His teddy bear was small whereas mine was larger and it growled when his tummy was pressed. We loved our teddies.

One day, I remember my mum shouting hysterically. She rushed to get the bread knife and started banging on the wall, much to my bewilderment at the time. A few minutes later our neighbour came running in as my mum loudly shrilled, "He's swallowed his rattle." The neighbour started shaking him upside down and slapping his back. My mum continued to shout, "He's going blue, he's going blue." My memory of that incident stops there but he lived to tell the tale, of course.

Who needed telephones in those days when you could call up a neighbour with a bread knife! By the way, my brother hadn't swallowed the whole of his rattle but the small top bit of it, which my mum saved with our severed umbilical cords in her special 'sentimental' box. It preceded the British Standard 'Kite Mark' branding on all baby items and toys.

The neighbour and her husband, who were older than my parents, had not been blessed with children. They would call my brother by his middle name as they would have liked a son of that name.

(Note: the British Standard 'Kite Mark' was stamped on baby items and toys, to endorse that they were safe with no 'add-on' parts

and no paint with lead content. Were children born in the fifties grow up with lead and smog dependencies?

As well as lead in paint, there were school cupboards lined with asbestos and the fifties 'smog cloud' hung over cities like an umbrella!

There were no crisp, black and white photographs of the city, from that era, as the thick fog made everything look grey and blurred. The smog was at its thickest above the steelworks and factories which bellowed out a cocktail of smoke and chemicals. This 'cocktail' drifted like deadwood towards housing estates and mixed with chimney smoke and ash from thousands of real coal fires. Often, people could see particles of soot in their own homes – making the inside almost as unhealthy as the outside!)

My brother's big pram, which had been mine, often graced the paved area in the back garden for some 'fresh' air as he slept.

Grandad had made a swing where he worked. This included two steel pipes joined at the top which had two metal rings welded on. One day he and Dad sunk the pipes into two large grindstones they had dug into the ground on the lawn. A grindstone was too heavy even for one man to lift and manoeuvre, so they rolled each one from the car to the lawn. They really struggled getting them out of the car and up the step at the start of the passageway. The steel frames were painted green.

The thick swing ropes were attached to the metal rings, ready for swinging…and swinging and more swinging. At first, my brother had to be held in the swing with ropes tied to the swing ropes.

(Over the years, no matter what we did or attached to the metal poles, they did not move 'a muscle' in those grindstones, even when we both sat on the swing and swung together.)

On Saturday mornings, grandad would pick me up and take me for a 'run' in the car. This would later include my brother as he grew into a toddler.

Usually it was a run round the reservoir and then parking on the drive into where he worked. I remember in his office, swivelling on his big black chair and picking up the receiver of his big black telephone. Once I dialled some numbers and I heard it warbling in my ear. I put the 'phone down quickly and carried on swivelling but couldn't quite understand why my face felt so hot.

Grandad was allowed to ring anyone, anywhere, but he never used it for personal calls because no-one he knew, family or friends, had a telephone. Most days he would drive home for lunch, except Monday's wash day, as it was best to 'keep out of the way'.

Another time, he bought me a replica of his car and I put it down next to his own car on the work driveway. He would buy us both a little car. Phil also remembers putting both our little cars next to his car. He also remembers picking up the big black telephone receiver to listen to it, but he can't recall dialling any numbers, as I had. I suppose I was the most silly and mischievous one of us with the grown ups using my most frequent nickname of 'giddy kipper'.

By 1955, motor cars were starting to be mass produced and thereby affordable with some 3 million on the road. It was the start of the motorways and ring roads being built. Britain was becoming a smaller island as more and more people 'took to the roads'.

Unemployed Irish workers were recruited in their hundreds to build the motorway complex and received a 'fortune' of £11 per week (higher than the average wage).

When the first part of the motorway was finished, it was said to be a 'joy' to drive along – no traffic jams, no speed limit and no restrictions on parking. I wish I could remember families having picnics on the hard shoulder!

My brother's first memory could have been the Saturday morning car runs with grandad, or sitting on our horse with its fluffy mane of white hair, or even an early seaside day trip. Or even my playful 'tormenting' of him.

It was none of those! My brother's first memory was of freak winds when he was five (he must have had a late developing memory as I have memories from at least aged three.)

In the middle of the 'freak winds' night, we were woken up several times by the wind blowing down the chimney which still went through our bedroom even though no fire was there. Next morning, we looked out of the bedroom window and it didn't seem like our garden anymore. Something was different. Something was missing. Dad came in and looked out and he suddenly said, "We'er's 'shed?"

The shed had been ripped from its foundation, blown straight over a high privet hedge between the two gardens and smashed into, and destroyed, next door's greenhouse. Now exposed, where the shed had been, were dad's tools and the lawn mower. Smaller contents, such as plant pots and trowels, were strewn about.

Everything in our garden seemed flat, but what had survived was my small apple tree perhaps because it was still small and was tied to a pole. Also, surviving and standing as majestic as its very first day, was the swing in those super solid grindstones!

There was debris everywhere – other people's rubbish, roof slates, broken plant pots, tree branches, rocks all over.

Dustbins on their side and contents spewed out. We had never seen such extreme weather or what that could do.

The official reason for the freak winds which hit the city was given as 'airflow enhancements downwind of the Pennines'. The wind in the night was recorded as reaching 96 mph and smashed a lot of store windows in the city centre – the police tried to post an officer per window display. At a fur store, a policeman and a passerby kept guard. By the next day, the wind had claimed three lives and damaged over 100,000 homes, including our home with missing roof tiles and a 'lost' shed!

After mother had cleared the area around the house, Philip and I went with her to the local shops to find only one shop open for business. The rest had started a clearing up operation – there were goods, groceries and glass everywhere. Dad had gone to work, but we didn't go to school. Back in our garden, we helped pile up some of the debris for dad to sort out later.

Dad's youngest brother, aged only 13 when mum and dad married, went to his sister-in-law's wedding on the day of the freak winds. Uncle Bert's new wife, Pat, was bridesmaid. Like most weddings planned months in advance the nearby park had been chosen for the photographs. What couldn't be planned was the actual weather on the day. Contingency plans for rain were solved with a few umbrellas. Contingency plans for the freakiest and strongest winds since records had begun a hundred years ago – errr, none!

The wedding party somehow walked, linking arms was safest, from the church and across the road to the park. The only way to move forward was to bob your head down. First obstacles were bits of debris, rubbish and tree branches in the road, and flying about. In the park, which was deserted, they had to step over branches and trees to get to 'their spot' by the river. Everything was wet and they had to hold onto everything – flowers, bags, veils and small children.

After only five minutes the photographer gave up and said they would have to be taken indoors. Apart from flying objects, the photographer was not able to stand still to even take one picture.

For some reason, this experience had made Uncle Bert need cups of tea. At the wedding reception, after his eleventh cup of tea, his wife told the caterers to keep the boiling water urn switched on for him to help himself. He drank over fifty cups of tea that day. As soon as he finished one cup, he went for another. So freak winds at a wedding = a desperate longing for tea!

(Bert's National Service had been from 1956 to 1958. He was so looking forward to travelling abroad like his two brothers before him. Dad had gone to Italy and Austria and Uncle Fred had gone to Hong Kong. So, would it be Austria or Malta or Egypt or even Hong Kong? Unfortunately, he only got as far as Swindon!

Near the end of his National Service he was sent for at home. His 'handicapped' brother was ill. Bert left straight away, but sadly he had passed away before he reached home. I have no memory of this, of course.)

My parents and grandparents loved the Royal Family, and I started to take an interest in the Queen, especially her two children, Charles and Anne. At Christmas, the dinner had to be eaten and cleared away for the Queen's speech and whenever the National Anthem rang out from the radio or television, we all had to stand.

Going abroad was still reserved for the Queen travelling

to Commonweath countries and other famous people. Very few 'ordinary' people ever left the country. School holidays were still enjoyed in parks, on day trips to the seaside or a week on the coast somewhere.

By the summer's six weeks holiday, the Hillsboro' Park picnic gathering now included father's younger sister and her daughter. His eldest sister's family now included another girl. So there were five girls running about trying to avoid the two boys. One boy was the oldest and the other was the youngest boy – my brother. As we grew a bit older, we girls would play together and the two boys would do 'boy' things.

Unfortunately, the oldest cousin wasn't always there at the picnics or when we went to their house. We girls would shush Phil away, which he hated us doing. (I didn't know how much until we were older.) Sometimes he would go to mum and she would come outside and say, "Let him play with you." We would let him play with us, for a while, and then he would be banished again to the sidelines.

The Park had almost everything – a library (in the former Hillsborough Hall); a bandstand for the Whit sings' band; a café (in a portacabin); a boating lake; a playground (of course); a bowling green (for grandad), and the largest of largest areas of grass. Also, tennis courts and next to those, another smaller grassed area. It was on this smaller grassed area, below the boating lake's embankment, that the extended family would play ball and picnic.

What it didn't have was a paddling pool and nature trail.

Up the grass embankment was the large pond or lake with two islands, home to swans, ducks and geese. Dividing the pond was a metal mesh in the water to stop the rowing boats for hire going round the islands.

(In fact, at the turn of the 20th Century, there had been three islands. By the time I was a little girl walking round this pond, three had become two.)

One of my girl cousins can remember me teasing my brother and chasing after him and when I caught up, he would get tickled or I would run off with his ball. He would say, 'stop it' or 'give it back'. Mum was never around for the tormenting sessions. A favourite of mine was hiding things and then watching him look for the item. Until I said, 'let me have a look' and after a few seconds, I would say, 'here it is' and he would be thankful, my teasing forgotten.

He was so very sweet and cute. Mum refused to cut his hair and at three years old it was shoulder length. I remember mum and dad 'having words' about him needing a haircut and mum had to give in and cut his hair a bit shorter.

He still sucked his thumb, despite attempts to stop him. Mum and dad tried bribery attempts like, 'you'll get nothing for your birthday'. I whispered back to him he would still get a present, so he carried on sucking. Philip's thumb, after being sucked, was now starting to look a bit shrunken and withered, as if he had stuck it in the bath for an hour.

(That brings back a memory of grandad's thumb and first finger on his left hand being a 'dirty' brown colour from smoking. It could not be washed off. He almost chain smoked which no-one thought of as anything unusual.)

The next summer 's six week school holiday, family visits to each other's houses now included father's younger brother, Uncle Fred, who had two boys. There were three families to separately visit us and then we would visit them within the six weeks. With the two boy cousins living the nearest to us, we would see them more often. So were the tables turned with three boys and one girl? No, because I was the eldest…and 'bossiest', thus earning another nickname of 'bossy boots'.

Due to no-one in the family having a telephone, there were two ways to make any arrangements – either by going to the house or by post. As a child, I would not know of any of these arrangements so they came as a surprise. I never quite got used to family turning up in the park or on a day trip to the seaside or even during a week's holiday away. At first, I thought the aunt, uncle and cousins were 'just passing' and had joined us, but growing older brings a realisation that the 'just passing' was, in fact, a prior arrangement between the two sets of parents.

Another park, two bus rides away from home, had a paddling pool. The pool water was river water. At the point where it flowed back into the river was a little bridge and a waterfall. You could walk around this waterfall and paddle in the river as well. This park had the longest slide with an enclosed wooden 'den' at the top of the slide. Next to the playground was a picnic area with wooden benches and tables and coloured building blocks. *(The building blocks are long gone.)*

This park also had a lido (outdoor swimming pool) so if the weather was really hot, we could go in there and have a swim and throw a ball about. It was better for me if father went with us to the lido as he and I could both swim. If mother went in, which was rarely, she would just stay at the shallow end with Philip. There was also a boating lake. All activities would cease for the picnic in the afternoon.

My brother had 'sinus problems' and had to keep his ears full of cotton wool which was not conducive to swimming pool water. He suffered a lot of colds and earache. At age five he went into hospital to have his tonsils out at the Children's Hospital. It was my first time in a hospital. I was not allowed to go onto the ward and had to stay at the door, but I could see my brother. He looked so small in the big hospital bed. I forgot about that by the time we got home as I had my parents all to myself again. He has no memory of going into hospital or after. (Remember, his memory didn't develop until he was five.)

No school for the next ten weeks so he had mother all to himself at home. Although I loved school, I felt 'left out' of their daily life especially as, to me, he seemed 'better' after the first week out of hospital. And to 'top it all', mother was advised to give him lots of ice cream 'for his throat'. Sure enough, he had lots of ice cream, mainly from the ice cream man as no-one had fridges and freezers were 'unheard of'. (In hot weather any milk was kept in the sink, half full of cold water as we had no cellar.)

The tonsils-out operation was common, at that time, for any child with even a hint of sinus problems, ear infections and/or frequent colds. Although the operation was a success, mother continued to be over cautious and over protective, resulting in Philip's ears *always* being stuffed with cotton wool. This 'stuffing', or 'molly coddling', resulted in Philip having a fear of water (he was excused from school swimming lessons) and the 'no splash' rule meant that I couldn't swish water on his face either in a paddling or swimming pool. He never did learn to swim.

The expression 'wrapped in cotton wool' was made for my brother!

We both loved ice cream and most other foods we shared

a liking for but animals that I perceived as pets or baby animals, I just could not eat. I did not want to eat any rabbit so mum would say 'try it first' without telling me what it was, but I refused until she told me what it was. When she said a stew had rabbit in it, I would not even try it.

How could anyone eat lamb when they had seen cute, little lambs jumping for joy in a field? I would not, could not, eat lamb. Mum admitted, years later, that she had pretended some stews were beef stews but they had been lamb. Since that admission, I can only say that I have 'knowingly' never eaten any lamb.

The same aversion applied to duck, pheasant and venison; the latter of which I had not heard of and I have no memory of mum, or nannan, ever buying any. Pheasants were hung up outside butchers shops, with 'poor' rabbits, but I have no recollection of anyone buying a pheasant.

Mum always refused to tell me what black pudding was, even though I asked her nearly every Sunday morning when dad cooked us a full English breakfast. When I did eventually find out what it was, that was the end of my eating black pudding. Mum had known that would be the case so she had let me enjoy it for as long as possible (which I did appreciate.)

I also had a dread of bones, fish bones in particular. This led to me only wanting to eat chip shop battered, filleted fish. If I found a bone then I would push the whole fish and the batter to the side of my plate. Occasionally, mother boiled white fish but she had to chop it all up in front of me in order to show me there were no bones.

My brother shared my dislike of anything to do with tripe or sheep's brains and when mum bought either of those two for Saturday or Sunday teatime, we would sit in the other room until the 'coast was clear'. We had separate eating arrangements for those times. We had noses which could detect tripe the minute it walked into the kitchen, despite it being wrapped up in a zipped shopping bag. We could not be in the same room as tripe. Mum would hide it away in a tin at the back of the pantry until she announced it was coming out for her and Dad to eat which was the cue for Phil and I to 'disappear'.

At home or at my grandparents, my 'quirky' (to everyone else) eating habits were accommodated, but when we went out or to functions they were sometimes an issue. For example, I would not eat pressed tongue sandwiches so I tended to avoid any meat sandwiches. But there was a wedding looming…

Mother's cousin Valerie was to be married. As mother had been bridesmaid for Uncle Walt and Aunty Cath, I was asked to be bridesmaid for their daughter. There were four young bridesmaids and the maid of honour, a schoolfriend of Valerie's. I was next to the youngest at seven years.

It was a 'rainbow' wedding with the five bridesmaids all wearing different pastel colours. The dresses were net over a silk material and billowed out from our waists and we wore white ankle socks and white shoes.

Mums and the four young bridesmaids, with Valerie, had all met together some weeks earlier to try on the same white shoes in a shoe shop. Our dresses had been made for us, but mums paid for the shoes and socks. The rainbow colours were pale green, yellow, purple and I was in pink. The maid of honour wore a more 'grown-up' designed dress of pale blue. We were all given a bracelet to keep.

I had my long hair cut, like the book's cover photograph. I wanted to leave behind ribbons and headbands but as my hair grew, back came the headbands. Some even matched my home-made dress material. All the bridesmaids now had the same length hair.

The wedding church, down a side road from the main Hillsboro' shopping area, dated back to 1893. Clearly, when this church was built it would have been surrounded by trees, grass and a graveyard. The houses, shops and a network of roads now surrounded the church. Next to it was a side road and on the other corner was a chip shop. I remember coming out of the church to the smell of fish and chips wafting across in the air. It made us bridesmaids feel hungry, but we knew the photocall would be next.

The photographs of the bride and groom had to be taken on the church steps as they led straight onto the pavement. The photo' with the bridesmaids was too wide for the steps so we lined up on the pavement. Two members of the family stopped what little traffic there might be and the photographer took the rest of the pictures from the middle of the road.

Of course, photographs at that time were all black and white so the rainbow colours had to stay in our memories. Dad took some impromptu photographs and one shows me smiling into the camera, every inch a bridesmaid, and in the background is a very bored little brother in a new shirt and short trousers.

The 'wedding breakfast' (it was never at breakfast time) or reception was at the bride's parents' home. Fortunately, there were no tongue sandwiches! I really enjoyed being a bridesmaid and all the attention it brought.

I loved staying at my grandparents' home as I got all their attention. I helped grandma with her chores (which were not chores to me), like holding the washing as it came out flat through the mangle and folding the dried clothes, setting the table for lunch or tea, dusting or fetching things from the cellarhead. I liked going shopping with her as she took her time and looked at everything and talked to everyone, including complete strangers.

By the time 'cheerio' was said they seemed like lifelong friends, but they would never arrange to meet. If the chatting took place in the city centre there would be no hope of ever 'bumping' into each other again.

Going into the city centre would mean a bus ride and more conversations like:

"Eyup, bit nesh today innit?"

"Aye, 'ad to put me cardy under 'coat,"

"So did ah – bus's full,"

"Aye dun't know we'er they're all comin' from,"

"Naw sales on, is the'er?"

"Not thar ah know on,"

"Is she yer grandaughter?"

"Aye, she helps me shop,"

"How o'd is she?"

"Jus' eight,"

"Ah, whar' a luv'ly age, ah've none yet," *(meaning grandchildren.)*

"How many yer got?" *(meaning children.)*

"Jus' three, all workin' naw,"

"Still 'ard to mek ends meet tho',"

"Aye. Oh this's my stop, bye,"

"Sithee."

('Eyup' is a greeting; 'nesh' is cold; 'ah' is I; 'aye' is yes; 'naw' is no; 'sithee' is see you.)

One day, my grandma and I were looking round the 'rag and tag' (open air) market. I once saw a lady lifting material through the bottom of her shopping bag which must have had a false bottom. I said in a whisper to grandma, "That lady's putting stuff in her shopping bag she's not paid for." Grandma 'shushed' me and took me away from the stall, obviously not wanting to 'get involved'. At the time I was disappointed as I thought she would alert the stall holder.

Women with children, and older women, walked about with 'turbans' on their head and at the front, curlers poked out. Shopping on a Saturday increased the number of headscarved women, and some would dispense with the turbans or scarves, just leaving a head of curlers 'on show'. They looked like 'Hilda Ogden' in the day and transformed into 'Elsie Tanner' at night.

(Hilda Ogden was a character from Coronation St who used to walk about with a headscarf and rollers jutting out at the front. Elsie Tanner was always heavily made up and wore short pencil skirts in the programme, whether it was day or night. (A bit like Mrs Jones!) Hilda was portrayed as a poor, downtrodden housewife and Elsie was supposed to be 'brassy'!)

Mum and grandma never went out with curlers in. They sometimes wore a hat or headscarf, but there was just hair underneath. The fact that they didn't frequent public houses may have had something to do with it, or they thought themselves 'one rung' on the ladder above the 'working class'? *(Well, neither of them worked!)*

At the other end of the city centre from the 'rag and tag' was the family run, large department store Atkinsons, now rebuilt to its former glory with both a waitress service restaurant and a self service one. Grandma would take me into the waitress restaurant and tell me stories from her life and from World War Two.

Some of the stories were repeats and I would endure, good humouredly, a 'running' commentary on which stores had been bombed and rebuilt and how grandma's favourite theatre had caught fire and had been demolished. I found it hard to believe that such large buildings could collapse to rubble in the 'blink of an eye'.

A surviving theatre, the Lyceum, had a pantomime each Christmas and a very early memory of mine was being taken to see Peter Pan. I remember Peter and Wendy flying across the audience on 'ropes'.

(Later productions of Peter Pan at the same, but refurbished, Lyceum Theatre, did not involve any flying across the audience – health and safety? Even so, it was still an enchanting production.)

On High Street there was a policeman (always a male) on traffic duty in the middle of the road and every few minutes he would stop the traffic and from each side of the road would walk a large throng of people. Then they all got mixed up in the middle and then separated again as they went on their way. My brother and I called this the 'charge of the light brigade'. After crossing, we would stand back and wait for the next people's crossing as we liked to see the policeman completely disappear in amongst the crowd, then miraculously reappear unscathed as the one throng became two again.

(Note: joining the police service was a career rather than a job. However, a policewoman would be expected to leave just before having a baby (still no maternity leave.) A woman could not go higher than the rank of superintendent – the ranks were constable, sergeant,

inspector, chief inspector, superintendent, chief super'; assistant(s), deputy and then chief constable. Unless a woman did not marry then it was extremely rare to find a woman reach a higher rank than Sergeant. If a woman got married, it seemed to turn her police career into a job while she 'waited' until she had a baby and left.)

In towns and cities, there would always be policemen on traffic duty, some were provided with a small square of poles to protect them in the middle of traffic. Also at traffic 'bottlenecks' there would be a policeman on 'point' duty.

In the six weeks holiday, mum and nannan would take us on a long bus ride to Chesterfield and in the town centre's main road there would be a policeman in a white coat and wearing large, white gloves. He would wave his arms about, swinging and pointing, making no sense to me, but thankfully making sense to the car drivers.

Chesterfield has a sprawling open air market with a compact area of shops, including a large department store with a café-cum-canteen where we would have a cooked dinner at lunchtime. I particularly remember Boots on the corner of the market square as it had high counters and everything seemed to be in a dark wood, incuding the walls and floors. It had a steep wooden staircase to the left of the entrance.

As the bus neared the town, Phil and I played at 'who can see the crooked spire first'.

(Chesterfield is a medieval market town in North Derbyshire, about 14 miles from Sheffield city centre. The 14th Century St Mary's & All Saints Church boasts a crooked spire, some 228 feet high, and is a well known and highly visible landmark in the area. It also attracts tourists from up and down the country, including Sheffielders! In the churchyard is the town's first gas lamp dating back to 1824. In the sixties, the town's population stood at over 70,000 and the *surrounding area was predominantly involved with coal mining.)*

When we went on our summer holiday to Blackpool, we would play a similar game of 'who would be first to spot the tower'. Phil and I were told when to start looking out for it. That would increase our holiday excitement, ten fold, necessitating a toilet stop.

The first time I went on a train was for dad's annual 'works do' on a day trip to Blackpool, which was the only time we went to the seaside without our grandparents.

We would sit in the seats with a table so that we could play cards. We hardly saw dad as he was up and down the train talking to work mates or 'muckers' as they referred to each other. He was social secretary so he organised a raffle with prizes and there was a prize for the first child to spot Blackpool Tower.

I won the competition one year, shrieking, "IT'S THERE!" But, I didn't get the prize as a few people, in good humour, shouted 'fix' and so it went to the next child. Dad said to me that it was only because I had shouted 'at the top of my voice' that it appeared I was first. (I did remember that I had made all those sitting around me jump like frogs with Phil leaping sideways on top of mother.)

We always enjoyed the day, sitting on the sands with his best 'mucker', a guy nicknamed 'Bunny' and his family. Later when walking down the promenade, looking for a prize bingo and hot dogs (in that order), dad would have to say, every few steps, 'eyup' to people he knew as we passed them. When walking back to the station it seemed like we had joined the longest queue of weary-looking 'muckers', some with 'kiss me quick' hats on. Dirty faced children would be eating candy floss or a toffee apple. We would be licking a

'Mr Whippy' and splashing blobs of ice cream down the front of our, already soiled, tee-shirts.

Twice a year we would go on holiday for a week to the seaside. That is, the six of us in grandad's new cream coloured car. It was brand new and he had to have a notice on the back window which said 'running in, please pass'. For a certain number of miles all new cars had to be driven slowly. There was no 'honking' from other drivers at going so slow as it was totally accepted, in the same way as going slow behind a tractor or learner driver.

The front was a continuous seat and my brother, as the smallest, sat in the middle as the gearstick was on the steering wheel. I sat in the middle of nannan and mum in the back seat. The 'clunk-click' of seat belts was still a generation away. Four gallons of petrol could be bought for a pound!

Grandad would fit a roof rack on the car before each week's holiday and then strap in our brown holiday suitcases. Our first week's holiday was to Great Yarmouth in Norfolk.

Did the Queen and her family travel by car or did they use the Royal Train to visit Sandringham near the Norfolk coast? The Queen and Prince Philip, in their role as young parents, would take Charles and Anne on the sands in one of the school holidays. This was unknown to the public at the time but what child doesn't like the sand and the sea? Home cine-films from that time show a young Charles and Anne paddling in the sea and being buried in the sand by their parents. Their corgis are also running about.

What was out of camera shot were the bodyguards keeping an 'out of sight, out of mind' distance.

(The Sandringham Estate has been the private home of four generations of British monarchs since 1862 when Queen Victoria

bought it for the Prince of Wales at age 21. The gardens have been open to the public since 1908 and the museum since 1930 for a charge of 3d. The Estate is well known for its apples and apple juice produced in the orchards planted by King George V. The aim of the Estate is to be self sufficient and is run like a Country Park.)

Did Charles and Anne play travel games? One favourite travel game for the two of us was writing down a list of car registration numbers. When we got to our destination we would count them up and the one with the most was the winner. A list of registration numbers, at that time, looked like:

Car Numbers

390 WB	410 TWJ
962 WB	582 DPW
955 PFC	918 EWW
5697 VX	90 DPB
447 LOV	9776 WA
753 AWJ	ANN 740
1175 WE	63 CWA
828 LWJ	194 WE
750 W	GHK 545
922 BWA	ETU 206
638 XET	

('W' was the letter for 'Yorkshire' cars)

Usually, after the first toilet stop, Phil would join me on the back seat and we would both kneel facing the back of the car to write down the registration numbers or play 'I-spy'. Mum and nannan would be either side of us, almost sideways to fit us both in the back.

The fifties was the first decade to set the tradition for a week's annual holiday.

In the north this was always the first week of the six week holiday, known as 'works week'. I didn't realise at the time how lucky we were to go on two separate week's holidays – one week in Great Yarmouth and one week in Blackpool – and to travel by car.

Blackpool had it all – pleasure beach; miles of sand; piers; theatres starring 'big names'; iconic tower with circus and ballroom; illuminations, and all the fun of the fair along the golden mile from the tower to the pleasure beach.

Along this golden mile were pubs, bars, variety clubs and theatres, slot machine arcades, prize bingo, cafes, restaurants and stalls selling gifts and novelties, candy floss, Blackpool rock and fast food. There were twelve piers, most with a theatre, cafes, amusements and Gypsy Rose Lee who would tell your fortune or guess your age.

Through the summer season there were millions of visitors pouring into Blackpool. Weekly trains were packed with over 4000 excited holiday makers with their straw hats and brown cases and children playing at 'who's going to see the tower first' as the train got nearer to their destination. As well as train passengers there were people in cars in bumper to bumper traffic winding back for miles, in the same queue as the packed charabancs. Most cars had roof racks loaded up with the brown cases and leather belted across.

The pleasure beach had a glass showcase with an adult clown and a child clown inside, both laughing so heartily with their heads bobbing forwards, that people walking passed were infected with laughter. The more you gazed, the more you laughed. Some people cried with laughter and had to hold their stomachs, it was so funny.

Miles away on the east coast of Norfolk, the same sort of

thing was happening, just inside Yarmouth's pleasure beach. This time, it was a laughing policeman inside a glass showcase on a raised plinth. He laughed with his hands on his stomach and made loud, guffawing noises. The policeman laughing was so infectious people would be bent over giggling, tears streaming down their faces. You were laughing so much you had to walk away to get control again and ease your aching stomach muscles. Once, mum had to rush off to the toilet – I wonder why?

In the pleasure beach amusements was a laughing sailor. A penny in the slot and there was a minute's worth of laughter from a loud speaker and the grinning sailor going from side to side.

One of the highlights of each holiday was the nonstop laughing at these figures and that rush of happiness which stayed with you for the rest of the night.

We had a later week in Blackpool. The family tradition of having a photograph with Blackpool Tower in the background continued with a picture of me on the sands in between mum and dad.

Our family would hire two deckchairs (for mum and nannan) and the rest of us would sit on either the sand or a stretched out car rug. Your 'own space' on the sand was mapped out by deck chairs and the bath towel or rug ('windbreakers' not yet in use.) Our sandcastles had to be mapped out to ensure that our 'own space' included sand to the front of the seating area. As a general rule, different families' towels could not touch and a short gap for walking through was normally left. I remember the sands of both resorts being packed right up to the wet sand and the sea.

Children would change immediately into swimming

costumes but the adults would remain fully dressed. Nannan would even leave her stockings on but mum would take her's off. Dad would leave his tie on, but grandad would take his off. Grandad always wore his light grey suit with an open necked white shirt and on his head a white handkerchief with four knots at each corner. Dad would wear a trilby hat while the ladies donned headscarves.

The same 'ritual' would be repeated, in various guises, up and down the beach.

Getting fully wet in the sea, riding a donkey and having an ice cream were obligatory for children. Before dad and grandad wandered off the sands (for a 'walk' but it was really for a drink, grandad to buy cigarettes and then playing prize bingo) they would help Phil and I make a large car in the sand so that we could sit side by side and pretend to drive it about. Pebbles were the car lights and our bucket the steering wheel.

When bored of that, we would build a sandcastle with a moat around it. The moat needed water so we would troop off to the sea, fill up our buckets, come back and pour into the moat. Several trips later, the moat was no fuller than after the first bucket, but it was all good fun and passed the time until dad and grandad came back. It would then be ball or frisbee throwing time (our frisbee was in fact a rubber ring, real rubber that is, painted different colours.) Playing any throwing games had to be done nearer the sea where the 'towel touching' finished.

At least once during each week's holiday we would go into a café and have 'proper' desserts or milkshakes. Phil and I would normally choose a milkshake each. The ladies would be treated to a knickerbockerglory which would cost 2/6d (75p) but due to the expense, they shared it. The chaps, if they came in with us, would not buy anything for themselves as they would be saving their 'pennies' for a pint of beer and more prize bingo.

When winning a line or four corners, a ticket was handed to the bingo winner. On the last night, grandad would take us to each bingo game where he had won tickets and saved them up for better prizes. Each holiday we would go back with a car boot 'full' of prizes, such as matching pillowcases, tablecloths, table mat sets, flasks, children's game for us, set of crockery or glasses, kitchen bowls and vases; to name a few which he won over the years – not all in the same week!

Around this time, mum started entering me in the 'Holiday Princess' beauty competition for girls up to age 15. Heats for different age groups were held in the City Hall and then those through to the final would get a free day at Cleethorpes on a coach. I always got through to the final.

Although wearing a swimsuit was optional almost all the girls wore one. One year, a girl in my age group actually came fourth wearing a flared skirt and blouse with white, net gloves, which mirrored a grown woman's fashion outfit. I came third that year which was my 'best' year with the number '296'.

I was pictured in the local newspaper with other contestants with the words, "And their costumes never got wet…this glamorous line up brought a breath of summer to the City Hall last night when they took part in the preliminary heats for the Cleethorpes Holiday Princess competition. They were among 250 girls going to the final."

The following year, a photograph made the local paper of me in a line-up of girls as we were about to get onto the coach to the seaside. I came fourth in a deep pink and white swimsuit with a short, flared 'skirt' and it tied behind my neck. Back home there was a photo call of me posing in the local paddling pool with my number '20' card. I came fourth again the following year with the number '150'.

Winning the top spot always eluding me!

My dad's boredom level at these finals, on the scale of 1 to 10 (10 being the most bored), was about 12. My brother's boredom level on the same scale was 102. The two of them normally leaving us 'to it', opting to go for a walk on the sea front or in amusement arcades.

My parents must have loved entering me in competitions so much that, one year, I was also entered in a talent contest at Yarmouth. I sung 'Around the World' and kept repeating the verse and the chorus until the commentator had to say, "Thank you and everyone clap, well done," and I stopped in mid-verse. I walked off with a very red face as I now realised why Mum was throwing her arms around in the front row to try and stop me singing. I didn't win, what a surprise!

The year after, a lot wiser and with a new song, I was entered again. This time I sung Doris Day's hit song, 'Que Sera Sera'. I sung the first verses with the chorus in between and stopped. I got a special mention in the children's category as a 'promising' singer. That was the start...and the end of my singing 'career'!

The following year, I did not want to enter as I remembered the laughter level of my brother, on the scale of 1 to 10, being 501 and he giggled the whole way through. Luckily, for me, he has no memory of it.

Generally, I have happy memories of those holidays, carefree days now long gone. There were no 'ring roads', only 'bottle necks' at each town, but when you stopped, you could park anywhere. As soon as we got to Yarmouth we begged (tormented, more like) to go on our favourite ride called the 'Snails' in 'Joyland'. It is a mini 'roller coaster' and one year, another 'up and down' hill had been added, much to our delight.

Some years, we would be taken straight on the Snails by dad or grandad and then on the sands. In the evening, it was on the Snails once again and each day after that.

('Joyland' was, and still is, a small children's funfair at the opposite end to the pleasure beach. As well as the Snails 'roller coaster' ride there was a Noah's Ark which was reached by a long flight of steps as the Ark appeared to be on the high seas. Inside were small animals, snakes, lizards and fish, and on the way out, you were given a small, wrapped present. There was a 'fast', circular car ride and a ride which went uphill and then twisted and turned downwards again. There was also a 'hook a duck' stall and a 'hoopla' stall at which you won a 'prize every time'. The prize was a plastic gun, a small bear, a balloon or a tub of bubbles. It was exciting to win at the time, but to an adult it was just a cheap, plastic novelty.)

One year, I had a new pyjama set which I loved and thought it was far too nice to wear just in bed. It was a white top with puffed sleeves and blue dots with the bottoms in blue with frills round the ankle hem. I 'nagged' my parents into letting me keep the pyjamas on outside and I was allowed to wear them for the morning. My dad took a picture of me wearing them, stood in front of grandad's car. I wore them for our first ride of the day on the Snails, unbeknown to everyone else, that I was still wearing pyjamas.

On the beach, dad or grandad helped make the obligatory large car in the sand. There's a picture of most years' sand cars in the family album.

At the end of the holiday, grandad would load sand into a large tin container to take back with us. Fresh sand for our sand pit kept in the porch. We played on a large wooden deck and when we were finished, mum would sweep the sand back into the container. As the sand pit was in the porch we could make sandcastles in any weather!

I have a scary memory from Yarmouth. My brother and I were wearing new yellow sweaters and tartan trousers (mum sometimes dressed us alike for reasons which still escape us) and we were walking along the promenade at dusk. Suddenly, hundreds of flies came from 'nowhere' and found a home on our yellow tops. Flies love yellow, which was unknown to us at the time. It was very scary and we had to take the sweaters off to get rid of the flies. We did not wear them outdoors again.

We went to the same guest house every year and the owners had a girl called Susan, who was a bit older than me. Mr and Mrs Reeves made a big fuss when we arrived and seemed sorry to see us go, but we were never invited into their living room at the back. Years later, they told us they were moving and didn't know if they would be running a guest house.

The following year we found another B&B but the detective sleuths, mother and grandma, tracked down where our former hosts had moved to. It was a posh looking, larger guest house. I remember them both being very hurt that we hadn't been welcome at their new place and it made them feel very 'working class' and northern. We never went in their new guest house.

In another seaside resort, Skegness, there was our favourite paddling pool with channels that meandered around in different shapes. It had a little stone bridge to go over or under it, with a large fountain as one of the channels opened up in the centre. The paddling pool water was sea water.

(The paddling pool is still there, but the little bridge over it became a casualty of 'health and safety'. The water is no longer from the sea and is chlorinated.)

Paddling pools in other seaside resorts are very 'ordinary' and 'run of the mill' compared to the Skegness one.

Before policemen had two-way radios, there were telephones in metal 'boxes' positioned at the top of poles which were at adult chest height. These 'phone stations' were located on pavements at the side of most roads and, if I remember correctly, displayed the words 'emergency use only'. There were also these 'phones behind a small door on the outside of police boxes.

We were walking back to the car at Skegness when I stopped at one of these 'phone stations'. Mum, who knew I liked to 'touch everything' warned me, in advance, not to touch it. But my curiosity far outweighed her warning. I opened the small door and a loud alarm was triggered. I quickly shut the door but the alarm kept beeping LOUDLY. I moved my hand away as if it was a red hot poker and stood dumb-struck.

People around us stopped what they were doing and looked over. Nearby cars stopped and people peered out. The alarm continued… alarming everyone. Mum and dad ushered us quickly on our way. An agitated dad, gruffly said, "Come on, hurry up." Phil and I looked back at the mayhem as we continued to walk briskly.

By the time we reached the car, luckily for me, mum and

dad saw the funny side of it and we all laughed. We stopped and listened and the alarm could still be heard in the distance which made us laugh again. Oh dear, another funny story to add to the growing list of mum's repertoire of her daughter's funny 'mishap' stories!

At Mablethorpe, a family member owned the chalet park and when we went for a holiday there, we stayed with them. At the time, I thought I would rather have a chalet to ourselves, but sleeping in bunk beds was fun – my brother and I took it in turns to sleep in the top bunk. He must have been five by then as he can remember the bunk beds, not the holiday, just the bunk beds!

We would visit the local park with a picnic hamper, balls and bats. Dad's sister, husband and our cousins would appear, from nowhere, and we would all play together and then picnic together. Unbeknown to us, the meeting had been pre-arranged, of course.

They would also come and visit us at home in the summer, travelling on two buses. I remember sitting on a small wall in our garden with the boy and the two girls, reading magazines. They thought it was great that we had a swing outside and a sand pit 'inside'. When I got my doll's house, it was brought outside on a small table and we girls would play with that.

We would visit them in the summer, on two buses. They hadn't got a very big garden so we would normally stay inside, drawing in the kitchen or playing a game.

At home, I have happy memories of playing in our long garden. In the glass porch we played with the 'Yarmouth' sand pit. Outside was a flagged area with a washing pole and line, then the bin, then two steps onto the lawn. There was a shared path down the middle of our garden and next door's.

(*My couple of memories of the big freeze of 1963 was dad standing on a stool with a long brush swiping snow from the glass porch's roof. And, sledging on our new home-made sledge. This was the worst winter for 200 years, lasting from Boxing Day to March 1963.*)

Behind our swing were two flower beds, one mine and one my brother's. Mum bought us packets of flower seeds each year to plant and to watch them grow. Phil and I would ask our parents who's garden was the best and they would reply, "They're both lovely." Secretly, I always thought mine was better – the flowers were spaced better and I had put seaside shells and pebbles in between. Along the front row of both beds were dancing, multi coloured flowers called Virginia Stocks.

Behind our two beds was a horse shoe rockery, my mum's pride and joy, but the inside was a house to Phil and I. Behind that were vegetable patches, my dad's pride and joy, alongside the shed. Our hiding places included behind the shed and underneath a big tree with overhanging branches at the bottom of the garden. That was our 'secret' den.

There were two sisters who went to our school, living at the other side of the wall, but their garden was just a flower bed and flagged stones. We sometimes talked over the wall. It was very rare that either one of us would climb over the wall into each other's garden.

Dad grew mint in his vegetable patch for mum to put in the Sunday roast. We would pick a piece of mint each and smell it until there was no more smell to smell. I didn't like the taste of mint but I liked its smell. I always said that I liked the hole bit in a polo mint but didn't like the sweet around it. I didn't know until years later that grandad didn't like the taste of mint either.

I have happy memories of my brother and I playing with the sand, splashing in a blow-up paddling pool, swinging on our swing, playing with our toys and playing at 'house' with my dolls and his doll. He was bought a boy doll wearing blue shorts and a white tee-shirt, which is an embarrassing memory for him now! Also, we loved playing Cowboys and Indians with a tent (a sheet over two chairs) as our home.

We had 'real' guns – silver ones where caps were inserted and when the trigger was pulled it went 'bang' and gunpowder smoke would rise from the spent cap. We loved the smell of the cap smoke. We played with a gun each, and on shooting each other, our noses would go straight to the cap to smell the aroma. In a 'real' gunfight we would carry on playing – one of us falling down 'shot', our body twitching and jerking and then lying still to appear 'dead'.

On the sitting room table we would play at 'farm' with small animals and cars. We had houses and tractors and a road network was made from playing cards. There were car crashes and high winds and road works and escaped farm animals.

An Aunty bought Philip a toy drum and a xylophone and they practiced a duet to play for us when they got back from the toy shop. Dad tried to cover up that he was covering his ears from the rather shrill noise. I was trying to cover up, and it was a huge effort, my laughter from the plonk plonk of the stick on the coloured metal. My Aunty was loving every minute of it and she became his favourite Aunt.

Meanwhile, a Royal Aunty was taking a little Prince to a toy shop in London. He was bought a tin trumpet and toy xylophone. Back at the Palace, they 'played' a duet for the family. Prince Charles became a great 'fan' of Aunt Margot.

Mum said that one of the few funny incidents which involved my brother was when they were walking down a road with a bend in it. She led him by the hand to cross the road, saying, "Let's cross here and cut the corner off." A little voice piped up, "Have we some scissors then?" He wondered why mum had to turn round and go straight back home due to laughing so much she had had a little 'incident' of her own. While rushing home he said in breathless gasps, "Are we going back for some scissors?" More laughing and mum said she could have 'rung out' her underwear by the time she reached the house!

When we were a bit older, mum and dad bought us a table tennis set which we played with the table's extensions out. The dining table instantly converted into almost a full length table tennis table.

We loved watching television and we could both now sit in the 'big chair' and watch children's shows like 'Sooty'. We would run and get our puppets – I had Sooty and Philip would 'wear' Sweep. As a general rule, Phil was more interested in the advertisements and their 'jingling' songs and tunes.

(The second channel, ATV, had advertisements in between television programmes. The very first two adverts were filmed to go 'on air' and there was strong competition and betting on which advert would be the first one ever. There were two contenders. The first, 'Gibbs SR' toothpaste, showed a tube of its toothpaste in a block of ice. This had been difficult to film as the ice had started to melt in front of the lights. The second advert featured two men singing the Batchelors' wonderful peas song. 'Gibbs SR' won!)

Dad had built a small brick wall especially for my doll's house to rest on outside. I had a little chair to sit on and play with it. My favourite large doll, Elizabeth, would play alongside me. Phil would be swinging or playing ball on the grass.

The local newspaper ran an 'Adettes' column which was for children's advertisements. My parents put an ad in as if it was from me when I was aged eight, 'WANTED large pedal car for my little brother, for a birthday present'. The ad worked. We both loved that second hand, red pedal car.

I have an unhappy memory of me, for some reason which escapes everyone (including myself), swinging on the washing line with my feet behind me in the air. Can you guess what happened next? The line snapped and I catapulted, but in a weird, slow motion way onto the flagged stones on my knee caps. Very, very painful and very, very bloody. I cried buckets and my knees got their very first scars.

Another painful memory was me on my scooter going round the nearby corner, on the pavement of a road with a slight incline. I can remember going so fast, the wind in my hair, feeling good…and then…I was down on the path. My knees were scraped and my left hand's skin hanging off with dirt and gravel on the raw, bleeding hand. I cried and was having difficulty walking and pushing my scooter. Philip came to the rescue and pushed both scooters back home.

My hand was put in warm water which hurt even more. The skin on my hand grew back over a couple of darker patches as if some gravel had healed into the hand. And, more scars for my knee caps!

A deeply embarrassing memory emerged from my desire to see my mum with no clothes on. I had only ever seen her in a nightie and in an underneath skirt over her underwear. I had never seen any pictures of a bare woman, or a bare man of course, but I wanted to see what I would look like when I became a woman.

In the bathroom, propped up on the back wall, was our old, redundant tin bath. This tin bath was overturned towards the wall. I had an idea! If I curled up behind the tin bath I could see what mum looked like without any clothes on, by peering out from behind the tin bath when she was bare.

What I hadn't thought through was how long I might have to be curled up and cramped behind the tin bath. Or, how I could peer round it but staying invisible only two feet away from mum.

One early Friday evening, I saw that my mum was gathering a clean nightie, clean knickers and a bath towel to go for her bath. Now was my chance to get into the bathroom and in position. I was sat with my knees drawn up against my chest and my feet on the inside of the tin bath to keep it in place.

Mum came into the bathroom and I could 'sense', as I daren't look, that she was checking the water and taking off her clothes. She turned off the water. She got in. Mum started splashing about, presumably washing, and then it went silent. I dare not breathe and I certainly daren't look.

What was I going to do? I was only five minutes into what was rapidly turning into an anus oribilus. I felt my feet 'twitching' with early cramp pains as they rested rigidly on the inside of the bath. My legs were already aching against my chest, after what seemed like half an hour but must have only been minutes. How long could I stay like this?

I started to think that not moving for any length of time would 'lock' my bones together and make me doomed to spend the rest of my life in this hideous foetus position. The future looked bleak – I would have to be rolled about and be force fed.

The steam in the bathroom was making me feel very sick and dizzy. What was I thinking of to get myself into this ridiculous predicament.

Yet without another thought, I suddenly popped up from my hiding place, shouted sorry, and rushed out. Mum let out an elongated scream. It lasted until I got to the bedroom and 'bomb dived' onto my bed.

I could hear dad 'belting' up the stairs. "Are you alright?" he shouted, still running towards the bathroom. She said in a shrill voice, "Jean was hiding in 'ere." I could hear him exclaim, "What?"

A hole in the ground was needed, NOW! Or the bed to suck me into its mattress.

Dad came into the bedroom, "What do yer think you were doin' in there?"

I could hardly lift my head up to reply, and in a feeble voice I said that I had hidden as a joke, not realising that mum would be coming in to have a bath, (I lied.) I said I was sorry (which I was, as I had frightened and upset mum) and dad said to me, "Well, don't do it again." *Believe me*, I had no intention of doing it ever again!

Why did I care what mum looked like without her clothes, and now, I didn't care at all.

I started reading on the bed without any of the words making sense. My face red and stinging with the embarrassment.

After the bath, mum came into the bedroom to me and

said I was a 'silly kipper' and I was to come downstairs. Everything was alright again.

Philip asked me at bedtime what mum was like without any clothes. I said I hadn't seen anything in my rush to get out, which was true.

The whole 'pantomime' had been in vain. After a few days, mum saw the funny side of it, but it wasn't a story she ever repeated (thankfully.)

I have a 'pride and joy' memory. I planted some apple pips and one started growing and kept growing. Mum eventually planted the seedling in the garden and it kept growing into a small apple tree. She grafted a branch onto it from next door's fully grown apple tree (while they were away on holiday.) My mum said it would turn the fruit into eating apples rather than be sour cooking ones. The grafting worked and the small tree, tied to a pole, survived the freak '500' mph gale force wind storm that followed.

(In years to come, it started producing tiny, tiny apples which were edible…and sweet.)

I have an embarrassing memory (though not in the same league as the 'tin bath incident') of reading my weekly girl's magazine 'June' and finding that my photograph was printed in it. A smiling picture of myself had been chosen as that week's 'June Rose' with six other birthday girls, called 'Rosebuds'. Mum had sent it to the magazine, she said, never expecting it to be printed. Well, it was! I never knew so many of my school friends read that magazine – 'everyone' seemed to have seen it, even my form teacher.

However, the prize was an iced cake and eight volumes of a 'Books of Knowledge' encyclopaedia set so it was worth the embarrassment, I suppose.

(I still have a copy of the magazine and the Books of Knowledge. In fact, on Coronation Street, in Ken Barlow's living room there was an exact set of books in a glass cabinet. Maybe someone who designed the 'Corrie' set had a sister or daughter who was a 'June Rose' and their prize was 'donated' to the set? Just a thought.)

At night, the 'big chair' was dad's chair to watch 'Corrie', but while Philip and I watched 'Children's Hour' on the television the big chair was 'our's'. The chair had large arms with a gap between the arm and the chair's cushion. We would also sit with our legs through the arms, one either side, and pretend that we were driving in a car. That was our 'indoor' pedal car.

Traditionally, settees were in the unheated front room instead of in front of the television.

We now watched 'Blue Peter' with it's 'Barnacle Bill' theme tune. This had started in 1958, originally for children between five and eight years. The first presenters we remember were Peter Purves, John Noakes and Valerie Singleton. Peter was very much the 'lead' host with John being the 'daredevil', attempting different, outdoor activities. Valerie tended to stay in the studio and show us how to make things out of household items such as empty, plastic washing up containers. As time was short, when she had to go onto the next stage she would produce one already made and glued, saying "Here's one I made earlier."

(It became a new 'cathphrase' when anyone hadn't a lot of time, for example on cooking programmes. After a dish was prepared, it would be put into the oven and then the chef host would produce the ready cooked dish saying 'here's one I cooked earlier'.)

The first 'Blue Peter' pet dog was like having a dog ourselves and he was called 'Petra'. Her puppy, 'Patch', also featured on the show. Phil asked if he could have a puppy. (Remember when I had asked for a puppy I was given a budgie!)

'Blue Peter's next pet was a tortoise which must have given mum an idea. Phil was given a pet tortoise but it wasn't the same as a puppy. However, it was slightly more fun than a budgie! Of course, you still couldn't take a tortoise for a walk in the park – unless you had a whole day to spare!

At the start of our favourite game show, a voice would sound: "It's Friday, it's five to five, and it's Crackerjack!" We would rush to get comfy in our big chair.

Leslie Crowther, the host, would ask three children questions and if the right answer was given, they got a present to hold. Another question right, another present. If a question was answered incorrectly, the child was given a cabbage. Contestants were allowed to have two cabbages but a third wrong answer meant you were out of the game. Also, if a present was dropped, it was lost, and a cabbage replaced it. Were they allowed to keep the cabbages?

(Such endless, innocent fun…and not a game boy or computer in sight!)

As young children, the year 2000 seemed so distant and futuristic. We had thought by then, that cars would be flying above motorways rather than running on the road.

If someone had said 'microchip', we might have thought it was a new sort of smaller chip from the chip shop. And, who could have imagined that the public telephone boxes would ever have anything in them except the mysterious (to us) push buttons 'A' and 'B'. Or even more far fetched that people would not need to use public telephones.

(Using a computer at work or at home, or walking about with a

wireless telephone – what's one of those – were things associated with science fiction and 'Dr Who'.)

For the record, 'Dr Who' first aired in 1963 with a Doctor, from another world, who time travelled in a blue police telephone box, the 'Tardis'. The early series featured his grandaughter. Dr Who was an instant hit with Phil and myself, but when an episode involved the Daleks, I would watch through my hands and a little boy would keep popping up from behind the settee.

Meanwhile, 'back on earth', I could now read most books and started to look through my parents' weekly newspapers, 'Weekend' and 'Weekly News'.

My parents must have so loved seeing the embarrassment and shock on my face when I saw my picture in 'June', that they repeated it a few years later. This time, sending a photo of myself to 'Weekend' for its 'Pleased to meet you' column.

On Saturdays, the 'Weekend' magazine 'appeared' and I always had a look through it around tea time. I would look at the inside page first, where the column appeared. However, on this occasion I flicked through and started reading the middle pages. My mum said, "I thought you always started with the first two pages?" I agreed, but carried on reading.

I noticed that I was being watched so I turned back to the first page. My face went the brightest of deep reds as I saw my picture and read alongside it '...and she's in for a big surprise this week when she sees her photograph – because she has no idea her mother sent it in ...' Yes, it was a BIG surprise!

The following week at school, the embarrassment continued, as numerous pupils, friends or not, referred to seeing my photo in the magazine. I didn't realise that so many people my own age would read their parents' magazine as I did each week.

On looking again at this magazine, there were seven separate, full page advertisements for cigarettes, common place at that time. The adverts made statements like, "The pleasure of fine tobaccos" and "There's 'no finer value in smoking."

Another cigarette advert read, "Have fun with … and keep smiling."

Yet another advert headlined, "A man gets real pleasure from …cigarettes."

How glamorous smoking was then. And how very ignorant everyone was and of where that misguided glamour would lead. When boys started work, they were encouraged to smoke and become 'a man', which is how grandad started smoking. Soldiers were encouraged to smoke and their army 'food' ration used to include cigarettes.

Interestingly, in this edition of 'Weekend' magazine, there were two pages promoting emigration to Australia. On offer in the early sixties was assisted sea voyages to Australia for £10 per person and free for children under 19 years. One advertisement heading was "Walk tall in Australia – a great place for families." I remember my parents talking about it, but it never came to anything more than a discussion, though my input had been, "Oh yes let's go!" My mother would not leave her parents. My father would not leave his job through loyalty and commitment as he had started there at 14, straight from school.

(Years later, that 'loyalty and commitment' would count for nothing.)

Grandma and I still visited her mother and disabled sister. On one visit whilst walking there, grandma explained that Aunt Harriet had been taken into hospital and her eldest sister, Emily, had moved back to stay with their mother. From listening to family conversations it was apparent that Aunt Harriet wasn't expected to come out of hospital and that my great grandma would be going to live with Aunt Emily and her two teenage boys. Her husband had already passed away. He had been a grinder by trade and couldn't get rid of a dry cough which eventually turned into bronchitis and resulted in an early death. He had smoked since the age of 12.

At the weekend, grandad took grandma, mother and I to visit Aunt Harriet in hospital. Grandad stayed with me outside the ward as children were not allowed in and it was two to a bed. Mother came out and grandad went in. Grandad came out and mother went back in. When we were ready to go, the ward door was held open as I waved at Aunt Harriet and she waved back from her hospital bed. That was the last time I would see her.

As mentioned in my mother's diary, two of grandma's sisters and her brother lived on the 'Bank. First up the hill, was Aunt Lily whose late husband, Fred, was the one who received the First World War Medal. Next door was Uncle Walt, Aunty Cath and Valerie.

Two doors up lived Aunt Minnie and Uncle Frank. Their son Frank, my godparent, had married and moved away. I visited the aunties and uncles with grandma or I would visit with mother and Philip. Where we lived was between the 'Bank and where Aunt Emily lived, which now included a bed-ridden, and almost blind, great grandma.

It's interesting to note that both of my maternal

grandparents and their parents had been part of large families, yet when the next generation married, they had such small families. Aunt Emily was the only sibling to have two children, the rest having only one child or none.

Grandad's two brothers, and himself, having one daughter each.

Passed the 'Bank was a winding country road to a park with the local paddling pool, 'up Rivelin'. The paddling pool water was river water. It would run in through pipes from the river with an overflow pipe at the other end so the water ran back into the river. My brother and I loved paddling in what was a series of four pools with a small, flat bridge over each pool area. After splashing in there we would go and get an ice cream from the café and then go into the playground. Next to the playground is an expanse of grass where we would picnic in the school holidays.

(This park was our favourite as it had 'everything' we could wish for in a park, including a 'nature trail' along the River Rivelin. There were rudimentary paths down to the river at intervals and Philip and I would meander down or walk on the bridges and throw in a twig to see who's twig floated the fastest. Happy, carefree times for the four of us. The trips usually included nannan who was company for mum as 'we two' paddled, played and dashed about.)

Most times, but not always, we would walk on the 'nature trail' along a path which took us over the bridges and over stepping stones. At the end was a large dam where, at the right time of year, you could fish with a net for tadpoles. We sometimes brought tadpoles home in a jam jar to keep them in the porch. As soon as they grew legs they jumped out and away.

We also caught caterpillars from the garden and placed them in little matchboxes with some grass to eat. They were kept in the porch, but sadly didn't live very long, even though we put holes in the matchbox. Another pastime, which seems cruel now, was to catch butterflies and put them in the shed. We would peer in through the window to watch their beauty as they flew and rested. When Dad went in for any garden tools they would fly out.

Philip's weekly magazine was 'Beano', but apart from that, he didn't much care for reading. I read books and magazines. I liked to draw and write. However, he was better at sums and arithmetic. All children learned the times table 'parrot' fashion. Phil and I used to test each other.

Selection of Blackpool photos –
all but the last one were taken
before WW2

National Service, 1948, dad and mate

Parents' wedding day, 1950

Aged 10 months in my big pram

My first blackpool photograph

3 weeks old, christening at
Sheffield Cathedral

2 years old – my first
Whitsuntide outfit

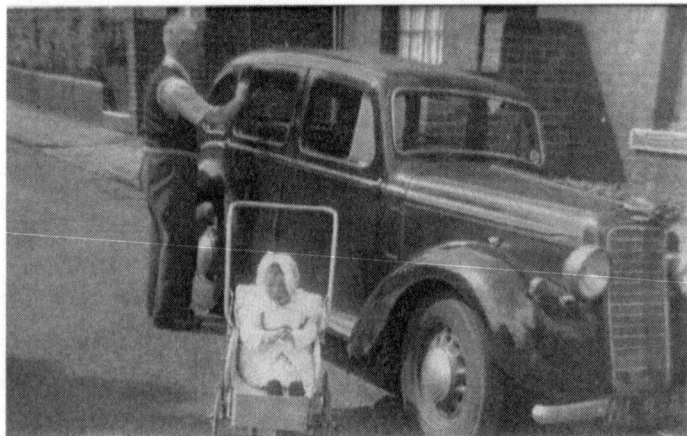

Grandad washing his car, the first one in Hillsboro'… me? I'm
parked in the road!

My brother and I, taken
in a studio

My first Whitsuntide
coat, aged 3

Pushing my new horse on wheels

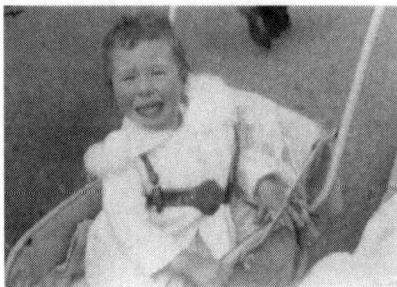

"Hang on while I take a
photo," said dad

My Whit turqoise suit
and 'pill box' bag before
being covered in soot

Fishing with grandad
(what a cheeky grin)!

Hurry up with the
ice creams!

Whit outfits – I wore a pink
fluffy bolero and Phil is in his
first shirt and tie

I realise 'baby' Elizabeth is
too big for my doll's house

Bridesmaid to Valerie –
I'm 2nd from right

Snails ride in Joyland – our favourite ride of 'all time'

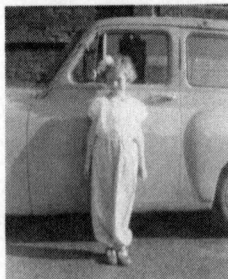

On holiday in front of grandad's car – I would not take off my new pyjamas

A Yarmouth pose. Note my mum-made dress and grandma's best 'holiday' suit

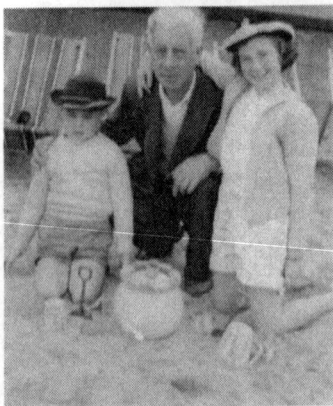

Grandad bought us 'cowboy' hats

374

The first photo I ever took!

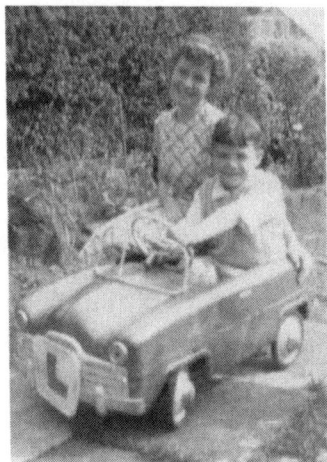

Our first car – note the mum-made dress

Us on the swing that grandad made

School Times

Before I started school, mum took me to look round the infants school and meet Miss Pass, the headmistress, who talked to mum about when I should start. I have a memory of her writing my name and age in a big 'ledger-type' book. Also, I noticed on her office wall that she had a gold framed portrait of a smiling Queen looking very beautiful.

After the Easter holiday, at aged four, my mum walked me to the infants school, one of her hands holding mine and the other pushing my brother in my grown-out-of-pushchair. *(On holidays though, I would call him 'baby' for being in it and when he got out, I got in!)*

I was ready to start school but I can't remember if I cried when my mum left me or not. I know she said that I waved once and was then 'swallowed up'.

(Malin Bridge Infants and Junior School was built for 800 pupils in 1904. The name and year set in stone signs on the central gables.)

The infants school was on a steeper hill than a '1 in 10' (it would have been '1 in 12' if they existed) and it was opposite the church where I went to Sunday School. The road was nicknamed 'Boulder Hill' by everyone.

(The 'nickname' actually originated from the area being called 'Boulder' and the road's former name had, indeed, been 'Boulder Hill'.)

About the same time, I also started going to Sunday School. As a very young beginner, mums stayed with their children while we drew and coloured in pictures of Jesus and heard stories about his miracles and parables. I liked Sunday School and mixing with different children to my school friends. The time there just seemed to fly by.

On special dates, such as Easter and Autumn, the Sunday School rooms would be decorated according to the time of year. I enjoyed Harvest Festival time as well as Easter. At Christmas, there was a nativity play and I remember being an angel when I really wanted to be Mary and hold the baby Jesus. I loved hearing about Jesus and how he grew up.

Opposite the church was the infants school and next to that was the juniors. Running alongside both schools was a walkway which linked the two schools onto the adjoining roads at either side. This saved mums living on the 'junior side' from going 'round the houses' to the infants and vice versa. *('Round the houses' meant a long way round.)*

In the infants school, classes were allocated to each room and you stayed in that room for the whole of that year. A lot of lessons were done in the school hall or on the floor of the classroom, like drawing and painting. Around the hall were the classroom doors.

After registration, it was assembly time. Piano music could be heard which signalled that a class at a time filed into the hall to sit in rows, cross legged, on the floor. Miss Pass would welcome everyone to school and say a short passage from the bible. We would all sing a hymn and say a prayer before filing out of the hall, a class at a time.

I remember one painting lesson on the floor in the form room. I had finished painting my picture so I started helping the girl sitting next to me, Norma, but the teacher said, "Jean, what are you doing?" I replied, "I'm helping Norma." The teacher said that I had 'spoiled her picture' so mine would not go onto the wall, she said. In my view, I had made her picture look better but that week my picture did not have the accolade of being put on the wall. I had a feeling of 'unfairness' for the first time in my life that someone had not believed me.

Another door off the hall led to the playroom which had a play house in it, a mini kitchen and a mini tools shed, the latter for the boys. There were blackboards and games for girls and boys. There were two boxes, one for girls to dress up in and one for boys. In the last week of the term, children could bring in a doll, teddy or a toy.

Most children were collected from school at lunchtime to go home for something to eat. A few children stayed behind and they had sandwiches. We were told they didn't have any parents so they had to stay there all day. I remember feeling sorry for them, especially as their clothes seemed 'raggy' when compared to children who had parents. Mum made a lot of my clothes which, at the time, I accepted as 'normal' but later on I realised that it was more usual for children to have 'bought' or 'hand me down' clothes.

Toilets were outside and at 'playtime' everyone had to go outside, in most weathers. In heavy rain, wind and snow, children were allowed to stay in the school hall and take turns in the playroom.

Children had milk to drink each playtime, taken from a crate outside in the yard. Each child punched a tiny hole in the top and inserted a straw to drink their third of a pint of milk. I can't remember anyone not drinking their milk. I can remember milk being spilt by misjudging the hole, drinking too fast and causing a liquid waterfall or the wet bottle slipping through tiny hands onto the ground.

Some mornings, there seemed to be as much spillage as there was 'drinkage'.

(The latter word is in quotes as it doesn't seem to have made its way into the dictionary!)

Although schoolgirls had separate entrances to boys, the playgrounds and classes were mixed. A teacher walked around the playground at playtimes.

When it was PE time, children got changed in the classroom. I wore a vest, a liberty bodice; a blouse in summer and a jumper in winter, with a skirt or pinafore dress. I also had a kilt in a pinafore dress style. Girls did not wear trousers or shorts. Boys wore shorts not trousers. In winter, children's exposed legs would be red from the cold. Coats were hung up and anything could be left anywhere. School blazers were worn in summer and in winter a big coat, called a gabardine, would be worn over the blazer.

Each child had a slipper bag hanging on their cloakroom hook. Inside would be black plimsolls, navy shorts and a white top. They would only be used for PE once a week. Socks worn that day would be kept on for PE and the rest of the day. I had clean socks on every other day, but the same underwear would normally be worn for the whole of that school week.

One day, after going home and taking off my liberty bodice (which I hated wearing as only the boys wore them, except me); mum noticed that it was not my liberty bodice. We had done PE but clothes were left on our individual chairs. I remembered that I had picked up my bodice from the floor to dress after PE. The next day, I wore my clean one and Mum went to school with me (brother and pram were left outside the school entrance).

(A liberty bodice is a sleeveless 'tank top' made of wool which was worn over a vest in winter.)

My deep embarrassment and red face began, as the teacher asked everyone to check their liberty bodices to the titter, titter of everyone. All the boys checked their liberty bodice. A boy had my liberty bodice on which had somehow got swapped yesterday. He had to take his off, there and then, and give it to my mum who dropped it into her shopping bag with her fingernails, like the bodice was infested with jungle ants. He spent the rest of the day 'bodice-less'. I hated liberty bodices even more after that.

(By the time I went to the junior school, I had persuaded Mum that only boys wore liberty bodices and I was being laughed at when we undressed for PE. Mum had agreed, at last, that I need not wear one.)

Mum arranged for a friend's daughter to walk me to school. I would walk to the top of the road and wait for Kathleen and then we would walk the rest of the way together. After leaving me at the infants, she would go down the walkway to the juniors. At lunchtime, we met at the walkway and then at the top of my road we parted. I would run the rest of the way home. Lunch was a sandwich or soup. After lunch, the whole thing was reversed with me running up the road and being met.

Kathleen was the middle of three sisters, the youngest was a year younger than me. I used to invite Kathleen to my birthday parties but she was too shy so her elder sister came instead. The other two children at my parties were my brother, obviously, and a boy who lived two doors away, John

Gold. I think my mum always thought, or hoped, we would grow up and fall in love!

(My mum kept in touch with Kathleen's mum over the years. I shall never forget when my mum told me that Kathleen had died, still only a teenager. My mum wouldn't tell me how at first, but as I persisted, mum said in almost a whisper that she had thrown herself off a local block of flats. I was totally shocked that someone I knew had died so young but more shockingly, if that was possible, in how she had died. To me, choosing to die was not something I had ever thought about or knew that it happened. Kathleen had helped my mum and befriended me and then no-one had helped her or knew how to. For a long time I could not look up at the flats when going passed them.

There was no suicide note but it was reported in court that Kathleen had been having problems with her boyfriend who had lived in one of the flats. Her mum also said that Kathleen was still a private, shy girl but if only she had tried to talk to her or knew that she needed help. The guilt overwhelmed her mother.)

That brings back another sad memory from the infants. We were all colouring, sticking and pasting pictures when a girl with blonde hair started shrieking and there was blood everywhere. The sharp end of a pair of scissors had somehow gone into her eye. She lost her eye and was off school a long time. When she did return, a black patch was worn over the lost eye and, eventually, she had a glass eye fitted which was very realistic.

Whenever mother repeated the incident to a neighbour, she added "…and she's a policeman's daughter."

At school dancing class in the juniors, the boys had to pick a girl to dance with. On one occasion, two boys wanted to dance with me and I chose the one whose dad was a policeman. Miss Thorpe played the piano.

When anyone spelled a word incorrectly, the word had to be repeated ten times at the end of the lesson on a thin strip of lined paper. Although time consuming, I'm sure this practice helped me to spell, even though I regarded myself as a naturally good speller. Also, at least once a week, the teacher would hold a 'spelling bee'. That is, the whole class would stand around the room and the teacher would say a word for each child to say in turn. Those who got a word wrong had to sit down.

I was one of only two children who would be the last two standing. More often than not, I would be the one to triumph. After quite a few weeks of consecutively winning, the class applauded when I eventually spelled a word incorrectly. I knew the word, but I had said it wrong, which made me seethe inside.

I loved those spelling bees as much as my brother hated them. The words got harder in the juniors.

In the junior school, again there were outside toilets and separate entrances, but the playgrounds were now separate. There was a stone wall splitting the playground in half with small gaps at each end. A teacher and a 'playground monitor' (a parent) would patrol outside and the teacher would shout at anyone who 'crossed over'. Our classes were still mixed.

Just outside the school gates was a 'tuck' shop. The shopkeeper sold penny drinks of Tizer (a red fizzy drink) or lemonade in small, 'shot' type glasses. 'Fruit salads' and 'Blackjacks' were four a penny. 'Blackjacks' had a golliwog's face on them and were made of liquorice which I didn't like. No-one could afford a Mars Bar at 6d. (15p in 'new' money.)

I now walked to and from the junior school with my brother who would leave me at the walkway and I watched him go into the infants side. Kathleen had moved onto comprehensive school. Mum would always be waiting outside for us at home time. On the way back, we would sometimes call in one or two of the individual shops which lined the route home. Sometimes, we would go round the corner to the co-op, which then took longer to walk home, but we always got back for children's hour on the television.

When Philip started school, mother must have missed him so much she volunteered as a 'playground monitor'. At both playtime periods, in the morning and afternoon, she would be in the playground with the children. If a child fell down, mum was to hand. If a child was upset, mum came to the rescue. If Philip missed his mum, well, she was there. I would go to the railings which separated the juniors from the infants' playgrounds and mum would come over and ask if I was alright. Sometimes, Philip would come over as well.

There was an A class, a B class and a C class in each year of the junior school. First of all I started in 1B class on the first floor. I remember 1C had their classroom in what was known as the 'comic room'. As pupil numbers were large enough for a third class, the 'comic room' had had to be used. It was most unfortunate that it was the C class in the former 'comic room' as they were the butt of jokes, like 'wish I could read comics all day like you can' or 'have you read any good comics today'?

The next year, I went up to 2A and was in the same class as the policeman's son. The top of the class would sit at one end, going through the room until the children in the end row were the ones at the bottom of the class. I had to sit in the end row when I first moved up, but in 3A, I was sat in the second from the end row which I was very pleased about. Some of the ones who had sat in the end row were now in

3B and some new children sat in their places. It was difficult at first to adjust from being the top, albeit in the B class, to then being near the bottom.

There was definitely a 'them and us' about being in the A class. When walking about the school with your A class friends, you could put on 'airs and graces'. I liked being in the A-team, I mean A class!

We used exercise books and pencils which we kept in our desk. We had to have a ruler, a rubber, a pencil sharpener and at least two pencils. I used a pencil case. As an exercise book got full, you put up your hand to show the full book. Any new book had to be 'backed', which I took home for Mum to do. She used clear cellophane paper which I was proud of, as other mums used brown paper or wallpaper.

There was a rumour in the A class that children in the C class had a ruler across their hands if misbehaving, but I never saw any evidence of it. Generally, children in the C class were not very well dressed, wearing what we would call 'raggy' clothes. Some of them did not wear any socks and did not have a school blazer which we were all supposed to wear. I did not want to be any different from what other girls wore. Any deviation from the 'norm' and you were made fun of or, even worse, shunned.

No-one from the A class was expected to talk to anyone in the C class. In fact, I didn't know anyone in the C class to talk to. I knew a few in the B class with whom I talked or played with at break time, but generally, A class children 'stuck' together.

There was only one male teacher in the whole of the infants and junior schools called Mr Martin, who was very nice, but I liked Miss Rogers the best. She wore a full skirt, just below the knee, with netting underneath to make the skirt 'flare out'. In between her top and the skirt, was a big black belt, making her waist look very tiny. She wore flat shoes and 'bobby' socks and was always smiling.

(Bobby socks were white ankle length socks, turned down to form a thick cuff.)

The male headmaster, Mr Courage, was very seldom seen outside of assembly time. As far as I recall, he didn't actually do any teaching and was not regarded as a 'teacher', hence Mr Martin being the only male teacher. Of course, Mr Courage was the butt of jokes like, 'he needed courage to teach 'ere' or 'he dun't teach 'cos he's run out of courage'.

Assemblies in the junior school were very much like the infants, children sat cross legged on the floor and the teachers sat at the front in chairs. Mr Courage would say a reading from the bible then we would have a hymn with Miss Thorpe playing the piano. Mr Courage then said any information we needed to know or any announcements, such as a school holiday coming up. At the end it was always 'heads bowed, hands together for the Lord's Prayer'. We would then leave in the same way as we had sat down, a class at a time.

The most popular playground game was 'tag'. There were four large grates, spaced out, which were 'bases' and when on a base you could not be 'tagged' (touched). If a girl was tagged, she would be 'on'. Sometimes, girls would play with skipping ropes, spinning tops or throw and catch. Looking over at the boy's side, it just seemed like a lot of running around and shouting, occasionally seeing a ball up in the air.

Some of my sentence work at school gives me an insight into daily life and what I was thinking around the time I was

7 or 8 years old. You were given a word then had to include it in a sentence (the word is in bold).

On **Sundays** we have bacon and eggs. (true).

You can touch my **fur** gloves. (a Christmas present)

My brother has **all** his teeth now. (milk teeth)

Last year my grandad gave us 50 **acorns**. (he didn't)

Sometimes my mummy runs **short** of lemons. (really, I think not)

My mum bought a **raw** lamb. (ugh, I know she didn't)

I have got a **lot** of uncles. (8, including my grandparents' brothers as uncles)

The cup final is **tomorrow**. (I liked football and my dad had started to take me to watch Sheffield Wednesday in the top division)

I love port, but mummy won't let me **drink** it. (I had never tasted or wanted to taste port)

I am very **clever** at sums. (I wasn't really)

You must not break your **knee** caps. (was I thinking of the washing line incident)

I do not like **people** with two heads. (I had never seen one and was never likely to)

Here is an account of what I do after school, taken from an English composition school book…

"After four o'clock I go into the cloak room and collect my things. I come down my road alone. I *(go)* up the passage *(in between our house and next door's)* very quiet and make my mother jump. My brother comes to the door. I play with them at Ludo. When it is 5 o'clock we set the table and have tea. After tea we watch TV. It is now time for 'My Friend Flicka' and then it is time for 'Just Dennis'. Daddy comes in and we all play games together. We watch 'Take your Pick' and we go to bed."

('Flicka' was a television programme about a child with a pet horse. 'Just Dennis' is similar to 'Just William'. 'Take your Pick' is a game show.)

Let's recap – 'Daddy comes in' and then 'we all play games together' – can you spot what is missing here? Is it mum putting on her make-up, being a 'little gay' and then putting a 'delicious meal' on the table when he comes in?

According to the above story, he comes straight in (leaves his coat on) and 'plays games', usually ludo. He can't have been one of those 'hungry' and 'work-weary' men in the 'Good Wives' Guide'? Or, I missed out the bit where he took off his coat, had a wash and ate his tea!

The annual school parents' evening was something to look forward to as, generally, my teachers had only positive things to say about me.

One report stated: "Jean is making good general progress. She remains just a little 'shaky' in arithmetic. Jean takes great pains with her work which is always very neat."

Best subjects – spelling (top marks), handwriting, English composition, reading and arithmetic tables. By this stage, I knew all the times tables 'parrot' fashion. If anyone got a table wrong or a spelling wrong or a sentence, it had to be repeated at least five times.

The remarks in next year's report: "Jean has put a great deal of effort into all her work and has made very good progress. She is very conscientious, a painstaking and a very careful worker. At times, however, she appears to become over-anxious." ('At times' meant before a test or exam.)

I could now add English composition (or English language) to the list of best subjects, but written and mental arithmetic remained 'shaky'. Although I had liked Mr Martin as a form teacher in the previous year, I much preferred Miss Thorpe, the current form teacher.

My sentences, though, seemed to remain a little 'far fetched':

Sue got in trouble with a policeman. (I don't think she did)

I have never seen a flying saucer. (I still haven't)

I only have one potato for dinner. (I don't)

Mind your own business Norma. (I never liked Norma after the infants painting incident)

Lesley has brought another biscuit to school. (no-one brought biscuits)

I love a bottle of tomato sauce. (not the whole bottle, obviously)

Oranges are winning now. (are they in a race with the apples?)

My picture has just gone up on the wall. (so there, Norma from the infants)

Marilyn has white socks on. (all the girls wore white socks)

Mum and I are going to clean the attic (oh no, we're not)

Susan is sucking her pencil. (did she?)

Here is another story from an English composition school book…

"I would like to go to Majorca, an island near Spain. I would like to stay in a posh hotel with servants to wait upon you, have a luxurious room and only the best of food.

Every day I would go on a sun-drenched beach and perhaps go swimming or even skiing. To meet lots of new friends or maybe movie stars.

Go to dances, meet famous people with dark glasses on, I might ask for a cha cha. I might not know why they are," *(why they are...what? I must have meant 'who they are'.)*

(Cha cha is a dance, but not sure why I would ask a famous person in dark glasses to cha cha with me?)

"I would buy presents for all my relatives and friends and also send them long letters and a coloured postcard with a picture of Majorca on it."

(But where would I find the time for all this present buying and letter writing – I've also got to make time for finding a famous person to do a cha cha with!)

"All too soon my fortnight would come to an end, so I would get on an aeroplane bound for Watford where the aerodrome is."

(Of course, Watford is where the aerodrome is...er, is there an aerodrome in Watford?)

"Once on the plane you do not know when you are in the air or on the ground because they run so smooth. The air hostess would bring the food in. Egg and bacon with some cooked tomatoes and tea.

On arriving at Watford I would get my luggage and go and stay with my Uncle George and Aunty Margaret for the night.

In the morning I would get on a train for Sheffield."

(Of course, I had never been on an aeroplane to know that you can tell when an aeroplane is taking off or has landed. I also thought

that 'real' meals would be served with real cutlery! It seems strange that I would go on my own though.)

This is an adventure story from the same school book…

"Stranded

I had booked a day trip to Norwich. The day before the trip I wished that I'd never booked the trip at all, the ground lay thick in snow, about two feet deep.

So at seven thirty I set of(f) for the coach yard with two friends of mine Susan and Gillian. After half an hour waiting we all set off for Norwich.

As we neared the crossroads the driver could not see any signpost. Then a passenger saw something above the depth of the snow. The driver and two other gentlemen went to investigate but the snow lay so thick they could not even budge it. So now the driver had just got to guess which way to go, there were two country roads covered in snow so we took the main road. After half a mile we all ran into the snow drift.

"Poop p o o o p p… *(the sound of the coach)*, it stopped dead, 'oh ouch ooooo,' that was the bumps and groans from the passengers who fell head first over the seat in front and landed on the floor with a bump.

Now we were stranded in the middle of nowhere. The driver and an engineer *(was there an engineer on board?)* looked at the motor part while two men walked one way and Susan, a lady, and two men walked the other way. That left nine of us – four ladies and five men including the driver.

Then one or two offered to clear the snow from under the coach wheels. Then the man who went with Susan's group came running up, so out of breath he could hardly splutter out the words, "We, we've found (gasp) a tele... phone and Susan's ring, ringing for help." Everyone was happy with the words, the driver insisted on all the ladies going in the coach out of the cold air.

In the next half an hour we thought we'd never live, for sleet and the snow came down so fast it came right up the sides of the coach *(that's incredibly deep!)* The way the snow came down the rescuers and passengers who was still looking for (the group that Susan was in, they were heading for the coach.) Help.

A(n) hour passed before the rescue party with the group that had just two men in came back in a bulldozer. After fifteen minutes of pushing and pulling the other group showed up and helped. It was so cold that I could not feel my hands and feet.

At last all the passengers and myself arrived safely at our destination being pulled by the bulldozer *(what a comical sight that would have been?)*

Glad to say half of our money was refunded because more than half the day was wasted on being stranded."

(It's strange, to me, that I should think of being compensated.)

The young teachers at school, including Miss Thorpe, were now wearing pencil skirts, just 'kissing' their knee, and tops in the new yellow and turquoise shades. Mr Martin's shirt collars did not grow and, although his ties got a bit wider, they did not reach the 'kipper' tie proportions I had seen younger men wearing in town.

Dad bought a red Scotch plaid tie, very near to 'kipper' size, but mum was still wearing flared skirts below the knee.

Her favourite outfit was still a red and white spotted dress with a matching bolero. The dress had a matching fabric belt making her look taller and slimmer, even though the whole look was now slightly 'last year'.

The television news showed young teenagers walking down the very trendy and 'vogue' Carnaby Street in London.

There were new clothing materials. Polyester, bri-nylon, tights and crimplene revolutionised high street clothes. They were easy to wear and easy to wash dresses and suits, and 'no need to iron' garments. They were very welcome when buying new school clothes, but mother still ironed everything.

The sixties heralded a colour and fashion explosion. All the 'rules' of convention seemingly broken forever as girls' skirts got shorter and boys' shirt collars got bigger. Not for schoolchildren, I might add.

I became aware of 'mods and rockers' and the emergence of teenagers as people with 'their own minds' and their own fashion trends. I saw more mini cars on the roads and more mini skirts on the pavements. The sixties' teenagers had more money to spend on clothes, at the cinema and in coffee shops.

Everything seemed a 'million miles' away from what their parents had experienced only 15 short years ago in the post war era of rationing and 'making do'.

The television news was full of the changes happening in the air as more people travelled by plane, making America that much 'closer' to Britain. On land, the mass manufacture of cars made them cheaper and more affordable to buy. By 1958 there were 8 million cars on the road. However, there were still no 'school runs' of any kind.

(The fifties 'Teddy' boys made way for the sixties 'mods and

rockers'. The rockers wore leather jackets and rode motorcycles. Mods were considered 'snobby' and somewhat effeminate, especially as they liked to wear clothes in the latest psychadelic colours. Rockers liked rock and roll, while the mods preferred pop bands like the Who and the Kinks. Clashes of mods with rockers were reported in some southern seaside resorts at Bank Holiday weekends.)

The news also featured screaming girls greeting the arrival of the Beatles or the Rolling Stones at an airport or at a theatre they were playing in. From the pop posters on the back of my 'June' magazine, I had seen several separate pictures of the four Beatles – John, Paul, George and Ringo.

In the school playground, in between our games, we sometimes talked about what a girl's older sister or brother was up to and I can remember one girl saying that her aunty and sister had seen the Beatles live on stage in Sheffield. To me, that would have been like stepping into the television set.

My school friend said she liked Paul the best. I liked John the best as, to me, he appeared to be the lead singer. Two others said that George was their favourite Beatle. No-one spoke up for Ringo, the drummer. We all knew the words to 'I wanna hold your hand'.

The most common school playground question became, "who's your favourite Beatle?"

(The Beatles first record was 'Love me do' but their biggest hit was in 1963 with 'I want to hold your hand'. John Lennon had founded the group, minus Ringo, billing themselves as 'Johnny and the Moondogs'. As a tribute to Buddy Holly and the Crickets (Buddy Holly was killed in a plane crash in 1959), their name was changed to the 'Silver Beetles' and later shortened to 'The Beatles'. The original drummer was replaced by Ringo. Their nickname became the 'Fab Four' and the rest, as they say, is history!)

Royal School Times

Traditionally, child members of the Royal Family did not go to school. They learned their lessons from governesses (they were mostly female) at home in a designated school room.

Though not royal until her marriage, Lady Elizabeth had been schooled at home with her younger brother because of their closeness in age, fifteen months. Their brothers and sisters were much older. The schoolroom was in the family's North London home, a grand house within its own grounds and so-called enchanted wood. I daresay with the customary aristocratic elephant foot stools and umbrella stands. That is, in the home not the schoolroom.

Morning lessons included music, dancing, drawing and French. The first World War was to interrupt the two siblings' happy, carefree childhood, including their education.

What was so much more interesting than their lessons was exploring outside in the grounds with its ponds and statues and the enchanted wood. In an old outhouse their favourite hiding place was in the attic. This had such a dilapidated ladder up to it that it would not take the weight of an adult, i.e. their nanny. *(What luck!)* There was no better place to hide for Elizabeth and David but in the attic where they kept a stash of apples and chocolate.

(Years later, Elizabeth had, in fact, finally accepted Prince Albert's

(George) marriage proposal while walking with him in the enchanted wood.)

The Prince had been educated at home with his older brother because of their closeness in age, eighteen months. They studied under tutors but without even a glimmer of the freedom that his future wife and her brother had been given. In the words of Prince Albert, his tutors had been 'old and crusty' who had been intent on learning him dates and grammar. He hated learning and could not spell. As a young man he found that he loved smoking.

In contrast, my own grandma, as soon as she could read and write, had only attended school from time to time but not through any exploration adventures. She was the one who had taught her 'invalid' sister how to read and write and to help her mother in their small house with a small, flagged courtyard. At the age of 13 she was found employment in Oldham with her aunt but with the onset of the first World War she was sent back home.

Grandad also left school at 13 years as he was bright enough to leave earlier than aged 14. At the same time as leaving school, he started his heavy smoking of untipped cigarettes.

The two Princesses, Elizabeth and Margaret Rose, had school lessons from a young and enthusiastic, but inexperienced, governess. She liked playing games with them and did not want to 'fill their heads' with regimented learning. Their father had said to the governess, "All I ask is that the girls learn to read and to write legibly." Most of all he wanted them to have the happy childhood that had so eluded him. Their mother had briefly attended a day school and hated it and was of the opinion that children should not be forced to learn, especially girls.

At 145 Picadilly, Princess Elizabeth would be given half hour lessons from 9.30am until 11am in the schoolroom. Her favourite subject was history as she said it was 'learning about her family'. After the short lessons came orange juice and games, sometimes joined by Margaret Rose. At 12 noon, it was 'quiet' time for the older girl and she was encouraged to lie down on her bed. This was followed by an hour of reading by the governess. Lunch would be with her parents, if at home, and her sister.

After that it was outdoor exercise, if weather permitted, dancing or singing. If there were any dentist or other appointments or commitments these tended to occur in the morning, thus interrupting her already inadequate education. The governess' inexperience was apparent… and she was not a qualified tutor. Her mathematics was reported as being 'hopeless'. Additional governesses were brought in and time was set aside for reading books. There were no examinations and no expectations for her to go to university. The emphasis for both Princesses had been in teaching them how to be 'ladylike'.

Learning did not become a priority for the Princess until the Abdication interrupted all their lives. She then started to learn how to greet and talk to distinguished guests, in theory as well as at first hand. On the academic side, twice weekly lessons in constitutional history had begun at Eton College in Windsor. Both Princesses were now being taught French, French literature and European history. However, they still had practical 'homemaking' lessons such as cooking and polishing furniture.

A clothes 'milestone' was reached at twelve as Elizabeth was able to discard her white socks for silk stockings (a birthday present from her mother.)

My mother went to school, like her parents, at a state run school in large separate-sex classes. She was bright and liked school and liked learning even though it was very much centred on 'all things' domestic. Girls did needlecraft, sewing, cooking, knitting and home making. Her schooling was interrupted by the second World War. Mother continued to wear white socks until she left school.

My father also went to a state run school, unlike his parents and grandparents, who had not attended school. His grandparents never learned to read and write. Boys learned about sums and arithmetic, metalwork and woodwork.

The first heir to the throne to go to school was Prince Charles which was a good thing and a bad thing. Good to mix and be challenged by other children but the 'bad thing' was the loss of privacy from being tutored at home.

At age eight he became a day pupil at Hill House School in West London but with the caviot that he be treated like any other boy. Of course, he wasn't like 'any other boy' as heir to the throne and with police protection (though it was kept at arm's length.) Ten months later he became a boarder at Cheam Prepatory School in Berkshire.

Charles did not enjoy the rigours of sporting life at public school but found refuge on the stage and in the art room. However, he was miserable and lonely at Cheam. Following again in his father's footsteps he then went to Gordonstoun in Scotland and when compared back to Cheam he found that had been a 'tea party'. He had many sleepless nights and felt more isolated than ever away from his family. Slowly, but surely, he found some confidence and managed to gain five GCE 'O' levels.

Due to the monarchy's links with the Commonwealth,

it was decided that he should spend a year in Australia. At last, he 'found his feet' and enjoyed his time at Timbertop, part of Geelong Grammar School near Melbourne. Although further away from his family, Charles was now 17 and free from many of the pressures on him in Britain.

Despite Princess Anne 'badgering' her parents to go to school at nine or ten, they resisted and she continued to be tutored at home. As a compromise, a few daughters of 'vetted' acquaintances came to join her lessons at Buckingham Palace and her mother's former Girl Guides' Company was reformed.

On her father's insistence, Anne wore more practical, outdoor clothes such as trousers and sweaters. She was never a 'girly girl' and loved 'all things' outdoors. She learned to swim, ride a bicycle and even drove a 'bubble' car round the private roads at Windsor. But her passion was always horse riding and she liked nothing better, in her spare time, than 'mucking' out the stables or sailing in a dinghy with her father.

As a more confident and less shy child than Charles, she still wanted to go to school. At long last, at age thirteen, Anne started as a boarder at Benenden School in Kent which she enjoyed, unlike Charles' early school life.

Like Anne, I loved school and liked to wear trousers and sweaters.

Like Charles, my brother hated school and was extremely shy.

First Diary

I was nine years old when I started to write my first diary about events and daily life. Unlike my mother's first diary they were events which did not involve evacuations, bombings and terrifying air raids. Just the daily life of an ordinary family.

But, like my mother's diary, there was quite a lot of general information at the beginning.

There was a general section, firstly about the cost of a driver's licence, 15 shillings for a full one and 10 shillings for a provisional licence (note, there were two 10s in a £.) Then information on car insurance, licence disks, lighting up time and car mirrors. Private motor cars, it states, are taxed at £17 10s per annum.

There was a paragraph on 'intoxication' and if driving a motor vehicle 'under the influence of drink or drugs' a person was liable to a £100 fine if a first offence, or after that, a four months prison sentence and/or 'disqualification of the driving licence for a period of not less than 12 months'.

The section on motorways stated what was not allowed on a motorway, including invalid carriages and animals. There was still no speed limit. However, the section on speed limits states that in 'built up' areas it is 30mph, but some roads which are technically 'built up' according to the definition of 'built up' are not restricted, and others which are 'built up' are not restricted. Well, that's very clear!

There was a section on 'Foreign Travel' about car regulations and which side of the road vehicles drove on, for several European countries. This section included international road signs.

The 'Postal Information' page gave the inland letter postage stamp as costing 4d and postcards 3d with the reply paid, 6d. Recorded delivery cost 6d on top of postage. Telegrams now cost 5s for twelve words and 5d per word after that. To send a parcel weighing less than 2lb (pounds in weight) it was 2s 9d. The cost of a stamp had more than doubled since mother's diary in 1939, then one and a half old pence to the cost in this diary at 4d. The cost of a postcard had trebled from 1d to 3d.

Some of the early extracts from my diary start with the precise time I got up, eg '10 past 9'. Some mention television programmes now archived and never known by today's younger generations. Here are some extracts:

Monday 31 December
I got up at 10.45. Then I went to Shepherd's (the corner shop) for mummy. Then I went to play in the snow, I made a snowman. When daddy came home he did the last things that wanted doing to our sledge (made by dad.)

Tuesday 1 January
I got up at 10.40. Daddy didn't go to work (as it was New Year's Day.) When daddy, Philip and me were ready we went to sledge in our front garden. Daddy made a super sledge run and daddy pulled us. A bit later we went to nannan's for

dinner (remember, we call lunch 'dinner') and tea. When we got back it was 10 o'clock.

(I'm sure I made an error in putting 'front garden' as it was so small, it would not have been long enough for a sledge run. It should have read, 'our back garden'.)

Wednesday 2 January

I got up at 10 past 9. At half past 10 we went to sledge again. mummy pulled us for about 5 minutes. Then we went back in for a bowl of soup (that was our dinner) (lunch.) Then mummy and Philip went in town with daddy (was I home alone?) When they came back (not daddy) we played at fishing game nearly all the rest of the day.

(I wonder what happened to daddy? Possible answers – he wanted to avoid the fishing game; he'd called for a pint of beer in the local; he'd got off the bus at his mother and father's home. I suspect it was the latter.

The fishing game explained – each player had a mini fishing line with a magnet on the end and you had to hook a magnetised fish from within an upright container. Each fish had a number and the largest number won the fishing game. This had been a Christmas present as the novelty was still new enough to play 'nearly all the rest of the day'.)

Thursday 4 January

I got up at 20 past 9. Then I saw the snow it was about 3 or 4 ins high. I played with Philip in the snow while mummy went shopping (we would have gone shopping but en route and outside the shop we would have been playing with the snow.) Then we had our dinner. Then mummy started washing. (She must have thought it was Monday?)

When Daddy came home (from work) we took the Christmas tree down and trimmings because we have to take them down by 6th January. Then we watched 'Bootsie and Snudge'.

(A British comedy starring Alfie Bass and Bill Fraser, set in a gentlemen's club. Bootsie was a down to earth character and Snudge was a 'snob'. Alfie Bass went on to join the cast of 'Are you Being Served', a comedy set in a department store.)

Saturday 6 January

I got up at 9.15. Then I wrote to those who had sent me Christmas presents (with a 'thank you' notelet set.) Then we had our dinner (lunch of course). Then we went to sledge with daddy. We had our tea then played at sixes and sevens (dominoes.)

Then we watched 'Black and White Minstrel Show' (a variety song and dance show where white men dubbed their faces black which was completely 'acceptable' entertainment in the sixties.)

Then I watched Sunday Night at the Paladiam. (Correct spelling 'Palladium' – I must write it again ten times!) Then I went to bed.

This programme was called Val Parnell's Sunday Night at the London Palladium and started at 8 o'clock. Val, short for 'Valentine' also ran the Theatre's stage variety shows.

The actual Palladium Theatre in London's West End opened in 1910 and became famous for its live variety shows. All entertainers wanted to be billed there. Bruce Forsyth, who came from a theatre in Eastbourne where he was playing to 'ten people a night', became a household name 'overnight' (within two months) of comparing at the Palladium. It did the same for Jimmy Tarbuck, club 'circuit' comedian, when he became Theatre compare in 1963, saying, 'it totally changed his life'. Bruce compared the television show from 1958 until Jimmy took over.

The TV show would open with the Tiller Girls dancing in 'can can' formation lines. Then came the lesser known artists and variety acts until my favourite 'Beat the Clock' game. This was where members of the audience took part in 'funfair' type games in order to beat the clock, usually set at 30 seconds. For example, throwing soft balls through a square hole or knocking down a pyramid of tin cans. A popular game was a board of magnetic words which had to be rearranged into a well known phrase or saying. My 'going to bed time' was usually after 'Beat the Clock' as it was school the day after.

The variety acts included jugglers, contortionists, bell ringers, magicians, comedians, acrobats, 'singing' ducks, performing dogs, horses and a baby elephant, dancing groups, clowns and high rise circus acts. Fifties' singers included Bob Hope, Frank Sinatra, Sammy Davis Junior, Danny Kaye and the Beverley Sisters.

If dad was on nights, mum would let me stay up to see all the artists at the end go round on a moving turntable and they waved when facing the audience. I loved that, but what a pity it was at the end!

The London Theatre's Palladium Variety Show was well established before television and during the War, Vera Lynn would sing 'We'll meet again, don't know where, don't know when, but I know we'll meet again some sunny day'. The audience would stand and join in, sometimes linking arms.

In war time, there had been patriotic shows by soldiers and comedy sketches about the war in order to make people 'feel good' about what was going on outside.

When listening to the show (before TV) the wireless commentator would say, "And everyone is all set on the moving turntable, they're off, they're waving and smiling as it turns them around slowly."

Now they could be seen on television going round on the famous turntable – when facing the front: wave, smile, wave, hold that smile; moving round to the back: put your arm down, tidy hair; facing the front again: arm goes up to wave and wave and smile; round the back: arm down, relax your mouth; at the front again: arms up, wave again…

By the time I remember watching the full show, there were singers like Tommy Steele, Cliff Richard, Adam Faith, Gerry and the Pacemakers and comedians Ken Dodd and Norman Wisdom. Apparently, in the early sixties, the man who was booking the acts did not know most of what or who he was booking and one Sunday night, on stage walked an 'up and coming' star, Jimi Hendrix.

Then they all went round and round and round –
at the front: wave, wave and hold that smile;
at the back: tidy hair or tie:
front again: wave, wave, smile and smile;
round the back: arm down and whisper: "Can't wait for a drink;"
front once more: wave again, grin, grin, and bear it, wave, wave…

Appearing in the Sunday night show meant you "had made it". Val Doonican, who had just been turned down by two record companies, appeared on the show and within days he had offers of three different record deals. In January 1960, Bruce introduced Cliff Richard and the Shadows to a TV audience of 20 million people. Frank Sinatra, Bob Hope, Liberace, Petula Clark and the Beatles, all 'topped the bill' in the early sixties. When the Rolling Stones 'topped the bill', they refused to go on the moving turntable and caused a furore, but everyone else jumped on!

And so the finale of going round and round and round –
at the front: wave, wave, hold that smile;
at the back: tidy hair, have a cough;
front again: wave, wave, aching arm and mouth but keep smiling;
round the back: rest arm and whisper, "Can't wait for a cig…"

Wednesday 9 January

I got up at 8 o'clock. It was school again. When I came home I didn't feel very well. We were going to Aunty Minnie's but we couldn't go (I must have been very poorly.) When we had tea we watched telly then we played at fishing game (I can't have been that poorly?) and later we went to bed.

Thursday 10 January

I got up at 8 o'clock. I didn't go to school for later the doctor came and told me it was 'German measles'. (I remember wondering how had I caught measles from Germany?)

Nannan came a bit later on. She took Philip to her house for tea. When daddy came home mum went to fetch Philip. (grandad would have run them back in the car.) Then we went to bed.

Saturday 12 January

I got up at 10 past 9. We had breakfast then I looked at comics. Grandad came and took Phil with him (I missed out on going for a run in the car due to being ill.) Then I had dinner.

(Philip was dropped off in the afternoon by grandad.) Then we had tea then watched 'Rag Trade' and then went to bed.

('Rag Trade' was a British comedy centred on a small clothing workshop where the female workers were led by a militant, female shop steward. Cast included Sheila Hancock and Barbara Windsor.

Years later, an episode where they make golliwogs for some extra money had its title renamed from 'Christmas Golliwogs' to 'Christmas Box' for release on video.)

Sunday 13 January

I got up at 9.30. We had breakfast. Then I read 'Sunday Pictorial' (newspaper which later changed it's name to the 'Sunday Mirror'.) Then we had dinner. Then we all played at miming then 'I Spy' then we had tea then watched telly. Then I went to bed.

('Then' seems to have been a very popular diary joining-up word!)

I didn't go to school the next day and in the evening I reported that it was 'I Love Lucy', an American slap stick comedy show starring Lucille Ball. Her husband was played by her real husband, Desi Arnaz, and their son was played by their real son, Desi Arnaz Junior!

Tuesday back to school and after that was my dancing class where I did tap and ballroom dancing. Dancing class was at the other side of grandma's house which was a half hour's walk. We would leave Phil with grandma, and then walk up the steep road, along a gennel and walk on the 'top' road to the dancing school. After the class, we walked back and grandad would run us back home.

I did not go to school on Wednesday or Thursday. I went to the doctor's on the Friday and again on Saturday the 19th with a rash which mum thought was mumps. (I'm not sure why she would think it was mumps as I had been diagnosed with German Measles.) The rash had disappeared by Sunday and, on Monday the 21st, I went back to school.

After that date, I started varying each day's finishing sentence, '…then I went to bed'. One was '…then I went to bed to go to sleep', which may have meant Philip and I didn't talk or throw pillows at each other and we just went to sleep. Another entry was '…then went upstairs to bed' which didn't add any further information as I always went upstairs to bed! If we went to bed late, I would add the time at the end of the entry.

Friday 15 February

I got up at 8.45. Then I went to school. When I came home we had tea. Then we watched telly then dad came home. Then we went to see Aladdin with nannan. She got on the same bus as us (that would have needed some prior organising without the use of a telephone as nannan lived about four bus stops away from us.) It was in that theatre where I went to see Billy Cotton (a dance band leader who used to start his television show with 'wakey wakey'.) Then at 11 o'clock we went to bed.

On the Saturday after dinner (lunch), I went with mother and grandma to look at a house. It was around this time that my parents were deciding to move to a larger house. Neither my brother nor I wanted to sleep in separate bedrooms which would have meant me going into the attic. They went through how it would be decorated with new, modern furniture but as I constantly refused to listen, they had decided, unknown to me at the time, to find a three bedroom, larger house.

On the way back from looking at the house we collected Philip, who was with grandad and back at home we played with our blackboard.

(The blackboard was a large, double sided one so we could sit either side and write and draw separately if we wished. Usually we would be at the same side drawing together.)

Monday the 18th, after school, we came home to find that the doctor had called to see mother who was ill and my grandma was there. After tea we watched 'telly' and I recorded that my dad and grandad came home. I then wrote, "At 8 o'clock nannan and grandad went home and at 8.30 I went to bed."

The next day after school I finished a drawing of a couple getting married. As mother was ill, I didn't go to dancing class. "Then dad came home and we played ludo," presumably after his tea. We then "watched telly and I went to bed at 8 o'clock." Nannan was a frequent visitor over the next few days. We were sent into the front room to play with our toys and when grandad came, he would join us. The gas fire was lit and…because it wasn't lit very often, it produced a 'funny' smell which we forgot about after a while.

By the weekend of the 23rd/24th, mother was 'up and about' again. She was quiet and didn't sing her usual repertoire of songs from the South Pacific film, 'I'm in love with a wonderful guy' or 'some enchanted evening'. There wasn't much ludo playing either.

(I only found out much later that we were set to have a new brother or sister. Unknown to Phil and myself, the planned larger family was one of the reasons for moving to a larger house. Sadly, it wasn't to be, as mum lost the baby. One of the few things that mum would ever say to me, was, 'it's nature's way'.

I would day dream about the baby being a girl and doing all sorts of things with my sister, like having a double pram buggy for our dolls or both of us playing with my doll's house. I thought we would have had bunk beds with Phil moving to the attic. We would have had a third more toys to play with but on the downside, there would have been a new baby taking all of mum and dad's attention and time.

The negatives, I thought, were far outweighed by all the great times I would have had with a sister. Of course, Phil would have day dreamed about having a little brother, had he known!)

I missed a second week of dancing class even though mother was a bit better. I was told that the walking was 'too much' for her. Her quietness made me sad and I wanted to be as good as possible for her. We stayed in that coming weekend and a couple of times I went to sit on her knee which I had got out of the habit of doing. She hugged me so lovingly and kissed me so tenderly that I didn't want the moment to end. I had no idea why she seemed so quiet and sad.

At the beginning of March I only went to school in the mornings as there were exams in the afternoon. It was great to be at home with mum while Phil was at school. We baked together, walked to the shops together and even went into town with nannan. The latter made me feel so grown up, as if we were three 'women' out shopping. We had our dinner in Atkinsons restaurant, but had to come back for when Phil came home from school. Nannan got off the bus at her stop while we stayed on for another four stops and then walked to the school gates.

Friday 1st March
I got up at 8.45. Then I went to school and in the afternoon at home we had records on. Then we played at ludo and then

had tea. When dad came home we gave him presents as it was his birthday. Then we watched telly and then we went to sleep on something called a bed. *(!?)*

Saturday 2nd March
I got up at 9 o'clock. Then a bit later on, grandad came and took us for a run and to nannan's. Then we had dinner and then played. Then we went home and had dad's birthday party. We played at card games and then nannan and grandad went home. We watched telly and then went to bed to sleep.

(Our favourite card game was 'new market'. From a second pack of cards, the Queen of Hearts, King of Clubs, Jack of Spades and Ace of Hearts are placed on the table. Before the full pack is given out to all players, a halfpence would be placed in the middle of the 4 cards, and a halfpence on a card. The lowest black would start, then a card with a black 2, then 3 and so on. If a player got one of the 4 cards out, they would take the money from that card and the winner would take the money from the middle.)

Sunday 3rd March
I got up at 10.45 and we had breakfast. Then Pic (Phil) and I played at farms. Then we had dinner but not on the table (the farms would have been set up on the table.) Then grandad called and he took Phil for a run. When they came back we played at farms (grandad would have gone home.) Then dad had a bath. Then we had tea and watched telly. A bit later we went to bed.

(As dad only had a bath once a week, usually on a Friday night, it was unusual enough, and newsworthy, to get a mention in Sunday's diary entry.)

Monday 4th March

I got up at 8.45 and went to school. When I came back we had tea. Then nannan called and we all went to look at a house. Then we played at blackboard. (That is, Phil and I.) Nannan went home. Later we watched telly and then went to bed.

Nothing different happened on the Tuesday, except that I resumed going to my dancing class after school. The only difference was that mother stayed with Phil and grandma walked me the rest of the way to the class. Grandad took us home in the car.

Thursday 7th March

I got up at 8.45. Then I went to school. When I came home mum told me I was allergic to 'that stuff they put in the baths'. (The rashes I had been having were due to an allergic reaction to the chlorine used in the swimming baths.) She said she knew because the doctor had been because she was poorly again. Then I had a bath (Phil would have had one after me) and then we had tea with nannan and grandad. Then dad came home and we watched telly.

Dad got a mention in Friday's entry, after we played ludo, he went to have his usual Friday bath.

Saturday 9th March

I got up at 9.30. Then we had breakfast. Then grandad took us for a long run (in the car.) We went into a shop and he bought a new tape recorder. Then we went to nannan's and had dinner. Then I went with nannan to the hospital (visiting Aunt Harriet) and grandad brought us home. We watched 'telly' and then grandad went out. Then I went to bed. (I was staying the night. Grandad went out to the Queen's Ground.)

The tape recorder was the very latest 'reel to reel', in two-tone blue and cream with a 'built-in' superimpose button. Phil and I, on numerous occasions, would have great fun with this button. We would start clapping which we recorded, then we superimposed more claps, and then more claps. When finished, the claps sounded like the clapping from a capacity audience at the Royal Albert Hall. One of us would carry on clapping a bit longer as there would 'always' be someone clapping longer in a real audience. We laughed almost as much as watching the 'laughing policeman' at Yarmouth.

(The tapes of me singing all the nursery rhymes could still be played on this new machine. What springs to mind is 'they don't make them like that anymore' as this recorder continues to work!)

Also, apparent from the diary entries around this time, was our game playing – snakes and ladders, miming, 'I-spy', bingo (board game), draughts, dominoes, cards (new market and rummy) – with our favourite and most frequent game, ludo.

Another popular board game had been free with Gibbs toothpaste. The Ivory Castle Game had an angry looking imp with a club to hinder you when you landed on 'wait here til you get a six', 'go back to 1', and 'it's a nice puddle miss a go'. A Gibbs fairy helped you towards winning with 'take a short cut', 'jump to 14' and 'here's my plane, go to 47'. To win took you through the gates of 'health and happiness'. (There was a Carries Wood in the game which I used as a nickname for the local woods where we picked bluebells in the spring.)

(The ludo and 'Ivory Castle' boards became old and tatty but still playable!)

'Coronation Street' gets a mention occasionally when I was allowed to watch it, or more often, when my brother would go to bed without me so I could stay up a bit longer. I remember some Saturday and Sunday nights going to bed with my brother and then when he was asleep, sneaking downstairs to watch television with my parents. In the weekdays Monday to Thursday our usual bedtime was 7.30pm, unless I was allowed to watch 'Corrie'.

On *Saturday 23rd March*, grandad called to pick Philip and I up in the car and he took us shopping. The diary records that his 'papap' (car) broke down and my brother and I walked to nannan's home and had 'dinner'. Then grandad went back to, and repaired, the car (this pre-dates vehicle breakdown services) and took us back home. In the afternoon we played in the garden.

The following day, *Sunday 24th March*, it was time to call on Aunt Minnie again, but we didn't go this time as Philip was feeling ill. However, not too ill to play with me in the garden or when it was Ludo time! Philip didn't go to school the next day and went to the dentist's with toothache.

I'd like to explain at this point that our favourite aunt was Aunty Minnie (even though it looks as though our visits kept being postponed!) We would visit normally about once a fortnight. Aunt Minnie had a very LOUD doorbell which we loved to ring at least twice each (sometimes more.) Then we would race to be the first one in her rocking chair, rocking vigorously, and looking towards the pantry door (which was a curtain.) She would disappear behind it and then produce a tin bursting with biscuits.

413

Tuesday 26th March

I got up at 8.45 then went to school. At 2 o'clock on the same day Aunt Harriet DIED (grandma's disabled sister). When I came home there was nobody in so I got the keys (from the 'bread knife' neighbour.)

When they (which included my brother) came home we had tea. Then I went to my dancing class (obviously keeping things as 'normal' as possible.) When I came back I wrote and filled up a book*. When dad came home at 8 o'clock we went to bed.

Wednesday 27th March

I got up at 8.45. Then I went to school. When I came out of school we went to nannan's. When I was there I wrote English. Then we had tea. Then we watched telly. Then mum, Phil and nannan went out (to the shops) and I wrote some more English. When they came back we watched telly. At 8 o'clock we went home in grandad's papap. At 8.30 we went to bed.

(I'm not sure why I had reverted to using our 'baby' word of 'papap' for car.)

Thursday 28th March

I got up at 8.45. Pic (Phil) and I didn't go to school. He had a cough and I had a black eye. Then I wrote. Then I read 'Judy'. When mum went shopping Pic and I played together at home. Then nannan came. Then we both had a bath and splashed each other. When mum came back we had tea. Then

*This referred to my first attempt at writing a magazine which I called 'Friendship Club Book'.

grandad came. Then we watched telly. Then nannan and grandad went. Then dad came home. Then we watched telly and then we went to bed at 8.30.

(There were a lot of 'comings' and 'goings' that day.)

Friday 29ᵗʰ March
I got up at 8.45. Then we went to school. (Mum and nannan went to the funeral in the day.) When we came home we watched telly with mum who was still a bit sad. Then dad came home and we played ludo and then he had a bath. Then at ten past eight we went to bed.

Saturday 30ᵗʰ March
I got up at 10.30. We had breakfast. Then I read 'June'. Later on, dad came home (he still worked Saturday mornings.) Nannan came and brought my 'Judy' and Pic read his 'Beano'. Then we played. Then we had tea. Then we watched telly. Then grandad came and we played ludo. Then nannan and grandad went. At 9 o'clock we went to bed.

Sunday 31ˢᵗ March
I got up at 10 to 10. Then we had breakfast. Then I read 'June'. Then we had dinner. Pic and I played together. Then nannan, mum and I went to Gram's (great grandma) and went to the cemetery. (Grandad drove us which left dad and Phil at home.) We had tea. Then grandad took them home (gram and nannan.) Then the four of us watched telly and played at ludo. (Surely not watching and playing at the same time?) Then we went to bed.

(We would have gone to the cemetery to see the flowers on Aunt Harriet's grave.)

Monday 1st April

Got up at 8.45. Then I went to school. When I came home we had tea and then went to the doctors. When we were there he said the little veins had been broken (round my 'black' eye) and it would take weeks to clear up. We went home and it was 7 o'clock and dad was having his cup of tea. At 7.30 we watched Coronation St and then watched I Love Lucy. Then went to bed.

Tuesday 2nd April

Got up at 8.45. Then I went to school and when I came back I had an apple. Then we had tea. Then I went to dancing class. When I came home we played at ludo. Then dad came home and tidied the boxes out upstairs while mum washed doors. Phil hindering (?) and Dad came downstairs at 8.30 and we went to bed.

Wednesday 3rd April

I got up at 8.45. Then I went to school and when I came home mum was waiting for me so we went to nannan's. There I did some English, then we had tea. Then I finished off my English and at 7 o'clock we watched 'Take a Letter' (game show) and then Coronation St.. Then grandad took us home and at 8.30 we went to bed.

Thursday 4th April

I got up at 8.45. Then I went to school and at 3 o'clock I went to the baths with school (swimming). Then went home and nannan was there. Then we had tea. Then we watched telly and grandad came home. Then I drew a picture. Then dad came home. Then we all watched Double your Money (game show) and Bootsie and Snudge. Nannan and grandad went home and we went to bed.

Friday 5th April

I got up at 8.45. Then I went to school. When I came home we played at ludo. Then we had tea and then we watched telly. Then dad came home. Then we took nearly all the furniture into the (front) room because of the chimney sweep. At 8.30 we went to bed.

Saturday 6th April

Got up at 9.30 and had breakfast. Then we took carpet up and covered everything. Then grandad came and then the chimney sweep came. He cleaned the soot up after but everything was still dirty. He went. Then nannan came. Then I helped clear everything up. Phil hindering (meaning 'getting in the way'.) Then they went at 8.30 and later we went to bed.

Sunday 7th April

Got up at 9.30. Then we had breakfast. Then I made an egg into a Queen for school and mum helped me. (Mum blew out the inside of the egg through a small hole in the shell. She had made some tiny clothes and a crown of gold paper. I painted the Queen's face on, of course it looked nothing like the Queen.) Grandad and Phil came back from the run and we had dinner. Then we all went to their house for tea. Then we played at cards. Then they took us home and they went at 9 o'clock.

Monday 8th April

Got up at 8.45 and went to school. When I came home, Pic

was at Steven's (boy across the road). Then Pic came home and we had tea. Then a bit later dad came home and went to football match. Then I posted a letter after I Love Lucy. Then we went to bed.

Tuesday 9th April
I got up at 8.45 and went to school. I took the egg dressed up as the Queen to school. In the afternoon, Miss Thorpe looked to see which was best. Mine came second. When I came home, Pic was at Steven's so I wrote his Easter card. Pic came home and we then had tea. Then I went to dancing class. When we came home I drew a pattern. Dad came home and then we played at ludo. Then we watched telly and we went to bed.

Wednesday 10th April
I got up at 8.45 and went to school. When I came home we went to nannan's. Then tea and then I did English. Then we watched Take a Letter and then Coronation St.. Then grandad brought us home. At 8.30 Pic and I went to bed.
('Take a Letter ' is a game show of the early sixties, hosted by Bob Holness.)

Thursday 11th April (the start of the Easter school holiday)
I got up at 9 o'clock. Then we had breakfast at 10.30. Mum went out with Phil and came back with some glue. Then we stuck paper on cardboard and then I drew a picture. Then we had dinner. Then we played at dressing up. Then dad came home and we watched telly. We watched Bootsie and Snudge and then Eric Sykes.
(The latter was a sit-com with Hattie Jacques as his sister – they kept their own names of Eric and Hattie in the show.)

Friday 12th April (Good Friday)
I got up at 9.30. Then we had breakfast and then listened to the wireless. Then I played with Pickle (Phil). Then we had dinner and later we had an ice cream. Then dad came home and we went to gramam's (dad's mum – going there and back on the bus.) Then we came home and played at ludo. Later we went to bed.

Saturday 13th April
Got up at 9.30 and then we had breakfast. Then dad and I went to the (swimming) baths. When we came back I played with Pic and we had dinner. We played again. Then we all went to the City Hall and danced.
There we had an ice cream. At home we watched telly and later we went to bed. (What no board games?)
(The City Hall held a 'tea dance', for all ages, every Saturday afternoon. 'Tea' referring to the availability of hot, cold and soft beverages only. It was ballroom dancing to a live brass band.)

Sunday 14th April
Got up at 8 o'clock and had breakfast. Nannan and grandad came and we went to Cleethorpes for 11.30 (arrival time.) We took car numbers on the way. We had fish and chips when we got there and then went on the sands. Grandad made a big car in the sand and Phil and I played in it. Mum and nannan went for a walk and when they came back we had tea. We walked on the front and had an ice cream before coming back home. At home we had a small Easter egg.
(We would also have had a Thorntons Easter egg from nannan and grandad with our names in icing which they gave us every Easter.)

Tea would normally consist of stew or mixed grill (the latter is like a Sunday 'fry up' breakfast), or potatoes, vegetables and a meat chop or sausages and on Thursdays it was 'pie' (homemade meat and potato pie). On Friday it was beans on toast. Saturday lunchtime was fish and chips from the 'chip shop'. Saturday tea was normally eaten at nannan and grandad's house. Sunday was a roast dinner eaten at lunchtime, except when we went for a day trip out.

The next school holiday after Easter was Whitsuntide (now called Spring Holiday) and we would visit Aunt Minnie and the other aunts and uncles who lived on the 'Bank in our new Whitsuntide clothes.

One Whitsuntide, I had a new red and white dress, red shoes and handbag. It was the first time I had worn any clothes in the colour red (mainly due to Sheffield Wednesday's rival team, the Blades, playing in red, hence dad's aversion to red.) In the garden we went into Uncle Frank's greenhouse as we were told, "Don't get dirty in 'garden." Oh dear, I found some paint which somehow splashed onto my dress, not a drop going on my brother. It was red paint which I thought 'oh good it will match my dress' but the paint had splashed onto the white areas.

From mum, I got a 'oh no, you've ruined your new dress' reaction. From dad, who had never liked the red and white dress, 'don't go in 'green'ouse again on yer own', and as an aside, 'ugh, I dun't like red an' white'.

The next year's Whitsuntide outfit was a pale turquoise suit with a pleated skirt and a matching pill-box handbag. Mum reminded us, "Now don't go in the greenhouse." So we went to the bottom of the garden and I, not my brother, somehow got a covering of soot (from a garden fire) on my now 'splattered grey' suit. After that, on future visits, we were not allowed out of the house!

What I could never understand was how the red paint and the soot came to my clothes like a magnet and completely repelled Philip's new clothes. He was stood right next to me and the soot billowed up in the air so how did it 'billow' down on me and not on Philip? Anyway, both 'funny' stories were told again and again by the family over the years causing much merriment!

Whit parades, and then the gatherings in the local parks, attracted thousands. At the helm of each church, in the parade, were two flag holders with a large banner of embroidered velvet and tassels depicting a bible scene with Jesus and the name of your church. Behind the flagbearers would be that year's May Queen and her rosebuds. I was a rosebud at the age of five with three others behind our 'Queen'. Then behind us were our parents and the rest of the congregation, all in their Sunday best with children in their new Whitsuntide outfits; except when I was a rosebud and I wore a long, white dress with a fine layer of net over it and a crown of flowers like a bridesmaid. I was given a bracelet to keep.

For at least a week in the six weeks holiday, I would go and stay with nannan and grandad. I loved staying there, even though I missed Philip and mum, but they would call round, of course. I loved sleeping in mum's old bed and looking in all of her old cupboards and the wardrobe. There was a lovely old, but redundant, 'Singer' sewing machine on a trestle table. A large iron pedal underneath operated the machine which I pedalled with my foot at every opportunity.

I also loved going shopping with nannan to the co-op

with the overhead money system and all the different shops. It still took a whole morning to shop as nannan spent so much time talking to people and the shopkeepers. But, most of all, I loved going up into the attic.

How did we fit so much into these six weeks – the holidays, the day trips, the visits to and from our mum's family and dad's family, the days in the park and at the paddling pool. And then the week I stayed with my grandparents. Also, the days we played at home and in the garden. At the time, six weeks seemed endless but I looked forward to going back to school as much as Philip did not.

That year's Christmas Eve was filled with the usual excitement and anticipation of Father Christmas bringing us lots of presents and then nannan and grandad coming round would mean more pressies. But, 'that year', we woke up on Christmas Day and dad wasn't there. Mum said that our 'other' grandad was ill and I remember asking why had dad gone visiting on Christmas Day. Mum had replied that it was because grandad was very ill.

Earlier that week, grandad had been taken ill and admitted to hospital with a suspected heart attack. He seemed to be improving and Uncle Bert, dad's youngest brother, rang the hospital from a public 'phone box on Christmas eve to hear that his condition had deteriorated. Uncle Bert then walked to where my dad worked and told him. They walked back home, collected gramam and caught a bus to the hospital. Dad had returned on Christmas Eve night.

Early on Christmas Day, dad walked the mile, or so, to the hospital as there were no buses. He met up with his mum and other siblings there.

When we went into our parents' room to open our

presents, mum said that dad had left early for the hospital and we would open them downstairs, which we did, but it wasn't the same without dad.

Phil and I played with our new toys and mum went into the kitchen to start the Christmas dinner. Nannan arrived early to help mum and we showed grandad our presents. There wasn't the same excitement and enthusiasm without dad. He missed Christmas dinner. He missed the Queen's speech.

Around teatime, dad came back but stayed in the kitchen with the sliding door closed. Mum went in the kitchen and we could hear dad crying. That made us upset as we had never heard him cry before. Mum came to us and said that grandad had died. Dad was trying not to cry when we went to put our arms round him in the kitchen. I cried more from seeing dad so upset than for our lost grandad.

Phil and I had never visited grandad and gramam on a regular basis and we never went to their house at Whitsuntide in our new clothes. Although they gave us a present, or money, at Christmas they did not give us an Easter egg or birthday present.

This was due to them having a large family with a growing number of grandchildren and they could not afford to give eggs or presents to them all. Our nannan and grandad had only the two of us as grandchildren and, of course, we saw them nearly every day. I understood the difference, but it meant we were not as close to dad's parents.

Philip and I went into the front room and played with our new toys and grandad came in to sit with us. In the living room, dad ate his Christmas dinner which had been warmed up for him.

We still played 'new market' and there was sherry and cigarettes, but Phil and I were quieter than usual as the grown ups were subdued. We watched television before the two of us went to bed.

On Boxing Day, after we walked to our grandparents, dad continued walking on to gramam's house. We waited for him coming back before having tea. We played 'new market' with our coppers and there was still the 'sherry and cigarettes' routine while watching television. Then the four of us all walked back home. The mood had lightened, a bit, as we had been laughing at a comedian on a TV variety show.

(The comedian would not have been Tommy Cooper as all four of the grown ups did not like his 'sort of humour'. It would not have been Charlie Drake as they didn't like his gravelly voice. Because of this, Phil and I grew up not to like them, especially when they appeared on the television someone would get up and switch over or turn the set off. Their favourite comedians were the 'slap stick' ones like Norman Wisdom.)

We had gone back to school when grandad's funeral took place.

During the following year, Uncle Bert had married and gramam had moved into a small flat. There was another reason she had moved – there were slum clearance notices coming through the estate's letter boxes like paper shooting through a printing press. Death warrants had been issued for the two up, two down homes and back to back houses, corner shops and the public houses on the 'estate side' of the main road. Portland Street was going to be wiped off the local map.

The right hand side of the estate where great grandma used to live had also had their 'death warrant' notices. Woollen Lane was set to disappear.

The acute housing shortage of the post war baby boom years had not been assuaged; but wait, how could a city afford to demolish a whole housing estate? The answer was in the planning of what promised to be a better way of living. It was going to be radical, ambitious, modern and … high rise! A new way of solving the housing crisis would be to build upwards.

Town planners were planning flats in the sky, a new way for people to live. This would solve the housing shortage and get rid of people being in cramped living conditions. People would be moved out and put back together to live in a dream, mini village. "Can't wait," said the planners. "What luck, a long term job," said the builders.

Of course, this pioneering utopia dream was still just a dream. No-one thought about what might be replacing the slums as families moved out one by one. Gramam was glad to be moving, the walls had been damp with green mould for some years, and the house was always cold, summer or winter. Over-riding that, she would 'desperately' miss her youngest daughter and her family who had lived two doors down. She would miss her friends Freda and Bill as their children had 'grown and flown the nest'. "We don't want to leave where we've all been so happy," the residents said.

Most of all, gramam would miss her best friend, Edith, from the same courtyard. They had grown up together, had children about the same time, been afraid together in the blitz, both supported each other as they lost their dear husbands and now they were to be parted.

As a child, a lot of things happen around you, but are unseen by yourself. All this was happening and being talked about, yet I was oblivious to what it all really meant. I knew gramam had moved, luckily in time for Christmas, I thought. I was not aware of any slum clearance orders or general rehousing.

Philip and I were in our own little childhood world and bursting with excitement in the build up to Christmas, especially as last year had been such a sad one for dad and for us all.

But this Christmas I had thought what a waste of money it was to buy cards. In the local co-op I had seen different novelties with chocolate buttons inside and that gave me an idea. Mum gave me some time, on my own, in the spice shop while we were out shopping.

The Saturday before Christmas when nannan and grandad were at our house for the evening, it was our Christmas card exchange time. I went to collect a bag hidden at my side of the bedroom.

Card opening began and I delved into this bag and gave everyone either a red postbox or red drum with chocolate buttons inside. Philip was pleased with his drum and chocolates. However, mum and nannan both said, "What's this, where's our card?" I replied, triumphant, "That's instead of a card, it's useful and you can eat it." Mum said back, somewhat glumly, "But this hasn't got a picture or a message inside." I was deflated and could not understand why my useful card substitute had been 'badly' received.

They smiled and thanked me and asked if they could have cards in future. So that became another funny story for my parents and grandparents to tell over and over again.

They couldn't stop laughing the next Christmas at my 'chocolate drop' cards and by then I had found it rather amusing myself. What would come out each year at

Christmas after that? Yes, you've guessed it, the empty postboxes and drums were placed on the sideboard with the decorated and illuminated tree.

In the home, lots of things were changing. In the kitchen were more labour saving devices such as food mixers, sandwich makers and electric washing machines. More and more sink units were being fitted which had a drainer and fitted cupboards underneath. Cleaning carpets made easier with cylinder vacuum cleaners, especially carpeted stairs. There were now electric irons and fold-away ironing boards.

Shops started advertising 'end of winter' sales or 'new year' sales. Newspapers started reporting queues outside stores, hours before the opening time. Inside, there would be a 'battle of the sales' as scores of women tried to grab a bargain.

There was also a lot of new car and road information, such as, "Don't stop in the middle of the road." One might think this is a ridiculous, unnecessary message, but looking through photographs taken in the early 'free for all' days there were motor cars parked in the middle of the city centre roads – not particularly in any line or order. All the driver had to do was avoid the tramlines!

More and more signs were going up on the roads, one way roads created, roundabouts built and traffic lights installed. However, still no speed limits and very few parking restrictions.

I was lucky to have grown up with a grandad who had a car. It meant we were able to go to so many places which would not have been possible or easy to get to by public transport or 'Shank's pony' (walking). As part of the euphoria of starting a diary, I asked my grandad for a 'potted' history of his early life and how he had met nannan. I also asked him questions along the way.

Grandad's Story

I was born above a shop at 'turn o' 'century, the second o' two boys. I knew later that me parents had wanted a girl so she could 'elp out in 'shop as soon as she was able to, but I 'wud 'ave to do fer naw'. Me mam said she said.

(Yorkshire slang explained: o' is of; 'fer naw' is for now; 'the'er' is there; 'we'er' is where. The general use of the apostrophe means that something is missed out, such as 'h' – 'ave; or in the phrase 'turn o' 'century', it has 'the' missed out and an apostrophe is used.)

I can't remember me little bruvver being born, he was 'jus' the'er', but again I know that me mam had wanted a girl and was even more disappointed this time. Both mam and father *(the 'a' in father is pronounced as in 'fat')* had come from a family o' girls so it had been 'teken fer granted' that we would 'ave girls and maybe a boy if 'luck would 'ave it, mind'.

When told 'it's a boy', me mam said father had said, "Ah'll go to 'bottom o' our stairs," meaning he was flabbergasted. His hopes dashed once again for a helper in the shop. Me mam said she had been distraught.

To 'soften the blow', I started fetching and carrying things in the shop – picking up candles from different boxes and giving customers their items wrapped in greaseproof paper or newspaper. My older bruvver had already been through my 'menial' stage with mam herself. He had 'graduated' to handling small amounts of money.

Let's face it, all amounts o' money were small. No-one EVER gave as much as a shillin' *(1s = 5p)* fer a penny *(1d)* or tuppenny *(2d)* item. Everythin' cost a copper or two an' people usually had reet *(right)* money, save fer per'aps the odd farthin' or two change *(a quarter of a penny)*.

A few weeks before Christmas, me older bruvver George and I would 'elp mam wi' baking. We 'ad to stone raisins and skin almonds for Christmas puddings which were fer 'shop but she'd save a small 'un back fer us.

She used upstairs wash bowl for Christmas bakin' as it was the largest she had.

The first day 'ome from work, after commandeering the bowl, father would shout from upstairs, "We'er's it, we'er's it, ger it 'ere." Mam would shout upstairs, knowin' he'd got a jug full of tepid water with nowe'er to pour it, "Use 'jug, I'm bakin." Mumbled words filtered down the stairs – words we shouldn't 'ear as father realised what 'ad 'appened to 'bowl. I deduced that he had a memory of less than twelve months as that scene played each year.

To skin the almonds, yer put some in yer hand and poured hot water o'er and the skins would slide off. Too hot an' yer own skin would slide off! Too cold an' the skins stayed put. I'm left handed so I used my left hand at first and yes, the water was too hot and I saw my own skin slide off an' mix wi' almond skins. Mother rushed to get a dollop of butter from 'tin tub, using her hand, and smoothed it into me blistering skin in order for it to 'eal quicker. I used my right hand after that and got to know temperature needed.

Nothing was added to the puddin' like brandy or a thrupenny *(3d)* bit as it was 'jus' too dear'. We would all have a stir for good luck, even father. If any salt or sugar wer' spilt this was bad luck and you had to throw some o'er yer shoulders. Playin' with either wer' also bad luck. We would get a rap on our knuckles if we were found playing with 'em, but sugar was the most fun. I liked to make as many holes as I could in the large sugar basin, which was difficult as it always avalanched back. Of course, I would forget what I wer' doing and then, rap, rap, rap. Red knuckles and buttered hand, but if father had caught me, red bottom an' all *('an all' means as well.)*

George and I would help with picklin', like cuttin' up cabbage fer mam to mix wi' vinegar and put in jars for 'shop.

Two weeks 'afore Christmas, mam would buy a pig's 'ead and trotters and boil 'em in water for what seemed like the whole day. (The farther away from Christmas it was, the cheaper it was to buy meat.)

She would cut 'meat up an' let it cool down in cookin' water. One year, father had to do it as mam was too heavy wi' little John and he moaned about it even on Christmas Day. He thought ought to do wi' 'ome or kids was 'women's work'. In the coming days, the meat in the cookin' water would all set an' then last longer so there'd be enough to sell in 'shop as well as for us on Christmas Day.

Did we 'ave Christmas presents? A toy each and somert useful to wear ('somert' meaning something). I remember gettin' a wooden stick with a rope attached and a top which father had made – it was a spinnin' top. The rope was wrapped round 'top and you flicked it to 'ground and it spun. I learned later that it had been made for George who said he'd outgrown it an' it wer' wrapped up for me one Christmas. I never had new clothes, save at Christmas, as I wore George's and if we'd had a sister then our aunts would have supplied her with second or third hand clothes. At least we wore sandals as a lot o' local children ran 'round in bare feet.

Those with bare feet were from large families and our's wer' small in comparison. Mam's mam and father's mam were sisters and between 'em they 'ad nine sisters. We had no blood uncles, save our grandparents' brothers, two I think.

The only great uncle I remember had been around at the start of Sheffield's trade union movement and that in later life he became a 'hermit'. I think I only ever met him the once when grandmam took me into his town office on a rare trip away from our shop. The office wer' in a four storey grand house in a large cobbled square, very 'high falutin' (posh). It had electricity which I thought would light up the whole room but it wer' still gloomy. He had a lit candelabrum on the cornish (mantelpiece).

As I gazed 'round his office – big chair and big desk – he bent down to my level and said to me in little more than a whisper, "When yer get yer sister, look after 'er." He was still bent down, for the longest time, and I thought he was goin' to say sumert else, but didn't.

I asked grandmam why he had said that and was I going to 'ave a sister? She said they'd grown up wi' a sister but she had ran off at fifteen and no-one had 'eard from her again. I didn't 'ave a sister in the end.

I never knew my great uncle's brother or me two grandads as they 'ad all died young. All of our aunties used our shop as mam would give 'em a 'bit extra' weight but she said in a whisper to me 'not too much mind'. She added that the secret was to look as though you were givin' more than a 'bit extra' and I 'ad winked back, knowing what she meant.

I can remember father workin' all hours in a grindin' mill and coming 'ome coughing all 'time. By bedtime he'd usually stopped but sometimes you still 'eard him coughing from 'bedroom. George and I slept together and when little John arrived 'e slept in our old crib but when he outgrew that we made 'im sleep in the middle of us with his head at our feet. He used to moan to mam that he would wake up with a toe in 'is mouth or he'd be kicked in 'night by one o' his sleepin' bruvvers. Mam would nod at 'is whining and give due sympathy but there was nowe'er else for him to sleep, save the floor.

By 'time I was five or six, I knew 'everythin' there was to know in the shop, like all the prices and we'er ought was. I could serve and work out money change which George 'ad struggled with. I could pick out all the different sizes of candles an' know we'er 'different pickle jars were kept. Mam sometimes trusted me in 'shop on me own for a while, but not George. I was eager to start school, couldn't wait, but George didn't want to go. After he'd started, 'e said 'e hated it.

When our fourth brother, Ted, died, the undertaker loaned us a makeshift coffin for 'im to stay in 'back room 'til the funeral. He died just before his second birthday. We were all very sad. Me mam distraught.

I remember an argument between mam an' father as to who would run 'shop during 'funeral. In 'end, the two aunts who had helped out with our births, stepped forward. On 'day o' funeral, the front shop door wer' closed. All the houses on 'street drew their front curtains, well, those who 'ad 'em.

Mam wore a borrowed black veil and father was lent a black jacket. He didn't own or wear a tie, ever, even on 'is wedding day, mam said. What 'e always 'ad wer a lit cig in his hand or a stub perched on 'is ear lobe ready to be relit. I do sometimes but not all 'time.

Can I remember being ill? Not really, but I do remember having an accident in 'shop, aged 'bout four. I know I weren't very old and I remember the large tin tub o' lard fallin' on me foot. The lard 'blobbin' on my legs. I sat the'er looking at 'mess and openin' me mouth and yelling the loudest ever yell. Mam said after, that my mouth opened but no sound 'ad actually come out. Funny, 'cos I'd heard the shrillest of yells, slowly coming up thru' me chest and out o' me' mouth. I thought, loud enough to stop a tram.

Mam said I 'didn't stop 'roarin' (crying). She ran wi' me to 'nearby workhouse, turned 'ospital, in our old pram. Due to 'high cost of an 'ospital doctor, a nurse looked at me foot and declared that it would 'ave to 'come off'. Mam said a firm 'no' and took me back 'ome. It were 'first time she had ever completely closed the shop. George had been told to sit in 'back and 'don't tek yer eyes off little 'un', meaning baby John. Mam said he were still sat in exactly same position when she came back, but his pants were wet. He had to take 'em off, dry 'em o'er fire, and put 'em back on.

When father came home he said that I 'ad to see the doctor (the local doctor was cheaper than at the hospital). Mam insisted on going wi' father, but the shop didn't close, so I think an aunt came round to serve an' look after little John which must 'ave been good news for George an' his pants.

The doctor also said me foot'd need amputating, but mam said that 'weren't goin' to 'appen in a month o' Sundays'. The doctor tried to persuade her, but she was adamant I was to keep me foot. It was 'patched' up an' bandaged. My foot hurt for months and I was carried everywe'er or pushed in 'pram wi' me legs o'er sides.

Eventually, I started to walk with a stick picked from the woods and I had to wear an 'ospital boot all time on me weak foot. Towards the end of needing the stick I was hobbling from wearing one big boot and a sandal. Mam told me it was just too dear to buy both boots.

In the long run, me mam was proved right an' I learned to walk without a stick an' after the longest time, I think gettin' on fer two years, to walk without limping. I went into the woods an' threw me boot as far as I could. It hit a tree and bounced back. So I picked it up an' threw it again an' it disappeared forever. Me ankle stayed bulky an' I were left wi' red marks on me foot but that's never bothered me.

After I started school, both George and I would 'elp out in 'shop at dinnertimes while mam were in 'back washin' and cleanin'. When we got 'ome from school we helped out again in 'shop and then after tea we might get chance to play outside for a while. We liked to be out o' house when father came 'ome as he would be coughin' and spittin' and we didn't like to see that. On Sunday we did the most playin' an' sometimes borrowed a cousin's bike (very old an' battered) and went riding round. Both o' us perched an' balanced on 'seat.

One Sunday we cycled to the park which 'ad a nature trail an' paddled in 'river. We forgot the time and when we got back, we both had the slipper from father – he said mam had been 'out of 'er mind wi' worry'. I 'ad to walk bike back (me bottom stung too much to ride) to our cousins' house and said we couldn't borrow it for a few weeks which seemed like, at the time, a month o' Sundays.

If father 'ad a lot to drink or if he couldn't stop coughin', he would make an argument wi' mam or George or I and then one o' us, or both o' us, would get the slipper. If we dared to ask 'what were tha' for', we would get more whacks so it was best not to say ought and just take it. He never hit our mam and very rare our younger bruvver.

I was ten when the King died and on day o' funeral, me mam din't open the shop at 'front. All shops an' schools were closed, but our shop stayed open at the back. Everyone wi' front curtains drew 'em 'til after 'funeral. The King's son became the next King and I read about his Coronation in the newspaper before all of 'em were sold.

Lots o' school kids celebrated the Coronation in schools, in town and in the parks, but George and I stayed at 'ome that week and 'elped out in 'shop as we had more customers than usual. We missed out on a bar o' chocolate all school children got which we were most upset about.

Most o' time I were bored at school. I were bored as teacher went slow for slow learners an' I had already learned what they were learnin'. I got the slipper's 'six o' the best' on me bum whenever I forgot to keep me attention on teacher. It were hard to keep attention as I'd been taught what he were teaching. I was bright enough to leave at age 13 years which wasn't really what I wanted. If it had been my choice I would have liked to 'ave missed a year and be in a class with the older kids but no-one had 'eard of anyone doin' that. I actually mentioned it to me mam at the time but she just said 'don't be silly' and that was that.

George had stopped going to school at age 13, not because he was bright, but because he hated school and just stopped going. He went wi' father to work in the same grinding mill. I didn't want a grinding job because of the dust and coughin' so I worked at a steelworks where everyone smoked so I started smokin'. I liked smokin', it made me feel like a man.

George started smokin' but he said he couldn't stand dust from work an' then cig smoke so he stopped smokin' which I thought was a bit babyish. He never really 'fitted in' at work, father said, which was partly due to not smokin' but also for his love of playing football. He practiced by 'imself all time an' joined a local side.

There was talk of a war and posters everywe'er saying it were 'your duty' to sign up. The war started the year father died. He were only just 50. Family and neighbours who 'ad front room curtains shut them as a mark o' respect 'til the funeral.

Mam said his lungs 'gave out' due to all the dust and coughin'. She hired a horse an' cart for his coffin and the shop was closed front and back on day o' 'funeral. We all walked in a sombre line behind the horse drawn hearse to the cemetery. Mam had borrowed the black veil which she kept on for rest o' day. The shop were open, as usual, the day after.

At the start o' War, there were celebrations all over and flocks of boys and men walking into town to sign up. Me an' George joined the steady stream of, almost marching, men. We were so proud and held our heads up high. Two boys me and George knew who were 15, but looked older, were signed up. George thought he would be signed up as he told them he was 15 and head o' household now. Much to our dismay and shame, we were both turned away. We walked back the long way round to avoid the queues of men still going into town.

(The Government had asked for 100,000 volunteers for what

436

would be a 'quick' war and certainly it would be over by the end of 1914. In the first month, 750,000 had signed up.)

We knew that Sheffield was so far away from Germany their planes couldn't reach us so no-one thought anyone wer' in danger at home or at work. Also, by January and February '15 it was jus' a matter o' time before the War was o'er.

As the year came and went hopes of a quick victory 'ad died, and then there were hundreds of wounded soldiers returning with horrific stories from the frontline. Huge airship Zeppelins started bombing London and other places bringing the frontline ever nearer to us. It was thought they couldn't reach as far as Sheffield.

I 'eard that on a night in September '16, there was a 'do' at the Grand Hotel in town which only left a few night watchmen doin' their jobs. So, almost unnoticed, a long airship sidled into other end o' city. The Zeppelin had followed the lit railway lines and dropped its incendiary bombs and high explosives. Even though it missed 'munitions factories they wrecked workers' homes, killing and injurying many people as they slept. When buzzers sounded people were supposed to go into their cellars but very few did. We 'eard some buzzers where we lived but not on that night.

(Around Sheffield there were anti-aircraft guns and searchlights but on the night of 29 September 1916, low cloud had prevented crews and watchmen from seeing the airship. One gun did take action but to no avail. 28 people died and many more were injured as well as nearly 200 damaged homes. Very few people went down their cellars – a lot went into parks and sheltered under trees and many more just carried on and went to bed. 'Gung-ho' attitudes changed forever after that night.)

By the end of '16, me mam told us she was goin' to cut down on what she sold in shop as food and other goods were not turning up. She 'ad to increase her prices and people were just too poor to buy ought except old food scraps. Me and George gave her all our wages now that father had gone. By the time food were rationed it was all too late for mam who had to close shop. Stale and leftover food from the shop kept us going for a while.

(Most imported goods were shipped in from America and Canada. After a successful U-Boat campaign by the Kaiser, food supplies, especially wheat, were not reaching shops or factories. Food prices rocketed and from 1918 food was rationed, e.g. wheat and bread. The Royal Family publicised that they were also taking part in the food rationing.)

Me mam opened up the shop again in '19 but she never sold food again and it became a hardware 'anything' shop.

On me nights off from shop, I'd hang round end o' street on main road, smokin' and talkin' to any girls who walked on by. That's how I got talkin' to Alice. She was attractive in 'er own way and seemed a bit better dressed than the local girls.

I took her for a walk and the following Sunday we walked into town. Not as many girls smoked as boys, but Alice smoked which I was right proud of an' bragged it to me friends. I also said we 'ad kissed but we hadn't. I also said that some walks were on our own but they weren't – her school friend always came along. A few times there wer' four of us.

One evenin' a week, I would call at me aunt's house with the old piano and practice making up tunes. She had a cornet and I started learning that. I sometimes borrowed the cornet to play at church. I taught meself.

I always talked to Shaw sisters in 'shop as they lived round corner. There were four of 'em and a fifth girl was an invalid in a chair. If one o' 'sisters brought the invalid she would be parked outside as the shop wer' too small, but I'd wedge open door so she could see in. Annie was the sister who brought her to 'shop the most. She was the most attractive of the sisters.

Before Alice, I was 'walking out' with Emily Shaw. Emily said she was trying to learn to play the piano and I asked her to me aunt's house to practice together. After that we went for a few walks and Annie came along.

John started courting Annie which 'peeved' me a bit at the time. Alice and Annie didn't know each other.

I think Emily only took an interest in the piano 'cos I were learnin' it but as I was servin' in 'shop most evenings I didn't 'ave a lot o' time so we drifted apart really. I started 'walking out' with Alice and then we started courtin'.

The difference between 'walking out' and 'courting'? I'm not sure, but when two people first go out it was called 'walking out' so I suppose 'courting' was a bit more serious. I asked Alice to start courting, thinkin' she may let me kiss her.

When John took Annie a walk, one o' her sisters or Nell would always be with 'em. John said he had kissed her, but I didn't believe him. In fact, Alice did let me kiss her when she turned up once on 'er own and we walked to the local park. I said let's go fer a short cut which I knew would take us behind some big trees. She let me kiss her wi' me arms around her waist.

John stopped going out wi' Annie. He said 'Annie had called it a day' but he wouldn't say 'owt else.

Annie seemed to come into shop a bit more which I

thought might be to see John. I would say, "He in't in tonight" and she would reply, "I've just cum in for …" whatever item she 'ad come in for. I felt very brave one evening in 'shop ('cos I'd 'ad a beer from keg barrel) and I asked her if she were free on Sunday and she said she was. When I knew she had gone, I 'whooped' round the shop which brought me mam in to see what was goin' on!

The next night, I walked to Alice's an' said I was just passin', which were a lie. We were in 'kitchen and I said I'd have to finish courting her. She asked a tearful 'why' and I lied and said I'd 'too much on' what wi' a twelve 'our shift at work, the shop and my cornet playing at church and jus' lately in the Cathedral an' all. Alice said she'd come and see me play and I said I'd let 'er know. She was still tearful as I left. I felt pretty miserable an' hoped that she wouldn't spot me 'walking out' with Annie on Sunday. I was playin' the cornet at the Cathedral so that bit were true, but it weren't 'til 'evening service.

I went walkin' wi' Annie and her friend Nell on Sunday afternoon and we walked to Botanical Gardens as I 'ad never been there with Alice. Nell walked behind us and sat down on a form. Annie and I carried on down a path to bear pit. Nell had brought some knittin' to do.

Annie told me that she had seen a bear in the pit when she was about 9 or 10 years old, but I knew she couldn't have as it was years ago since bears were kept down there. She insisted though, and I sort o' believed her.

It was so easy to talk to Annie and we always found somert to talk about. I knew why I had been so 'peeved' when John walked her out – I had been jealous. That afternoon I fell in love with Annie – I didn't give a damn if the bear pit story was true or not. I could have 'whooped' round bear pit, but I jus' lit another cig instead. I offered Annie one and she gave me a funny look as I'd jus' remembered, in my head, that it was Alice who smoked, 'whoops'.

I still felt guilty 'bout Alice so I said to John that she liked him. He asked her out and they got on really well which were a great relief to me. John said I 'was a fool' to give up Alice and that she smoked, as John did. I didn't really care if Annie smoked or not.

John and I made the mistake of going out on a foursome with our young ladies.

It led to Alice an' Annie 'having words' though we had called it a 'spat' at the time. They had only just met each other an' they seemed to take an instant disliking to each other.

To be 'onest though, I think Annie didn't like her 'cos I had courted Alice. They never became friends and there was always an 'undercurrent' of tension between 'em.

But, they 'had to put up and shut up' when they became sisters-in-law, but it were a sort of 'surface politeness'. Annie got on wi' everyone and she liked everyone and everyone liked her, except Alice. That was jus' the way it was.

Did I know that Annie had written to a soldier? Aye, Annie had told me some time before we wed. There was a small case which Annie said had got her 'childish things' in but I knew that this included many postcards he had sent her during the Great War. I didn't mind as I was the one Annie had chosen.

Annie was painfully shy so I just held her on our weddin' night and then we fell asleep.

We spent that first night in our new bedroom at me mam's. The bed had been mine an' me bruvvers' old three quarter sized bed. In the room 'cross 'landing was Mam an' George, still living at home. Annie an' me moved bed round and turned mattress o'er to try an' make bed an' room feel a bit more like our own.

I was earning quite good money at the steelworks and Annie helped me mam in 'shop – though it were unpaid, mind. She gave up 'er filing job the week before we married as all women had to so they could look after 'ome and 'usband. Me mam said Annie were the daughter she never had which filled me wi' pride and love.

What an even prouder day when Annie said, "I think I'm with child." The day little Annie was born was the second best day of our lives – the first best day had been our wedding. Me shirt buttons were in danger of 'popping off' with swollen pride when I told 'chaps at work an' gaffer 'bout sweet little Annie.

Did we think about calling her Elizabeth? There were never any question we would be callin' her ought other than Annie. If she'd been a boy, he would 'ave 'ad my name, Wilf. Princess Elizabeth had been born in April as Annie was born in July – there'd been a picture in 'paper o' new princess but we 'ad our own princess in little Annie.

We started lookin' round for somewhere else to live and found a little house no more than a quarter o' mile away from 'shop. It had a tiny, tiny front wi' paving slabs an' a privet hedge. At the back was a shed, a tiny, tiny lawn an' a small garden wi' paths an' flowers. The outside closet stood alone rather than in a row o' closets. House had both a cellar and an attic. We felt we had moved into Buckingham Palace! Well, it was like that to us.

We'd not been renting the house very long when the

steelworks started laying off workers in the recession in the late '20s. Annie had carried on helping mam in 'shop, going there every day wi' little Annie in her push chair and we were now grateful for the bit o' money me mam was givin' us for that help. In fact, it was our only source o' money.

Me mam told Annie how to save on meat by buying offcuts, boiling 'em up, and then letting 'em set so that we could at least 'ave some meat in stews an' for Sunday dinner. It seemed like we had potatoes for breakfast, potato soup for dinner and then potatoes with somert else for tea. I drew the line at anything 'potato-ey' for supper, so it were dry bread!

We got by wi' Annie's sisters givin' us clothes for little Annie which we didn't like but we had no choice. They brought stew round an' all. All our plans to buy bits o' furniture for 'house went out o' window so to speak. Annie offered to pawn her engagement ring which I said a BIG 'naw' to an' not to even think it. I had bought the ring from Pond Street which was a road in town full o' little jewellers' shops and had been a stagecoach terminus. The ring was 22 carat gold with three small diamonds, set at an angle. I even said, "I'd move us back in wi' me' mam than pawn tha' ring."

In me search for work I spent hours, days, walking round the local steelworks and the ones not so local, but there were no work anywe'er. I decided to try me luck at small tools firms and file cutters' works. I spent more hours, days, doin' that. Then, 'bingo', a small tools engineering firm, 'jus' down road', needed someone to start straightaway. I started straightaway.

I wanted to learn everythin' quickly an' I talked to most o' workers to see what they did an' to build a picture up about their work. This seemed to impress Mr Wing, the gaffer, and he'd just had a new baby girl an' all. I went wi' him in his big, black car to larger works, 'touting' for business so to speak. He liked my easy talking manner an' he gave me an office and his big, black car (he bought a new one) to go round the firms on my own. I loved it, and I could use the car on Sunday and anytime.

I loved being wi' me family, me music an' billiards.

We 'ad a bit o' money now to start buying bits o' furniture from Patnicks, the nearby second hand shop. George helped me carry a piano up the hill and along the road to 'house. What a 'pull' that was up the hill and we drank a full pot o' tea each when we'd done. We had such a laugh pushing an armchair on castors up the same hill that I nearly wet me long johns.

What did I think of Joseph, yer dad? Well, I liked him and I did invite him to the Queen's Ground to play billiards and 'ave a pint but yer nannan quashed it as not right and proper. She thought he weren't good enough for our Anne, as she wanted to be called. He came from a large, poor family but of course Annie had. He came from a 'two up, two down, back-to-back' housing estate, but so did we. He was very, very shy and blushed which I very, very much liked. He was so shy I think Anne was the first ever girl he'd courted.

Anne had already courted Ralph who 'ad been a soldier in the Second World War and when he called for her, he were always smartly turned out in his uniform. They had met at a dance. Annie thought he was 'just the sort o' man for our Anne to wed'. I think she was 'reliving' her time with her Great War soldier but I said nowt.

Annie was polite to Joseph but no more. She wanted Anne to 'better herself' and wed someone who 'ad a good job an' maybe she would have if she hadn't changed jobs to work in the wages office where Joseph worked. That's where they met.

We asked Anne to have a long courtship. We met Joseph's mother and father one evening at the Speedway. They announced at Christmas they were to wed in March. Was four months a long courtship – yer nannan didn't think so!

Their wedding day should 'ave been the third best day of our lives, but I can honestly say that it wasn't. Annie had no teeth in. Annie's gums, minus teeth, were still healing. It certainly spoiled the day for us. I felt so sorry for Annie who couldn't laugh, even smile, or eat ought at the wedding breakfast.

There's no doubt though that our third best day of our lives was our first grandchild coming into the world. Annie wanted yer to be called 'Annie' or 'Anne' but the compromise was 'Jean Anne'. Yer mum favoured 'Carol Anne' but Annie quashed that as it was nowhere near to Christmas. So you became our little Jean Anne. *(Grandad smiled and touched my cheek.)*

"Our 'ome wer' your 'ome for first three years o' yer life." We put a crib into second bedroom, as well as a new wardrobe and matching dressing table. Yer Aunt Lily 'ad made a rug out o' material scraps and it were placed between 'bed an' crib. Lily had also crocheted a tiny blanket and then she crocheted yer christenin' shawl.

As I played the cornet for the Cathedral, I asked the Vicar if my little Jean Anne could be christened there, and he said 'yes'. I were o'er moon – we all were.

It was like going to a christening in Westminster Abbey, it was grand, jus' grand. You couldn't make up yer mind when the holy waterfall started falling, whether to cry or not, but we needn't 'ave worried as you were as good as gold.

We felt like the Royal Family when we emerged from the Cathedral in our Sunday finery as people walking passed and came over to 'bill and coo' over our newly christened baby.

By age o' three yer knew all nursery rhymes an' I taped yer singing 'Jack and Jill' and 'Humpty Dumpty'. I was so proud o' yer, still am. Yer mum taught you to read the 'Janet and John' books.

I really missed yer when yer mum and dad moved to your own home, but there was a second baby on the way, our Philip. We were so blessed to have a grandaughter and then a grandson, one of each.

I started pickin' yer up on a Sat'day mornings to take yer fer a run round in 'car and we'd call in at work. You loved havin' a swivel on me big black chair and pickin' up the big black 'phone. I rang someone from another works and asked him to ring at a set time so that yer could hear what the sound was like. You nearly fell off the chair and I picked the receiver up and gave it to you. You looked into that phone's ear piece as if the man was inside it. *(I said, I couldn't remember that.)*

When Phil got a bit older, I took both of you for a run before calling in at work. You'd lift Phil onto the swivel chair and spin him round, 'not too fast, mind', I'd have to say. Once or twice he'd come off that lookin' a sickly shade o' green. We all loved those Sat'day runs. *(I nodded.)*

Yer nan wouldn't let me boil the fish bait at 'ome, so I had to do it at work. They were pellets or a paste which thickened when heated. I loved it when all six of us went out on a Sunday fishing in Newark or Knaresboro' or going to the seaside.

We helped your mum and dad wi' money side o' things when we went on a week's holiday. At the seaside we all had an ice cream and one o' me favourite sayings was 'we all scream for ice cream'. And when we first saw the sea we'd shout, 'I can see the sea and the sea can see me. *(I said, I could remember that.)*

At Yarmouth, yer dad asked me to take yer both on the Snails ride early on or we'd be 'tormented all day'. And if we walked near 'Joyland' at night yer went on the Snails again.

When Phil or you looked glum or you'd jus' been told off for somert, I would stick my thumb up at yer and say 'laugh at that' and I always got at least a smile out o' yer. *(I just can't think why we thought that was so funny.)*

When we went fishin' no-one liked to catch eels, but you made such a 'song an' dance' about it. One Sunday in Lincoln your float went down and you started shrieking, "I've caught a big fish, it's a whale." Of course, it wasn't a whale, but what came out of the water was a big, fat slimy eel. I positioned the keepnet alongside the moving line in the water and with my spare arm I tried to help you lift this 'monster' out o' water.

You started shrieking again so I put the keepnet down and took the rod from you, lifting it high enough to expose the 'whale'. What a performance!

Grandad carried on, "Only we never landed it, did we? I had to cut the line and lose a good float which was not uncommon with an eel."

I recalled that we had quite a crowd of people watching to see what was going to emerge from the water after I'd sounded the 'shrieking' fish alert siren. People came off their boats and passers by stopped passing by to see this spectacle, this 'monster fish'. There was muttering that it could be a 'big daddy' trout or salmon, but as the eel flapped and wriggled on the water's surface, the embarrassing titters started. Passers by started passing by again and the crowd thinned, thank goodness!

Grandad asked me if I could remember when he came down the helter skelter bowl at Yarmouth. No-one watching would ever forget it!

After you moved into yer new home, I made you a swing at work. Yer dad and me put it up one spring evenin' after you'd both gone to bed. When you went outside the next day Phil thought a swing had 'grown' in the garden overnight. I was told you were both swinging that much and for so long, yer mum brought your dinner out to you. Yer were still swinging when yer nan and me arrived later on. I had a swing as well – that made you all laugh. *(I smiled.)*

When you weren't playing you were reading or writing. Phil didn't like either reading or writing. "I'm so, so proud o' yer both," he said. *(I hugged him.)*

I know that you were ahead in your school class for reading and writing. And by eight or nine you'd started a diary and were writing poems in an exercise book. When yer stayed at our house in the school holidays, you'd bring your writing and the book you were reading.

First Poems

My first poems were in my head before I put them to paper.
I wrote the rhyming words first and then made them into
the following two poems:

What did you pay
For that stack of hay
What did you say
I said what did you pay
For that stack of hay
One pound that's what you pay.

What did I win
A rusty old pin
A shiny new bin
A big heavy tin
It was nice to win.

I started writing 'books' as a vehicle for my poems. I pulled
out a few double, centre pages of an exercise book, which
became the first attempt at putting together a book-type
magazine. I called this the *Friendship Club Book* with the front
page having a message from the editor.

Grandad was never too busy to look at what I had done

when he came home from work. If I asked nannan she would say 'in a bit' or after whatever she was doing. Sometimes she forgot. I knew never to ask her just before grandad came home as that was the time she got out the 'donkey' stone for the steps and then started making the tea.

Nannan liked the fashion pages, especially the underwear section, as she wore the same featured long vest. I cut underwear pictures out from advertisements in one of our newspapers or magazines, then stuck them next to my narrative.

I wrote a 'Dear Readers' section with a 'lovely selection of snaps' *(they were actually pictures I'd drawn)*. Under a landscape scene I wrote, "The one on the right is very colourful indeed."

On the front page, I tried to tempt readers into buying the magazine: "I wonder what Little Sport and Saturday Sammy are up to – turn to back page and find out," they were characters from a daily newspaper. My made up name as editor was 'Lindy'. Also, on the front page were three letters to 'Lindy' from 'readers'.

Turning over was the 'Pets Page'. I'd cut out a picture from a magazine of a girl throwing bread in the air for birds but her dog was jumping up for the bread. I wrote, "My dog loves bread which is very unusual for a dog. We are on holiday in Yarmouth, we are on the pier. I am throwing bread to the seagulls but my dog Bret is having it instead." *(The dog was completely made up.)*

On the next page was a form with details on how to join the Friendship Club. All you had to do was complete the form and send with a 1/6d (old money of one shilling and sixpence). It stated that you had to put a 3d stamp on the envelope (postage rate at that time – a straight conversion of 3d to the money of today, would be 15p.) After joining the Friendship Club, you would be sent a badge, a 'few books', a membership number and your own secret code. *(Wow!)*

Over the page was 'Safari Sue', part of a picture story I had cut from one of my two girls' magazines, 'June' and 'Judy'.

A woman's dress and coat was stuck into a fashion page opposite the picture story. Opposite was the page on 'underwear' (featuring a 'vest and panty all in one' for 29/11d which was £1.9s.11d – half of an old pound was 10s. In the 'new' money this would be written as £1.50p.)

Then there was a page on 'wooliwear', featuring a cut out picture of a 'charming wool hat and scarf with red and white bits at both ends'.

The two centre pages were called 'Fun and Puzzle' pages with spot the difference pictures, a crossword and 'a sweet treat to try by Sweety Pye' the latter cut out from a magazine. There was a puzzle column, a numbers game and a 'Hello Everyone' letter from the Editor (Lindy). Also, packed into these two pages were cut out and stuck on photos of a Rose and her rosebuds (from 'June' magazine.)

Before the back page, there were pop pages, more picture stories and an article (cut out and stuck in) of a boy who had tattoos over his chest and arm with the heading 'the man who did this needs whipping'! On the inside back page were cut out and stuck in picture jokes.

Sport on the back page included jokes of 'Little Sport' and 'Saturday Sammy'. Also, tomorrow's weather, local football news and an article on Stanley Matthews.

(Stanley Matthews is an England football legend. Although I knew of him, I was too young to have seen him play. He kept fit

enough to play top level football until he was 50 and was the oldest player to ever represent England. He moved from Stoke to Blackpool for a record £11,500 at the age of 32 and earned the maximum a footballer could earn, at that time, of £12 per week. He later returned to Stoke before he retired.)

I was also writing a magazine called *'Star Book'* (as I had stuck some gold stars on the exercise book cover.)

This magazine included articles on the Queen, her family tree, a timetable of when children should go to bed, some French translations, drawings I did of my brother, a list of names of girls and boys in my school class, my own family tree and an imaginary one. Also, a crossword I had written with the answers at the back of the book.

There was an account of a meeting with an aunt and uncle (grandad's brother and his wife who had made their home in Watford after he finished his football career.)

An Account of the Meeting with Uncle George and Aunt Margaret (as I had written it)

The couple had not set foot in the city for five years and everything (so they said) had changed, the Estate where they had lived was still one mass of rubble.

(Due to slum clearance rather than WW2 bomb damage.)

Aunt Margaret has goofy teeth which are going bad, they are her own. Her hair is dyed a kind of beige colour to match her suit. *(Really?)* She loves children and has Sophie and Stephen *(their grandchildren)* for a week while Christine *(daughter)* and her husband have a holiday undisturbed.

Uncle George has false teeth and wore a dark grey suit. His hair was brown, but receding at the temples. He obviously likes his brother (my grandad) better than his other brother, for he spent one afternoon and one night with Grandad and only a morning with his other brother.

(Note the quite graphic teeth descriptions, e.g. 'goofy' teeth, which were not meant unkindly. They were, in fact, my favourite aunt and uncle on my grandad's side of the family. 'Favourites' due to them sending Christmas presents through the post.)

At 4.30 in the afternoon of Good Friday, Mum, Philip and I were watching 'Black Beauty' on television. A car drew up at the bottom of the steps, it was a blue estate car with a white bonnet. Aunt Margaret and Uncle George descended with a knock on our door. I turned the telly off and awaited a shake of the hand, a hug, and a kiss.

They sat down, the man on the settee and my aunt on the easy chair. We all talked, talking about my education was one of the subjects. After some time Mum showed them around upstairs of our house. Philip and I remained downstairs. Another talking session followed when at 6.15 they went for tea at Gram's *(for the purpose of the book I had put Gram's instead of Nannan and Grandad.)*

By 7.00 Dad, Mum, Philip and I walked to Gram's to join them for the night (not all night.) I had changed from my jeans into my torquise *(turquoise)* suit, I also put a teeny bit of lipstick on my lips.

After watching TV we all had a game of bingo for 1d a game. I checked for the caller and won twice. We were then given Easter Eggs. Mum handed round small chocolate eggs and they sure were delicious.

We all had a drink of either sherry or whisky (Philip had lemonade). I had sherry diluted, so did Aunt and Mum, the others had sherry or whisky strong.

Later on, supper was got ready by the ladies, excluding our lady guest. I had two pickled onions and some corned beef. A piece of cake afterwards. It was a most enjoyable meal.

At around 11 o'clock Uncle George took the four of us home in his car. It made a lot of noise, but it was better than walking. Aunt Margaret remained behind as they were sleeping at Gram's. I went to bed at 11.30 and was asleep at 12.10. *(How did I know what time I fell asleep?)*

* * * * *

There is a page on 'how I dislocated my elbow' while at school, which seems not in the least bit interesting, but gives an insight into what happened at that time. For example, dislocated bones are not left dislocated but the joint is pushed back as quickly as possible which reduces swelling and any potential impairment.

The day I dislocated my elbow

On the Friday I had my medical and then went to gym where only having spent 10 minutes there I bounced on the trampette and over a trestle, but instead of landing on my feet I landed on my left elbow which came out of its joint. The school 'phoned an ambulance where I went with Joy *(my school friend)* to the Infirmary Hospital, *(it was nearer than the Children's Hospital.)* I was still clad in gym blouse, skirt with shorts underneath and Joy's stockings on my feet. *(Joy had lent me some socks rather than go bare foot to the hospital.)*

(The doctor at the hospital said to me that I should feel quite

'grown up' for coming here than to the Children's Hospital and I did feel very 'grown up' after he said that. It didn't last long as the pain took over.)

Mum and Dad came at 11.30 after a black doctor had x-rayed my arm and I waited in a wheelchair to have my arm put in place again. The doctor closed the cubicle screens and pressed on my elbow and with no anaesthetic, no screaming or crying it clicked back in place. I was x-rayed again and strapped up for 6 weeks. I was discharged on Thursday 16th Feb still not straight.

(Afterwards, the arm was extremely swollen and painful underneath its tight bandaging. I wore a sling except in bed and could not bathe properly until the bandaging was removed. Mum had to help me in and out of the bath. I was told by the doctor that I would never straighten my left arm again, but perseverance and pushing it outwards every day ensured that eventually it became straight again. I was determined that I would not be going through life with a half-bent left arm and my daily efforts, over the next year or so, finally paid off.)

Poems from the '*Star Book*'

Thinking
If I had a boat,
Then I'd put on a coat,
For if it splashes
I'd get wet through.

I would advertise for a crew,
One or two girls and maybe a boy,
Every kind of equipment,

But! Not one single toy.
I should take something to eat
And put on the seat
Of my small, compact boat,
Beside the red and blue coat.

My School
This School of mine is Malin Bridge,
Where the teachers are hazy
And the pupils are crazy,
Because of the time between lessons.

My teacher's name is Fred esquire.
He's a nice, tall, bearded man,
On all pupils pranks he makes a ban,
Proud he wants to be of his form.

In winter it is very bleak
And leaves the pupils rather weak,
The teachers think, "Ah! cold weather,
Now shall I go to school or whether…"

Music, Maths, Science, Scripture,
The lessons really are enough
When homework being easy or tough
Is done to the teachers delight.

From early days the school has grown,
Working our fingers to the bone,
Who knows that in the future
There might be a young year tutor.

The Hare and the Tortoise

A hare and a tortoise
Were out racing one day,
I was so very fortunate
Because they came my way.

I tried to speak to them
But they raced on by,
And when they got out of sight
I gave a little sigh.

The next day they came again
A racing once more,
And as those two went on by
I saw the hare's sharp claw.

I'm sorry to have to say
They never came another day
They must have gone another way
That tortoise and that hare.

A story about my brother in the *'Star Book'*

My brother is called Philip and he is six years old. He enjoys stamp collecting and I like that as well. We stick stamps into a stamp book and we have one each. He has not many stamps, they are mostly English ones, only four are foreign. Philip had five but I did swap with two of my English stamps for a stamp he had from Spain. It is red with a picture of a house from Valencia on it.

Philip does not like going to school and he is good at arithmetic sums. He does not know his times table. He likes taking toys to school – a toy car, a toy bulldozer, and a gun.

He is very handsome and good looking and cannot stand his hair being cut which is well over his ears and eyes. He likes brown shoes and does not like any others.

★ ★ ★ ★ ★

(I had wanted the Valencia stamp for my collection ever since Phil was given it. I 'bribed' him into thinking he was getting a 'good deal' of two stamps for one. It seemed I was being 'unfair' to my own brother, but the feeling of pleasure in owning that stamp far outweighed any other feeling, sorry bro.)

As a child, I remember feeling many emotions but without the wisdom of knowing what was behind that emotion. I remember the next door neighbour coming round to see mum and she said her daffodils had been trampled on by us. My mum and the neighbour 'had words' and mum had promised to talk to us about it. The neighbour grunted and went home.

Mum asked us if we had trampled the daffodils and we both said, "No." In fact, we knew that it was the boy from across the road who had called to play with Philip and he said as much to mum. But instead of saying thank you and going to tell the neighbour it wasn't us, she became cross and angry that she hadn't known the boy had come round to play. She said they had both trampled the daffodils, even though I said it wasn't Philip.

When dad came home, mum told him about the trampled daffodils and Philip got a smack on his legs from dad. I had one a few weeks later.

Philip and I were playing in the garden, throwing a long

cane at each other like a javelin. We were playing rather than trying to hit each other. My cane, however, accidentally struck Philip on his head and he went inside crying to Mum.

When dad came home, mum told him about my cane hitting Philip and I got a smack on the legs from dad.

Even at the time, I felt both smacks were unfair as Philip did not trample the daffodils and I hadn't meant to hit him with the cane. My heart is pounding just writing this as I, once again, feel the injustice of the two incidents.

The feeling of unfairness was a lot stronger than what I felt when the teacher said I had spoiled Norma's painting. I was learning that strong emotions helped me to write poetry.

We laugh
We play
Each day

We think
We make
And bake*
We jump
We run
In the sun

He pushes
The ball
And I fall

I push
The balls
And he falls

I cry
We cry

He is crying
I am crying

*Bake is a reference to Phil and I helping Mum in the kitchen.

The crying at the end was inferring that even when we were happy playing, it might all 'end' in tears. That is, one of us would be hurt playing or mum would tell dad of something and one of us would get smacked on the leg.

When we thought we were being 'naughty' like hiding in our tree den at the bottom of the garden, mum took it very well and even joked about it. Both mum and dad took the 'soot' and 'red paint' incidents at Aunt Minnie's very well, to say that my red and white dress had been ruined.

Some aspects of growing up were very confusing!

Just After Spring

It was around the time of my early poems and magazine writing that my parents put their names down against a plot of land. It was for a semi detached, 3 bedroomed house nearer to the main road and opposite the local park. The land was a rose garden and orchard within the grounds of a convent.

One day, the four of us were walking back, on the main road, from visiting grandma and grandad but we passed the side road we normally walk up. We asked why we were going the 'wrong way' and our parents said, "Wait an' see, we're gonna show you something."

We walked up the next road, and dad pointed to a convent's rose garden with tall trees surrounded by a high wall. Phil and I exchanged puzzled glances. Dad said, "We've put our names down for a new house to be built on there." The garden didn't seem large enough for two houses, let alone the five dad said were going to be built.

Over the coming months, our new route home took us up the 'new' road as we saw the houses take shape. There was a detached next to 'our' new semi-detached house. After a second semi detached pair of houses was a driveway to the garages round the back. At the top of what would be our garden was the detached house's garage and our own, making our garden smaller. Dad said that hadn't been on the original plan for our garden to have both garages. He complained to the builders but no avail. The builders were hardly going to say, "Oh dear got it wrong, we'll move one of the garages!"

There was still enough room in the garden for our own flower beds, in front of our garage's side wall. My growing apple tree was uprooted, to be replanted in my new flower bed. Our swing was dug up by dad and grandad to be rebuilt on the new lawn.

(Left behind in the ground were the two grindstones, deemed far too heavy to be moved again – if anyone ever dug up that lawn they would find the two grindstones. Any diggers may even bring in historians who may declare 'what a discovery, this lawn must be on the site of an old mill'. The 'discovery' could become part of an archeological dig with television coverage. Or am I getting a bit carried away, reminiscent of my 'giddy kipper' days?

Seriously though, the two grindstones are still embedded there as the lawn appears to be untouched – following a clandestine visit to check!)

In the new garden there were two large pear trees in the middle of what would be the lawn and where our swing would be going. The trees, unfortunately, had to go. As no-one had collected the pears, the fruit was rotting, smelly and strewn over the whole garden. I would have liked to have seen the trees being taken down, but on our next passing visit, the trees had 'disappeared'.

When it was time to pack all our belongings for the move, we sadly took our posters down off the bedroom wall. We were under strict instructions they were not to go up in the new house. The posters of pop stars collected from my magazine 'June' were all over my side of the bedroom. Pride of place had been John Lennon and Cliff Richard. We packed our toys and books into boxes one weekend and the move took place while we were at school.

We had set off for school from home and returned to a new, different home after school.

Walking the new, longer route home seemed strange. We hesitated at the back door and on hearing voices, we slowly opened the door. A barrage of do's and don'ts came our way – do come in, don't put anything down; please help, but don't touch anything. Dad was not at work and looked dishevelled. Mum looked completely in control except her hair was dusty and messy.

How could we help, we asked. "Make your beds upstairs," shouted mum.

Apart from a few kitchen items and a tea towel, everything was in boxes and crates. There was no evidence of any tea and where was the television? It turned into the day we had to have toast for tea and missed children's hour on TV.

Upstairs was worse than downstairs. Phil's bed was on its side and mine had two large boxes on top. In the bathroom were two mounds of bedding tied together with rope. Mum and dad's room had a larger mound of bedding propped up between the wardrobe and dressing table. Boxes were everywhere.

We could hear grandma's voice from downstairs and then we watched her slowly come to join us. She said, "Let's start with the bedding and see if we can make the beds." The three of us somehow got our two beds made up. Phil and I did not speak as the realisation of separate bedrooms 'hit home'.

We went downstairs and grandma made a pot of tea using

the new automatic kettle. Grandad had unearthed the television and was busy fiddling with the knobs to get it to work again. Dad was playing at musical boxes in and out of the living and dining rooms.

Phil and I went outside in the garden and collected some of the smelly rotting pears in a discarded box. The swing poles were laid across the lawn ready to be erected. There was a bag of cement and two spades there as well. We realised that the concrete would be replacing the grindstones.

This new kitchen looked very different from our old one and very modern with fitted cupboards next to a fitted sink unit. The cooker was an oven with hobs and an open grill above. There was a hatch over the two fitted cupboards which divided the dining room and kitchen. The stand alone kitchen unit, still popular, fitted next to the cupboards and hatch. In fact, that space was left for a kitchen unit. There was still a walk-in pantry from the kitchen which went back under the stairs.

Mum had bought an electric twin tub. This had a washer in one half and a spin dryer in the other. A rubber pipe was attached from the hot tap into the washer to fill it with water. In went the washing up powder and the electric motion washed the clothes. The electric twin tub, a revelation at the time, did leave the housewife free to do other chores while her clothes were washed.

However, once washed, the housewife was back in the kitchen. The clothes had to be moved into the spin dryer side and rinsed with water through the pipe attached to the tap, then a short spin. Clothes rinsed for the second time followed by a longer spin. Meanwhile, the water from the other half had to be emptied using a second rubber pipe from the washer to the sink. This could only be done by moving the pipe up and down in a rhythm conducive for manually emptying the water. If the water was not too 'murky', mum would use it again for the next load of washing (but we weren't to tell grandma.)

Dad's shirt collars and socks were still rubbed with soap before they went into the washer. Woollens and other delicate garments continued to be hand washed at the sink, rinsed twice and squeezed instead of spinning.

The radiogram was in the dining room with the table and chairs. The television was now in the living room on a table. The settee from the previous front room was now used to watch the television along with the 'big chair'. Along the back wall was the sideboard.

From the sitting room there was a door into a small hallway for coats and shoes at the front door and bottom of the stairs. The front door was never used. To hang up your coat and leave your shoes in the hallway meant walking through the living room, but that was just how it was.

At the top of the stairs was a window looking out from the side of the house (useful to 'monitor' the family in the detached house next door).

(The reason my parents had not chosen the detached house had nothing to do with money. They did not like the side door opening onto the high stone wall of the convent. For the record, each of the four semi-detached houses cost less than £1000.)

Upstairs the bathroom was the first on the left, then my bedroom with both rooms overlooking the back garden. Beyond the two garages, over an old stone wall, was a large courtyard where children were playing. Until we moved in we hadn't realised that the catholic convent was also an orphanage.

The master bedroom had the large mahogany wardrobe and the matching dressing table. The other, smaller front bedroom was my brother's with a single bed and cupboard. Next to the door was an 'imposed' shelf which formed the 'head' space for coming up and downstairs. He used this shelf for his airfix aeroplanes, dumper truck and toy cars.

In my room was my three quarter sized bed, a chair and a 'tallboy' which was part of the master bedroom suite. Next to the window was my mum's old desk which was now mine. I did not want the 'tallboy' in my room as I regarded it as 'old fashioned' and 'spoiling' my new bedroom. Grandparents came to the rescue and they bought me a 'combination' wardrobe. There was only one condition – I had to keep the 'tallboy' in my room.

(A 'tallboy' is a cupboard for sheets and linen with a drawer underneath. My new 'combination' wardrobe had a half wardrobe door and in the other half from the top: sliding cupboard mirrors over a pull down door which acted as a writing desk and then three drawers underneath that. Similar wardrobes would have different combinations of cupboards and drawers.)

This house had no attic, but there was a white trapdoor in the ceiling outside my brother's bedroom. "Is the attic up there?" I asked. "Naw, it's a loft," said dad.

I further asked, "How do you get up there?" Dad showed me by getting the wooden stepladder, climbing up and sliding the trapdoor open.

He climbed down and I climbed up. All I could see, in the darkness, was a lot of golden coloured 'cotton wool' (fibreglass) in between wooden planks and the sloping roof above. I had no desire whatsoever to actually go into the loft.

Our old attic, though, had been nowhere near as

interesting as my grandparents' attic. Our's had housed only the television aerial, a couple of old chairs and boxes of uninteresting things like winter bed linen (if it was summer) or summer bed clothes in winter.

The only interesting thing in the old attic was a square cut-out in the wall, which had four corner screws keeping it in place. One evening, Phil and I had quietly gone into the attic with a screwdriver and took off this loose piece of the wall. It was cold and dark and we heard bird sounds which frightened us. We quickly screwed it back. (That had been our secret reason why we didn't want to sleep in the attic.)

We never realised that our parents would buy a three bedroomed house to give us separate rooms. At the time, we had not known that a third sibling had been planned.

One advantage of being in separate bedrooms, for me, was that I could stay up a bit later at night, albeit under protest from my brother – 'why do you let her stay up'? Mum would answer 'because she's older' or 'you need more sleep 'cos you're younger'. On weekend mornings, my brother and I would take it in turns to go into each other's bed after we woke up.

For my mum, there were endless shops up and down the main road. It was also the main road to and from our grandparents so the walk to their home was made about fifteen minutes shorter.

Hillsborough shopping 'mecca' still included a lot of the older established shops, like the Woolworths store; the ladies' clothes shop; the large co-op, now with a café; the butchers shops; fishmongers; card shops; the spice shop; a pet shop; hardware stores; the 'selling anything' shops; cobblers and key cutting and the two banks.

Gone was the post office in someone's front room. Kinema Cinema had closed along with the alternative entertainment at the dentist-cum-chemist shop. Gone were the tram lines on the main road.

There was now a Burton menswear store; both gas and electric showrooms; a purpose built post office; a new chemist and a grocery store which had become self service.

A housewife was still involved with shopping over several hours through the week, especially if she did not have a fridge. (Nannan remained 'loyal' to the cellar, buying fresh food in small quantities and needing to visit the shops each day.)

Our new fitted kitchen did not include a space for a fridge, so it had to go in the corner of the dining room, next to the radiogram. They went together like chalk and cheese but at least we could have iced lollies 'on tap' in the fridge's small freezer compartment.

Converting grocery stores to self service was the start of easier and quicker shopping. At first, these stores were cramped for space, but very soon purpose built, larger self service shops started opening. The introduction of frozen foods completely speeded up the whole shopping 'experience'. Bird's Eye fish fingers had arrived!

(Three cheers for Mr Bird's Eye – in fact, there really was a Mr Birdseye. He was born in 1886 in New York, a taxidermist by trade, who had an interest in cooking. He wished he could have fresh food all year round. While fishing in the Arctic, he saw that locals preserved fish in buckets of sea water which froze quickly in the Arctic temperatures. In 1926, armed with buckets of brine and ice, he set about perfecting the process of putting fresh food into waxed packets and quickly freezing them. In 1930, a company under the name of

'Bird's Eye Frosted Food' started selling frozen vegetables, fruit, seafood and meat. It took a 'little' longer to reach Britain!)

There was the new power of television advertising, not least the one depicting 'Captain Birdseye's new frozen peas and fish fingers'! Any new product promoted in a popular family scene and with a catchy tune ensured good, if not phenomenal sales, in the next few days and weeks. Especially if advertised around the showing of Coronation Street.

Some foods were specifically aimed at children during their television programmes. Sugary cereals 'took off' – 'Sugar Pops', 'Sugar Frosted Flakes' (29% sugar) and 'Sugar Smacks' (over 50% sugar). I started the day with 'Sugar Smacks', but my brother had toast.

Sweets and biscuits galore! Chocolate, in some form or other, was in nearly every advertisement. Remember, 'a Mars a day helps you work, rest and play'!

Special chocolate shops had opened in the form of 'Thorntons' Chocolate Kabins. As we were children who had never known 'sweets rationing', it was the 'norm' for us to have lollies, bags of dolly mixtures and jelly babies, sherbert and chocolate. Not forgetting the Victoria sponge cakes, vanilla custard slices and iced buns.

Shops were now selling tinned Spam (pressed 'leftover' pork shoulder meat), corned beef and tinned Coronation Chicken. Along had come gravy salts and custard powder, as well as tinned golden syrup for pancakes. And, tinned fruit with Carnation cream for dessert.

For dad, the new house's close proximity to the main road (as opposed to the actual shops) meant he only had a short walk to the bus stop for going to work. Also, the route to the football ground was literally across the main road and through the local park. The route took less than ten minutes. Leaving the park at the other side and turning left, passed three hotdog stalls, some houses and a car lot, and you were walking into the ground.

The Christmas after moving, we were bought an 'intercom set' which meant we could talk to each other from our own bedrooms. What fun! After going to bed, we would activate the walky-talky devices and speak to each other. Such as, "What are you doing?"

"Can you hear mum and dad?" (we only ever heard whisperings from the bedroom.)

"Let's play I-spy," or, "Are you asleep yet?" No answer meant you were already asleep…obviously!

In the '*Star*' *Book*, I recorded what I had received for Christmas.
(Those without recipient names were from Father Christmas)

What I got for Christmas, aged 8
A handkerchief embroidered as a ballerina and a notebook from nannan and grandad
Four 'ashes of violet' bath cubes and soap from Philip
Three handkerchiefs in a box from Uncle Bert and Aunt Pat
One pound from gramam
A pencil sharpener in the shape of a dog from Uncle George and Aunt Margaret
A game called 'Tell me' and a set of cards
Dolly mixtures with a fairy
A white embroidered handkerchief with 'Jean' on
A snowman with fruit gums in
Six assorted 'daintee' lollies

A pink dressing gown in flanelette *(flannelette)*
Nine chocolate cigarettes *(now called 'candy sticks')*
New money – 2 pennies, 3 sixpences, 1 shilling, three threepenny bits
(this was the tradition of putting new money minted that year in the bottom of your Christmas stocking)
  (Note: there was an 'outbreak' of 'hankies'!)

What I got for Christmas, aged 9
One doll called 'Honeybunch' with long auburn 'real' hair
A blue pleated dress for Carol *(renamed from 'Honeybunch')*
Blue anorak from mum and dad *(I loved that anorak)*
Pair of 'nylons' from dad *(he wrote 'to cover up your pretty legs')*
Set of perfumed bath cubes and talc
Kinky *(?)* boots from nannan and grandad
2 silk padded coathangers from Philip *(thoughtful but boring)*
A white sailor blouse from mum *(which I didn't like)*
Lemon and orange slices from dad
Box of crackers from mum and dad
Pair of longjohns (pink with a white frill) and notebook from nan and grandad
Scarf and flowered handkerchief from Uncle George/Aunt Margaret
Informal notes (perfumed) from mum and dad
Diary from Joy
A cosmetics bag from another school friend
6 bath cubes and talcum powder from Uncle Walt and Aunt Cath
Perfumed talcum powder (pretty peach) from dad's sister Aunt Margie/Uncle Ted
A pound from gramam

New money which was put in my money box
(Note: there was an 'outbreak' of bath cubes and talc!)

I received the 'Honeybunch' doll as I'd liked combing Tressy's hair so much. (Tressy was a 'Barbie' sized doll with hair which retracted or lengthened by turning a key.) Rooted 'natural' hair on dolls was still a relatively new innovation.

I've no recollection of what the 'kinky' boots looked like!

The following Christmas was the Christmas I had asked for a puppy. Did I get a puppy – no! Did I get a kitten – no! Was my new pet a hamster or was it a rabbit, er no, it was a budgie!

On Christmas morning there seemed to be a continuous 'tweet tweeting' coming from downstairs. In the living room stood a new cage and stand with a baby blue chested budgie perched inside.

I could not even choose a name for my new budgie as all the family's budgies were called 'Peter'. I had to call him Peter, which I was not happy about. I had wanted to call him 'Bluey'.

I hid my disappointment that it wasn't a puppy, but in fact, I was secretly thrilled with this pretty bird and he would fly round the room when mum said I could open the cage. When we wanted to close the door again, one of us would stand next to the cage so the next time Peter went inside, the string was unhooked and the door closed.

Each Christmas followed the same routine in the build up to the big day, which we all looked forward to. Our big day was Christmas Day but I had read that the Royal Family, at Sandringham, opened their presents on Christmas Eve.

I had read about the Queen, as a child, buying small gifts

from Woolworths for her family while out shopping with her sister and Nanny (as in governess not their grandma.) On Christmas Eve, the young princess received books, chocolates, dolls and toy horses. Both princesses were sometimes bought, what my nan would call 'trinkets', likw brooches or bracelets. As I did, the two girls wrote neat lists of what they had been bought and from whom in order to send the right 'thank you' cards. My list was written in the diary my school friend Joy had bought me.

In that first diary, I wrote about Peter the budgie alongside an entry about what pets were given to the two Princesses. My entry was, 'my doll is called Elizabeth but the real Elizabeth had puppies when she was a little girl'.

Part of our routine before Christmas was to go shopping with mum but without Philip. Another day, mum would take Philip shopping for a little 'trinket' or bath 'stuff' bought for me from his spending money. Our parents would have wrapped up our own presents after we were in bed.

Near to Christmas, Phil and I would be taken to Santa's Grotto which was on waste ground in the city centre (this waste ground had not been built on since the Blitz.) Trees and bushes were planted forming a path through the fairy lights and illuminated nursery rhyme characters.

When getting closer to Father Christmas, there was fake snow everywhere and a big Christmas tree all lit up. His sledge would be full of presents and Rudolph was a life size illuminated reindeer with a flashing red nose. His head went up and down. Oh, the excitement as you got nearer and nearer to Father Christmas and then you had to wait for the children in front to finish talking and taking their presents. It was our turn and he would ask what we wanted for

Christmas and had we been 'good' which we always said we had been. Small children he would lift up and sit on his knee.

We gave our wrapped up presents to mum to save for Christmas Day – we never opened them before.

A week before Christmas, the tree would be brought out of storage and placed in the living room and then filled with decorations, baubles and lights. Nannan and grandad would do the same with their own tree. At their house, on the sideboard, was a row of glass candles and when they were switched on and got hot, bubbles would bubble inside the candle. They were all different colours. We loved watching them and had 'bets' on which colour would start to bubble first.

Two days before Christmas mum would start to cook buns, cakes and parkin. At nannan's house, she was cooking the same things. When mum called us to the kitchen, we would scrape out a baking bowl, 'yum yum'. A turkey would appear, along with eggs, lots of vegetables and at least three loaves of uncut bread.

The day before, nannan would call and they would both scrape out the soft bread from the uncut loaves and mix with sage and onion – no ready made stuffing in a box! Vegetables would be peeled, cut and left to soak in water, except the potatoes which were prepared on the day.

Phil and I always went to bed early on Christmas Eve so that we would be asleep when Father Christmas came.

On *the* morning, Philip and I would wake up really early and we would pick one present each from the presents at the bottom of our beds from Father Christmas. One year, my secretly chosen present was a pair of real fur and leather gloves. Phil's was a wind up racing car. We then had to wrap them up as before.

There would be a stocking each full of smaller presents. The stocking bottom jangled with the traditional new money. 'Stocking fillers' included fruit, unshelled nuts and sweets. The socks were a pair of grandad's large, brown woolly fishing socks.

When we couldn't wait any longer, we would walk into mum and dad's bedroom and ask when we could bring our presents in. If around 7 o'clock then it was OK. We carried in our presents and then got into their bed. A mad frenzy of opening by Philip and he had soon finished opening all of his. As I took my time, my present opening lasted longer. It then looked as though I had two or three more presents!

By now, toys, gloves, hats, sweets and chocolates were everywhere. Mounds of discarded wrapping paper all over the bedroom – what fun! After getting out of the bed, Phil and I would screw up pieces of wrapping paper and throw them at each other, wildly, until we were told to pick up our presents and take them downstairs.

We would play together with our new toys while mum and dad got dressed and tidied up. One year, I received a doll's crib complete with pillow and duvet and Philip had a racing car circuit, the latter of which was great fun for both of us.

We were allowed to have some chocolate after breakfast.

We always had a new game, like the magnetised fishing game. 'Tell me' had little cards with a name or phrase written on. There was an A-Z spinning wheel. The caller would spin the wheel and say from a card, 'a girl's name beginning with C'. Any answer could be said to some of the cards, like 'something in this room' or 'something you want the most'.

The first to shout out an answer would win the card. The winner was the one with the most cards.

Another year, Uncle George had sent us two games in boxes, both called 'Beetle Drive'. One depicted a beetle and the other a giant ant.

('Beetle Drive', a British party game, where a dice is rolled and the number decides which part of the body is drawn. A leg could not be drawn before the body and an eye could not be drawn before the head, and so on. The winner is the first player to complete the insect.)

By about 10 o'clock, mum would be in the kitchen and the turkey in the oven.

Nannan and grandad would arrive about 11 and we would all stop what we were doing and sit in the living room. We gave our presents out and opened our parents' and grandparents' presents to us. We would also open the presents Uncle George had sent through the post from Watford. What a huge pile of used and torn wrapping paper in the centre of the room. Another opportunity to squeeze some into a ball and start throwing them around the room and at each other, presents momentarily forgotten. Grandad and dad would join in.

Paper throwing was mum and nannan's cue to disappear into the kitchen.

(Note, toys were still gender specific – for me, a doll's new outfit, a fold up small pram, a miniature brush and pan set; and for my brother a meccano construction set and a cricket bat. A game, like Mr Potatohead, would be for both of us.)

Dad and grandad would either watch television or put some Christmas hymns on the record turntable in the radiogram. The deck could take about ten records at a time, when one finished, another would drop down to play.

Mum would shout when it was time to set the table and dad would extend the table outwards from underneath. The best 'bingo' won glasses, crockery and cutlery set would be used.

Christmas dinner was piled high on each of our plates, 'yum yum'. We would drink lemonade with the meal. Only grandad liked Christmas pudding, so a small one was made for him. Phil and I would just have custard – homemade with no lumps!

Christmas dinner always had to finish in time for the Queen's speech. At ten to three, we would all sit round the television and be upstanding for the National Anthem. We loved it when her message included family pictures of her children. Mum and nannan usually shed a few tears between them.

We would then start to watch the customary family film. One by one, the grown-ups would fall asleep and we would go back to our toys. (I vowed never to be so boring as to fall asleep after Christmas dinner when I grew up.)

In the evening, the grown-ups would have their traditional sherry drinks and one of grandad's cigarettes each. It was very amusing to Phil and I to see mum and nannan inhale on their cigarette and then blow smoke out. They would both cough after a few puffs. We would then all play card games until it was time for nannan and grandad to go home.

On Boxing Day, we walked to their house in the afternoon, having our tea there. In the evening, we would watch television, then repeat the previous night's sherry drinking and cigarette smoking, followed by the same card games, which we never tired of. The four of us would walk home about 10.30, tired but happy.

On New Year's Day, we would go to my grandparents' house for a roast dinner, with all the trimmings, and then spend the day there; singing along to grandad on the piano, playing card games and watching television. Sherry drinking in the evening, but only grandad smoking now for the rest of the year. Mum, dad and nannan had had their quota of two cigarettes for the year!

On Valentine's Day, mum sometimes sent dad a card and one year mum had written:

Oh Joe
Oh Joe
Where for art thou,
Mr Joseph?

Your feet are huge,
Your jumper is holey,
But in spite of all that,
I still love you.

But will you be mine,
On Saint Valentine?

They never had any serious arguments, only what Phil and I would call 'spats'.

About a week before Valentine's Day, Philip and I would have secret, separate periods of time to cut, paste, draw and to colour. We would both make a Valentine's card for each other. Mum helped us with our early attempts. One year's card from me was of a boy's head cut from a magazine and stuck on a piece of heart shaped card with a large '?' inside.

Philip's card back to me was a girl's head stuck onto card with the words 'guess who?' inside. (No guess needed, of course!)

The cards got more elaborate each year. One card to Philip showed a picture of two mail boxes and above I'd written in purple pencil crayon, 'Why wait for a postman to bring a Valentine…' Inside was the message in blue pencil crayon '…when I am sending you one'. Then on the opposite heart shaped page, 'Love from an Admirer?' and written underneath was 'not from a postman.' *(Phil would not have thought it was from the postman!)*

His Valentine to me was a folded card with a red shaped heart with tiny hearts around it on a background of blue pencil crayon. Inside it read, 'To Jean, one day you will be rich forever, from ?' *(When does the 'rich forever' start?)*

One year, my card to him was a folded piece of paper with 'To My Valentine' on the front. Inside was a small, heart shaped card with a cut out boy's face and kisses underneath. On the other side was a girl opening a card.

His card to me was a girl smiling on a heart shaped card with red pencil colouring around it. Inside he had written,

'The Day
is going to may
you are so sweet
and come and meet
To be my Valentine
From?'

(…and that's a poem made up by my brother!)

During the Easter school holiday, there was the Cleethorpes Holiday Princess beauty contest and a free coach trip to Cleethorpes for the final.

We would also have day trips to the seaside in grandad's

car and to where he liked to fish, such as Lincoln and Knaresborough. In Lincoln, mum and nannan would go shopping while we fished or fed the ducks. In Knaresborough, there was a paddling pool high up near the top of the castle which we would walk up to and paddle in. We would have our sandwiches there before walking down to grandad and going home.

There was always a 'guessing game' as we approached grandad as to how many fish he had caught. Most times, it was between 12 and 20.

Also, lots of Easter eggs to and from the six of us, including the Thorntons egg in a box for Phil and I with our names iced across them (across the egg, not the box.) We weren't allowed to start an egg until we came back from church on Sunday.

In May's Bank Holiday, Whitsuntide, heralded the church processions through the streets, with May Queens and their rosebuds, behind their own church banner held aloft by two flag bearers. All meeting together in the local park for the Whit Sing. We would be wearing our new Whit outfits which were bought or made for us. One year, mum had a pink dress made for me which I loved and it made me feel so special. That year, Philip had his first suit and tie – he looked so small and so cute. The suit was a brown tweed with short trousers. That year's photograph of us in our Whitsuntide clothes is one of my favourite pictures of the two of us.

By this time, the bandstand in Hillsborough Park was minus the covered part of it leaving just the steps up to the flat, raised platform.

Then there was our annual week's stay in Great Yarmouth.

(This seaside resort had once been a thriving fishing town with its 'heyday' in the 1920s. There were so many fishing boats, over a 1000, a fisherman could walk from boat to boat and reach the other side of the harbour without getting his feet wet. The boats ran on steam and everything was done manually without winches. Fishermen had to haul in large nets full of fish, by hand. The men would say that fishing was not a job, it was a way of life and an apprentice, someone's son, would start work on the boat from as young as 12.

While still a fishing town, there were 365 public houses – one for each day of the week! Of course, a few have closed since then.

The fishing industry began a steady decline in the 50s and 60s due to dwindling herring stocks and rising imports of fish. It was still an interesting sight when driving through the harbour docks where grandad would take us for a run most mornings before breakfast.)

The '*Star*' *Book* continues with diary extracts of that year's
Yarmouth holiday (*stated as it was written*)

Saturday
Started off at 7 o'clock. Stopped at East Dereham for dinner. Arrived at 2.30.

Note: it was a journey of about seven and a half hours, due to there being no ring roads around towns or villages.

(Before our 'car games' started, we had to go through the different districts of the city. This took us through a district where, we thought, only 'coloured' people lived. One had to bear in mind, that our only experience of people of a different colour or race to ourselves was the 'Black and White Minstrel Show' and we knew that they were white people dressed up as black people.

Everyone travelling in cars seemed to set off on Saturday morning at about the same time – 8.00am. This meant that by mid-morning cars going to the coast were in traffic jams through busy high street shopping areas. Also, on the approach to Yarmouth, there was only one road in and over the bridge so grandad would always say 'so near but yet so far'. By this time, we had got bored with our games of writing car registration numbers down and 'I-spy', and the grown-ups had run out of conversation.

At Mrs Reeves, my grandparents slept in a double bedroom. In our room would be a double bed, a wardrobe, chair, a single bed and a washbasin. Philip and I would share the single bed. There were no en-suite facilities, all guests shared a toilet and bathroom.)

Went to Mrs Reeves and emptied luggage. Then Dad, Mum and me went to Marks and Spencers. Then had ice cream then went on the Snails *(as already mentioned our favourite ride of snails going round on a mini 'roller coaster' track in Joyland.)*

Then at 4.30 we headed back for Mrs Reeves. For our tea we had first a veg soup then salad, after we had sponge fruit pie with cream.

After tea we went on the crazy golf. We went in the Pleasure Beach after. I won a pot of flowers on Crackerjack *(a game on a stall which boasted 'win a prize every time'.)* We went all round *(the pleasure beach)* then Philip and I went on the old cars *(pedal cars around a track.)* Then we went back to Mrs Reeves. At 11.30 I was in bed. I coughed a bit then went to sleep.

Sunday

I woke up at 7.15. At 7.45 I got up and went for a ride in Grandad's car round the docks. Breakfast was at 8.45. We had – cornflakes then eggs and bacon, beans and fried bread then tea and toast. After that we went on the Snails then on the beach, then went down to the sea, but didn't go in only paddled. *(Isn't that going in?)*

At five to one *(not one o'clock)* we went for our dinner and we had – tomato soup then peas, potatoes, Yorkshire pudding and gravy. *(I think I missed out the 'roast meat' bit?)*

(On Sundays, guest houses serve Sunday dinner rather than a meal at teatime.)

After dinner we went to Potter Heigham. Philip caught five fish, Grandad caught ten, oh he's just caught some more – fourteen. I've caught one roach and Dad caught one.

At 5.30 we had tea in a restaurant. I had beans on toast and tea. Then I watched Philip and Grandad fish.

Then at 8.45 *(that's 3 hours watching them fish, surely not)* we went back to Gt Yarmouth and into the bowling alley. I had a cheese roll and orange. At 10.30 I was in bed. At 11 o'clock I was asleep. *(I must have had an illuminated watch which I would look at just before falling asleep… or I guessed the time!)*

Monday

Woke up at 7am. Got up at 7.45 and went with Grand and Phil for a walk along the seafront – Grand bought a newspaper and some cigarettes. At 8.45 we went in for breakfast we had – cornflakes and after had egg, fried bread, tomatoes and bacon. After breakfast we went to Lowestoft.

I made a sand castle with a tunnel under it. I took a photo of Dad and Phil at the back of it.

Then I went with Nannan and Grandad to the car. But half-way it rained so we sheltered in a launderette factory *(is that where they make launderettes?)*

When getting to the car we went to Oulton Broads. At Oulton Broads I walked up to the fair, but wasn't open. Then I went in the playground and went on the slide and swings.

Then I went and watched Phil and Grandad fish.

I went back to the car and with Mum and Nan, I sailed Philip's red and white boat *(…in the car?)*

After that at 4.45 we started back for Great Yarmouth. For tea we had – oxtail soup then chips, fish and peas. After it was plum pie with custard.

After tea we (Philip and me) went on the Snails. Then we all went on the Pier. Nannan won on the bingo and got a tablecloth.

Then we went on the front and I had some soup in cups *(that's cup-a-soup!)*

At 9.30 I was in bed and asleep at 10 o'clock *(let me check what time I'm going to fall asleep, yawn.)*

(Note: the phrase 'I went to bed' which would have included Philip at the same time, remember, we're sharing a single bed.)

Tuesday

I woke up at 7 o'clock and got up at nearly 8 o'clock. I went with Grandad and Phil for a run round and called for a paper and cigarettes.

At 8.45 we had breakfast we had – flakes, sausage, egg, fried bread and beans. Tea and toast.

Mum and Dad, Phil and me went on the sand and everyone except Mum went in the sea *(that would be the three of us, not 'everyone on the sand'.)*

For dinner we all had cheese and tomato roll, a choc roll and coffee (Phil had lemon.)

After dinner we went to Hickling. But the water was too rough so went to Potter Heigham. I looked in the shops with Mum most of the time, or watched Grand fishing.

(Potter Heigham, on the Broads, has an exceptionally low bridge

over the river and catches out numerous boats whose owners think that they can get their boat under the bridge. 'Oh dear, we forgot the sail is up' and crash; or 'oh dear, the top of the boat is sliced off' and crunch; 'oh heck, I only just ducked down in time'. We have witnessed many accidents, including boats getting stuck under the bridge. Only once did we see anyone fall into the river and we never saw anyone injured.)

At nearly 5 o'clock we set of(f) for Gt Yarmouth. For tea we had – vegetable soup, meat, potatoes, beans. *(No dessert or, more likely, not recorded.)*

After tea we went to Gorlstan *(Gorleston.)* At about 9 o'clock we went home and took the car in *(parked it.)* Then went on the Snails and Noah's Ark and then went for our supper at a snack bar. At 9.45 I was nearly home. At 10.15 I was in bed.

Wednesday

I woke up at 7.50 went with Grand and Phil for a walk on the front and he bought a newspaper, sweets for us to have later on, and packets of cigarettes. At nearly 8.45 we arrived in time for breakfast we had – corn flakes, fried bread, tomato, egg. Tea and toast.

At 9.30 we set of(f) for Wroxham. We met Uncle Ted and Aunty Margie and Janet with a broken leg *(dad's younger sister, her husband and our cousin.)*

In Caister we stopped to look in the shop *(is there only one shop, I think not.)* Then just outside it started to rain and when we got to Wroxham it hadn't stopped. As soon as we had parked we went for our dinner I had – a tomato sandwiche *(is that French for sandwich)* and a cup of tea. After I had a choc roll.

Then Nan, Mum and I had a look in the shops. Wadso *(Dad)* and Pickle *(Phil)* watched while Grampse fished.

At 3.30 we went back to Gt Yarmouth and arrived in time for tea. We had – bacon, egg, beans and fried bread *(that's a second breakfast or 'all day breakfast' in today's 'speak'.)* After that it was pineapple with cream *(my favourite fruit.)*

We went on the Snails, then at night at 8 o'clock we went (excluding Nan and Grand) to a carnival dance. At 11 o'clock balloons and party hats came from an extra big light.

At 11.15 arrived home. At 11.45 in bed.

(The time from enjoying balloons and party hats (11pm) to arriving home (11.15pm) appears to be incredibly short, unless the dance was next door, which it wasn't!)

Thursday

Woke up at 8 o'clock but tried to go to sleep again (but didn't succeed.)

For breakfast we had – flakes then bacon, egg, fried bread and beans. After breakfast we went on the beach and met Uncle Ted and Aunty Margie and Janet who were with Marion and Eric and there *(their)* children, Andrew and Ray. *(The latter were the aunt and uncle's family friends.)*

At 12.30 I had a cup of tea, a cheese and tom sandwich. Then everybody except Eric and Marion went to the swimming baths. Everybody except Janet, Phil, Margie and Mum went in. *(It would have been easier to record who went swimming.)*

At 4 o'clock we had a look round Uncle Ted's flat. At 4.30 we went in for tea *(at Mrs Reeves.)* For tea we had – soup, potatoes, cabbage, carrots, gravy and meat and onion pie. After we had bannmange *(blancmange)* on jelly and peaches.

After tea, Phil and I went on the Snails then went on the Noah's Ark *(in Joyland.)*

Then we went in Majestic Bingo and Grandad won. At 7 o'clock we went to the bowling alley. Dad, Uncle Ted, Aunt Margie and Eric had a go – they won in the order I wrote. *(I take it everyone else just watched, surely not!)*

At nearly 9 o'clock we went on the waterways *(a motorised boat ride next to the sea front)*. At 10.45 we were making our way home. At 11 o'clock I was in bed and asleep at 11.30. *(Let's check that late night clock, yawn and check, nearly asleep, check, eyes closing, check, zzzzzz.)*

Friday

Woke up at 7.30 and got up at 8 o'clock in time to go with Grandad for a run round and called in a shop for cigarettes and a paper. At 8.45 we went in for breakfast. For breakfast we had – flakes, fried bread, egg, bacon and sausages. Then toast and tea.

After breakfast we went shopping for half an hour *(that long.)* Then went on the beach and joined Uncle Ted, Janet, Aunt Margie, Eric and Marion, Andrew *(what had happened to their other son, Ray, or did I forget to mention him.)*

The boys digged *(dug)* a hole and tricked me into getting in it. So buried me up to the end of my legs. Dad took a photo of me holding a real white cuddly poodle while paddling.

For dinner we had a cheese and tomato *(sandwich)* and tea. Then went back on the beach until 3.30.

Dad, Ma, Pic, me went of(f) the beach to where we go on the trampoline *(which is on the sand.)* While on the trampoline a wasp stung me and so went to the Red Cross first aid, where they put vinegar on it. We walked to the Snails and went on two times.

Then we went back for tea. For tea we had – potatoes, Yorkshire pudding, meat and gravy.

After tea we got the bingo prizes on the pleasure beach and everywhere.

(Grandad was always winning at prize bingo and a card is given to the winner. Cards were saved up for better prizes. Over the years, there have been clocks, table sets, tablecloths, bed linen, lamps, torches, crockery sets, pans, picnic sets, toys and games for us, large cuddly bear, food mixer… This list is starting to sound like the Generation Game's conveyor belt of prizes at the end of the gameshow!

Just to mention here that gameshows started to replace large variety shows. An early one was the Generation Game. The finale was one of the winning pair of contestants memorising as many prizes as possible from a moving conveyor belt. After the conveyor ended, the contestants won all the prizes he or she could recall.)

At 10.45 we made our way home, sad that the holiday was gone. At 11.15 I was asleep.

Saturday

I woke up at 8.15 and got up at 8.30. At 8.45 went down for breakfast and had – flakes, pouched egg on toast and tea.

We went on the Snails while Mum and Nan did the packing.

At 10.30 we set of*(f)* for home. We stopped at – Swaffam, Myro's café and one or two more. *(That would be one or two more stops, not one or two more cafes.)*
Arrived home at 6.30. *A journey of 8 hours…*

★ ★ ★ ★ ★

(In those days, all families seemed to set off on Saturday morning

causing traffic jams on the way to the coast and then everyone sets off home the following Saturday morning causing traffic jams on the way back! Did anyone not think to set off earlier or later?)

One year, during the school holidays, the four of us went on a day trip by train to London. Phil and I were in awe as we walked around. Although we were used to living in a city, this was a kind of 'future city' with such tall and grand buildings. To see Trafalgar Square and walk down the Mall to Buckingham Palace, well, what a tremendous sight. We stood by Queen Victoria's statue for the longest time to see if we could see the Queen or her children at one of the windows. *(We were not aware that a certain flag would fly if the Queen was at home.)*

My souvenirs included a piece of tree bark from Hyde Park and a piece of cement from Buckingham Palace wall. We had walked all round the wall in case there was a gate we could see through and see the Queen or one of her family in the garden. *(What naivety on the part of my parents!)*

We walked to the Houses of Parliament and all the way along Downing Street. Phil and I had our photograph taken next to the policeman at no 10.

We ate sandwiches beside the River Thames and then sadly made our way back to the railway station.

The next 'big' event after the six weeks school holiday, was bonfire night with lots and lots of fireworks. *(I have no memory of Halloween as, to be truthful, nothing was 'made' of it.)*

We looked forward to 'bonfire night', as we called it. Our grandparents would buy us a selection of individual fireworks, several rockets and sparklers. Mum and dad would buy a few. Nearly every garden would have individual bonfires, a Guy Fawkes to burn and fireworks to set off. Our favourites were the rockets which were launched from an empty milk bottle.

Here's an account of 'Guy Fawkes' night from a school book:
"On November fifth we had our bonfire and fireworks display. I saw the bonfire with its fiery flames dancing in the nights cold air. The fireworks were of red, yellow, blue and the lovely snow storm with its shower of white. I saw many colours of the sparklers – greens, reds, yellows and whites.

"Zoom" went the rocket high into the sky. Mum lit it and ran away not being able to see it. I heard many a cackling from the flames of the fire. Also when Philip threw a box and bags onto the blazing fire.

The lovely smell, the lovely taste of chestnuts roasting and the red toffee apples all sticky and hard. The nasty smell of the fireworks after they had done, they were smouldering away too hot to move.

I think that the whole idea of fireworks and bonfires is silly, ridiculous and thoroughly dangerous for children up to the age of twelve. There are more and more people getting either killed or injured. They ought to ban fireworks altogether."

(Where did that last paragraph come from? I can't ever remember thinking that they should be banned.)

Roasted chestnuts were a favourite of my grandad's and he always roasted some on bonfire night and at Christmas on a long metal handle in the open fire.

Our birthdays were conveniently dispersed through the year: dad's in March, Phil's in May, mum's in July, mine in August and both grandparents in October. Apart from when we were little, where we might have had one or two neighbours' children round, we celebrated by having a birthday tea at our house.

Or the four of us would have a meal in the newly opened Chinese restaurant above some shops at Hillsboro' corner. What a treat to go into a restaurant within walking distance from where we lived and the first Chinese one in the area.

(The magnificent building where this restaurant was located can be seen in the very first photograph in this book which shows Hillsboro' corner. It's the building behind the tram. Ironically, this building was demolished, years later, to make way for the city's new supertram network.)

On schooldays we would open family cards in the morning. After school, we would open posted birthday cards and our presents. As there were six of us, we received five presents per birthday, along with some smaller surprises.

One year, nannan had bought me a book on Princess Margaret. Philip had bought me a loose leaf notebook with a bird on the front cover.

I used this notebook for my next magazine and called it the *Bird Notebook*.

On the first page: "Dear Readers, I hope you enjoy this thrilling, most exciting notebook with tearaway pages. It is excellent for both boys and girls." However, the words "for boys and" had a line through. As the book took shape, it became clear that its contents, in my opinion, would not be of interest to boys!

The first two pages were 'pretend' questions by my brother and then my answers. My brother was not involved, of course.

Question: How many brothers and sisters have you?
Answer: One brother!

491

Question:	What are your hobbies?
Answer:	Ballroom dancing and swimming.
Question:	What are your likes and dislikes?
Answer:	I like vegetable soup and fishcake and chips.

I dislike almond and marzipan and crusts off loaves.

Question:	What is your favourite singer?
Answer:	Cliff Richard and the Rolling Stones.
Question:	Have you any pets?
Answer:	Yes, a budgie called Peter.
Question:	When did you get this book?
Answer:	My birthday.

Then I had drawn a map of the local park, the one where my parents had spent so much time walking during their courtship (which I had not known at the time of writing the *Bird Notebook*.)

The next article was 'How To Write A Play' which started with a flowchart on the steps to make it a success:

Story
Characters
Make into a play
Persons taking part
Whether make up, dress, etc, needed
How long it takes
Type it out neatly (if possible)
Rehearse a lot
Get experts to see it
And finally put it on stage

On the next page: "First of all think of a suitable story, one made up or one you've seen or read about. Characters you must must *(written twice)* not have more than about eight and not less than three. One or two adults and all the rest children will make a nice play." *(Would it?)*

"Scenery should not be too fussy or to the last very small detail. If it is not done in front of spotlights, make up is not necessary and neither will dressing up in the costume of the play. When having thought of a story make an outline of the entrances and exits of the people taking part. Do not make the main person yourself, unless the part suits you."

There was a section on the 'Don'ts' of writing a play:
"Don't have about seven adults and one child or there won't be much fun in it.
Don't make the play have triplets in it or twins, etc. *(I wonder why not?)*
If doing it for only your family don't wear make up or dress up and
don't rearrange the furniture."

And the 'Do's' of writing a play:
"Do have feeling and act it just as the play says.
Write or type a copy of the play for each actor.
Don't *(er, this is the Do's)* have any children under the age of 9 or 10 as they won't learn their parts because of their age.
Do have some scenery, but not unnecessary things."

The next section was a play written by myself, or in fact, a rewriting of Jane Eyre in play format. There were two adults and five children in the play with one of the children acting as Jane Eyre.

Following the play, some light relief in a 'Puzzles' page with answers later in the *Bird Notebook*.

1. When does a fire show anger?
When it flares up.
2. From what can you take the whole and still have some left?
'Wholesome'

Cooking hints
3. How to make the pudding stretch far?
Put elastic in it.
4. How to make a cake last longer?
Don't eat it.
5. How to make peas stick to the knife?
Apply a little glue.

Just Joking
6. If the clock strikes thirteen what is the time?
One o'clock.
7. What must you do before you get out of a train?
Open the door.
8. When is the letter 'a' hard to see?
When in darkness.

In the same *Bird Notebook,* there was a section on 'Ballet Hints and Photos'. Then a page on 'Formation Dancing', 'Ballroom Dancing' and 'Stars on Skates'.

Also, 'Cookery Corner', 'Beauty Hints' and a 'Modern Miss' page'.

(Note: so these sections give clues as to why "for boys…" was crossed out. That is, my own thinking that most boys would not be interested in ballet, cooking, beauty or fashion.)

There were sections to interest both boys and girls in the *Bird Notebook,* such as 'Spelling Bee', 'Words pronounced

Alike', a 'Mathematics' page and a story about a mischievous squirrel.

I wrote an article called 'Our Dream Princess', which was based on the book about Princess Margaret. The article looks back at her younger years and then her role as a wife and mother. I was too young to remember her wedding.

(Princess Margaret's wedding to Antony Armstrong-Jones in Westminster Abbey in 1960 was the first televised Royal Wedding. The ceremony was watched by 300 million worldwide. The honeymoon was aboard the Royal Yacht Britannia on a six week Carribean cruise and, on their return, the newly weds lived in Kensington Palace. Antony became the Earl of Snowdon.)

Following the article on the Princess, were several blank pages for readers to write in their chosen TV programmes. They are still blank, of course.

A section on 'School Games' stated that, "When teachers are away or there are too many pupils absent to continue the normal lessons, the teacher will tell you to get on with anything you want to do." *(Did that actually happen, I very much doubt it!)*

The 'School Games' listed were:

Noughts and Crosses

Dotto

Hangman

I-spy

At the end of 'I-spy explained', were the words "Have Fun!"

Poems from the *Bird Notebook*

On the Kitchen Mat

The great, big rats

The owls and bats

Our big, black cat
All on the kitchen mat

A Horrid Blister
I've got a sister
She's got a blister
I'm gonna ' kiss 'er
Oh dear, I missed 'er

Little Mabel
Hello little Mabel
Sitting on a table
Looking at a
Pretty little stable

A cold
Nose
blow blow blow

Nose
glow glow glow

Nose
sore sore sore

Nose
blow some more
The Willow Tree
I like the huge, old willow
You know of course it's a tree
Which often stands by me

I like its old, green leaves
And best of all I love to see
Them glittering high above me

I like the big, brown bark
And the sweet little honey bee
Which sometimes buzzes round me

I like the enormous branches
They sway so full and free
I look up at them, they look down on me

I like the wise old tawny owl
Which lives in the willow tree
Which often stands by me

The Swordfish at Work
Swordfish has to find a job soon
He needs to buy himself some food
He thought what can I do?
Make things as good as new!
I'll use my sword to bevel wood
That would be so very good

So he makes a chair or two
Tables and cupboards too
He sells to folk beneath the sea
And soon he's as busy as can be
He's making this and making that
Even a great big wooden mat

The fish shouts out a yelp
He now needs lots of help
To deliver his goods of course
And hires a strong sea horse
His work needs painting too
But he hasn't got a clue
So an octopus will do just grand
With a brush in every hand!

Going into the sixties, my girls' magazine 'June' continued to print a full page photograph of a different 'pop' star each week which I now had to save instead of putting on the bedroom wall. I can remember Cliff Richard singing 'Bachelor Boy'.

The Beatles regularly had an individual photograph printed in the magazine as well as different pictures of the group. At school, you were asked who your favourite Beatle was, and I would answer, "John Lennon." All my school friends had a favourite Beatle.

The Rolling Stones featured in the very first 'Top of the Pops' on television.

At the cinemas, there was a British Pathe News special with the 'cockerel sound' announcing a special broadcast. The title was 'Rolling Stones gathers moss' from the phrase 'a rolling stone gathers no moss'.

('Top of the Pops' started in 1964, filmed live from a converted church in Manchester. It meant that artists, whatever party they had been to the night before, had to catch the 6 o'clock morning train from London. Jimmy Saville hosted the weekly show in casual t-shirt and jeans which was a huge change from the traditional suit and tie of TV presenters at that time and with his distinctive voice gave the show

added entertainment value. According to Jimmy, there was never any problem booking artists as it was the 'top pop programme in the world'. Artists such as The Supremes, Everley Brothers, Chubby Checker appeared, as well as 'home grown' stars like Cilla Black and Adam Faith.)

For three years, the 'Top Ten' record charts were dominated by the Beatles, Rolling Stones, Bob Dylan and theme songs from the film 'The Sound of Music'. At that time, I was more interested in the film and its songs having gone to see the film with mum and Phil and then again with nannan. Mum and dad bought the sound track LP and it was played over and over again. Mum and I knew all the songs 'by heart' and we would sing "the hills are alive…" together. Phil would either join in or, if dad was there, he would roll up his eyes.

There were regular updates on the Royal Family at the cinema (and on television news programmes.) Cinema performances were continuous so any short film was played before or after the 'A' film. I had read that the Queen did not carry anything in her handbag which made me wonder why she carried one. In fact, the Queen does carry items in her handbag.

Do you know what items they are?

Let's test your knowledge of the Queen:

Q1. Name two of the items she keeps in her handbag.

Q2. Who keeps her other 'emergency' items –

a)her bodyguard; b)Prince Philip; c)Lady in Waiting; d)in the car/train.

Q3. Name three of the 'emergency' items.

Q4. How does the Queen keep her hair in place?

a)wears a wig; b)hair lacquer; c)she always wears a hat; d)a hairpiece.

Q5. The Queen never sneezes in public – true or false?

Q6. If true, can you give a reason why not?

Q7. If false, when have you seen the Queen sneeze?

Q8. How does the Queen keep her dress/skirt from flying up in the wind?

Q9. How are the Queen's clothes cleaned?

a)always dry cleaned; b)put in the washer; c)handwashed; d)given to charity.

Q10. What helps the Queen staive off minor illnesses?

a) keeps cotton wool up her nose;

b) stops breathing if talking to someone with a cold;

c) homeopathic medicine;

d) eats only organic food.

(Answers at the end of the book.)

At school, you were expected to know who the British Prime Minister was. To me, it always seemed to be an 'old man'.

I had also read that America had a young President. At age 43, John F Kennedy became the youngest American President.

(His parents had been appointed Ambassadors for the USA in the mid-1930s and as a young family, they had visited the UK and stayed with the Royal Family at Windsor Castle. Two of John's siblings, Teddy and Jean, were the nearest in age to the two princesses and the four of them played together in the Castle grounds. Elizabeth, at nearly 12, was still dressed identical to her sister but they were now hatless; gone were the more childish bonnets they had been used to wearing).

While in office President JF Kennedy saw the building of the Berlin Wall and was involved with the Cuban Missile Crisis, the Space Race and the African/American Civil Rights

Movement, all of which I knew nothing about at the time.

(After WW2, Germany was split between the four major allies, UK, France, Russia and the USA. East Germany was the Russian side, but due to indoctrination and an increasing 'police state', including food and other supply shortages, more and more people moved over to the 'free' Western side. Checkpoints were set up in the fifties – people checked out and didn't check back in. By 1960, the building of two walls began with a 'no man's land' in between them. A 'cold war' had started, mainly between Russia and America.

Meanwhile, America was leading in the 'nuclear arms race' but the Russian missiles could reach the UK but not the USA. Russia set up nuclear weapons in Cuba. All this was done in secret, until an American spy plane spotted what was happening. The Russians said they would use battlefield nuclear weapons if the island was invaded. President Kennedy and his advisers imposed a quarantine around Cuba. He then gave the Russian President assurances that he would not invade Cuba if they dismantled their missiles. The world held its collective breath. Russia removed them and war was averted.)

A few years later, I asked my parents about this time. They said the 'Cuba Crisis' seemed to be turning into a third world war and that it had been a very worrying period, especially so because of the nuclear threat. Then suddenly it had fizzled out over there, but we in Britain still thought that Russian nuclear missiles were aimed at key cities. My parents said that Sheffield was one of those 'key cities' and that, in some ways, it was more frightening to think of someone 'pressing a button' and them being 'wiped out' than to remember waiting in an air raid shelter during WW2.

(Meanwhile further, there was a 'Space Race' going on! The Russians beat the Americans by launching an artificial satellite into

space. Russia then put a dog into orbit around earth. The 'Moon Race' started with the USA launching humans into orbit around the moon, that is, inside a rocket. President Kennedy asked the Russians 'why not join together'?

Everything was racing ahead, except the African/American Civil Rights Movement which was going too, too slow for Bobby Kennedy, as Attorney General. The President, with his brother Bobby and the Movement, wanted to 'put things right' and end racial discrimination. Even though many services and facilities were available for African/Americans, they were of lower quality than for white people. There was also segregation – a black person drinking only from a 'coloured' water fountain and black people could only wait in a 'coloured' waiting room in a bus terminal.

A lot of protests took place, including a successful bus boycott (black Americans had to give up their seat if a white person got on the bus); sit-ins at food stores (e.g. black people could buy food in stores but were not allowed to sit and eat at the lunch counters); and marches (e.g. thousands walked into Washington to support the ending of employment discrimination.)

Sadly, President Kennedy would not live to see the success of this Movement or see a man on the moon.

There is a saying that anyone 'old enough' can remember exactly what they were doing when President Kennedy was shot. I can remember being in the bath, being washed by mum. We heard dad shouting up the stairs, "Kennedy's been shot" and mum said to me, "Can you dry yourself", and she was gone.

There was no satellite link to America! The television newsreader was talking through what had happened and by the time I got downstairs, President Kennedy was 'fighting for his life' in hospital. A picture of the hospital was on the screen as the newsreader 'went over' what had happened. I then had to go to bed.

The next day, I remember feeling sad when told that he had died as it was so tragic and so early in his life. I saw the newsreel of his little boy saluting at the funeral and feeling sad all over again. Mum shed a few tears.

It was about this time that I started looking through dad's daily newspaper. I can recall the newspaper headlines that the death penalty had been abolished, though in reality, it had been suspended rather than abolished. I never liked the thought of purposely taking someone's life, even though they might have taken someone else's.

Abolition of the death sentence had been debated in Parliament as early as 1938 and it was decided, that year, to suspend corporal punishment for five years which continued until after WW2. As the pre-war support for the abolition had disappeared, the death penalty by hanging was reinstated.

In 1957, crimes punishable by the death penalty were reduced to six categories of murder:
 – in the course of theft
 – by shooting or causing an explosion
 – resisting arrest/escaping
 – of a police officer
 – of a prison officer or prisoner
 – the second of two murders committed on different occasions in the UK.

Although I didn't agree with the death penalty, I was fascinated by how the smallest of crimes, up to the 1850s, were punishable by death. Up to then, you could be hung for stealing as little as a few pennies or food or for pick pocketing, whether you were a child or adult. So, during the century in which I was born, and in the lifetime of my grandma, a child could still be hanged for a 'petty' crime, but fortunately wasn't.

The last woman to be hanged was in 1955 and the last man was in 1964.

Also making the front page in 1964 was the happier news that the Queen had given birth to her fourth child. In true Royal birth tradition, the announcement was pinned to Buckingham Palace railings after the birth of Prince Edward. At the time of his birth he was third in line to this country's throne, and that of ten independent Sovereign states, (as Commonwealth realms); Head of the Commonwealth (54 nations) and Supreme Governor of the Church of England.

Prince Edward was born at the Palace and baptised at Windsor Castle. He was the fifth grandchild of the Queen Mother – the Queen's four children and the son of Princess Margaret. That same year, the Queen Mother had her full complement of six grandchildren as Princess Margaret gave birth to a daughter.

Nearer to home, Phil and I had a new cousin, born to Aunty Pat and Uncle Bert. As dad and his brothers became supporters of the local BIG football club, Sheffield Wednesday; Bert became a supporter of the rival 'small' club, the Blades. Bert did that on purpose as his brothers expected him to be an Owls supporter. This led to much rivalry within their household.

Wednesday's ground was one of the largest in the country and always hosted semi finals for the FA Cup competition. It was going to be one of the grounds for the World Cup as well, which made us feel very proud. We were also 'riding high' in the Top Division of the Football League, playing the likes of Manchester United and Liverpool.

(The Club got its name from playing their football matches on a Wednesday. So if they had always played on Tuesdays, or a Thursday, the Club could have been called Sheffield Tuesday or Sheffield Thursday!)

Around this time, Dad started taking me to some of the football matches. We sometimes called into the Club's shop which was a small portercabin in the car park. It was single file in and single file out due to lack of space. The single file in snaked round the car park – join the queue too late and you risked missing the kick off. Mum had knitted me a blue and white striped scarf and a blue and white jumper which I proudly wore and made me 'stand out' in their uniqueness.

We stood up to watch the match as there were only two stands with seats. (What a contradiction – a stand having seats!) Occasionally Dad would take my brother instead of me (due to costs) and very occasionally he would take the two of us.

Grandad used to go to all the matches and he would tell stories of a sea of flat caps on the kop and at some of the games with regular crowds of up to 30,000. The record gate at Hillsborough ground was 72,841 to see Wednesday play Manchester City in 1934. It was a 1-1 draw. If Grandad hadn't gone, it would have been 72,840.

The following year, 1935, the Owls beat Arsenal in front of a crowd of 66,945 and went on to become FA Cup Winners at Wembley with a crowd of 93,204.

Gate numbers inevitably became restricted, but on the kop there were still surges forward, up to the advent of seats, and it was best to avoid standing behind a steel barrier, 'ouch'!

As there was still no restriction on where anyone stood in the ground, there were frequent fights between rival supporters on the kop.

When there was a fight, a hole would appear in the crowd and everyone would move backwards to watch. Then police officers would wade in through the crowd, but most fights were over by the time they reached the 'hole'. There was only an arrest if the police spotted someone who had been in the fight and may be a bit bloody or dishevelled. Due to the unpredictability of the kop, dad would take us in the opposite stand where most family groups went.

There was a 'park' football team so whenever I played, I was usually the only girl playing. I really enjoyed playing, but it was before any female football teams had started so my only chance of playing was in the park with local boys and my brother.

I remember dad telling me about the 'yo-yo' years of the 1950s when we were promoted to the First Division four times and relegated three times. Then we had the 'glory' years as I started to take an interest in the sixties. Dad had told me about the 'glorious' away match of 1961 when we beat Manchester United 7-2 in front of their home crowd of 65,243. Dad didn't go to any away matches.

When Sheffield Wednesday got to the FA Cup Final in the sixties, we asked dad if he would take us, but he said it would cost too much and we would have to watch it on television. Grandma and grandad came to watch the match with us. 'Everyone' would watch the FA Cup Final, even mum and grandma, and others who weren't really interested in football.

An FA Cup Final had a unique standing of followers and

it was a great family occasion to watch it on television, whichever teams were playing. I remember going down the road to a shop in half time and there was not a soul in sight. Amazingly, to say we lived off a main road, there was no traffic either. (It made me feel like the planet's sole survivor of some catastrophe.)

At the start of any FA Cup Final there was singing to a marching band and the conductor would be on an elevated small stage in the centre of the pitch, waving his hands in unison to the singing. The climax was a full stadium of spectators 'belting' out the National Anthem, "God save our Queen..." especially if the Queen was actually watching from Wembley's Royal Box.

On this Owls versus Everton Cup Final at Wembley, we started celebrating at home during half time as we were playing so well and two goals ahead. My dad and grandad had some beer and we were all laughing and looking forward to seeing the Cup brought back to Sheffield. No-one ever said 'let's not count our chickens' as we all thought it was 'in the bag'.

Oh dear, we had to settle for the honour of being in the Final, but our defeated team was the first to do a lap of honour around Wembley. Back in Sheffield, when the team toured the city streets in an open topped bus we shouted and cheered as if we had won!! Hundreds lined the main roads.

Then the World Cup brought lots of foreign visitors to 'our' football ground and our area. Along the main road of shops there were lots of German speaking people, mainly men. Nannan said it was like we had been 'invaded' but in a good way, rather than the fear from yesteryear.

Dad couldn't get any tickets or I think that he just didn't know how to get them.

(Online? What on earth was that? In fact, what on earth was a computer?)

Philip and I had gone to the park to play footie, but we decided to go and see if we could get into the ground for the World Cup game. We had no money and no ticket, so we climbed half way up the pylon type floodlights to watch the game. We were shouted down and told we could go in at half time free which we did and saw West Germany playing Uruguay.

In the fifties going into the sixties, it was a time when the Chairman (it was then always a man) ate sandwiches in the Directors' box, footballers were unknown outside of their local area and they were paid peanuts (not literally.) Being a footballer's wife was 'nothing to write home about'. In fact, a woman telling her parents the man she wanted to marry was a footballer got the answer 'you could have done better and met someone with a 'proper' job'!

A new girlfriend of a footballer in the late fifties actually thought her boyfriend had a 'proper' job in the week and only played at the weekend. She was 'dumb struck' when told he got paid for playing football and trained during the week. Pay was 'capped' by the Football Association until 1961 at £20 per week. The new girlfriend actually earned more working in a bank, £11 pw, than her footballer boyfriend who earned £8 pw. Very few earned anything like the £20 'ceiling' wage.

Football spectators? Thousands of them, a 'sea of men' and boys (with a few women and girls 'dotted' about.) It was the age of politeness in queuing and little bad language. But lots and lots of smoking. It was still a 'man's world'.

Footballers' wives and families weren't seen and they weren't heard. England's World Cup Coach took the squad

508

away for training in the build up to the competition. The wives would see their husbands after two months, but only from the terraces, and it would be three months before they met each other again.

At the opening of the World Cup at Wembley, the Queen made a speech. The players then came out from the tunnel to the roar of the crowd, and the Queen went down the line of players shaking hands. The National Anthem was played by a band on the pitch and the England fans, almost all the way round Wembley, 'belted' out the National Anthem. However, it was a disappointing start as England drew to Uruguay with no goals to 'shout about'.

The next match at Wembley was England versus Mexico and another packed stadium. Hanging in the air was a mixture of nervousness, tension and excitement. This time we won and went on to beat Argentina in the quarter finals. It was at this point of the competition that many people thought 'we can win this'.

The England players were slowly becoming more and more well known and they were invited to a day at the Pinewood Studios. It was still very much a male 'affair' without female partners and few female actors. The players met Cliff Richard and a 'larking about' Norman Wisdom, as well as other actors.

England 'sailed' through the semi final, beating Portugal. They just kept playing better and better with more and more confidence. The eyes of the world was now on England as they prepared to take on the Germans…on a football pitch this time!

The night before the final, the wives and girlfriends had been brought down to stay in the Royal Garden Hotel in

London, though not the hotel where the players were staying! Envelopes had been left for some of the wives with £50 in each. Those wives went shopping in Harrods – one 'blew' the lot on a top to wear at the banquet planned for after the final.

The throng of people walking up Wembley Way was just "phenomenal", said an England supporter, "To feel the surge of people, the energy in everyone." Union Jacks were waving, people were singing and 'jigging' along. Someone had a dancing monkey in a little top emblazoned 'World Cup Champions'. "Just being there was an experience," said another supporter.

The roar from 98,000 people when the players came out of the tunnel could surely be heard in Watford? Back at home, we were 'jumping up and down' with excitement as grandad sang a few chants of 'we won the war'. Germany took an early lead and our hearts sank through floor. Geoff Hurst headed in a goal and our hearts came back up. A second goal and our hearts took off towards the roof. But the Germans weren't ready to surrender just yet, and they scored.

Thump, thump, thump, went our hearts, our mouths were dry and our throats sore. It was like a bomb had been dropped on Wembley as a stunned silence was broken by the whistle for extra time to begin.

Geoff Hurst scored a goal which was vehemently disputed by the Germans, as the referee (from neutral Switzerland) walked over to the linesman. Our hearts had stopped. The goal stood! Spectators stood. We stood. And, just when you 'think it's all over', it was, and we WON – we beat the Germans on our own soil.

The stadium erupted as the whistle blew. At home, we

linked arms. Grandad lit up a cigarette and dad went for some more beer. Mum and nannan had a sherry each (normally reserved for Christmas.)

For the first time I knew what winning was, and as I knew something about the two world wars, I felt elated that it was the Germans we had beaten at football. The victory had made the players heroes but, this time, without casualties.

The Queen looked radiant in (neutral) canary yellow and beamed as she gave the Jules Rimet Trophy to Bobby Moore, the captain. More cheers as he held it high and then he kissed it. Wembley Stadium was swept away with pride and patriotism. We were all jumping about at home as the Trophy and players did their lap of honour.

(The Queen presented the real *Trophy, but it could so easily have been a replica.*

In the build up to the competition, the Trophy had been stolen from an exhibition display. A nationwide hunt revealed nothing. A replica was quickly commissioned, just in case.

Out walking with his owner, a small dog called Pickles, sniffed something wrapped in newspaper behind park bushes in London. It was the Jules Rimet Trophy! Pickles 'saved the day' and became a hero off the pitch!)

To celebrate, the players and their wives now in the same hotel, stepped out together onto the hotel balcony and waved to the crowds below. One player said to his wife, "I like your top," and his wife answered, "I blew the £50 on it." "What," he exclaimed, "You blew all that on a top!" *(Note: a well-made 'high street' top could still be bought for under £5.)*

On going back inside the hotel, the wives were ushered to the left as the players went into the banquet on the right.

The wives were 'treated' to a 'low key' meal together and the players were dining 'alone' again. What made the injustice worse, was the FA Officials had their wives sat next to them.

At the press conference the next day, the players made sure their wives and girlfriends were with them.

An exceptional year of excitement and pride.

But, before the year was out, grandad started feeling ill. He just couldn't keep his food down. He tried 'Complan', which he hated but he knew he had to try and eat something. *('Complan' is a protein filled powder that is mixed with milk or water.)*

He thought it might be his teeth which he had kept but were now bad. He went through the trauma and upset of having his teeth out. But, false teeth did not help and he grew thinner. In fact, grandma wrote on her calendar, 'had his teeth out and never been well since'.

He cut down on the number of cigarettes he smoked, but he didn't stop, couldn't stop. Almost a lifetime of smoking untipped, strong cigarettes but even then cigarettes were not associated with any illness whatsoever.

(A fact not known until years later, was that during the fifties and sixties, lung cancer in men had doubled. This seemed to reflect the smoking trends of earlier decades.)

In the new year, his illness remained undiagnosed, therefore, no treatment. Grandad was in and out of hospital as they tested for this and tested for that. As smoking was allowed in hospital he continued to smoke. He had constant back pain which 'wore him down'.

At home, he ate and slept in the front room, only venturing out to occasionally watch television. The piano lid was left shut. His billiard cues in their box. The shiny and clean yellow car stayed put. When he wasn't well enough to walk to the outside closet, he used a bucket in the front room.

I wasn't sad or anything as I just took it for granted that he would get better. Though he was 'old' to me at 65 years, I knew that a lot of people lived to be much older than that. (In fact, great grandma was already 88.)

On the first Monday in March, Nannan had a new gas cooker fitted – it was an 'all in one' oven and hob. On her calendar after that she wrote, 'wash day as usual'. Up to then, nothing and no-one had ever interrupted Monday's wash day!

Grandad lost more weight and he was admitted to hospital on the first Monday in April. There was no washing done that day, or the Monday after.

He looked so small in a high hospital bed when we visited him that evening. The rules were relaxed so one child could be with two adults around the bed. Dad would stay with Philip outside the ward, then he and I would swap places.

Grandad said on one hospital visit, "When I get out o' 'ere I'm goin' all o'er damn show." This meant he would be driving his little yellow car to all the places he loved where we had gone on Sunday fishing trips to the countryside and holidays at the seaside. He knew his shiny and clean, yellow car was parked outside his house waiting for him.

Talking about 'getting out of hospital' and about the seaside made me think grandad was getting better. If someone, even mum, had said he might die, I'm sure I would not have believed them. He was my grandad, part of our world, and he wouldn't leave us.

Indeed, the following weekend he was feeling a bit better

and Monday's wash day was reinstated. Up to then, nannan had been doing a bit of housework and washing 'here and there' on any day except Sunday.

When Philip and I visited grandad, dad would take us for a walk around the hospital after we had said 'hello'. On the next Sunday afternoon he looked tired, but we were all allowed round grandad's bed for a short time. To me he just appeared to be sleepier than usual.

Mum said I could stay with them, but I wanted to go on the walk with dad and Phil. I was to regret not staying for that further precious time with grandad.

Like the Queen all those years earlier, if only she had been told how ill her father had been, she could have stayed with him for his last days. I wanted that time again by grandad's bedside so that I could have cherished his last hours.

The Queen's father had been a heavy smoker like grandad. Yet at the time of both deaths, smoking was just never thought to be a contributory factor, never mind the cause of any deaths. Even though the King's lung cancer had been diagnosed and his left lung had been removed, his death was officially recorded as 'coronary thrombosis' (clotting of the arteries around the heart.)

'Pneumonia' was recorded on grandad's death certificate.

How many other deaths were caused by 'lung cancer' but the actual death 'masked' by what had officially caused their death? Consequently, they would not have been included in the lung cancer 'statistics'. Maybe the doubled statistics of the 1950s/60s for that disease in men was even higher?

If grandad's 'lung cancer' had been diagnosed, would he have lived after treatment? The only comparison I have is that the King was ten years younger and had treatment, but still lost his life. I could write a list of 'what ifs'. But at the top of the list would always be 'what if they hadn't smoked'!

On the night grandad died, I was at home in bed. In the middle of the night, I woke up suddenly and saw light in the shape of road markings down my bedroom wall, but the room was in darkness – how could any light come in? I looked at my clock and it was about quarter past one and I just knew grandad had gone. I cried and cried. I must have cried myself into some sort of sleep.

I was awakened by the back door opening and closing. It was very early, but already light. I could hear my mum and nannan crying downstairs and my dad's voice. I'm tearful as I write this as he was such a funny and loving grandad.

I lay in bed, not crying, and my mum came in and laid on top of the bed with me. We cried together and she said, "We've lost your grandad." Before my mum left me I asked what time we had lost him and she replied, "About one." Did my grandad's spirit give me a sign that he was with me? I like to think he did.

Grandma insisted that he be brought home a day ahead of the funeral and he lay in the front room with the furniture pushed back and the curtains closed. All the nearby houses had closed their curtains, even the Jones. Mum went to stay with nannan so they could both be there when he came home.

Dad walked us there after school, the day before the funeral. We said prayers in the front room and then Phil and I went to watch television in the living room. I knew that the lid was not fastened down and that they were paying their last respects to grandad.

Philip didn't have to go to the funeral and I said I didn't

want to go without him. I was told I had to go to represent the grandchildren. Also, that Philip was 'too young to go' and he would be going to school.

I was glum on the morning of the funeral. I was made to wear a black coat I didn't like, and I thought grandad wouldn't have made me wear it. Looking back, I was just being childish and selfish.

I realised how popular grandad was, as a person, from the number of sympathy cards, over a hundred, and the large number of people at the funeral.

Everyone from the Queen's Ground had come. Everyone from where he worked had come as well, including Mr Wing. People in firms he visited in his little yellow car had turned up.

There were band members from the band in which he played the cornet. There were 'Sally's Army' representatives. Fellow players from the Hillsborough Park Bowls Club had arrived to pay their respects.

Friends and neighbours, his brothers and their families, his sisters in law and brothers in law and their families. The church was packed 'to the rafters' as people stood to the sides and at the back.

I heard phrases like 'what a great chap he was', 'he was always up for a laugh, 'a lovely family man', and 'what a talented chap'. More than one person had remarked what a shock it had been that he had died. Grandma's brother in law, Uncle Frank, had been poorly 'on and off' for ages and it was whispered at the funeral that he had been expected 'to go first'.

As grandad had given me a sign that he was still with me, had made me feel calmer through the funeral though I still cried buckets in the church and by the grave. Grandma's legs gave way at the top of the grave and she nearly fell forward on top of the coffin. She was caught by dad as a few people gasped. She was held up by Uncle Walt and dad after that. I was with my very sad mum, her shoulders hunched, her eyes red and her head bowed.

So the year of pride was followed by a year of great sadness and the end of my childhood happy 'bubble'. I wrote a poem dedicated to my grandad:

I love fishing and maggots
And going for a run
In the rain or sun
I love card games
And your funny tricks
I love our Sundays
I love our holidays
At the seaside
On the Snails ride
Or in the sea
I'll miss everything
But most of all…
I'll miss you

The first line, '*I love fishing and maggots*' is a reference to the Sundays when the six of us would go in grandad's car to a place where he could fish. Philip and I would fish as well but when we got bored we would play with the different coloured maggots, watching them squirm about and we would race them. He put the fish he caught in a keepnet, secured below the water line. He always held his catch aloft with pride for us to see the fish squirming about and then he put them all back in the water. It made us feel good to watch them happily swim away.

As I got a bit older, while grandad fished, I sometimes went with mum and nannan to the nearby shops, especially if we were in Lincoln. Our favourite place was Newark as there was an outdoor swimming pool, a lido, so on sunny days the four of us would go there, leaving nannan behind with grandad and his fishing line.

What I didn't like about fishing was retrieving the hook from a fish's mouth which grandad had to do for me. Eels were so slithery to catch and net that grandad had to cut the line and throw the eel back with the hook still in its mouth, sometimes losing the float as well. *(My brother still has our fishing rod.)*

'Going for a run' refers to grandad picking us up most Saturday mornings for a run in the car. A favourite run was to Bradfield which had a stream (for paddling), a cricket pitch and surrounding grass (for ball playing) and there was always an ice cream van there in summer. On the way back, calling in his work to boil bait for the next day's fishing and then the newsagents for his cigarettes.

'I love card games' line referred to Saturday nights at my grandparents. The four of us would walk the quarter of a mile to their house to have tea, play cards and watch a game show on television. Our favourite card game then and at Christmas was 'new market'.

Grandad's *'funny tricks'* included a trick box where you put a red counter in it and you said a magic word and the colour changed to blue (the trick was turning the box round which we didn't know at the time.) He did card tricks as well and made coins disappear from his hand.

The best 'trick' he ever did, and the funniest, was when he came down the helter skelter 'bowl' at Yarmouth!

As I've written earlier, but worthy of being repeated, was the large wooden bowl at the end of the ride that everyone spun into with their mats. When picking up your mat, you were knocked down again by the next child sliding into the bowl. There was always a crowd around the top of the bowl, peering down at everyone speeding in. Getting knocked over and over was all part of the fun.

Grandad zooming into the bowl was so hilarious. We held our breath as he was knocked down but then laughed again as he tried to get up. He stood up, waved, and then promptly got knocked over as he picked up his mat. There were loud cheers for grandad's attempt, the likes of which I had never heard before. The cheers from a larger than average crowd as he walked up the step ladder were quite deafening!

Grandma had a 'weak' attempt at 'telling him off' but otherwise it was grandad just wanting to make us all laugh.

'On the Snails ride' refers, of course, to our favourite mini roller coaster ride in Yarmouth's Joyland.

Reference to *'in the sea'* was about us paddling in swimsuits and the adult family members rolling up trousers or tucking skirts into knickers. There was no changing into shorts. Grandad, or dad, always started the car made out of sand or we would build a road network with a tunnel and sandcastles.

The six of us had our last holiday only a month before grandad started to feel poorly. We had gone to Blackpool on the Friday and stayed with some relatives in their B&B on the front.

In my diary, I wrote:

On the Saturday morning after breakfast we went into Stanley Park. Phil, dad and I kicked a football around. In the afternoon, we went to see the Tower Circus. On the Sunday, we went to Cleveleys on the tram.

In the evening we went to the Pleasure Beach. Phil and I rushed over to the laughing policeman at the Fun House. Then we hooked a duck and won a toy each.

(I can still remember grandad laughing, tilting his head back and ruffling up Phil's hair affectionately as we laughed at the chuckling policeman. Phil and I linked arms with him, one on either side, and we went to play prize bingo. We were still there when the others joined us later. Grandad, as usual, had managed to win a game.)

Monday morning, dad and I went in the swimming baths. Phil came in but he stayed in the shallow end. Mum watched. Nannan and grandad had gone for a walk on the front. In the afternoon, the four of us went up to the very top of Blackpool Tower and bought some cards from the little post office. We tried to spot nannan and grandad below but everyone looked like flies. At night we went to Fleetwood on the tram.

It was our sands day at last and after picking up deck chairs we walked across the sand. Phil and I ran to the sea after taking off our clothes to reveal our swim costumes. We came back wet and had an ice cream. Grandad tied four knots at each corner of a hanky and he ate his ice cream like that, making us all smile.

Dad made us the car in the sand and he had dug down to the wet sand to make a really large car. After that, we got mum and grandad to walk down to the water's edge with us. Grandad actually rolled up his trousers to the knee and got his feet wet. Mum just lifted her skirt a bit but the water was nowhere near her knees. *(I had pretended to splash mum and she had said, "I'm going back if you splash me.")*

That evening we were all sad as the next day we would be going home.

(Mum wrote on the kitchen calendar after the holiday, "Came home from Blackpool, we had a lovely time.")

It takes time to realise just how much you would miss the happy and carefree times with grandad.

One evening, a few weeks after the funeral, Mr Wing called on grandma. She gave him a cup of tea and they had a chat. He very kindly said that he would have to take the car back (it still belonged to grandad's work). No more rides or day trips in 'our' little yellow car.

Grandma had a 'trick up her own sleeve', so to speak, and gave mum and dad some money to buy a car for future Sunday trips and holidays. It was a Vauxhall Victor, 'gull grey', registration number 864 AWF.

However, dad could not afford to keep the car going all year round so in winter he would take the car off the road and lock it away in the garage. That saved car tax, insurance and petrol. He went on the bus to work all the year round anyway. Neither mum nor nannan could drive.

Like grandad, dad had never taken a driving test. Driving tests were introduced for people who had started to drive on or after 1 April 1934. My dad should have had to take a driving test but didn't. This was due to him driving during his National Service and being given a driving licence on discharge.

After grandad's funeral, a lot of people came back to my

grandparents' house and it seemed to take a long time for them to have a cup of tea and leave. Dad left early to walk home for Philip returning from school. I wanted to go with him, but I felt I ought to stay with mum. We were given a lift back home.

I started leaving things 'for grandad' on the top of my desk in the bedroom. One of the things was a bracelet bought for me at the seaside which grandad had particularly liked. It was a bracelet with different coloured, very tiny beads. I laid it gently on my desk before going to bed.

The next morning the bracelet had gone. I asked mum if she had seen it and she said no. I asked Philip, more than once, and he said 'no' each time. I asked him if he had hidden it, and his answer seemed sincere that he hadn't. I asked him some weeks later but he didn't waiver in his reply. I concluded that grandad was finding comfort in keeping the bracelet and I never saw it again. *(It is truly inexplainable, even now.)*

A light still appeared at night from nowhere and sometimes my bed seemed to be depressed on one side. I thought if I told mum, then grandad would not come back. Weeks later, I did tell mum, but there was to be no further sign or any light markings down the wall. I know it was not childhood imagination or 'wishful' thinking, but what I do know is that a part of the child still inside me died in the bedroom's new darkness.

Looking back, it was quite a privileged childhood having access to a car when there were so few cars around, 'posh' even. Two holidays a year and fishing days out and about could also be regarded as 'middle class'.

I had sometimes resented having my everyday clothes

made for me by mum, but now I feel so proud of those mum-made dresses and home knitted garments. My brother and I always had a new outfit at Whitsuntide. We always had plenty to eat and drink with lots of presents at birthdays and Christmas. We had a garden with a swing, thanks to grandad.

There is no doubt that I had a happy and carefree childhood, made possible by loving parents and grandparents. I knew Phil and I were the centre of their world and that we were lucky to be growing up as best friends and sharing so much together.

I thought it would all last forever, but losing grandad was the start of the childhood bubble bursting. A child's future, mine in this case, then rested on a single examination at the young age of 11. In complete contrast was the royal children's education and the fact that my brother and I were born in the middle of the Queen's family.

My life had changed and was going to change again, but that's a story to be told in 'My Summer, more Royal times and Ordinary lives'.

Answers to the 'Do you know' quiz about the Queen:
Q1. Name two out of the items kept in her handbag?
A1. They are known to be – lipstick, comb, small mirror, handkerchief, a fountain pen, her reading glasses, sweeteners and a copy of the day's programme of events. The Queen has been known to produce a bag hook from her handbag which she wets (very discreetly) and then sticks the suction hook on the underside of the meal table to hang her bag.

Q2. Who keeps her 'emergency' items?
A2. c) a Lady in Waiting, in what is known as the 'brown bag'.

Q3. *Name three of the 'emergency' items?*

A3. *These include: a pair of tights, spare pairs of gloves, a moist lavender cloth, needles, thread and safety pins for emergency repairs and hay fever antidote (for the 'I'm going to sneeze moment'), and hair lacquer.*

(Her private secretary keeps the texts of her speeches.)

Q4. *How does the Queen keep her hair in place?*

A4. *b) hair lacquer – in her own words "liquid concrete on hair!"*

Q5. *The Queen never sneezes in public – true or false?*

A5. *It's true because she uses a hay fever 'remedy' with a spare antidote in the 'brown bag'.*

Q6. *Related to Q5, if true.*

A6. *Although the Queen has never been known to sneeze in public, I have seen an 'off camera' moment when the Queen perchanced to sneeze while inspecting the fire damage at Windsor Castle but she was recovering from a bad cold.*

(Note: a Lady in Waiting, with the 'brown bag', does not accompany her on 'private' visits.)

Q7. *Related to Q5, if false.*

A7. *It is false, of course.*

Q8. *How does the Queen keep her skirt/dress from flying up in the wind?*

A8. *The garment's underskirt is made slightly tighter so under any circumstances that would not lift above her knee.*

Q9. *How are the Queen's clothes cleaned?*

A9. *c) handwashed... and her clothes are made from natural fibres!*

Q10. *What helps the Queen staive off minor illnesses?*
A10. *c) homeopathic medicine.*

How many did you get right?
5 or more and you're a bit of a Queen 'buff'!
8 or over and you *are* a Queen 'buff'...well done.

Epilogue

Although the Royal Family and my humble northern family live in very different circles of people and customs, there were similarities of dates for different occasions and events, as we've seen through the book.

There have been phenomenal changes through the passage of time. At the start of Queen Victoria's reign, it was still the law to publicly hang someone, including children, and a child could work down a coal mine. At the end of her reign, Britain was head of a vast Empire and cars were about to hit the roads.

At the start of King George V's reign, women could not vote and were 'just' home makers. At the end of his reign, women had a voice and he had taken the first steps to close the class divide between the monarchy and its people. One of those first steps was to broadcast an annual Christmas message to the nation.

In the year he died, the King praised his second son and that of his good family values. He doted on Princess Elizabeth, calling her Lilibet. Who would have known, at that time, she would one day become Queen?

There is no doubt, in my view, that Queen Victoria 'set the scene' for our royal dynasty to become top of the premier league of the world's constitutional monarchies. Since

Queen Elizabeth II took her solemn vows at the start of her reign she has been committed to, and has ensured, the continuing popularity of a 'family monarchy' that is revered and envied throughout the world.

Yet, some things can change very little over time as I can recall the shouts of a rag and bone man with his horse and cart in the street. And there were still no restrictions on people driving cars or where they were parked or what speed they went.

But, my generation and after did not have to live through a world war. This makes it difficult for us to comprehend what it was really like.

My grandparents, and their brothers and sisters, lived through two world wars. They lived through unimaginable horrors and experiences whether at home, in air raid shelters or nearer the frontline.

Grandma and the Queen Mother both suffered the loss of close family members in the First World War and nearly everyone knew of someone who had lost family and friends.

My parents lived through the second of the world wars, and although too young for war work or service, they lived through fears of invasion and horrific blitz nights.

Some things are beyond imagining what might be felt or feared, like fighting at the front whether it was in dire conditions of the trenches, on beaches, at sea or in the air. Knowing that a frontline order to charge or move forward would mean the end of a life for so, so many young men! No battle or war since can compare.

But marching soldiers then, and marching soldiers since, have seen the glory of the sun rising, and been cheated out of its setting. Those fallen, but not forgotten, heroes. Remember that war, any war, is not worth one life!

MARCHING

Youth, no job
He signs up
For King and Country
Smart uniform
marching, marching
marching, marching
Bayonet charges
And rifles shooting
marching, marching
Pride and glory
Ready for war

Marching youth
Going afar
For the Empire
Smart soldiers
digging, digging
waiting, waiting
Bayonets ready
Rifles and guns
charging, charging
Pride, no glory
This is war

By me, then aged twelve and a half.

Finally, a poem about war and its transcending fear on a sailing ship...

ATTACK

I can see the dead bodies all around
Flapping sails, cannons shooting,
Sinking boats, we should have invented floats
I can hear cannon balls splashing in the sea
People screaming, including me
I can feel a terrible cold sea spray in my face
Sweat on me and my mates
Getting more and more frightened.

By Thomas, then aged nine and a half.

'Princess' photoshoot in the local

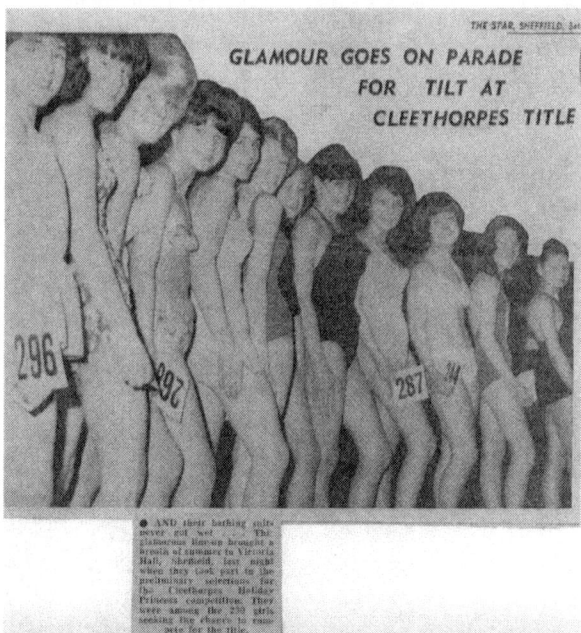

GLAMOUR GOES ON PARADE
FOR TILT AT
CLEETHORPES TITLE

Would-be princesses line up for the Sheffield 'STAR' – I'm on
the left

THE *June* CLUB

The June Club,
26/27 Farringdon Street,
London, E.C.4 (Comp.)

OUR JUNE ROSE AND HER ROSEBUDS

Jean Southate is our June Rose — winner of the Book of Knowledge prize. She is from Sheffield and she's ten this week. Jean tells us her hobby is ballroom dancing, for which she has won a medal and a certificate.

Hello, Everybody!

I'm Club Leader turned reporter this week! Thought you'd like to hear about the French girls' fashion ideas. I saw a party of them on a train—smart they looked, too. Grey, pleated skirts with plain-coloured blouses, many of them prettily trimmed with broderie anglais were very popular, and the ones who obviously preferred sweaters to blouses had gone for the trim vee-necked variety. A favourite colour combination seemed to be navy blue and green . . . and the latest hair-bows had obviously taken their fancy just as they have yours. The other thing that struck me about the girls was the way they all sat and walked. They held themselves beautifully and looked as though they were proud to be alive !

Au revoir till next week, *June*

P.S. A happy slice of news for everyone ! JUNE BOOK 1963 is on sale from 1st September, so place an order for yours NOW !

With my 'June' Rose prizes – a set of books of knowledge and birthday cake

Our last photo with grandad

5ᵗʰ March '66 What Time Should Children Go To Bed

BEDTIME	6	6	6½	7	7	7.30	8	8½	9	9	9.30	10	10	11
HOURS OF SLEEP	14	17	13	12½	12½	11½	11	10½	10	10	10	9½	9	8
AGE	1	2	3	4	5	6	7	8	9	10	11	12	13	14	15	16	17	18

Above: 'going away', in the hospital drawn landau. Left: This is a drawing of Princess Elizabeth's wedding day photographs. The train, is 15 feet long, is of transparent ivory silk. The veil of crisp white tulle was held by a team of pearls and diamonds

Excerpts from the 'Star' notebook (I had stuck coloured stars on the cover)

Excerpts from the 'Bird'
Notebook, so called because
of a bird on the front cover

But the work has its lighter
moments, too. Fun can be had by
taking part in pantomimes at
Christmas. These revenues are
useful, too, for in them, the art
of mime — a most important part
of a ballerina's training — can
be learned and practised.

Stars in the making

All senior students must master
the art of make-up. It is

important that the most
distant member of the audience
be able to distinguish features
clearly.
Even if girls pass the
first audition very few become
ballerinas like the ones below.

The picture on
the left is a
ballerina from Russia
who years back
must have started
out at an audition.

The Italian
ballerina on the
right once said
to her mother, "I
want to be a ballet
dancer."

One of the
girls who, after
eight years of
Ballet School life, made it.

534

My last photograph in the junior school